CONVENT NETWORKS IN EARLY MODERN ITALY

Convent Networks
in Early Modern Italy

Edited by

MARILYN DUNN and **SAUNDRA WEDDLE**

BREPOLS

British Library Cataloguing in Publication Data
A catalogue record for this book is available from the British Library.

© 2020, Brepols Publishers n.v., Turnhout, Belgium.

ISBN: 978-2-503-58607-6
e-ISBN: 978-2-503-58608-3
DOI: 10.1484/M.ES-EB.5.118310

ISSN: 2030-3068
e-ISSN: 2406-5838

Printed in the EU on acid-free paper.

D/2020/0095/19

Table of Contents

List of Illustrations

Ludovica Galeazzo

Marilyn Dunn

Sheila Barker and Julie James

Acknowledgements

This volume emerged from panels convened at the 2013 Sixteenth Century Studies Conference — two on 'Convent Networks', organized by the co-editors, and another on 'Dynastic Convents', organized by Sheila ffolliott. Also significant to this project's development was a roundtable discussion on the theme 'Interrogating Monastic Enclosure', organized by Elizabeth Lehfeldt for the 2015 Sixteenth Century Studies Conference. We would like to thank everyone who participated in and attended these events for their stimulating questions and observations, which have informed our approach to this book.

Resulting from several years of work and collaboration, this book's scope and focus have changed over time. We are very grateful for the persistence, patience, care, and creativity of the authors whose work is collected here. Their contributions have inspired and challenged us with new perspectives.

We would like to extend our sincere thanks to Peter Howard, General Editor of the Europa Sacra series when our volume was first proposed, and Guy Carney, Publishing Manager for the Europa Sacra Series, as well as the Series editorial board for their support of this project. We would also like to express our appreciation to the anonymous reader who helped us refine the book's content.

Saundra Weddle is grateful to the many colleagues and friends who have generously offered insights, criticisms, inquiries, and assistance throughout the course of this project. First among them is Marilyn Dunn, whose deep and broad knowledge about Italian history and convent culture has been an invaluable asset throughout the writing and production process. Her ability to identify connections and inconsistencies, her extraordinary attention to detail, and her collegiality and friendship have made work on this book a great pleasure. Special thanks are also due to Robert Weddle and Adam Weddle for their unwavering support.

Marilyn Dunn is especially grateful to Saundra Weddle, who has been an ideal collaborator and friend. Her cogent articulation of key ideas, insightful questions, and organizational skills have added immeasurably to this volume and have made work on this project a rewarding experience. Marilyn also wishes to thank her colleague Paula Wisotzki for her support and Carolyn Valone for many conversations in Rome about women and convents. Very special thanks are owed to William McGuire for his steadfast support and help in a multitude of ways over the years of this project.

MARILYN DUNN and SAUNDRA WEDDLE

Introduction

Christian monasticism's origins are usually traced to the ancient eremitic practices of men who embraced seclusion and asceticism in order to cultivate religious devotion and faith. As life in community guided by a rule became the standard, the ideal of separation from society found expression in the three solemn vows of poverty, chastity, and obedience, ultimately professed not only by men, but also by women who committed their lives to the service of God. The regulations, practices, and architecture of enclosure served to sequester nuns, who were perceived to be more vulnerable to temptation than male monastics, from the secular world to maintain their spiritual focus, develop their piety, and preserve the purity of their thoughts, words, and deeds. And yet, convent communities cannot simply be characterized as homogeneous groups made up of women living solitary lives, side by side within the same complex, absolutely separated from secular society, and disconnected from other religious communities.

Historians have long understood that nuns maintained personal, religious, social, political, economic, and cultural connections with individuals and institutions, serving both personal and collective purposes.[1] A long-standing debate asks whether the convent — as an institution and a spatial condition — facilitated or hindered nuns' agency. The answer is both. With the opportunity to assume offices that governed and organized the community, women religious were more likely to acquire and exercise power than most secular women, but that power was circumscribed by male-dominated institutions that supervised and checked their activities. The enclosure both literally and figuratively contained convent communities, making it a fundamental

---

1   See for example, Kent, 'Lorenzo de' Medici, Madonna Scolastica Rondinelli'; Strocchia, *Nuns and Nunneries in Renaissance Florence*; Evangelisti, 'We Do Not Have It'; and the substantial and wide-ranging body of work by Gabriella Zarri and Kate Lowe, including Zarri's *Recinti: Donne, clausura e matrimonio*, and Lowe's *Nuns' Chronicles and Convent Culture*.

Marilyn Dunn (mdunn@luc.edu) is Associate Professor of Art History and associate faculty member of the Women Studies and Gender Studies Program at Loyola University Chicago.

Saundra Weddle (sweddle@drury.edu) is Professor of Architectural and Urban History and Theory in the Hammons School of Architecture at Drury University, Springfield, Missouri.

Convent Networks In Early Modern Italy, ed. by Marilyn Dunn and Saundra Weddle, ES 25 (Turnhout: Brepols, 2020) pp. 13–30   BREPOLS PUBLISHERS   DOI 10.1484/M.ES-EB.5.119511

conceptual datum for the study of convent history. This context inspires a more pertinent question, which this collection of essays aims to address: how did nuns respond to the ever-present (if sometimes only implied) referent of enclosure to pursue and realize their desired outcomes? This volume focuses on one of the most important tools deployed by early modern convents: the cultivation and maintenance of relationships, alliances, and networks, both inside and beyond the enclosure.

Over the last three decades, historians with diverse interests have produced an evolving and nuanced understanding of how and why enclosure was observed — or not, and an overview of this theme provides necessary context for nuns' experiences. Case studies from the Italian peninsula (and indeed, from all over Western Europe) reveal that enclosure was as frequently disregarded as respected, to greater or lesser degrees depending on location and time period, even as civic and religious authorities regularly re-stated the ideal of absolute separation of life inside and outside the convent.[2] From at least the late thirteenth century, when Pope Boniface VIII issued his decretal, *Periculoso*, prescriptive rules sought to control the body, describing enclosure either as active, meaning that nuns could not leave their convent except in the case of an emergency, or as passive, meaning that individuals from outside the community could not occupy areas of the convent intended for female religious.[3] But the categories of active and passive enclosure were compromised in a number of ways. Convent architecture seldom incorporated definitive separations between religious and laypersons; the boundary between 'inside' and 'outside' was often mediated by openings like doors and windows, so that the physical limits of *clausura* changed from time to time. Furthermore, exceptions to enclosure rules, approved by the very authorities charged with monitoring them, could permit abbesses and office holders to leave their convent.[4] Sometimes, the right to breach the enclosure was formally written into a convent constitution, or was tacitly acknowledged as a matter of long-established tradition. Nuns' family members, their associates, and visiting dignitaries also occasionally treated enclosure rules as if they simply did not apply to them. Heike Uffmann and Sharon Strocchia have advanced the notion of 'open reclusion', which

---

2   The importance of considering specific contexts is discussed in Lowe, 'Nuns and Choice'. An example of how location and temporal context could influence observance of both active and passive enclosure can be found at Roman convents, particularly after the Council of Trent, with active enclosure becoming more strictly applied, while passive enclosure remained somewhat more flexible.

3   Makowski, *Canon Law and Cloistered Women*.

4   Examples abound. For a fifteenth-century excursion by a group from S. Zaccaria in Venice to view the church of S. Croce alla Giudecca, see Radke, 'Nuns and Their Art', p. 449. For the practices of the canonesses at S. Maria delle Vergini, see Venice, BMC, MS Correr 317, fol. 58ʳ. For the various motivations for and programmes of licencing in Florence, see Strocchia, *Nuns and Nunneries in Renaissance Florence*, pp. 123, 175. For a licence that allowed nuns to leave their enclosures to attend the 1515 entrance of Pope Leo X into Florence, see Weddle, 'The Ritual Frame and the Limits of Spatial Enclosure'.

describes a situation (in Germany and in Italy, respectively) in which nuns did not practice strict enclosure, but might still have upheld other standards of monastic discipline, especially in the fourteenth and early fifteenth centuries.[5] By the mid- to late-fifteenth century, convents began to face more assertive efforts on the part of religious and civic authorities to restrict contact between female religious and laypersons, but observance and enforcement of these rules remained problematic. With a broad geographical and temporal scope, examining both major centres and regional hubs in Italy, and covering the fifteenth through the eighteenth centuries, this volume reflects changes in both rules and observance over time and in relation to place, revealing how these factors may have influenced convent networks.[6] The focus on Italy takes advantage of the relatively coherent cultural context south of the Alps, allowing the chapters to enter into conversation with one another, while also articulating the idiosyncrasies of particular locations, which possessed their own peculiar social networks, institutional structures, and practices.[7]

The reasons for movement in and out of convents are significant and relate to this volume's principal theme of alliances and networks. Neither reformers nor their rules adequately accounted for the practical motivations for nuns' pursuit of connections, particularly those that extended to the outside world; they focused instead on the ways in which these activities were incompatible with monastic ideals (at best) or flagrantly immoral (at worst).[8] Indeed, interpersonal relationships, especially those that reached outside the convent, were an investment for these communities, which — to greater or lesser extents — supplemented their income and supplies, and accumulated comforts and privileges, with support from others. This state of dependence persisted even after the reform movement reached its peak with the Council of Trent's sweeping and stringent decrees, which were issued in the late sixteenth century and then followed by a spate of papal bulls and briefs intended to further tighten convent practices.[9]

---

5   Uffmann, 'Inside and Outside the Convent Walls'; Strocchia, *Nuns and Nunneries in Renaissance Florence*, p. 154.

6   The chapters collected here not only address the centres of Florence, Venice, and Rome (Callahan, Turrill Lupi, Llewellyn, Weddle, Galeazzo, Montford, Dunn, and Barker and James), but also touch on a range of locations of varying scales and degrees of reputation from small towns to more prominent regional cities across the Italian peninsula. These include Brescia, Mantua, and Soncino (Cavalli); Borgo San Lorenzo, Paradiso, and Ferrara (Callahan); Prato (Callahan and Turrill Lupi); Pistoia (Turrill Lupi); Bologna, Siena, Milan (Montford); and Marino and Avezzano (Dunn).

7   Of course, early modern monastic life was, by its nature, defined by rules and governance structures designed to create consistencies in the way of life observed by convent communities, regardless of their location. These inevitably created some affinities between houses sited on the Italian peninsula and those situated in other locations where the Western Christian Church dominated.

8   For example, see Girolamo Priuli's comparison of Venice's convents to bordellos in *I diarii*, p. 115.

9   See Makowski, *Canon Law and Cloistered Women*; Medioli, 'An Unequal Law'; and Medioli,

Convents could be quite creative in their use of both verbal and non-verbal communication that mitigated enclosure's limitations. Nuns, acting either individually or on behalf of their community, often availed themselves of strategies, tactics, and modes of communication more commonly associated with the laity, building connections with individuals, families, and institutions that could support their interests, both sacred and secular. The nature and success of these interactions hinged on expressions of identity, as models from the secular realm demonstrate. A useful and illustrative example of how relational identities could be expressed and leveraged comes from Patricia Waddy's analysis of the architecture and uses of the seventeenth-century Roman palace:

> Rank itself was established by several considerations: the distinction between ecclesiastical (higher) status and secular (lower) status; particular offices held; the distinction of one's family or, in the case of ambassadors, the prince or nation served; one's position within that family; and one's age. Signs of rank included the number and quality of carriages in the guest's train; the clothing worn for a visit; the announcement of the guest's arrival by the ringing of a bell in the stair; the points in the guest's progress toward the audience room at which he would be met, first by gentlemen attendants and then by the host; forms of address used; compliments paid; the offering of the left or right hand by the host; the arrangement of chairs in the audience room; the lowering of the *portiera*, or door hanging, during the interview (for guests of higher rank) and, on departure, the points in the suite at which the guest was bade farewell, first by the host and then by his gentleman attendants.[10]

This description demonstrates how not only status, but also spatial context and accompanying objects inflected receptions, meetings, and other kinds of interactions. Waddy's study focused on male actors, but non-verbal modes of communication also applied to women. While it is generally acknowledged that elite laywomen led modest and circumscribed lives, they still expressed their rank and identity, which were defined not only by gender, age, and socio-economic position, but also included their marital status. Before entering the convent, most women likely witnessed and absorbed this repertoire of behavioural norms and their potential consequences and benefits. Understanding the role these practices played in the manifestation and the pursuit of status, favours, and personal attachments in the secular world allowed convent communities to use these gestures as a kind of currency. Interactions with and between nuns, whether informal or formal, would have been influenced by decorum, but this was especially the case for ritual receptions and ceremonies, which might extend inside the enclosure and out into the urban fabric, demonstrating how

---

'Dimensions of the Cloister'.

10   Waddy, *Seventeenth-Century Roman Palaces*, p. 4.

different constituents used spatial and gestural meanings within a dynamic
and discursive context to confirm or establish identity, power, and privilege.[11]

Convents also communicated through the presentation and exchange of
gifts, both tangible and intangible. Convents' economic strategies usually relied
to some extent on nuns' labour, especially textile work involving sewing and
spinning, copying manuscripts, or producing religious objects like Agnus Dei;
such products, along with fruit from the convent garden, sweets, and other
foodstuffs were used as gifts to make manifest the ties between convents and
others.[12] Such gestures were governed by expectations not unlike those that
guided the ritual and reception behaviours of laypersons, and depended largely
on the status and identity of the parties involved, implying certain proportional
and reciprocal rights and obligations.[13] Intangible gifts, namely prayers,
were even more valuable. Strocchia has shown that 'the explicit exchange of
prayers for financial favors was one of the key mechanisms by which convents
were transformed into full-fledged civic institutions'; and that prayers were
'the crux of [nuns'] social and spiritual power'.[14] The benefit of gift giving,
regardless of the nature of the exchange, surpassed the value of the gift itself or
monetary compensation; it served as a transactional act of relation formation
that extended and multiplied beyond those directly involved. As Jane Bestor
has observed, 'Through gifts, persons and the social relations objectified in
persons are continually remade'; 'effective gift giving is socially productive'.[15]
As the essays gathered here will show, such activities yielded connections and
assistance that were uniquely significant to the convent context.

Relationships were not only enacted in space and time; they also began
increasingly to be recorded in ways that provide lasting evidence of the
transactional, intangible, and ephemeral nature of personal and institutional
associations. Diaries, letters, inventories, account books, contracts, ceremonials,
chronicles, *vitae*, and other written sources proliferated and, importantly, many
such documents survive. Each engages a documentary typology that provides
a lens for interpreting the identity and status of writers and intended readers,
not to mention others who might be named in the text. Letters directed from
petitioners to patrons, for example, tend to include devices like flattery and
expressions of deference that acknowledge the asymmetry of the relationship.[16]

---

11 For one of the best documented and most studied examples, the investiture of the newly
    elected bishop of Florence at the Benedictine convent of S. Pier Maggiore, see Miller, 'Why
    the Bishop of Florence Had to Marry the Abbess'; Strocchia, 'When the Bishop Married
    the Abbess'; Fabbri, 'La sella e il freno del Vescovo'; and Weddle, ''Tis Better to Give than to
    Receive'.
12 Weddle, ''Tis Better to Give than to Receive'.
13 Bestor, 'Marriage Transactions in Renaissance Italy', p. 13, with reference to Mauss's *Essai sur
    le don*, and Emile Durkheim's *Leçons de sociologie*.
14 Strocchia, *Nuns and Nunneries in Renaissance Florence*, pp. xiv and 104.
15 Bestor, 'Marriage Transactions in Renaissance Italy', pp. 19 and 45.
16 McLean, *The Art of the Network*.

At the same time, writers often selected plural pronouns — 'we' and 'our', 'they' and 'theirs' — that signal shared experiences, perspectives, and interests as a way to confirm or build alliances. Letters exchanged between relatives are another example, providing insight to structures of power and authority that were internal to the family and could be replicated among kinswomen within the convent; these structures could also shape relationships between those inside as well as outside the enclosure, where the influence of family status and alliances held sway in a broader, secular realm.

Patronage studies have loomed large in early modern history during the last forty years, considering motives and methods, and interpreting evidence that extends from the documentary and literary to the artistic and architectural.[17] A patron's identity strongly influenced the character of his or her projects, resulting in a 'presentation of the self' that raised the stakes for patronage activity.[18] It is now clear that women were active patrons, not only in the commissioning of works of art and architecture, but also as negotiators, agents, and brokers of various means of support and advantage, financial and otherwise. Patronage, defined more broadly, has not been fully explored in the context of monastic institutions.[19] Members of a convent were simultaneously individuals and part of a collective; those who did act individually claimed a measure of autonomy but were never completely independent of their community's hierarchies and standards, so the 'self' being presented cannot be reduced entirely to either the individual or the collective. The convent's religious order and rule provided a meta-structure that shaped communal identity, but a standard internal and interconnected hierarchy also differentiated women from one another. At the top was the abbess, who exercised an executive authority that all in the convent were charged to obey; she might be assisted and counselled by a group of elder nuns.[20] Next, office holders had responsibility and a modicum of control over the particular convent functions they oversaw, such as maintaining accounts, supervising the sacristy, or monitoring the doors. Professed choir nuns ranked above novices and unprofessed nuns, with lay sisters or servant nuns at the bottom of the pecking order.[21] Charismatic nuns might gain a kind of informal status and

---

17 See, for example, Reiss and Wilkins, *Beyond Isabella*; McIver, *Women, Art, and Architecture in Northern Italy*; Hickson, *Women, Art and Architectural Patronage in Renaissance Mantua*.

18 Goffman, *Presentation of the Self*.

19 Regarding nuns' and convent patronage of art and architecture, see for example, Roberts, *Dominican Women and Renaissance Art*; Thomas, *Art and Piety in the Female Religious Communities*; Wood, *Art and Spirituality: The Poor Clares of Early Modern Italy*; Hills, *Invisible City*.

20 The first superior might also be referred to as a prioress, and prioress is also sometimes used to refer to an assistant to the abbess whose rank was slightly lower than hers.

21 These servant nuns are called *converse* in Italian; the term can also be translated as lay nuns or lay sisters. *Converse* typically performed manual labour and served other community needs and, although they participated in the convent's religious life and enjoyed its spiritual benefits, they were not obligated to say the Divine Offices as choir nuns were.

influence at the centre of a circle of disciples; sometimes these figures served as monastic mentors, but in other cases their group might function more like a social clique, something Church authorities tried to discourage. Convents might also house laywomen — annuitants, boarders, and pupils — who did not figure in the religious hierarchy and technically had no voice in the convent's affairs, but who were influential nonetheless and represented a sure link to the outside that could extend over time even after the layperson left the convent. The personal and family status distinctions that identified both religious and laywomen in their secular life did not entirely disappear when they entered the convent, and this affected the relational forces operating within and beyond the community.

The coincidental individual and collective identities within convents call for a mode of analysis that acknowledges the complexity of polyvalent relationships. Whereas patronage studies tend to emphasize the dichotomy of client and patron, network analysis instead considers the individual as an embodiment of a unique collection of interpersonal and group associations, and examines her relationships to numerous others through connections that are dynamic and extend exponentially. An important contribution to our understanding of the nature and function of networks in historical contexts is sociologist Paul D. McLean's *The Art of the Network: Strategic Interaction and Patronage in Renaissance Florence.*[22] McLean describes networking as an intention-driven social process enacted by individuals whose 'personhood [is] constructed out of a number of different identities' that are adopted 'singly or in combination, in different interactional settings', with the goal not only of entering into a given circle of influence, but also 'branching out, moving up, and attaining control'.[23] Deliberately inventing and projecting one's identity was a familiar practice during this time period, codified in Baldassare Castiglione's *The Book of the Courtier*, published in Venice in 1528.[24] Leaving aside the question of whether the modern concept of the individual self was born during the Renaissance, our focus is rather on the relationships between individuals: why and how were certain kinds of connections cultivated and expressed within the common context and shared culture of the early modern Italian convent?[25]

The still evolving field of network analysis provides a useful theoretical and conceptual framework for addressing these questions. Emerging from the discipline of sociology in the 1990s, network analysis employs both qualitative and quantitative methods.[26] Catherine Medici provides a helpful overview of

22   McLean, *The Art of the Network*.
23   McLean, *The Art of the Network*, p. 2.
24   Castiglione, *The Book of the Courtier*.
25   Burckhardt, *The Civilization of the Renaissance in Italy*; Greenblatt, *Renaissance Self-Fashioning*; and Becker, 'Individualism in the Early Italian Renaissance'.
26   Medici, 'Using Network Analysis to Understand Early Modern Women', p. 153 describes it as a methodology 'of Digital Humanities'.

key concepts and terms, pointing out their value for understanding women's place within their communities, the agency of lesser-known actors, and the overall functions of networks, defined broadly as 'interconnected systems of people or things'.[27] Network analysis identifies 'nodes', individuals who produce links or connections called 'edges'. The qualitative characteristics (or 'attributes') of these nodes and edges shape relationships and determine the network's effectiveness. For example, the method considers the number of shared connections within a given network and the hierarchy of its nodes: when a node possesses a high number of connections, it is identified as a 'high degree node', while the high degree node that possesses the most connections within the network is referred to as a 'hub'. The distance and directness of a node's connection to the hub reflects that node's status within the network, thereby clarifying power structures and revealing the diverse configurations of associations inherent in complex relationships, including those that have long been ignored because they have not been considered central to dominant historical narratives.[28] The concept of propinquity is particularly relevant to convent studies. A community's shared, enclosed residence served to reinforce the bonds between nuns and others who resided within the convent complex so that, even in houses where factions and discord existed, physical proximity and monastic vows inextricably tied the women together, usually for life. In addition, convents were never completely self-sufficient and inevitably relied upon relationships with locals for essential support and resources. But as the chapters in this volume demonstrate, nuns frequently extended their reach beyond their house, neighbourhood and city; letters, gifts, and works of art crossed the distance to make connections tangible, while prayer offerings and other devotional acts served as intangible, ephemeral links extending and reinforcing convent networks.

Networks are products of and contributors to particular cultural contexts, and change over time. These dynamic forces affect a given network's efficacy, and promote or constrain an individual or collective actor's action within the network.[29] As several of the authors here explain, the concerns and conflicts of a specific place and time not only influenced the roles played by nuns and their communities, but also determined the modes of establishing connections they employed.

Unlike quantitative approaches that assign fixed values and weights to the properties of human relationships, qualitative approaches consider individual, collective, and institutional actors within the contexts of their relationships in order to assess their nature, durability, and implications as they change over time.[30] The strength and potential of a given network is informed by multiple

27   Medici, 'Using Network Analysis to Understand Early Modern Women', pp. 153–55.
28   See, for example, Granovetter, 'The Strength of Weak Ties'.
29   Emirbayer and Goodwin, 'Network Analysis, Culture, and the Problem of Agency'.
30   Scott, *Social Network Analysis*, pp. 2–45. Medici, 'Using Network Analysis to Understand

factors that stem from the negotiated, contested, and relational qualities of identity and status. Recognizing that these variables can shift and overlap, the connectedness of social networks correlates with the number and nature of shared characteristics; reciprocal relationships; symmetrical or asymmetrical links; longevity and physical proximity of associations; and kinship.[31] The ways in which the ties are recognized, cultivated, expressed, and reinforced are as significant as the actors, governed as they are by norms and explicit or tacit practices of decorum. Further, different kinds of transactional exchanges can help cultivate the establishment and maintenance of valuable connections; the perceived value of tangible objects and intangible favours can serve the interests of multiple parties, and can catalyze reactions that extend meaningful associations. Network analysis proposes that the study of all these conditions helps to clarify the nature, significance, and impacts of human relationships. While none of the essays assembled here explicitly applies network analysis, each provides examples of these relational dynamics in practice. The method offers a useful conceptual structure for the reader's engagement with these case studies of convent communities and individual nuns acting simultaneously at the centre and at the margins of a variety of complex networks. Early modern nuns and convents were well aware of the social capital inherent in the networks they participated in, and they deftly navigated the dynamics of these complex relationships to advance their own agendas.

The essays in this collection examine multiple kinds of networks established and engaged in by early modern Italian convents. Their authors draw upon an extensive use of archival materials, such as letters, convent chronicles, nun-biographies, financial and property records, and other documents, as well as look to the visual record of material culture to investigate the character and function of networks formed within and beyond Italian convents. They explore how these enclosed communities were both affected by external networks that penetrated their walls and extended their own networks into the social and urban context beyond the cloister, with each constituency exploiting these associations to serve its own aims. Through the case studies, situated within specific local contexts, authors address diverse network relationships as well as elucidate interwoven types, mechanisms, and patterns of networks that are related across time and place. The organization of the volume reflects

---

Early Modern Women', p. 155 describes how the quantitative approach to network analysis deals with large data sets and applies algorithms to measure relationships and network operations.

31   Sociologists and anthropologists acknowledge different kinds of kinship — consanguinal, which is biological and based on birth and blood relationship; affinal, meaning that it is based on marriage; and some also recognize social kinships, for example as a result of affiliation with a religious community or other group, like a guild. The nature of the kinship relationship can be expressed in terms of degree; for example, primary consanguinal kinship involves direct blood relationship between parents and children, and between siblings. Secondary consanguinal relationships extend from these primary ones.

the kinds of connections that create networks, the means by which networks are forged, and the purposes that resultant networks served. But within this basic organizational scheme, types and patterns of networks can be found to frequently overlap and create links among the various examples of convents examined within the book's chapters.

The first two chapters (Cavalli and Callahan) explore networks established and promoted through shared spiritual values, and examine the role of letters in documenting and maintaining relationships between female spiritual advisors and their female advisees. Letters from religious women created an epistolary network of nuns, convents, and laywomen that could substitute for the physical presence of their writers. Cavalli and Callahan address the function that these epistolary networks served among network participants.

Based on the correspondence of Augustinian nuns, Francesca Caprioli and Laura Mignani, from S. Croce in Brescia and Dominican tertiary Stefana Quinzani from Soncino, Jennifer Cavalli's chapter investigates spiritual advising relationships between holy-women nuns and noblewomen in north Italian courts in the midst of political turmoil during the Italian Wars in the early sixteenth century. While male rulers valued holy women's intercessory powers and advice on governance, noblewomen sought spiritual comfort and fortitude from these female advisors associated with diverse monastic orders. Through epistolary networks, female spiritual counsellors circulated among laywomen who were connected by marriage and courts as well as by the convents with which they maintained ties. Networks extended between spiritual advisors, between court women, and between courts and convents reaching out from and penetrating into convents through multiple points of connection. Cavalli examines the content of spiritual direction, the circumstances under which it was solicited and delivered, and the purposes that spiritual advice served to distinguish the unique function that these epistolary spiritual advising networks fulfilled for women who were not necessarily physically present in one another's immediate sphere. Not only did aristocratic court women rely on female spiritual advisors and their prayers, these holy women were, in turn, embedded in female networks that crossed geographical, social, and political spaces. Cavalli argues that convents were nodes in a network that connected religious and laywomen in a collaborative piety, and reinforced the stability of female sociability.

Letters also form the basis of Meghan Callahan's analysis of networks forged by Suor Domenica da Paradiso, who founded the convent of La Crocetta in Florence (1511) in order to continue Girolamo Savonarola's reform movement. Although Suor Domenica corresponded with male ecclesiastical and political authorities, Callahan's chapter focuses on letters written to women in Florence and Tuscany and beyond, in Emilia Romagna and Le Marche, which created an epistolary network of nuns, convents, religious women, and laywomen of various social classes. As a tertiary, the charismatic Suor Domenica was not strictly cloistered and sometimes visited other convents. She also defied Church rules by preaching in her convent and inviting followers to hear her sermons. Nevertheless, as Callahan demonstrates, Suor Domenica's letters of advice to women helped her to foster and maintain a network of followers who adhered to Savonarola-inspired reform after the friar's execution (1498). Suor Domenica's letters served as substitutes for her desired physical presence and helped her maintain the image of an obedient nun. Much like the female spiritual advisors discussed by Cavalli, Suor Domenica offered spiritual solace, but encouraged women to endure their troubles with patience. She urged cautious restraint to women contemplating abandoning husbands to embrace a monastic life, reminding them of the difficulties of the religious vocation, and she warned advisee Caterina Cibo, duchess of Camerino, of her dangerous association with the accused heretic, Franciscan friar Bernardino Ochino. Callahan highlights how Suor Domenica employed her letters strategically to fashion a self-image as a religious reformer who appeared to remain within the bounds of Catholic orthodoxy whilst she sometimes transgressed those boundaries.

Essays by Catherine Turrill Lupi and Laura Llewellyn focus on networks bound by shared religious affiliations in which works of art linked nodal points. Turrill Lupi continues the exploration of Savonarola-inspired networks addressed by Callahan's essay in a chapter that pursues the Savonarolan thread through an examination of networks of patrons, painters, and *piagnoni* ('big weepers', a pejorative nickname for Savonarola's followers) at the Dominican convent of S. Caterina in Cafaggio in Florence, whose foundation had been inspired by Savonarolan reform. In the 1500s, many of the convent's nuns and patrons came from families that had been followers of Savonarola, and *piagnoni* patronage tapped into the kinship networks that linked the convent with networks of shared veneration for the Dominican friar. Drawing on new archival research, Turrill Lupi examines the art patronage at S. Caterina by generations of women associated with these networks, elucidating an interwoven web of connective relationships. The works these women sponsored in the public church and convent spaces fostered the cult of Savonarola well into the sixteenth century in a convent environment that continued to be devoted to him as a prophet, saint-like figure, and martyr, long after his dramatic and violent death and subsequent, sustained repudiation in dominant political circles. Further, Turrill Lupi demonstrates that the commissioned paintings participated in artistic networks shared by S. Caterina and its sister Dominican convents in Florence, Pistoia, and Prato.

Laura Llewellyn's chapter focuses on a broad network of Augustinian interests in Florence's Oltrarno neighbourhood with Francesco Botticini's *Saint Monica Altarpiece* (c. 1485) in the Augustinian church of S. Spirito as its visual nexus. Based on newly discovered sources and a reinterpretation of previously identified documents, Llewellyn untangles the complicated and confusing archival record related to this painting of St Monica enthroned and surrounded by women of the Augustinian order. Formerly placed in a chapel allocated to the Augustinian *mantellate* in the hermit friars' church, the painting traditionally has been interpreted as being under the purview of the Augustinian nuns of the nearby convent of S. Monaca. Challenging this assumption, Llewellyn argues that the term *mantellate* identified a female tertiary branch of the Augustinian order, distinct from the second order nuns of S. Monaca, and she suggests that the women who surround St Monica represent both second order nuns and tertiary *mantellate*. As the mother of legendary founder St Augustine, St Monica, since the early fifteenth century, had been embraced as a unifying figure among Augustinians. Through a detailed analysis of documentary sources and visual evidence, Llewellyn proposes that the chapel and its painting of St Monica served the devotional needs of the various branches of the Augustinians — friars, second order nuns, and tertiary women — and created an Augustinian identity in which women played a key role. Her investigation reveals a more complex and nuanced interpretation of the interconnections between these branches of the order in Florence and Tuscany, and proposes that consistency of visual imagery may have helped proclaim this wider network.

Chapters by Saundra Weddle and Ludovica Galeazzo turn to a different region of Italy in their focus on convent networks in Venice. Both authors place emphasis on architecture and the built environment to explore various conceptions of networks that existed within convents and extended convents' reach into the social and urban fabric of the city. Saundra Weddle sets the 1519 reform of Venetian convents into new contexts by examining how the targeted convents were viewed as a cohort by reformers, and how reform efforts fostered a network of alliance between these elite convents and their patrician allies. Reforms instituted by civic and ecclesiastical authorities thrust convents into a lengthy period of transition from Conventual to Observant communities, in the course of which convent identities and alliances were thrown into a state of flux. Weddle notes how this uncertainty affected patronage, while demonstrating how new connections were established both within convents, amongst Observant nuns, and also outside the cloister with their lay benefactors, as the Observant character of convents emerged and evolved.

Her essay focuses on the 1519 reform's architectural expression, a salient and distinctive feature, which has been largely neglected in previous scholarship. Observant nuns, introduced to reform convent communities, and recalcitrant Conventual nuns, bent on defending their traditions and privileges, were physically separated by architectural partitions that divided the convent spatially, a strategy that was complemented by prohibitions on new professions among the Conventuals. Together, these initiatives functioned as an instrument of authorities' control, serving to reinforce and construct identities, and producing competing alliances amongst Conventual and Observant nuns. Throughout this process, Weddle argues, art and architecture at the targeted convents expressed these identities and alliances, which continued to shift over time. Weddle further observes how, by the late sixteenth century, the Observant nuns who had replaced the Conventuals fashioned an identity that embraced the convent's pre-reform prestige and privileges. As renewed and rehabilitated Observant convents stabilized, they asserted themselves within Venice's urban and patronage networks and contexts.

Ludovica Galeazzo's chapter examines the entrepreneurial networks engaged in by the Augustinian nuns of S. Caterina dei Sacchi in Venice. Like Weddle, she frames her study within the context of the tensions and conflicts of government-sponsored efforts at ecclesiastical reform in sixteenth- and seventeenth-century Venice. One of the less-studied Venetian convents, S. Caterina dei Sacchi was located at the northern extremity of the city, but its inhabitants derived from elite patrician families that dominated Venice's centres of power. Galeazzo demonstrates that the well-educated and resourceful nuns of S. Caterina, who defied governmental legislation regarding convents to serve their own best interests, managed to elevate their peripheral community into one of the wealthiest Venetian religious institutions. She argues that, similar to their male relatives who served as members of the Venetian bodies of government, S. Caterina's elite nuns possessed an administrative and managerial acumen that empowered the convent to actively engage in the social, cultural, and urban development of the northern rim of Venice despite *clausura* regulations. Galeazzo's chapter elucidates the convent's adoption of a strategically calculated financial policy that enabled it to gain control of surrounding property, embark on projects of land reclamation, urban development, and real estate investment in the area around the convent and on the Venetian *terraferma*, and undertake a campaign of architectural and artistic patronage to embellish their church and convent. These initiatives strengthened, expanded, and made manifest the convent's wide spectrum of networks, through which S. Caterina dei Sacchi actively participated in the cultural, socio-economic, and political dynamics of Venice.

Weddle's and Galeazzo's chapters span an interval before and after the Tridentine reforms of convents in the late sixteenth century. The time period after the decrees of the Council of Trent (1563) imposed stricter regulations on enclosure and other convent practices is also addressed in the chapters by Kimberlyn Montford, Marilyn Dunn, and Sheila Barker and Julie James. Although the Tridentine decrees and subsequent regulations did bring transformations to convent life and modes of engagement with social structures of the world beyond the cloister walls, as these essays attest, convents of the seventeenth and eighteenth centuries continued to establish and maintain a wide range of diverse networks that linked female monastic communities through family ties, religious affiliations, social class, female sociability, music, artistic production, and art and architectural patronage to the public world in which they remained actively engaged despite enclosure.

Scholarship of recent decades has brought to light the significance of nuns' music in the early modern period.[32] Chanting the Divine Office in their interior choir was the essential part of nuns' religious duty, and nuns'

---

32 For example, Monson, *Disembodied Voices*; Kendrick, *Celestial Sirens*; Reardon, *Holy Concord*

singing was compared by contemporaries to celestial choirs of angels. The introduction of polyphony created a new aural richness as the 'disembodied voices' of the nuns filtered into their public churches.[33] Music-making could provide agency for nun-musicians and functioned as a primary networking tool that connected many Italian convents to a broad spectrum of the public, but it was also a source of controversy and battles with paternalistic Church authorities determined to exert control over female religious. Kimberlyn Montford's chapter surveys the musical networks of early modern Italian convents within the context of the post-Tridentine reforms, examining the diverse and uneven application of reform in various Italian cities. She identifies different kinds of music-centred networks that nuns adroitly utilized to maintain their presence in the musical and urban landscape. They engaged in networks within the Church hierarchy that oversaw their convents, as well as in networks cultivated amongst laywomen and through connections within the elite social and political structures of their cities. Montford particularly emphasizes the key role of nuns' musical programming and convent music's place in the celebration of Holy Year festivities in the establishment and maintenance of convent connections. She shows how strictly cloistered nuns exploited the power of sacred music to extend their presence into the public realm to gain prestige and fortify patronage relationships.

Noting that one of the aims of the Tridentine reforms imposed on convents was to curtail family influence and interference in convent life, Marilyn Dunn argues that, nonetheless, many convents in seventeenth-century Rome continued to be favoured sites for patrician families to place their daughters, creating clusters of related nuns who often represented multi-generational family lineages or dynasties within their convents. She points out that, although convents were subject to male ecclesiastical control, nuns who were empowered by family prestige and wealth were able to assume their own active agency as administrators and art patrons, an observation that demonstrates parallels to Galeazzo's argument for S. Caterina dei Sacchi in Venice. By cultivating networks of alliance between family and convent, like the Venetian convents discussed by Weddle, cloistered women in Rome mutually benefitted both their convents and their families and produced a public impact through their artistic and spiritual patronage. Dunn begins with an examination of the elite Dominican convent of SS. Domenico e Sisto in Rome, a nexus for aristocratic women — both from the secular world and also within the convent community — to investigate family, sibling, and other alliances operating inside the convent and extending beyond its walls. Her chapter proceeds to explore the dynamics of networks of alliance formed between male and female siblings of the Colonna family, a broader network

---

within *Sacred Walls*; Harness, *Echoes of Women's Voices*; and Glixon, *Mirrors of Heaven or Worldly Theaters*.

33   Monson, *Disembodied Voices*.

of Dominican convents, and female supporters of Catholic reform that proved crucial in the early history of two little-studied observant and austere Dominican convents founded outside of Rome by two Colonna family nuns from SS. Domenico e Sisto with the assistance of their brother. Although the character of SS. Domenico e Sisto and its daughter convents differed, Dunn's chapter demonstrates the integral nature of multiple network relationships within these diverse post-Tridentine convents.

Networks of family alliances and aristocratic nuns' roles in the construction of family identity, similar to those noted by Dunn, are also evident in Sheila Barker and Julie James' examination of the art production of aristocratic artist-nun Suor Teresa Berenice Vitelli at S. Apollonia in Florence. Their chapter carries the volume's investigation of convent networks into the early eighteenth century and, like those of Turrill Lupi and Llewellyn, positions art as the link that connected a complex network. Barker and James' essay considers how Suor Teresa Berenice used her art to maintain or create connections with elite nodes of secular culture to project her individual, corporate, and family identities beyond the cloister. The circulation of her art in the secular world enabled her to transcend enclosure and assume a virtual presence in the Medici court culture and artistic community of Florence. Specializing in miniatures of flora and fauna and exotic luxury objects, she exploited her familiarity with her father's refined collection of artworks, curios, and natural specimens, and his shared cultural interests and relationship with the Medici family. Barker and James examine Suor Teresa Berenice's strategies of linking herself to family identity through her artistic imagery and directing her artworks as gifts to family and the Medici court, and for display at a public exhibition organized by the Accademia delle Arti del Disegno. Suor Teresa Berenice's artistic production significantly differed from earlier forms of convent income-generating artistic enterprises, like lacemaking, or the production of religious paintings and artworks for the convent or other lay and religious patrons, such as those produced by Suor Plautilla Nelli and her workshop at S. Caterina da Siena in sixteenth-century Florence. Barker and James demonstrate that convent enclosure posed no impediment to Suor Teresa Berenice; through mutual cultural interests she forged connections to a broader network of intellectual and politically elite patrons and the artistic community outside her convent. Nevertheless, although Suor Teresa Berenice's art surely gained prestige for her convent, Barker and James argue that it brought little practical benefit to it.

The essays assembled here reveal the many ways in which nuns and their convent communities participated in and contributed to diverse relational networks. Despite physical and institutional barriers designed to control their thoughts and activities, these women occupied important positions within constellations of individuals and groups that shared and served their interests. Those interests intersected with family ties, social alliances, civic bodies, and entrepreneurial enterprises, as well as with religious structures, including relationships between and within monastic orders, and men at various ranks of the Church hierarchy. In this context, women religious exercised their agency, using letters, works of art, music, business transactions, and patronage to express and assert their own and their community's identity. While nuns and their convents cultivated, enjoyed, and often depended upon such alliances, these examples reveal that those outside the enclosure not only acknowledged but also sought out these relationships, thereby challenging the characterization of enclosed women as existing on the margins of society and culture in early modern Italy.

Works Cited

Manuscripts and Archival Sources

Venice, Biblioteca del Museo Correr (BMC)
    MS Correr 317

Primary Sources

Girolamo Priuli, *I diarii di Girolamo Priuli*, vol. IV ed. by R. Cessi (Bologna: Zanichelli, 1938)

Secondary Works

Becker, Marvin B., 'Individualism in the Early Italian Renaissance: Burden and Blessing', in *Florentine Essays: Selected Writings*, ed. by James Banker and Carol Lansing (Ann Arbor: University of Michigan Press, 2002), pp. 258–84
Bestor, Jane Fair, 'Marriage Transactions in Renaissance Italy and Mauss's *Essay on the Gift*', *Past and Present*, 164.1 (August 1999), 6–46
Burckhardt, Jacob, *The Civilization of the Renaissance in Italy* (New York: Harper, 1958)
Castiglione, Baldassare, *The Book of the Courtier*, trans. Charles Singleton (Garden City: Anchor Books, 1959)
Emirbayer, Mustafa, and Jeff Goodwin, 'Network Analysis, Culture, and the Problem of Agency', *American Journal of Sociology*, 99.6 (May 1994), 1411–1545
Evangelisti, Silvia, '"We Do Not Have It, and We Do Not Want It": Women, Power, and Convent Reform in Florence', *The Sixteenth Century Journal*, 34.3 (Fall 2003), 677–700
Fabbri, Lorenzo, 'La sella e il freno del Vescovo: privilegi familiari e saccheggio rituale nell'ingresso episcopale a Firenze fra xiii e xvi secolo', in *Uomini Paesaggi Storie: studi di storia medievale per Giovanni Cherubini*, ed. by Duccio Balestracci, and others (Siena: Salvietti e Barabuffi Editori, 2012), pp. 895–909

Glixon, Jonathan E., *Mirrors of Heaven or Worldly Theaters?: Venetian Nunneries and their Music* (New York: Oxford University Press, 2017)

Goffman, Erving, *Presentation of the Self in Everyday Life* (Edinburgh: University of Edinburgh Social Science Research Centre, 1956)

Granovetter, Mark S., 'The Strength of Weak Ties', *American Journal of Sociology*, 78.6 (1973), 1360–80

Greenblatt, Stephen, *Renaissance Self-Fashioning: From More to Shakespeare* (Chicago: University of Chicago Press, 1980)

Harness, Kelley, *Echoes of Women's Voices: Music, Art, and Female Patronage in Early Modern Florence* (Chicago: University of Chicago Press, 2006)

Hickson, Sally Anne, *Women, Art and Architectural Patronage in Renaissance Mantua: Matrons, Mystics, and Monasteries* (Aldershot: Ashgate, 2012)

Hills, Helen, *Invisible City: The Architecture of Devotion in Seventeenth-Century Neapolitan Convents* (Oxford: Oxford University Press, 2004)

Kendrick, Robert L., *Celestial Sirens: Nuns and their Music in Early Modern Milan* (Oxford: Clarendon Press, 1996)

Kent, F. W., 'Lorenzo de' Medici, Madonna Scolastica Rondinelli e la politica di mecenatismo architettonico nell'convento delle Murate, Firenze (1471/72)' in *Arte, committenza ed economia a Roma e nelle corti della Rinascimento (1420–1530)*, ed. by A. Esch and C. L. Frommel (Rome: Einaudi, 1995), pp. 353–82

Lowe, Kate, 'Nuns and Choice: Artistic Decision-Making in Medicean Florence', in *With and Without the Medici: Studies in Tuscan Art and Patronage 1434–1530*, ed. by Eckart Marchand and Alison Wright (Aldershot: Ashgate, 1998), pp. 129–53

Lowe, K. J. P., *Nuns' Chronicles and Convent Culture in Renaissance and Counter-Reformation in Italy* (Cambridge: Cambridge University Press, 2003)

Makowski, Elizabeth, *Canon Law and Cloistered Women: Periculoso and Its Commentators, 1298–1545* (Washington, DC: Catholic University of America Press, 1997)

McIver, Katherine A., *Women, Art, and Architecture in Northern Italy, 1520–1580* (Aldershot: Ashgate, 2006)

McLean, Paul D., *The Art of the Network: Strategic Interaction and Patronage in Renaissance Florence* (Durham, NC: Duke University Press, 2007)

Medici, Catherine, 'Using Network Analysis to Understand Early Modern Women', *Early Modern Women An Interdisciplinary Journal*, 13.1 (2018), 153–62

Medioli, Francesca, 'An Unequal Law: The Enforcement of *Clausura* before and after the Council of Trent', in *Women in Renaissance and Early Modern Europe*, ed. by Christine Meek (Dublin: Four Courts, 2000), pp. 136–52

——, 'Dimensions of the Cloister: Enclosure, Constraint, and Protection in Seventeenth-Century Italy', in *Time, Space, and Women's Lives in Early Modern Europe*, ed. by Anne Jacobson Schutte, Thomas Kuehn, and Silvana Seidel Menchi (Kirksville: Truman State University Press, 2001), pp. 165–80

Miller, Maureen C., 'Why the Bishop of Florence Had to Marry the Abbess', *Speculum*, 81 (2006), 1055–91

Monson, Craig A., *Disembodied Voices: Music and Culture in an Early Modern Italian Convent* (Berkeley: University of California Press, 1995)

Radke, Gary, 'Nuns and Their Art: The Case of San Zaccaria in Renaissance Venice', *Renaissance Quarterly*, 54.2 (Summer 2001), 430–59

Reardon, Colleen, *Holy Concord within Sacred Walls: Nuns and Music in Siena, 1575–1700* (New York: Oxford University Press, 2001)

Reiss, Sheryl, and David Wilkins, *Beyond Isabella: Secular Women Patrons of Art in Renaissance Italy* (Kirksville: Truman State University Press, 2001)

Roberts, Ann, *Dominican Women and Renaissance Art: The Convent of San Domenico of Pisa* (Aldershot: Ashgate, 2008)

Scott, John, *Social Network Analysis*, 4th edition (London: Sage, 2017)

Strocchia, Sharon, 'When the Bishop Married the Abbess: Masculinity and Power in Florentine Episcopal Entry Rites, 1300–1600', *Gender and History*, 19 (2007), 346–68

——, *Nuns and Nunneries in Renaissance Florence* (Baltimore: Johns Hopkins University Press, 2010)

Thomas, Anabel, *Art and Piety in the Female Religious Communities of Renaissance Italy: Iconography, Space, and the Religious Woman's Perspective* (Cambridge: Cambridge University Press, 2003)

Uffmann, Heike, 'Inside and Outside the Convent Walls: The Norm and Practice of Enclosure in the Reformed Nunneries of Late Medieval Germany', *Medieval History Journal*, 4 (2001), 83–108

Waddy, Patricia, *Seventeenth-Century Roman Palaces: Use and the Art of the Plan* (Cambridge, MA: MIT Press, 1990)

Weddle, Saundra, 'The Ritual Frame and the Limits of Spatial Enclosure in the Early Modern City', *Repenser les limites: l'architecture à travers l'espace, le temps et les disciplines* (Institut national d'histoire de l'art, 2005) https://journals.openedition.org/inha/72

——, ''Tis Better to Give than to Receive: Client-Patronage Exchange and its Architectural Implications at Florentine Convents', in *Studies on Florence and the Italian Renaissance in Honour of F. W. Kent*, ed. by Cecilia Hewlett and Peter Howard (Turnhout: Brepols, 2016), pp. 295–315

Wood, Jeryldene M., *Art and Spirituality: The Poor Clares of Early Modern Italy* (Cambridge: Cambridge University Press, 1996)

Zarri, Gabriella, *Recinti: Donne, clausura e matrimonio nella prima età moderna* (Saggi, n. 516) (Bologna: Mulino, 2000)

JENNIFER A. CAVALLI

Advising Women

Holy Women and Female Advisees in Early Modern Italy

Nuns who assumed the role of spiritual advisor in early modern Italy used letters to establish and maintain their personal and, one might say, professional networks beyond the convent walls, producing documentary artefacts that took the place of personal visits. In 1502, the holy woman Suor Stefana Quinzani, a Dominican tertiary, wrote to her 'sister and daughter in Christ', Isabella d'Este, marchioness of Mantua. In her letter, Suor Stefana describes her words as a 'segno de vera amicitia spirituale, la quale quello sanguinolento et ingiodato crucifixo voli usque ad mortem intra noi conservare' (a sign of true spiritual friendship, in which the blood and nails of the cross will preserve us unto death).[1] She went on to profess her devotion to the marchioness, writing 'le mie oratione per le Signorie vostre mandate a quello, et fate com quello poco spirito lo qualo a mi è concesso' (I send my prayers for your Highnesses, made with that little spirit with which I was granted), and then extended her greetings to Isabella's family, ladies, and individuals with whom they were both familiar, including the marchioness of Cotrone, and Osanna Andreasi, a Dominican tertiary, who advised Isabella and the Gonzaga court in Mantua.[2] Then Suor Stefana turned to the spiritual matter at hand: the season of carnival. She advised Isabella to 'siati cauta, madona mi cara, molti lazi lui ve aparegiato a voi e a tuta quanta la corte e familia vostra' (take care, my dear Madonna, for he [the devil] has many temptations even for you and for the whole of

---

1 Stefana Quinzani to Isabella d'Este, 2 February 1502, reprinted in Cistellini, *Figure della riforma*, pp. 176–77. Cistellini's book helpfully includes fully transcribed letters from a number of female and male religious in the appendix, which readers of this volume may find useful. He also includes important documents and correspondence relating to Angela Merici and the Company of St Ursula, and the Oratory of Divine Love.
2 Stefana Quinzani to Isabella d'Este, 2 February 1502, reprinted in Cistellini, *Figure della riforma*, p. 177.

Jennifer A. Cavalli (j.a.cavalli@gmail.com) is Honors College Faculty Fellow at College of Charleston and holds a PhD from Indiana University.

Convent Networks In Early Modern Italy, ed. by Marilyn Dunn and Saundra Weddle, ES 25 (Turnhout: Brepols, 2020) pp. 31–51   BREPOLS🕮 PUBLISHERS   DOI 10.1484/M.ES-EB.5.119512

your court and family), exhorting her 'fati bene; fati bene, fati bene, filiola in Christo mia carissima; non più: non più per amore de Dio' (do right; do right, do right, my dearest daughter in Christ; nothing more; for the love of God, nothing more).[3] In this initial letter to Isabella — the earliest from Suor Stefana preserved in the Archivio Gonzaga in Mantua — Suor Stefana's advice, caution, and assurance of spiritual protection through intercessory prayers foreshadowed the ways in which she would connect to and guide Isabella and other elite women as their spiritual advisor.

In her study of female spiritual advising, *A Woman's Way: The Forgotten History of Women Spiritual Directors*, Patricia Ranft defines spiritual direction as that which 'helped, advised, guided, inspired by example, instructed, preached, cajoled, reared, chided or directed … toward the spiritual realm'.[4] In this regard, Suor Stefana Quinzani (1457–1530) assumed the similar but perhaps less formal and less authoritative role of spiritual advisor. In her letters to various women of high status, such as those to Isabella d'Este, Suor Stefana offered examples for contemplation, sought to inspire by her own example, and offered comfort, advice, and instruction.[5] She was among a growing number of religious women who dispensed spiritual guidance to a laity increasingly desirous of it in late fifteenth- and early sixteenth-century Italy. Religious women, whether in convents or living as tertiaries, symbolized purity as brides of Christ and their intercessory prayers for individuals and entire cities were believed especially efficacious. Those women, who experienced visions and ecstasies, were particularly valued as mediators because of their 'daily dialogue with heaven', through which 'they have foresight, they can advise and protect'.[6] They had universal appeal across genders and social status, but for women of the elite and ruling classes in particular, female spiritual advisors represented a type of piety and spiritual companionship with which many laywomen were familiar from their awareness and experience of convent life. Laywomen of ruling families, such as Isabella d'Este (1474–1539), marchioness of Mantua; Lucrezia Gonzaga (d. 1505), countess of Verola; Elisabetta Gonzaga (1471–1526), duchess of Urbino; and Lucrezia Borgia (1480–1519), duchess of Ferrara, sought out and relied on holy and prophetic women for comfort, support, encouragement, and guidance.[7] Their correspondence with Suor

---

3   Stefana Quinzani to Isabella d'Este, 2 February 1502, reprinted in Cistellini, *Figure della riforma*, p. 177.

4   Ranft, *A Woman's Way*, p. 6.

5   In 'A Key to Counter Reformation Women's Activism', Ranft distinguishes between pre-thirteenth-century spiritual directors, who did not forgive sins, and the development of the confessor-spiritual director of the late medieval and early modern period who could offer absolution. I am using the term advisor to capture the more general and universal spiritual advice the women in this study dispense to several women.

6   Prosperi, 'Spiritual Letters', p. 118.

7   My goal in this argument is to stress the norms of convent spirituality as the reason for confiding in religious women. However, it would be worthwhile to explore how this context and type of advice compares to the context of courtly advisors and advice giving.

Stefana Quinzani, who founded a community of Dominican penitent women in Soncino, and Francesca Caprioli (d. 1516) and Laura Mignani (1482–1554), Augustinian nuns at the convent of S. Croce in Brescia, reveals the content of spiritual advising, the circumstances under which women solicited and delivered advice, and the role spiritual advising between women played in shaping forms of spiritual expression. Their letter exchanges demonstrate that women spiritual advisors provided care and direction consistent with the collaborative piety of a larger network that revolved around convents, reinforcing the stability of female sociability during a period of political upheaval, personal loss, and health concerns.

The importance of holy and prophetic women stemmed from their intercessory powers. While these noted holy women were important to noblemen, especially rulers, and cities, they were also important to noble and ruling women in their own right. Laywomen turned to women spiritual advisors to ease anxieties about uncertain futures and for the general care of their souls. The ability to aid in the salvation of others, most often through prayer and directing another's thoughts, was a prominent feature of holy women's identities in their advising relationships with the laywomen in this study. The image of the saintly woman who guides others, especially the female mystic, was already familiar by the late Middle Ages. With it came an epistolary tradition 'of personalized spiritual guidance'.[8] In his study of female saints and their male hagiographers, John Coakley traces the development of female sanctity through nine partnerships, beginning around 1150. He identifies three main tropes in the hagiographies that construct the sanctity for which women became revered: their ability to care for and aid souls through intercession; their capacity to reveal important messages about ecclesiastical and political matters; and their insight into religious doctrine, including Scripture.[9] For example, the Dominican tertiary Catherine of Siena (1347–1380), perhaps best known for the latter two capabilities, provides what may be considered a guide to caring for souls in her *Dialogue*. Responding to her worries about how to discern goodness and provide the proper advice to those seeking it, God spoke to Catherine, outlining the main duties of her role. Above all, she was to guide others to perfect union with the Godhead — the definition of human happiness — through affection, love, and compassion, abiding by the call to love thy neighbour. This meant offering material and spiritual assistance, instructing the advisee on the principles of Christian virtue, steering the advisee toward self-knowledge, and leading the advisee to recognize free will and the role of suffering in attaining happiness.[10] Later women who acted as spiritual advisors, both from the Dominican order and other religious orders, such as the subjects of this chapter, emulated these

---

8 Benvenuti, 'Le religiosae mulieres', p. 385.
9 Coakley, *Women, Men, and Spiritual Power*, p. 13.
10 For a full discussion of Catherine as spiritual director, see Ranft, *A Woman's Way*, pp. 87–93.

precepts. Like St Catherine of Siena, who wrote during the papal schism of the fourteenth century, they did so at a time of political upheaval.

Political instability and displacements in the period of the Italian Wars during the first three decades of the sixteenth century, when European powers disputed territorial claims and jockeyed for alliances on the Italian peninsula, inspired individuals from threatened states to seek spiritual comfort and advice from holy women with mystical and prophetic gifts, including the holy women under discussion here.[11] Prophetic women protected cities, princes, and their families in periods of upheaval and, as Gabriella Zarri writes, served as an 'irrefutable sign of the presence and protection of God over the city'.[12] Moreover, they held appeal for both women and men, either as individuals, couples, or families. Suore Francesca Caprioli, Laura Mignani, and Stefana Quinzani all advised Lucrezia Gonzaga and her husband Nicolò Gambara, and Stefana Quinzani regularly advised Isabella d'Este, her husband Francesco Gonzaga, and their son Federico. Stephen Bowd links Suor Stefana, a recipient of the stigmata, to 'an interconnected web of Dominican religious women and the ruling families of Ferrara and Mantua', and Isabella's father, Ercole d'Este, duke of Ferrara, even attempted to convince Isabella to bring Suor Stefana to Ferrara.[13] When holy women advised women's husbands and sons, they often provided guidance on governance and reminders of their civic responsibilities as Christian leaders in a cautioning, maternal tone. For instance, writing to Francesco Gonzaga in 1502, Suor Stefana cautioned him about the serious task of leadership, underscoring his responsibility to prevent evil and protect his people, especially those of humble means.[14] She took a similar maternal tone with Isabella d'Este's son, Federico, urging him to model his leadership on his late father, writing, 'Cerchàti le bone compagnie et li salutiferi consilii' (Seek out good companions and salubrious counsellors) from those who had surrounded his father 'et della Ill[umina] Madre V[ostro] et Rev[erendissim] mo Cardinale' (and from your Illustrious Mother and the Reverend Cardinal).[15] Suor Stefana stressed her singularity as spiritual mother in her letters to the Gonzaga men, but she switched between mother, daughter, and friend in the way she presented herself in letters to Isabella and other laywomen, reflecting

---

11 Zarri, *Le sante vive*, p. 62, and 'Living Saints: A Typology', p. 248. Zarri has thoroughly documented the appeal of prophetic and visionary women during the Italian Wars when their spiritual gifts took on an increasingly political character. Among the powers vying for control on the Italian peninsula were France, Spain, and the Holy Roman Empire.

12 Zarri, *Le sante vive*, p. 57. Zarri argues that prophetic women and spiritual advisors were especially prominent during the Italian Wars, but that they became less conspicuous after the wars concluded.

13 Bowd, *Reform before the Reformation*, p. 223.

14 Stefana Quinzani to Francesco Gonzaga, 16 August 1502, reprinted in Cistellini, *Figure della riforma*, pp. 177–79.

15 Stefana Quinzani to Federico Gonzaga, 13 June 1519, reprinted in Cistellini, *Figure della riforma*, p. 187. The cardinal Stefana Quinzani referred to was Cardinal Sigismondo Gonzaga, Federico's uncle.

the multifaceted nature of female relationships and convent networks. While at times advisors adopted a commanding tone, such as in Suor Stefana's aforementioned February 1502 letter to Isabella d'Este, their advising of women more often emphasized contemplation of core precepts of the faith meant to cultivate the spiritual strength needed to withstand suffering amidst uncertainty and turmoil.

Such was the case when Elisabetta Gonzaga, duchess of Urbino, sought advice and comfort from Suor Laura Mignani, an Augustinian nun at S. Croce in Brescia, after being forced to flee from Urbino to Mantua at the advance of Pope Leo X's troops.[16] Founded in 1471, S. Croce quickly became a favoured convent among the Brescian ruling class, which endowed the convent with material goods and financial support.[17] As symbols of purity, convents protected the state. In return for their invaluable prayers, the state protected convents through material and financial — and at times, managerial — assistance, a configuration Zarri refers to as 'civic religiosity'.[18] S. Croce garnered a reputation for divinely inspired nuns with extraordinary intercessory powers, and its first two prioresses, Suore Timotea and Francesca from the aristocratic Caprioli family, cultivated relationships with the Brescian elite, including the ruling Gambara family. Suor Laura Mignani, known for her intercessory and prophetic abilities, added considerably to the convent's reputation.[19] Members of prominent families near and far sought her counsel and intercession, especially when facing extenuating circumstances as Elisabetta Gonzaga was in 1517. Continuing the attempt to assert the papacy's claims on cities and install relatives as their rulers, which had been a prerogative of the papacy during the Italian Wars, Pope Leo X accused Elisabetta's son, Francesco Maria della Rovere, duke of Urbino, of treason. Francesco Maria fled to Venice and Elisabetta and her daughter-in-law, Eleonora Gonzaga, went to Mantua.[20] It was from Mantua that Elisabetta appealed to the sister's intercessory powers in a letter of May 1517.[21]

---

16 Laura Mignani (1482–1554) was born in Brescia to a noble family, taking the habit in 1491 at the Augustinian convent of S. Croce in Brescia. She was spiritual mother to Bartolomeo Stella, leader of the company of the Oratory of Divine Love in Brescia in the 1520s, and Gaetano da Thiene, co-founder of the Theatines. Among Stella's circle was Angela Merici, founder of the Company of St Ursula. See Cistellini, *Figure della riforma*, p. 56.

17 Suor Timotea Caprioli from the convent of S. Giovanni di Beverara in Verona was S. Croce's first abbess.

18 'Civic religiosity' is a theme appearing in many of Zarri's writings. For a discussion of princely protection, see 'Monache e sante alle Corte Estense', especially pp. 424–25, where she details the types of interventions the Este family made on behalf of Ferrara's convents and the motivations for these interventions.

19 Cistellini, *Figure della riforma*, p. 57. An example of her intercessory powers described in S. Croce's chronicle includes an entry about Suor Laura personally interceding to remove an individual from Purgatory, the evidence of which was a painful burn on her hand.

20 For the role of the papacy in the Italian Wars and the practice of papal nepotism during the period, see Shaw, 'The Papacy and the European Powers'.

21 Elisabetta Gonzaga to Suor Laura Mignani, 20 May 1517, reprinted in Cistellini, *Figure della riforma*, pp. 241–42.

A month later Elisabetta acknowledged Suor Laura's response, writing that her letter and the regards she sent through Elisabetta's nuncio left her 'di tanta sodisfatione, quanto alcuna altra cosa avessi potuto conseguire' (most satisfied, as much as anything I had hoped to obtain), thanking Laura for the charitable love expressed in her letter.[22] Explaining that there was a contingent aligning against her son, Elisabetta sought Suor Laura's intercessory prayers for him. Because of the strength of Suor Laura's prayers, Elisabetta used her as a conduit to help her son 'quanto più posso d'intercedere per il prefato Signore alla Maestà Divina, ed alla Gloriosa Vergine Madre' (inasmuch as possible to intercede for the aforementioned lord with the Divine Majesty and the Glorious Virgin Mother).[23] Putting her full trust in Suor Laura's spiritual help, Elisabetta closed her letter by professing 'che io ancora per il singolar affetto, e devotione, che ho nella Vostra Carità spero, come buona figlia spirtuale che io gli sono, debba esser io esaudita, e soddisfatta di questa mia dimanda; ed alle sue orationi di continuo me raccomando' (that, for the singular affection and devotion I have for Your Grace, I hope, being the good spiritual daughter that I am, that my request should be fulfilled; and to all your prayers I commend myself continually).[24] Elisabetta sent another letter to Suor Laura in 1521, still worrying about her son and suffering what she referred to as 'travaglii di mente' (afflictions of the mind), to confirm that the sister 'far continue orationi per la salute di sua Signoria' (make continuous prayers for the health of his Lordship). She acknowledged that it had been a long time since she had received correspondence from Suor Laura, and Elisabetta prayed she would resume writing, as it would be a 'gran consolatione' (great consolation) to her.[25] What Elisabetta sought, especially in this last letter, was not only intercessory prayers but also instruction on how to direct her thoughts.[26] Positioning herself as a 'good spiritual daughter', Elisabetta cast herself as a spiritual client seeking the patronage of Suor Laura. The machinations of patronage suggest that the support Elisabetta sought and gained from Suor Laura also meant gaining the support and prayers of all the sisters at S. Croce.

The letters laywomen sent to religious women seeking protection, advice, and spiritual support, such as those from Elisabetta Gonzaga to Suor Laura

---

22 Elisabetta Gonzaga to Suor Laura Mignani, 21 June 1517 from Mantua, reprinted in Cistellini, *Figure della riforma*, p. 242.

23 Elisabetta Gonzaga to Suor Laura Mignani, 21 June 1517 from Mantua, reprinted in Cistellini, *Figure della riforma*, p. 242.

24 Elisabetta Gonzaga to Suor Laura Mignani, 21 June 1517 from Mantua, reprinted in Cistellini, *Figure della riforma*, p. 242.

25 Elisabetta Gonzaga to Suor Laura Mignani, 24 November 1521 from Mantua, reprinted in Cistellini, *Figure della riforma*, p. 243.

26 Elisabetta Gonzaga to Suor Laura Mignani, 24 November 1521 from Mantua, reprinted in Cistellini, *Figure della riforma*, p. 243. '[...] et oltre a questo a volerci mandar a dire qualche cosa in quello vi pensate abbia da essere, che non ci potrete fare il maggior piacere'.

Mignani, were addressed to spiritual patrons and thus follow the formulations and commonplaces of patronage letters.[27] These laywomen employed common salutations and ingratiated themselves; they communicated deference, at times placing the spiritual status of an advisor above their own elite secular status, such as when Elisabetta addressed Suor Laura as 'Your Grace'. They used the language of fictive kinship, referring to themselves as 'good spiritual daughters'; they communicated an expectation of help. And they closed their letters with expressions of loyalty and recommending themselves, such as when Elisabetta professed her 'singular affection' and devotion to Suor Laura. For their part, the advisors returned the maternal imagery by referring to themselves as spiritual 'mothers'; they expressed favour while acknowledging the laywoman's elite worldly status, as Suor Stefana Quinzani did in her 1502 letter to Isabella d'Este; and they closed their letters by reiterating their loyalty, promising assistance in the form of prayers — their own and those of the entire convent or community, such as when Suor Stefana offered her prayers 'cum tuto el Colegio nostro' (with all our College), whose members always pray 'per voi et stato vostro, qual Idio renda felice in terra poi in cielo' (for you and your state that God renders it happy on earth and then in heaven), and returning the recommendation sentiment.[28]

Within the context of patronage, the letters served to unite individuals into a network of association, but instead of securing material aid, the laywomen secured spiritual aid. Suor Laura Mignani's spiritual patronage presumably connected her spiritual clients to an entire network of favour and mutual support, in this case, the convent of S. Croce and the networks with which its members interacted. By seeking the spiritual patronage of a prominent member of a convent, as Elisabetta Gonzaga did with Suor Laura, a high-status laywoman like Elisabetta expanded the number of convents with which she networked and on which she could rely. The convents, on the other hand, expanded the number of benefactors on whom they might call for assistance. The economy of convents meant that they depended 'on networks of supporters to provide donations and political help'.[29] The ability to attract spiritual clients beyond their immediate environs created opportunities for new sources of financial assistance. Whether directed to persons close by or farther away, letters were the primary avenue to meet material needs of a convent and an opportunity to enlarge a 'community of clients and benefactors'.[30] For instance, it was likely Lucrezia Gonzaga provided financial assistance to the penitent community Suor Stefana founded in Soncino, S. Paolo e S. Caterina da Siena, and a number of the letters between Isabella d'Este and Suor Stefana indicate

27 For a detailed discussion of patronage letters and patron-client expectations, see McLean, *The Art of the Network*, especially pp. 51–52, 58.
28 Stefana Quinzani to Isabella d'Este, 23 November 1527, reprinted in Cistellini, *Figure della riforma*, p. 189.
29 Baernstein, *A Convent Tale*, p. 9.
30 Scattigno, 'Lettere dal convento', p. 323.

Isabella's regular financial contributions to the community.[31] The fame of spiritual advisors extended the reach and reinforced the prestige and status of a convent or penitent community among local benefactors.

The desire to have holy women ease anxieties about an uncertain future reflected the important civic role convents fulfilled in protecting states during the period. It also reflected shifting political alliances, which, as Christine Shaw notes, often resulted in divided family allegiances.[32] As such, the safety of husbands and sons was a prominent feature of the correspondence, including that of Suor Francesca Caprioli, prioress of the convent S. Croce in Brescia, and Lucrezia Gonzaga, countess of Verola. Suor Francesca reassured Lucrezia that, despite the anxieties caused by several setbacks in her husband's military commission in 1498, 'Dio ama il caro fratello nostro [...] ben ne ha bona cura cum custodia' (God loves our dear brother... and keeps close guard over him).[33] She attributed this assurance to Suor Laura Mignani, who was a young nun at that point, and her gift of prophecy. Isabella d'Este consulted Suor Stefana Quinzani in a similar manner in 1523 when the French were once again moving into Italy. Faced with similar anxieties, Isabella wrote to Suor Stefana on behalf of her son, Federico, who was leading opposing troops.[34] Writing that Federico's life was in danger, Isabella asked 'la R[evernda] V[ostra] per quella grande fede che havemo in lei voglii fare et far fare a tutte quelle sue matre ferventi orationi pregando Nostro Signore Dio lo deffendi la periculo cussi de la vitta sua come dil stato non cessando da questo suo sancto officio' (Your Reverence, because of that great faith that we have in you, that you and all your mothers make fervent prayers to Our Lord God to defend him [Federico] and the state, not ceasing from your holy duty).[35] For this Isabella would be perpetually obliged. She went on to indicate that she herself had been suffering from stomach pains but 'hora per gratia de Dio stiamo benissimo' (now through the grace of God we are well).[36] Suor Stefana responded to these

---

31 On Lucrezia Gonzaga and Suor Stefana, and Isabella d'Este and Francesco Gonzaga's initial financial support of the community, see Herzig, *Savonarola's Women*, pp. 147–48. Several letters preserved in the Archivio Gonzaga in Mantua reference alms, including F.II.9, b. 2999, libro 45, 67ᵛ–68ʳ, #175 from Isabella and EXI.1, b. 1897, folder III, #44 from Stefana as just two examples.

32 Shaw, *Barons and Castellans*, p. 198.

33 As quoted in Cistellini, *Figure della riforma*, p. 66. Lucrezia Gonzaga was the daughter of Francesco Gonzaga of Novellara. In 1492, she married the condottiere Nicolò di Brunoro Gambara, who fought for Pope Alexander VI's armies during much of their marriage. See Cistellini, *Figure della riforma*, p. 63. She had three children from the marriage, Auriga, Emilia, and Lucrezio.

34 Federico commanded the Papal and Florentine troops as part of the anti-French alliance between the Italian powers and the Hapsburgs. He led the troops into French-controlled Milan in 1523.

35 Mantova, ASMn, F.II.9, busta 2998, libro 43, 15ʳ⁻ᵛ, #35. Isabella d'Este to Stefana de Soncino, 12 February 1523.

36 Mantova, ASMn, F.II.9, busta 2998, libro 43, 15ʳ ᵛ, #35. Isabella d'Este to Stefana de Soncino, 12 February 1523.

circumstances by instructing Isabella that God, who bound them together, would watch over her: 'non dubidar fiola che dio te aiutara pur che sia bona' (do not doubt, daughter, that God will help you in whatever way is best). Isabella had to have patience, hope in God and pray that He would help her withstand 'discordie tale ne ha seminate' (such discord sown [by the Devil]).[37] In all these instances, the laywomen's appeals address anxieties stemming from external political circumstances, over which they had little control. What they sought, however, was an easing of their minds and individual comfort of the soul. In response, their spiritual advisors sent instructions to fortify their advisees' soul, at times for self-assurance, and at other times, such as in this last example from Suor Stefana, to do spiritual combat. The imagery of struggle and battle against temptation encouraged self-reflection and discernment. The theme of spiritual combat against the machinations of the devil, a prominent theme in Suor Stefana's letters, 'increasingly characterized a conception of an interior life'.[38] This interiority was nevertheless collaborative: the advisor was there to guide the laywoman in her experience of spirituality and prayer, and to remind her of the practices she must engage in to keep faith and her relationship with God at the forefront of her life. Among these practices was striving for self-knowledge and discerning what made one most susceptible to temptation and sin, such as despair.

The desire, indeed need, for reassurance and special intervention expressed in the above examples was not focused exclusively on the well-being of husbands and sons on the battlefield. Equally prominent was concern for the advisees' physical and emotional well-being. Lucrezia Gonzaga, the countess of Verola, regularly relied on Suor Francesca Caprioli of S. Croce in Brescia for guidance and care, especially as her health steadily declined after the birth of her last child in 1501. Suor Francesca consoled Lucrezia with prayer and instructed her to 'confortative cum bona pacientia nel dolce Jesu, e desiderati de meritare per gaudere cum il dillecto Jesu' (take comfort and have patience in sweet Jesus, and wish to be deserving of the joy of beloved Jesus), and regularly sent additional words of encouragement and prayers.[39] In this case, the spiritual advisor came from a convent to which the laywoman was already connected. The ruling Gambara family into which Lucrezia Gonzaga married favoured S. Croce through regular patronage, establishing a relationship of mutual obligation and reciprocity. The convent's prioresses had frequent contact with daughters and wives of the Gambara family, which continued from one generation of women to the next. Indeed, Suor Francesca and, later, Suor Laura Mignani, Francesca's successor as prioress and who Francesca often

37 Mantova, ASMn, E.X.I., busta 1897, folder III, #44. Stefana de Soncino to Isabella d'Este, 21 February 1523.
38 Zarri, *Le sante vive*, pp. 61–62.
39 Francesca Caprioli to Lucrezia [Gonzaga] a Verola, 6 July 1496, reprinted in Cistellini, *Figure della riforma*, p. 213. Suor Francesca addressed Lucrezia Gonzaga as 'Lucrezia a Verola', whereas Suor Stefana Qunizani addressed her by her married name 'Lucrezia Gambara'.

referenced in her letters to Lucrezia, continued to serve as spiritual advisors to Lucrezia's young daughters after Lucrezia's death.

At times, however, personal struggle, whether from physical illness or mental turmoil, prompted women to go beyond their immediate convent network. This was what Lucrezia Borgia, the daughter of Pope Alexander VI, who married Alfonso d'Este and became duchess of Ferrara in 1502, did when she wrote to Suor Laura Mignani about the desolation she felt in 1512. In that year, her son from a previous marriage died and the army of Pope Julius II was advancing on Ferrara. Invoking maternal imagery in the opening of her letter, Lucrezia expressed that she had been waiting for a quiet time to write but decided to do so now because of how events were moving forward, presumably referring to the impending threat of war. Lucrezia explained that she desired Suor Laura's help in devoting herself to God so that 'per la Sua misericordia liberarci' (through His mercy, we are freed) from travails, and that 'saressimo sommamente desiderosi che volesse continuare in quel modo l'inspirasse Nostro Signore Iddio, in quello s'aspetta [sic] la salute nostra e di questo Stato, che si accrescerà l'obligo, che gli tenemo; e la preghiamo voglia raccomandarci all'Orationi di quelle Venerande Madri e Sorelle' (above all, we desire and want you to continue in that way, inspired by Our Lord God, [interceding for] our health and this State, which increases our obligation [to you]. We ask that you recommend us to the prayers of the venerable Mothers and Sisters [at S. Croce]).[40] Lucrezia's appeal carried the same overtones as those of Elisabetta Gonzaga, with whom she formed a friendship after her marriage to Alfonso d'Este. Their choice of Suor Laura in similar circumstances of political uncertainty and emotional strain was not a coincidence. While it is not known if Lucrezia had a connection to Suor Laura prior to writing to her, Elisabetta's appeal to Suor Laura five years later most likely stemmed from her relationship with Lucrezia.[41] Laywomen used their court network to expand their spiritual network, which can be seen not only in the sharing of spiritual advisors, but also through negotiating and providing dowries for ladies-in-waiting who later decided to pursue convent life.[42] In turn, spiritual advisors like Suor Laura Mignani expanded their convent's network by connecting with laywomen who were linked to one another by marriage and courts.

Such was also the case with Suor Stefana Quinzani. While Lucrezia Gonzaga had steady advising from Suor Francesca and Suor Laura in her immediate convent network, she also reached out to Suor Stefana requesting intercessory prayers as her physical health faltered. Taking a similar approach

---

40   Lucrezia Borgia to Suor Laura Mignani, 4 December 1512, reprinted in Cistellini, *Figure della riforma*, p. 241.

41   Zarri, *La religione di Lucrezia Borgia*, pp. 78–79.

42   For example, Isabella d'Este had Beatrice Contrari and Cassandra Corrigia, both former ladies-in-waiting, negotiate the placement and dowry for Joanna Boschetti, another lady-in-waiting, at the convent of St Catherine in Ferrara. See Cockram, *Isabella d'Este and Francesco Gonzaga*, p. 125, n. 40.

as Suor Francesca, Suor Stefana counselled Lucrezia that the love of God would support her through illness and all other sadness. Addressing her as daughter, Suor Stefana reassured Lucrezia by confirming that many other holy people were praying for her.[43] Saddened by news of Lucrezia's worsening condition, Suor Stefana assured her that while she had no doubt physical illness weighed on Lucrezia, the soul must bear with patience all that befalls it in this world, because 'come credemo possi essere la veritate, non ne pigliamo tanta tristicia si che in ogni occorentia che acada, persuademo la pr[aetere]a V[ostra] M[adonn]a ad tal effetto et per amor di Dio supporter pacientemente infirmita' (as we believe it is possible to be true, we do not take on so much sadness from every occurrence that happens, [and] we also [wish to] persuade Your Ladyship of this fact and of God's love [in order] to withstand patiently this illness).[44] She went on to write, 'et se havemo fare altra cosa per V[ostra] M[adonn]a quella advisi che, per quanto se potra extendere de porzi nostre, non mancaremo per dar compita satisfattione ad quanto richiedera' (and if we can do anything else for your Ladyship, we will extend ourselves to satisfy your request).[45] In caring for her soul, both Suor Francesca and Suor Stefana encouraged and guided the ailing Lucrezia to focus her thoughts on maintaining and increasing her spiritual strength as her physical strength declined.

Whether to cultivate fortitude or prepare one to battle against temptation and sin, care for the soul often came through instruction for individual contemplation. In her July 1496 letter, Suor Francesca Caprioli encouraged Lucrezia Gonzaga to consider St Augustine's counsel: 'se vogliamo gaudere cum li Sancti nela gloria triumphante, bisogna patire in questo mondo et seguitarli nele tribulatione cum essi loro' (if we want to enjoy glorious triumph with the Saints, we must suffer in this world and follow in tribulations like theirs).[46] Suor Francesca again counselled Lucrezia in 1499 to shift her focus away from her tribulations and toward engaging her spirit: 'debe exultare e rendere gratie e laude alo eterno Dio nostro, perché dice Paulo glorioso per multe tribolatione ne bisogna caminare se vogliamo intrare in el regno di Dio' ([one must] exalt and give gratitude and praise to our eternal God because, as the glorious Paul says, we must walk through many troubles if we want to enter into God's kingdom).[47] As Lucrezia's health faltered in 1503,

---

43 Stefana Quinzani to Lucrezia [Gonzaga] Gambara, 20 October 1504, reprinted in Cistellini, *Figure della riforma*, p. 190.

44 Stefana Quinzani to Lucrezia [Gonzaga] Gambara, 20 October 1504, reprinted in Cistellini, *Figure della riforma*, p. 190.

45 Stefana Quinzani to Lucrezia [Gonzaga] Gambara, 20 October 1504, reprinted in Cistellini, *Figure della riforma*, pp. 190–91.

46 Francesca Caprioli to Lucrezia [Gonzaga] a Verola, 6 July 1496, reprinted in Cistellini, *Figure della riforma*, p. 213.

47 Francesca Caprioli to Lucrezia [Gonzaga] a Verola, 6 July 1499, reprinted in Cistellini, *Figure della riforma*, p. 215.

Suor Francesca wrote that during those days of strain and weariness, Lucrezia should meditate on and contemplate how Jesus bore his suffering.[48] Even when threatened and denounced by those who scorned and railed against him, 'afatichato sudato cum li piedi nudi discalco vano per terra patisse fame e sete et affani asai solum per amor nostro per darne exempio et insegnarne che anchora noi dovemo portare volontiera le tribulation de questo mondo' (tired and sweating, going about with bare feet, enduring hunger and thirst and breathlessness, practically alone, he gave us an example through his great and certain love for us, [and thus] we should carry willingly the tribulations of this world).[49] Likewise, Stefana Quinzani redirected Isabella d'Este's thoughts in her letter of condolence to Isabella over her husband Francesco's death in 1519. She instructed Isabella on how one should respond to such a loss. Expressing maternal affection, she conveyed the support of higher powers: 'Iesu et Maria cum S Paulo ve diano consolatione' (may Jesus and Mary with St Paul offer their consolation).[50] Acknowledging the great void such a loss had left in Isabella's life, Suor Stefana counselled that 'tuta volta al tuto dobbiamo conformarse com el volver di Dio et acceptar ogni cosa per el melio' (at all times [and] in all things, we must adapt ourselves to the will of God and accept that everything is for the best).[51] Isabella must continue in the spiritual fortitude she had been demonstrating to that point for her own well-being.[52] The type of advice spiritual advisors offered — encouraging their advisees to understand challenges as coming from God, to focus on the sacrificial model of Jesus, to prepare oneself to combat spiritual doubt in times of physical weakness — promoted an interiority consistent with the affective piety associated with visionary holy women. They urge those they advise to come to self-knowledge and strengthen their faith by meditating on Jesus's life. This type of piety was exemplified in the sanctity for which advisors like Suor Stefana were renowned: one that endowed holy women with extraordinary intercessory powers, and in some cases, such as Stefana's, the visible signs of the stigmata.

All of the laywomen discussed here had other outlets for spiritual guidance and advisors. In fact, they had access to many of the most reform-minded and celebrated male religious of their time, owing to their elite status and range of social connections. For instance, Lucrezia Gonzaga received numerous letters from men such as the Dominican Onorio Pezzi, a noted and sought-after confessor to the Venetian aristocracy.[53] Lucrezia Borgia was the dedicatee of spiritual texts, including *Expositione ingeniosa et accomodata a nostri tempi*

---

48 Brescia, ASB, AG, filza 88. Francesca Caprioli to Lucrezia [Gonzaga] a Verola, 22 March 1503.
49 Brescia, ASB, AG, filza 88. Francesca Caprioli to Lucrezia [Gonzaga] a Verola, 22 March 1503.
50 Stefana Quinzani to Isabella d'Este, 3 April 1519 in Cistellini, *Figure della riforma*, p. 185. 'Ill. ma filiola mai honorandissima, e memoria [...].
51 Stefana Quinzani to Isabella d'Este, 3 April 1519, reprinted in Cistellini, *Figure della riforma*, p. 185.
52 Stefana Quinzani to Isabella d'Este, 3 April 1519, reprinted in Cistellini, *Figure della riforma*, p. 185.
53 Cistellini, *Figure della riforma*, p. 63.

Figure 1.1. Francesco Bonsignori, *Blessed Osanna Andreasi*, Mantova, Complesso Museale di Palazzo Ducale. *c.* 1519. Bridgeman Images.

del XIIII, XV, et XVII Psalmo by the Augustinian friar Andrea Baura. She also communicated with Antonio Meli da Crema, Anselm Botturnio, and the Savonarolan Dominican Tommaso Caiani.[54] Nevertheless, all of the women

54 For discussion of the work and its dedication to Lucrezia in 1513, and for Lucrezia's

in this study sought out and maintained similar relationships with women religious who took on the role of advising. What did female spiritual advisors provide that male advisors did not?

Female spiritual advisors exemplified a type of piety cultivated in convents, a space filled with other women, both religious and lay, who would share in their spiritual practices in ways that were familiar. In her analysis of Francesco Bonsignori's *Veneration of the Blessed Osanna Andreasi*, an altarpiece completed for the Dominican convent S. Vincenzo in Mantua, Sally Hickson argues that what one really sees in the piece is the complexity of female religiosity and women's relations with one another (Figure 1.1).[55] In the centre of the composition is a towering Blessed Osanna, holding white lilies in one hand and a human heart pierced with a knife and crucifix in the other. She stands on a horned beast representing her triumph over the devil. Above her on either side are angels, one holding the same flowers as Osanna and the other bearing a cross. Around the venerated Osanna are five kneeling women: two laywomen in widow's garb, largely accepted to be depictions of Isabella d'Este and Margarita Cantelma, duchess of Sora, and three women in nun's habit, among whom may be Suor Ippolita Gonzaga, Isabella's daughter who took vows at S. Vincenzo in 1511. Hickson sees the inclusion of these women as weaving 'an intricate pattern of relations between sacred and secular and public and private devotion', calling the altarpiece 'a "city of women"'.[56]

Bonsignori's altarpiece may also be seen as a reflection of the regular sharing of space, practices of piety, and sense of spiritual community of convents with which elite women in the period engaged. What female advisors provided that male advisors did not was their familiarity with convent life's spiritual devotions and disciplines, as well as gender dynamics both inside and outside the enclosure. Like almost all laywomen of their status, those in this study had varying degrees of experience behind convent walls. For instance, Isabella d'Este preserved her connection with a number of convents in her natal Ferrara, and many of the letters from nuns in Ferrara refer to Isabella's past and anticipated visits to their convents.[57] In Mantua, she kept especially close ties to the Dominican convent S. Vincenzo where she attended her daughter Ippolita's (1501–1570) profession of vows in 1511, documented in detailed letters

---

relationships with Antonio Meli di Crema and Anselm Botturnio, see Zarri, *La religione di Lucrezia Borgia*, pp. 80–83. For letters between Lucrezia Borgia and Tommaso Caiani, see Zarri, *La religione di Lucrezia Borgia*, Appendix I.

55 Hickson, *Women, Art and Architectural Patronage in Renaissance Mantua*, p. 7. The altarpiece's current location is the Museo della Città, Palazzo di San Sebastiano, Mantua. There is some dispute over the altarpiece's date, which ranges from 1508 at the earliest to 1515, the year of Osanna's beatification, to 1519, the year Isabella d'Este and Margarita Cantelma became widows, consistent with the widow's garb in which they are depicted. For further discussion of the date, see Nigrelli, 'Le Gonzaga', p. 132.

56 Hickson, *Women, Art and Architectural Patronage in Renaissance Mantua*, p. 7.

57 I offer an extended discussion of Isabella's convent ties in both Ferrara and Mantua in 'The Piety of Female Friendship'.

to her half-sister, Lucrezia Bentivoglia, whose daughters were also taking formal vows at the convent.[58] Isabella's sister-in-law Lucrezia Borgia had even more familiarity with life behind convent walls. She received her education at S. Sisto in Rome and later became a Franciscan tertiary. In Ferrara, she embraced the relationship between the Este court and the convent Corpus Domini, where her husband's mother, Eleonora d'Aragona, had maintained her own cell. She also founded the convent S. Bernardino for her niece in 1509, and sent alms to convents in Mantua, Brescia, Milan, and Florence.[59] She, like her late mother-in-law, often retreated to Ferrara's Corpus Domini. In 1502, the chronicler Bernardino Zambotti recorded that Lucrezia Borgia was staying for a few days at Corpus Domini 'con poche donne [...] per il male epsa ha patito del parto che ha facto' (with a few women [...] due to the illness she suffered after childbirth). An extended stay after an illness, domestic or political strife, or personal loss all occasioned noblewomen's stays.[60] While Lucrezia may indeed have needed further physical convalescence, she would also have been retreating to Corpus Domini for emotional convalescence. In the convent, she would receive the care, guidance, and support she sought after a difficult childbirth, all delivered in a familiar and comforting environment.

These women were not unique in their connections with convents. In addition to continued contact with professed aunts, sisters, daughters, nieces, and friends, women inside and outside of convents maintained relationships with each other through patronage, letters, personal visits, and events and activities within convent walls. These ties created a spiritual community of lay and religious women connected through shared spiritual concern, collaboration, and the space of the convent. Women in this network sought out the intercessory prayers of their friends, asked for spiritual guidance, and encouraged piety and charity by giving gifts intended for spiritual edification.

The accepted model of the nun's life resonated with the accepted model for the laywoman's life, further supporting connections between women religious and laywomen. Manuals of Christian doctrine and those for female behaviour prescribed similar rules of comportment for religious and laity alike.[61] In her study of instructional literature dedicated to women between the mid-fifteenth and seventeenth centuries, Zarri notes the close association between female behavioural models and religious ideology in texts of spiritual advice. She contends that devotional literature during this period made little distinction between religious and laywomen in terms of its audience and

---

58 Mantova, ASMn, F.II.9, busta 2996, libro 29, 60. Isabella d'Este to Lucrezia Bentivoglia, 3 October 1511 and 5 October 1511. Another of Isabella's daughters, Paola (1508–1569), took vows at the Clarissian convent Corpus Domini.

59 For a discussion of the role S. Bernardino played in Lucrezia Borgia's financial activities, see Ghirardo, 'Lucrezia Borgia as Entrepreneur', and 'Lucrezia Borgia duchessa'.

60 Lombardi, I Francescani a Ferrara, p. 161.

61 Knox, 'Civility, Courtesy and Women', p. 6. Knox cites Nicholas Jenson's 1471 manual of Christian doctrine Palma virtutum and Giovanni di Dio da Venezia's Decor puellarum (1461).

that by the end of the sixteenth century, monastic discipline constituted 'the behavioural norm for all the states in the life of a woman'.[62] Similar findings led Sharon Strocchia to argue for a 'continuum of urban and monastic culture' as the basis of good morals, citing women's 'deep, personal familiarity with life behind the convent walls that was not shared by their male counterparts'.[63]

Convents served laywomen in a variety of ways throughout a woman's life. They were settings of early education for girls; places of safety during familial or political unrest; spaces in which to await an impending marriage; a retreat for rest and consolation after the death of a child; and residences for widows who did not remarry. The result was 'distinct continuities to the female life cycle within and across generations'.[64] Monastic life was, as Strocchia puts it, the 'common currency' of female community.[65] For example, Leonora Cibo, daughter of Ricciarda Malaspina and Lorenzo Cibo, rulers of Massa and Carrara, had extended stays at the Florentine convent Le Murate on several occasions during her life. She was educated there as a girl, left eight years later to marry, returned four years after that as a widow, and then returned a third time after the death of her second husband.[66] Within convent networks, this spiritual community perpetuated and advanced existing bonds between women, as many of the relationships mentioned in this chapter demonstrate.

Female spiritual advisors, irrespective of the religious order to which they belonged, reconnected laywomen to the community and fellowship convents provided, even when laywomen were not physically present within their walls. Suor Stefana, for example, was keen to identify other women who were familiar to Isabella d'Este, both lay and religious, reminding Isabella of her place in an extended support network that operated in a spiritualized context that lent structure and familiarity to their relationships. Similarly, in addition to referencing Suor Laura Mignani, Suor Francesca Caprioli often mentioned and sent regards to a Madonna Gabriella in her letters to Lucrezia Gonzaga. In September of 1504, Francesca described the joy and consolation brought to her by Madonna Gabriella's visit to the convent on Lucrezia's behalf, writing, 'mentre non li posiamo dimonstrate per visitation corporale non di meno alcuno signo de carita et amore' (while it is not possible to demonstrate it through a physical visit, nevertheless I can demonstrate my care and love for you) through the special prayers the sisters say every day 'como promisseno a vostra Mag.tia' (as promised to Your Magnificence).[67]

---

62 Zarri, 'Christian Good Manners', pp. 82, 78.
63 Strocchia, 'Taken into Custody', p. 197, and 'Learning the Virtues', p. 20.
64 Strocchia, 'Taken into Custody', pp. 188–89.
65 Strocchia, 'Taken into Custody', p. 190.
66 Lowe, *Nuns' Chronicles and Convent Culture*, pp. 181–82. Leonora's first marriage was to Gian Luigi Fieschi. She then married Gian Luigi (Chiappino) Vitelli, during whose absences Leonora 'returned to Le Murate for visits'. When Leonora returned to Le Murate for the third time she was granted leave three times a year.
67 Brescia, ASB, AG, filza 88, Francesca Caprioli to Lucrezia Gonzaga, 10 September 1504.

It worked the other way, too. Laywomen drew on their female connections to access spiritual advisors, thereby multiplying the individual nodes within a given network. For example, in 1509, Lucrezia Borgia attempted to convince her sister-in-law Isabella d'Este to bring Suor Stefana Quinzani with her when she came to Ferrara for the Christmas season. She wrote, 'Et circa la resposta la mi fae de la Matre sore Stephana, no dirò altro […] Ma ben la prego che, qhando [sic] seremo a questo Natale et che epsa Stephana sia tornata a lei, come la dice avergli fermamente promesso' (And concerning your response regarding the Mother Suor Stefana, I will say no more […] But I pray that when we are together this Christmas that Stefana returns with you, as she [Stefana] had firmly promised).[68] The desire Lucrezia expressed to her sister-in-law reveals how spirituality permeated women's lives and networks were under ordinary conditions in addition to the extraordinary circumstances discussed elsewhere in this chapter.

Spirituality constituted a key part of laywomen's relationships with one another in large part because of the shared experience of convents. Women who shared the experience of courts also shared the experience of convents and convent spirituality. This shared experience was also reflected in the letters of spiritual advisors. In their spiritual advising, women varied their frames of interaction to suit the particular need of the moment. Sometimes they referred to themselves and their addressees as mother, sometimes friend, and sometimes daughter. Suor Francesca Caprioli, for instance, most often referred to Lucrezia Gonzaga as 'our most obedient mother' in her letters, whereas Suor Stefana more often referred to herself as mother in her letters to Isabella d'Este, such as when she sent Isabella 'un pocho di lino in segno de materno amor, acciò possati filar una corda che ve tire fina al tercio Ciel' (a little linen as a sign of maternal love, so that you are able to spin a cord that pulls you to all the way to the third heaven) as a sign of her 'gran desiderio di vederve coniuncta cum lo dolze amator Iesu Christo et talmente cum luy unita che non ve curati de cose transitori ma solum de le perpetue' (great desire to see you joined with the sweet lover Jesus Christ and so, united with Him, you do not care for transitory things but only those of that last).[69] This flexibility points to the larger community, one to which advisor and advisee both belonged, but that also extended beyond the particular advising relationship.

The letters between spiritual advisors and advisees reveal ruling women's reliance on holy and prophetic women in providing spiritual guidance and protection, but also the embeddedness of these women in convent networks that crossed geographical and political spaces. Although they had male confessors with the power to absolve sins, laywomen solicited advice and spiritual comfort, whether through prayer or reassuring words, from religious women

---

68   Lucrezia Borgia to Isabella d'Este, 13 September 1509, reprinted in Zarri, *La religione di Lucrezia Borgia*, Appendice II, p. 303.
69   Stefana Quinzani to Isabella d'Este, 31 July 1518, reprinted in Cistellini, *Figure della riforma*, p. 183.

when they faced new challenges and struggled to persevere through on-going challenges. Many called on the women within their convent networks, and thus operated through its norms. The spiritual community these networks constituted was characterized by regular expressions of the necessity and desire to keep one another spiritually close, and the cultivation of spiritual fortitude. Moreover, extending the reach and range of spiritual support was a priority in this community. In addition to instructing, comforting, and reiterating existing connections between writer and addressee, letters from advisors more often than not also directed the advisee toward other women on whom they might rely, such as Suor Francesca Caprioli's references to Suor Laura Mignani in her letters to Lucrezia Gonzaga, thereby expanding the network. These connections did not only project into the future cultivation of the web of relations, but could also extend back in time to older associations that might be reinforced, as in the case of Suor Stefana's words of guidance to Isabella d'Este regarding the death of Isabella's previous spiritual advisor, the Dominican tertiary Osanna Andreasi, in 1505. Here, Suor Stefana promised to imitate Osanna in piety and devotion, and urged Isabella to take comfort in contemplating all that Osanna had overcome with divine help.[70] Female spiritual advisors represented the support and experience of the communal piety of convents available to religious and laywomen alike. As such, women's spiritual advising represented continuity, piety, and spiritual growth through companionship, and across space and time.

---

70 Stefana Quinzani to Isabella d'Este, 7 September 1505, reprinted in Cistellini, *Figure della riforma*, p. 180.

Works Cited

Manuscripts and Archival Sources

Brescia, Archivio di Storico Civico (ASB)
    Archivio Gambara (AG)
Mantova, Archivio di Stato (ASMn)
    Archivio Gonzaga
    ——, E.LXI.1
    ——, F.II.9

Secondary Works

Amadei, Federigo, *Cronaca universale della città di Mantova*, vol. II, Edizione Integrale (Mantova, C.I.T.E.M., 1955)

Baernstein, P. Renée, *A Convent Tale: A Century of Sisterhood in Spanish Milan* (New York: Routledge, 2002)

Barette, Rev. Gene, 'Spiritual Direction in the Roman Catholic Tradition', *Journal of Psychology and Theology*, 30.4 (2002), 290–302

Benvenuti, Anna, 'Le religiosae mulieres tra cura animarum, cura monialium e direzione spirituale', in *Storia della direzione spirituale*, vol. II. L'età medieval, ed. by Sofia Boesch Gajano (Brescia: Editrice Morcelliana, 2010), pp. 373–85

Bowd, Stephen D., *Reform before the Reformation: Vicenzo Querini and the Religious Renaissance in Italy* (Leiden: Brill, 2002)

——, *Venice's Most Loyal City: Civic Identity in Renaissance Brescia* (Cambridge, MA: Harvard University Press, 2010)

Cavalli, Jennifer, 'The Piety of Female Friendship: Convent and Court in Sixteenth-Century Mantua', *Sixteenth Century Journal*, 50. 2 (2019), 31–53

Cistellini, Antonio, *Figure della riforma pretridentina: Stefana Quinzani, Angela Merici, Laura Mignani, Bartolomeo Stella, Francesco Cabrini e Francesco Santabona* (Brescia: Morcelliana, 1948)

Coakley, John W., *Women, Men, and Spiritual Power: Female Saints and Their Male Collaborators* (New York: Columbia University Press, 2006)

Cockram, Sarah D. P., *Isabella d'Este and Francesco Gonzaga: Power Sharing at the Italian Renaissance Court* (Farnham: Ashgate, 2013)

Dunn, Marilyn R., 'Spiritual Philanthropists: Women as Convent Patrons in Seicento Rome', in *Women and Art in Early Modern Europe: Patrons, Collectors, and Connoisseurs*, ed. by Cynthia Lawrence (University Park: Pennsylvania State University Press, 1997), pp. 154–88

Evangelisti, Silvia, *Nuns: A History of Convent Life* (Oxford: Oxford University Press, 2007)

Ghirardi, Angela, 'Osanna Andreasi e Isabella d'Este. Tracce artistiche di un'amicizia', in *Osanna Andreasi da Mantova, 1449–1505: L'immagine di una mistica del rinascimento*, ed. by Renata Casarin (Mantova: Casandreasi, 2005), pp. 65–77

Ghirardo, Diane Yvonne, 'Lucrezia Borgia as Entrepeneur', *Renaissance Quarterly*, 61 (2008), 53–91

——, 'Lucrezia Borgia duchessa, imprenditrice e devota', *Quaderni Estensi*, 2 (2010), 195–211

Herzig, Tamar, *Savonarola's Women: Visions and Reform in Renaissance Italy* (Chicago: University of Chicago Press, 2008)

Hickson, Sally, *Women, Art and Architectural Patronage in Renaissance Mantua: Matrons, Mystics and Monasteries* (Farnham: Ashgate: 2012)

Hillman, Jennifer, 'Soul Mates and Collaborators: Spiritual Direction in Late Medieval and Early Modern Europe', *History Compass*, 13.9 (2015), 476–84

Knox, Dilwyn, 'Civility, Courtesy and Women in the Italian Renaissance', in *Women in Italian Renaissance Culture and Society*, ed. by Letizia Panizza (Oxford: Legenda, 2000), pp. 2–15

Laven, Mary, *Virgins of Venice: Enclosed Lives and Broken Vows in the Renaissance Convent* (London: Viking, 2002)

Lehmijoki-Gardner, Maiju, *Dominican Penitent Women* (Mahwah: Paulist Press, 2005)

Lombardi, Teodosio, *I Francescani a Ferrara, vol. 4. I monasteri delle Clarisse: S. Guglielmo, Corpus Domini, S. Bernardino, S. Chiara* (Bologna: Antoniano, 1974–1975)

——, *Gli Estense ed il Monastero del Corpus Domini di Ferrara* (Ferrara: Centro Culturale Città di Ferrara, 1980)

Lowe, Kate, *Nuns' Chronicles and Convent Culture in Renaissance and Counter-Reformation Italy* (Cambridge: Cambridge University Press, 2003)

Luzio, Alessandro, and Rodolfo Renier, *Mantova e Urbino. Isabella d'Este ed Elisabetta Gonzaga nelle relazioni famigliari e nelle vicende politiche* (Turin: Roux e C., 1893)

Matthews Grieco, Sara F., 'Models of Female Sanctity in Renaissance and Counter-Reformation Italy', in *Women and Faith: Catholic Religious Life in Italy from Late Antiquity to the Present*, ed. by Lucetta Scaraffia and Gabriella Zarri (Cambridge, MA: Harvard University Press, 1999), pp. 159–75

McLaughlin, Mary Martin, 'Creating and Recreating Communities of Women: The Case of Corpus Domini, Ferrara, 1406–52', in *Sisters and Workers in the Middle Ages*, ed. by J. Bennett and others (Chicago: University of Chicago Press, 1989), pp. 261–88

Mecham, June L., 'Cooperative Piety among Monastic and Secular Women in Late Medieval Germany', *Church History and Religious Culture*, 88.4 (2008), 561–611

Monson, Craig, *Disembodied Voices: Music and Culture in an Early Modern Italian Convent* (Berkeley: University of California Press, 1995)

Nigrelli, Gianni, 'Le Gonzaga, priore e committenti d'arte in San Vincenzo', in *La beata Osanna e i domenicani a Mantova. In memoria di Nicola Fiasconaro*, ed. by Angela Ghirardi and Rosanna Golinelli Berto (Mantova: Casandreasi, 2011), pp. 125–38

Prosperi, Adriano, 'Spiritual Letters', in *Women and Faith: Catholic Religious Life in Italy from Late Antiquity to the Present*, ed. by Lucetta Scaraffia and Gabriella Zarri (Cambridge, MA: Harvard University Press, 1999), pp. 113–28

Ranft, Patricia, 'A Key to Counter Reformation Women's Activism: The Confessor-Spiritual Director', *Journal of Feminist Studies in Religion*, 10.2 (1994), 7–26

——, *A Woman's Way: The Forgotten History of Women Spiritual Directors* (New York: Palgrave, 2000)

Russell, Camilla, 'Convent Culture in Early-Modern Italy: Laywomen and Religious Subversiveness in a Neapolitan Convent', in *Practices of Gender in Late Medieval and Early Modern Europe*, ed. by Megan Cassidy-Welch and Peter Sherlock (Turnhout: Brepols, 2009), pp. 57–76

Scattigno, Anna, 'Lettere dal convento', in *Per lettera: la scrittura epistolare femminile tra archivio e tipografia: secoli 15–17*, ed. by Gabriella Zarri, Series I libri di Viella (Rome: Viella, 1999), pp. 313–57

Shaw, Christine, 'The Papacy and the European Powers', in *Italy and the European Powers: The Impact of War, 1500–1530*, ed. by Christine Shaw (Leiden: Brill, 2006), pp. 107–26

——, *Barons and Castellans: The Military Nobility of Renaissance Italy* (Leiden: Brill, 2015)

Sperling, Jutta Gisela, *Convents and the Body Politic in Late Renaissance Venice* (Chicago: University of Chicago Press, 1999)

Strocchia, Sharon, 'Learning the Virtues: Convent Schools and Female Culture in Renaissance Florence', in *Women's Education in Early Modern Europe: A History, 1500–1800*, ed. by Barbara Whitehead (New York: Garland, 1999), pp. 3–46

——, 'Taken into Custody: Girls and Convent Guardianship in Renaissance Florence', *Renaissance Studies*, 17. 2 (2003), 177–200

——, *Nuns and Nunneries in Renaissance Florence* (Baltimore: Johns Hopkins University Press, 2009)

Warr, Cordelia, 'Performing the Passion: Strategies for Salvation in the Life of Stefana Quinzani (d. 1530)', *Studies in Church History*, 45 (2009), 218–27

Zarri, Gabriella, 'Monasteri femminili e città (secoli XV–XVIII)', in *Storia d'Italia: La Chiesa e il Potere Politico dal Medioevo all'Età Contemporanea*, vol. 9, ed. by Giorgio Chittolini and Giovanni Miccoli (Turin: Giulio Einaudi, 1986), pp. 360–429

——, 'Monache e sante alle corte estense, XV–XVI Secolo', in *Storia Illustrata di Ferrara*, vol. 2, ed. by F. Bocchi (San Marino: AIEP, 1987), pp. 417–32

——, *Le sante vive: profezie di corte e devozione femminile tra '400 e '500* (Turin: Rosenberg and Sellier, 1990)

——, 'Living Saints: A Typology of Female Sanctity in the Early Sixteenth Century', in *Women and Religion in Medieval and Renaissance Italy*, ed. by Daniel Bornstein and Roberto Rusconi, trans. by Margery J. Schneider (Chicago: University of Chicago Press, 1996), pp. 219–303

——, 'Christian Good Manners: Spiritual and Monastic Rules in the Quattro- and Cinquecento', in *Women in Italian Renaissance Culture and Society*, ed. by Letizia Panizza (Oxford: Legenda, 2000), pp. 76–91

——, *La religione di Lucrezia Borgia: Le lettere inedite del confessore* (Rome: Roma nel Rinascimento, 2006)

MEGHAN CALLAHAN*

Nuns' Networks

*Letters from Suor Domenica da Paradiso
at La Crocetta in Renaissance Florence*

In Renaissance convents, *clausura* kept nuns from the public eye, but inhabitants maintained and developed social networks with the outside world through meeting with family and friends.[1] Visitors delivered gossip, gifts and letters, creating a web of exchange between nuns, their friends and families, and business associates. Letters were an especially important part of early modern networking, and favours and recommendations were requested and fulfilled through missives sent within city walls and out to the wider world.[2] In Florence, secular women such as Alessandra Macinghi Strozzi (*c.* 1408–1471) maintained her family's status and managed her exiled sons' affairs through letters.[3] In a similar fashion, religious women, some of whom no doubt felt exiled to convents, sent letters to their counterparts in other convents, to family members, and to their neighbours to maintain social bonds or to discuss issues of inheritance, disputes over shared walls and communal property, or political news.[4] They even wrote to communal officials about trouble in their own

---

* I thank Marilyn Dunn and Saundra Weddle for their dedication to this project. I am grateful to them and the anonymous reviewer for their insightful critiques and corrections. Any errors remain my own. I have retained the original spellings and forms of words in my transcriptions. The archive of La Crocetta was housed in the cloistered convent on Via Aretina in Florence until 2016, when the convent closed, and the documents were transferred to the Biblioteca Domenicana di S. Maria Novella Jacopo Passavanti, Florence.

1 See among others Monson, ed., *The Crannied Wall*; Weddle, 'Women in Wolves' Mouths'; Dunn, 'Nuns, Agents and Agency'.

2 On the tradition of letter writing in fifteenth-century Florence, McLean, *The Art of the Network*. For early modern England, see Medici, 'Using Network Analysis to Understand Early Modern Women'.

3 *Selected Letters of Alessandra Strozzi*, ed. by Gregory, p. 6; *Letters to Her Sons*, ed. and trans. by Bryce. The Strozzi sons were exiled in 1458.

4 On feeling imprisoned, see the seventeenth-century Arcangela Tarabotti, *Semplicità ingannta*, ed. and trans. by L. Panizza; for Tarabotti's letters see Tarabotti, *Lettere familiari*, ed. by Ray and Westwater.

Meghan Callahan (macallah@syr.edu) is Assistant Director of Teaching and Learning at Syracuse University London.

Convent Networks In Early Modern Italy, ed. by Marilyn Dunn and Saundra Weddle, ES 25 (Turnhout: Brepols, 2020) pp. 53–84   BREPOLS✠PUBLISHERS   DOI 10.1484/M.ES-EB.5.119513

Figure 2.1. Anonymous, *Portrait of Suor Domenica da Paradiso*, Florence, Palazzo Pitti. *c.* seventeenth century. Reproduced with permission of the Gabinetto Fotografico delle Gallerie degli Uffizi, Florence.

convents, accusing clerics of violating the nuns.[5] Religious women managed artistic commissions from behind the grate by sending descriptions of the images they wanted to adorn their chapels, and sometimes were permitted on visits arranged by letter to inspect paintings in other convents.[6] The letters preserved in convent and state archives allow us to hear the voices of early modern religious women and understand their agency.

5 Strocchia, *Nuns and Nunneries in Renaissance Florence*, p. 183, citing a 1481 letter from a nun at S. Caterina in Florence.

6 Radke, 'Nuns and their Art'; Thomas, *Art and Piety in the Female Religious Communities*; Hayum, 'A Renaissance Audience Considered'.

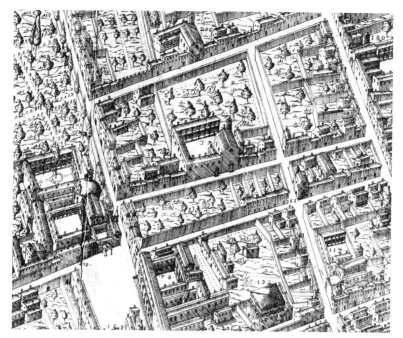

Figure 2.2. Stefano Buonsignori, detail of *Pianta di Firenze*, showing La Crocetta (number 37), Florence Kunsthistorisches Institut Florenz. 1584. With permission of Kunsthistorisches Institut Florenz.

One such voice is that of the Dominican mystic Suor Domenica da Paradiso (1473–1553), who founded the Florentine convent of La Crocetta in 1511, and occupies an unusual place in history as the only lower-class female patron of monastic architecture in Renaissance Florence (Figure 2.1).[7] As seen in the Buonsignori view of 1584, the convent was once located near the church and friary of SS. Annunziata, on today's via Laura, but the original building was largely destroyed in the nineteenth century (Figure 2.2).[8] Copies of over ninety letters sent by Domenica survive.[9] Domenica's missives allowed her to

---

7 Callahan, "'In her name and with her money'". I thank Anna Bisceglia for alerting me to the image in the Palazzo Pitti collection.

8 The Crocetta nuns moved to a building on Via Aretina in the nineteenth century, and the convent officially closed in 2015. I thank the former archbishop of Florence, Ennio Cardinal Antonelli, and his successor, Monsignor Giuseppe Betori, for granting me permission to enter the cloistered areas of the convent of La Crocetta between 2003 and 2005 and again in 2009, and the nuns for welcoming me into their home. On Domenica building the convent see my "'In her name and with her money'", and my 'The Politics of Architecture'.

9 Contemporary copies of Suor Domenica's letters are held in the BDSMN in Florence. I thank Ughetta Sorelli for her invaluable support and help in the archives. In Domenica dal Paradiso, *Scritti spirituali*, ed. by Antignani, Antignani used MS H Epistole della Ven.l. Mre S.r Dom.ca Fondatrice et dotatrice del Monast.° della Croce di Firenze, dll'[*sic*] ordine di S. Dom.co, (then

reach beyond the walls of her convent and build her reputation as a visionary, healer, and leader of a Dominican-affiliated reform movement, despite not taking full vows as a nun until the year before she died.

From the first decades of the 1500s to her death in 1553, Domenica used scribes to write to people from all levels of society, including her artisan and noble followers, friars, the archbishop of Florence, popes, and rulers such as Duke Cosimo I, creating an epistolary network that crossed classes and spanned the Italian peninsula. Though she wrote to both men and women, in this essay I will focus mainly on Domenica's letters to women in convents or to those who were considering life inside the walls. Elite women such as Caterina Cibo (also spelled Cybo) the duchess of Camerino, and Ginevra Tiepolo, the signora of Pesaro, communicated with Domenica to share bonds of faith and interest in reform. Women from the artisan class, who were probably not literate, would have heard the mystic's advice in letters read aloud to them. Domenica's letters reveal her determination to expand her reach beyond Florence and beyond her social class, to promote her vision of Church reform to men and women searching for a new prophet in the years after Girolamo Savonarola's death, and to insert herself into the chain of communication that linked women beyond convent walls throughout Renaissance Italy. Fully aware that letters were often read by others than the intended recipients, Domenica and her confessor Francesco da Castiglione, (1466–1542), a canon at S. Lorenzo, used epistles to bolster her image as a holy, obedient woman who kept within the boundaries of Catholic orthodoxy, even if she sometimes transgressed them.[10]

Francesco assisted Domenica in all of her activities. He assiduously recorded her sermons, wrote some letters for her, and detailed the miraculous events of Domenica's life in unpublished biographies.[11] Convinced he was in the presence

---

in the cloistered convent, now in Florence, Biblioteca Domenicana di S. Maria Novella Jacopo Passavanti, Archivio di Monastero della Crocetta (BDSMN, AMC)).

This is a bound book of copies of Domenica's letters written in the sixteenth century by various hands. The letters are numbered in the manuscript, and are organized loosely by subject and recipient, but in his publication, Antignani reordered and renumbered them, in an effort (he claimed) to better understand Suor Domenica's 'spirit and teaching' and 'according to a logical and chronological succession'. Domenica dal Paradiso, *Scritti spirituali*, ed. by Antignani, p. 87. Of course, Antignani's logic is different to that of the original compilers, for that reason I have referred to his numbering system of the letters simply as 'no.' in subsequent citations.

10   I thank Marilyn Dunn for this thought.

11   On their relationship see Callahan, 'Suor Domenica da Paradiso as "alter Christus"'; Valerio, *Domenica da Paradiso*. For Domenica's sermons see Librandi and Valerio, *I sermoni di Domenica da Paradiso*. Carolyn Muessig also discussed Suor Domenica's preaching in her paper 'Breaking the Silence: Female Preaching in Late Medieval and Early Modern Europe', in the session *Female Religious Authority in the Late Middle Ages*, sponsored by International Medieval Sermon Studies Society, 17 March 2019, Renaissance Society of America Annual Meeting, Toronto, which is included in her book, *The Stigmata in Medieval and Early Modern Europe*.

of a 'living saint', Francesco hoped Domenica's biography would be used in a future canonization process. This later occurred after Maria Maddalena de' Medici joined La Crocetta in 1611 and her mother, Grand Duchess Christine of Lorraine, instigated a committee to beatify Domenica.[12] Despite this Medici interest, because of Domenica's reputation as a Savonarolan, the mystic was never canonized, though she is listed in the Index Causarum as 'venerabile'.[13]

Domenica and Francesco met in 1506, seven years after she moved to Florence from the farming town of Paradiso, outside the city.[14] Despite not belonging to a convent or group of tertiaries, she was called 'Suor Domenica' because she wore a homemade habit and had a reputation as a healer. Even then she was rumoured to be a follower of Girolamo Savonarola, the recently deceased Dominican preacher who had attempted to transform Florence into a New Jerusalem through religious and political reform. Savonarola's sermons had shaken the city as he attempted to convince Florentines to reform to a fully Christian life.[15] Though initially supported by many, Savonarola's political involvement and public charges against Pope Alexander VI led to his death under accusations of heresy. Hanged and then burned at the stake in Piazza della Signoria in Florence, Savonarola died in 1498, but his followers continued his movement through the mid-1500s.[16]

By about 1501, Domenica was the beneficiary of some of these followers' attention as she became known within a small group for her visions, prophecies, and rumoured stigmata.[17] She lived in the home of a *stamaiuolo*, Giovanni da Sanminiato, and worked as a weaver or servant with other women in the house.[18] These women, along with men from the artisan class, Giovanni, and some of his children, became her first followers. After predicting the death of a child in Giovanni's family, Domenica was accused, then absolved of heresy in 1501. Several charges seem to have been brought against her, including wearing a Brigittine habit without permission, not having a fixed confessor,

---

12 See Callahan, 'Suor Domenica da Paradiso as "alter Christus"'; Calvi, *Histories of a Plague Year*, pp. 199–226. The grand duchess commissioned Ignazio del Nente to write a new biography of Domenica using Francesco's sources in 1611, which he dedicated to Princess Maria Maddalena. See Callahan, 'The Politics of Architecture', p. 28.

13 Catholic Church, Congregatio pro Causis Sanctorum, *Index ac Status Causarum*, p. 98 as 'congr. Antepraep s. virt. 10 mar. 1761'. This indicates that Domenica's candidacy had reached the pre-preparatory phase of consideration of virtue, martyrs or miracles (see p. lxxiii for definitions). Antignani, *Vicende e tempi*, p. 236 n. 37, noted that Domenica's writings were approved on 28 July 1742, citing the 1975 edition of the Index. This was also cited in Gagliardi, *Sola con Dio*, p. 240. Antignani, *La Crocetta di Firenze* pp. 55–58, 60, reproduced the text of an eighteenth-century copy of a convent manuscript detailing the arrival of Maria Maddalena at the convent. Claudia de' Medici (1604–1648) was Maria Maddalena's sister and a widow when she stayed at the convent for two years (1623–1625).

14 Callahan, 'Suor Domenica da Paradiso as "alter Christus"'.

15 Weinstein, *Savonarola*.

16 Polizzotto, *The Elect Nation*; Herzig, *Savonarola's Women*.

17 Callahan, 'Suor Domenica da Paradiso as "alter Christus"'.

18 A *stamaiuolo* delivered combed wool to spinners. See de Roover, *A Florentine Firm*, p. 14.

having raptures, and claiming the stigmata. According to Francesco, the archbishop's vicar was swayed by Domenica's arguments defending herself.[19] She later became embroiled in a fight with the Savonarolans of S. Marco over her right to wear the Dominican habit, with which she had vested herself in 1506.[20] The friars wanted to control Domenica and her group, but she resisted.

Despite the controversy with the S. Marco friars, a positive reputation was growing for Domenica among elite men such as Girolamo Gondi, Marco del Nero, Federigo de' Ricci, and Francesco Inghirami, all of whom financed Domenica's new convent of La Crocetta.[21] The connections between these men were reinforced through marriage. Marco's second wife was Nannina di Bernardo di Gondi, (a cousin of Girolamo), and Federigo de' Ricci married her sister Alessandra.[22] After Marco died in 1528, Federigo replaced him as procurator (legal representative) at La Crocetta.[23] In the same election, Francesco Inghirami was voted in as procurator.[24] His wife was Maria di Bernardo di Gondi, sister to Nannina and Alessandra. All of these men served the convent as procurators, and some had their daughters join the convent. Federigo eventually had two daughters join La Crocetta, while Girolamo Gondi installed one daughter, Costanza, who adopted the name Serafina in her new life as a nun.[25]

---

19 For a full account see Callahan, 'Suor Domenica da Paradiso as "alter Christus"', p. 329.

20 Polizzotto, 'When Saints Fall Out'; Callahan, 'Suor Domenica da Paradiso as "alter Christus"', p. 331.

21 See Callahan, '"In her name and with her money"'; Callahan 'Suor Domenica da Paradiso as "alter Christus"'.

22 Toccafondi Fantappie, 'Marco del Nero'. For references to the del Nero family see also Fra Vincenzo Mainardi, 'Epistolario di Fra Vincenzo Mainardi', ed. by Verde and Giaconi, vol. 1, pp. 195, 196; vol. 2, pp. 413, 554. I thank Alessio Assonitis for this reference. See also Corbinelli, *Histoire genealogique de la maison de Gondi*, vol. 1, frontispiece, p. 102.

23 Florence, BDSMN, AMC, unnumbered MS Libro dei Partiti, fol. 4[r], Procuratori del monast[o] Giovanj [sic] dibanco deglialbizj, Federigo di ruberto de'ricci [sic], Francesco di Girolamo inghiranj [sic] 1528.

24 Corbinelli, *Histoire genealogique de la maison de Gondi*, vol. 1.

25 Florence, ASF, CRSGF 107, filza 1, Giornaliere, Libro A, 1518, fol. 2[v]. Two other Gondi cousins were in La Crocetta. Caterina di Carlo Gondi, called Suor Colomba, entered the convent on 22 October 1526, was vested on 10 June 1526, professed on 11 October 1528 and died on 16 October 1528. After her death, her sister Lisabetta di Carlo Gondi (b. 1 January 1518), replaced her by taking the name Colomba and entered the convent on 3 April 1529, vested on 21 September 1529, professed on 14 April 1532, and died on 9 May 1563. Caterina de' Ricci adopted the name Arcangela and entered on 24 December 1530 at the age of ten. Her sister Susanna took the name Alessandra and entered on 10 September 1531 at the age of eight. On 20 April 1521, it was decided that four girls would be accepted as nuns, when they reached the correct age. They were 'una nipote dibernardo ghondi n[ost]ro procuratore ... una figluola di brunaccio brunacci ... una figluola di Philippo ghondi ... una figluola di Federigho di ruberto dericci' (a niece/granddaughter of Bernardo Gondi our procurator, a daughter of Brunaccio Brunacci, a daughter of Filippo Gondi, a daughter of Federigo di Ruberto de' Ricci). Florence, BDSMN, AMC, unnumbered MS Libro dei Partiti, fol. 1[r]. Immediately after, it was decided that except for the four above-named girls, anyone wanting

The documents do not reveal who the first man to meet Domenica was, but Marco del Nero was an early contact. He knew Domenica when she lived in Giovanni da Sanminiato's home, and he later encouraged a friend's daughter to join her group, saying that no convent in Florence was run as well as Domenica's.[26] The connection may have come from shared industry ties; in 1506 Giovanni da Sanminiato purchased combed wool [*stame*] from the wool company of Simone del Nero, Marco's father.[27] This wool was probably destined to be spun by Domenica and the women who worked in Giovanni's home.

Despite her followers' belief that Domenica was close to God, the impact of Savonarola's fiery death on Florentine political life prompted the mystic and her group to remain fairly quiet about the funding of Domenica's convent, her preaching, and meetings to ensure survival. They had seen fellow Savonarolans exiled, and Marco del Nero's father Simone was fined 200 florins for his support of the friar.[28] These repercussions lasted for years after 1498, as has been demonstrated by Lorenzo Polizzotto.[29] When an accusation was made in 1519 that Suor Domenica was 'speaking against the Scriptures' in illegal pro-Savonarola conventicles held at her convent, she staunchly denied it in a letter.[30]

Domenica chastised a certain unnamed group for gossiping about her, claiming: 'Io non so nè leggere, nè scrivere, et sono usa amazolare cavolo et cipolle, perchè da piccolina fui hortolana. Se voi trovate ch'io exponga la Sacra Scriptura per virtù del mio exercitio, riprendetemi come presumptuosa' (I don't know how to read, nor write, and I'm used to digging up cabbages and onions, because as a little girl I was a gardener. If you find that I expound on the Sacred Scriptures per virtue of my work, reproach me as a presumptuous [woman]).[31] Her claims of illiteracy neatly aligned with Savonarola's

---

to enter the convent in future had to be between thirteen and eighteen years old, and *converse* had to be between eighteen and twenty-two. It is not clear if the girl accepted in 1521 was Caterina (who would have been one year old) or another daughter who decided against joining and therefore was not recorded.

26 Florence, BDSMN, AMC, MS 4 Libro dei Miracoli, fol. 45ᵛ, see also Callahan, 'The Politics of Architecture', p. 177.

27 Edler, *Glossary of Mediaeval Terms of Business*, p. 325. For the purchase see Florence, AOIF, Estranei 122, 419, Memoriale Segnato C, 'Libro di Simone del Nero e chompagnia di lanaiuoli in garbo 1504–1511', fol. 25ʳ. I am grateful to Dr Lucia Sandri who helped with the transcription. Giovanni's brother Jacopo's name appears in Simone di Bernardo di Simone del Nero's *quadernuccio* (small notebook): AOIF, Estranei 122, 434, 1501 Segnato E, 40ʳ, 1503. See also Callahan, 'The Politics of Architecture'.

28 Toccafondi Fantappie, 'Marco del Nero', p. 176.

29 Polizzotto, *The Elect Nation*.

30 Callahan, 'Preaching in a Poor Space', p. 227.

31 Florence, BDSMN, AMC, MS 7 Epistole Morali, letter no. 133. Cited in Borghigiani, Parte Terza, p. xv; Domenica dal Paradiso, *Scritti spirituali*, ed. by Antignani, p. 167, no. 52, and Gagliardi, p. 165. Each author used different accents (Borghigiani: none over 'ne', 'perchè'; Gagliardi: 'né', 'perché') I have followed Antignani. On Domenica's sermons see Librandi and Valerio, *I sermoni di Domenica da Paradiso*; Callahan, 'Preaching in a Poor Space'.

assertions that it was often the simple — among whom he included women and children — who best knew God.[32] Suor Domenica's public insistence that she was an 'illiterate and simple woman' cloaked the mystic's abilities in a mantle of humility that allowed her to act independently without excessively disrupting the established social order.

Domenica's letters share certain conventions seen in writing by religious women, especially those who were lauded as living saints.[33] Like Domenica's near contemporary Battistina Vernazza of Genoa, and their predecessor St Catherine of Siena, Domenica was always careful to claim she was channelling God's voice in her prophecies, sermons, and letters.[34] But Domenica's voice comes through clearly. Her description of the dictation process reveals that she saw the amanuensis's hand as an extension of her own, and Domenica was frustrated by delays.

Watching the scribe painstakingly take down the words that flowed out of her in a torrent of inspiration often proved too much for Domenica, as she noted:

> Però non vi dolete di me ch'io exponga la Sacra Scriptura. Io vo allo studio quando ho a scrivere, inginocchiomi et fo Orazione, et priego Dio che mi facci dire quel che è l'honor suo [...] Dico quel chel mio sposo Jesu mi manda a bocca senza pensar nulla, et dico ch'io mi struggo di vedere scrivere si adagio, perché mi abondano tanto le sententie, tanto le allegorie, ch'io mi distruggo avere aspectare lo Scriptore, et dire si adagio, et batto di qua et di là, piglio que sensi et quelle allegorie, che giungono in su la lingua senza pensarle. Però rispondo ch'io non expongo la Scriptura quando è in me, ma porgo quello chel Signiore mi mette in bocca [...] Allui non è impossibile alcuna cosa [...] Quando mi è letto quel chi'io ho dittato, triemo, perchè veggo et conosco ch'io non harò scusa alcuna, perchè sono tenuta a mettere in opera quel che Dio mi fa parlare [...] Però, dilectissimi mia, non via maravigliate ch'io scriva, et chio dica le Laude del mio Sposo Jesu Xpo, benchè io non habbi studiatio, el mio Sposo sa ogni cosa lui, fece parlar l'asina, non è gran cosa che facci parlar me.[35]

> (But do not worry that I expound on the Sacred Scripture. I go to the study when I have to write, I kneel down and pray, and beg God that he makes me say that which is to his honour [...] I say what my husband Jesus sends to my mouth without thinking, and I say that I struggle to see it written so slowly, because there are so many pronouncements coming to me, so many allegories, that it kills me to have to wait for

---

32 Savonarola, *La Semplicità della Vita Cristiana*, trans. P. Tito S. Centi.

33 Zarri, *Le Sante vive*.

34 Camillocci, 'La monaca esemplare'.

35 BDSMN, AMC, MS 7 Epistole Morali, letter no. 133; cited in Domenica dal Paradiso, *Scritti spirituali*, ed. by Antignani, p. 167, no. 52. For the reference to Christ making an ass speak, see 2 Peter 2. 16.

the writer, and to speak very slowly, and I go back and forth, I take those senses and those allegories, that come together on the tongue without thinking about it. So I respond that I don't expound on the Scripture when it is in me, but I put down what the Lord puts in my mouth [...] Nothing is impossible for him [...] When what I dictated is read to me, I tremble, because I see and I know that I would not have any excuse, because I have to put into words what God makes me say [...] Therefore, my dearest ones, don't marvel that I write, and that I praise my husband Jesus Christ, even if I have not studied, my husband, he knows everything, he made the ass speak, it is not a great thing that he makes me speak ...).

Despite the difficulties of remaining patient, Domenica viewed suffering through the long writing process as a devotional exercise. She knew the power of transforming the spoken word into the written for posterity, and as a means for increasing support for La Crocetta.

The written word was not the only medium Domenica employed to connect with her network of associates. She also went in person to other convents and on begging excursions in the streets of Florence. Not being a nun, Domenica was not cloistered, but she also could not leave La Crocetta whenever she wanted. In 1516, the archbishop's vicar, Pier Andrea Gammaro imposed an order that Domenica become the prioress of La Crocetta because the elected abbess was not up to the job. In exchange, Domenica was allowed to leave the convent if she had her confessor Francesco's permission.[36] The deal allowed her to keep her freedom of movement, while Gammaro insured that Domenica would run the convent.[37] Gammaro was one of her 'spiritual sons' and was concerned that Domenica's convent would fail if she did not run it, though he also knew she was giving sermons and may have wanted to protect Domenica from the promulgations against preaching by unauthorized persons issued the previous year by the authorities.[38] He knew Domenica's charisma and personality drove the convent, and kept funding coming in during the early years. Yet at the same time, he recognized her need for independence, and wrote:

Cr[e]dete vi voglia legare? no, voglio possiate portar el pan al forno, possiate andar accattando, Et q[ua]n[do] sara el tempo andar q[u]ᵃlch[e] giorno Con i [uno] muletto, si, sedovremmo M[esser] fran[cesco] et io

36 Because Domenica had not fully professed as a nun, she should not have been elected prioress, but Gammaro ordered her to take the position because she had founded the convent, and he might have wanted to protect her against accusations of illegal preaching, see Callahan, 'Preaching in a Poor Space', p. 225.

37 Florence, BDSMN, AMC, 'Originali di lettere missive della BMSD', Filza C, 3, 'Di Monsigre. Pietro Andrea Gammaro V(icari)° archiepij. ecopale [*sic*] alla B.M e di lej a lui', letter no. 14, 9 April 1516. On the promulgations see Polizzotto, *The Elect Nation*, p. 280.

38 Callahan, 'Preaching in a Poor Space', p. 225.

inq[ue]lmezo hav[er] cura al monasterio: no[n] dubiate, purch[e] vi
trovj ubidie[n]te.[39]

> (Do you think I want to restrain you? No, I want you to be able to take
> the bread to the baker, for you to be able to go around begging, and
> when it will be time to go some day with a little mule, yes, if we have
> to Mr Francesco and I [in that way will] take care of the monastery,
> don't doubt it, as long as you are obedient).

Francesco noted in his biographies of Domenica that she often wanted to leave
the convent to beg for money to help support her 'daughters', but he was more
circumspect about her visits to other convents and did not mention them in
his texts. In the wake of Leo X's 17 April 1515 papal brief, which condemned
all remaining Savonarolans, and commended the canons of the Duomo and
the Florentine archbishop for ridding the city of the itinerant preacher Don
Teodoro, Francesco would not have wanted Domenica to be painted with the
same brush.[40] A 'living saint' visiting convents could have led to suspicion that
Domenica was rabble rousing among the nuns. Gammaro's written permission
protected Domenica's freedom. Domenica knew how to demonstrate qualities
of obedience that she in fact often resisted, and letters allowed her to build
her network when she could not leave the convent.

There are twenty-one transcribed letters to nuns from Domenica that
have been published, and it is unclear how many others were written and later
lost.[41] Several of the extant letters emphasize her obedience to her superiors.
In an undated letter to the nuns of an unnamed convent, Domenica told them
'Avvisovi come io non potetti venire a visitarvi, perche la mattina che io ero
rimasa di venire mi prese una gran febre … Ora non ho licenzia di venire' (I'm
letting you know that I couldn't come to visit you all, because the morning
I was going to come I was overtaken by a great fever. And now I don't have
permission to come).[42] Since her confessor Francesco was not at the convent,
he could not give her leave to go.[43] Continuing the theme of obedience,
Domenica remarked that 'servants of the Lord' should obey God at all times:

---

39 Florence, BDSMN, AMC, 'Originali di lettere missive della BMSD', Filza C, 3, 'Di Monsigre.
    Pietro Andrea Gammaro V(icari)° archiepij. ecopale [*sic*] alla B.M e di lej a lui', letter
    no. 14, from Pietro Andrea Gammaro to Domenica 9 April 1516; Callahan, 'The Politics of
    Architecture', p. 97. The reference to going somewhere with a mule refers to Domenica's
    desire to go on pilgrimage to Mary Magdalene's grotto in France, which she had earlier
    expressed to Gammaro and Francesco.
40 For Don Teodoro, see Polizzotto, *The Elect Nation*, pp. 288–89.
41 For the letters see Florence, BDSMN, AMC, MS 7 Epistole Morali; Domenica dal Paradiso,
    Scritti spirituali, ed. by Antignani, pp. 171–91.
42 BDSMN, AMC, MS 7 Epistole Morali, letter no. 129, Domenica dal Paradiso, *Scritti spirituali*,
    ed. by Antignani, p. 172, no. 56.
43 The letter may therefore date to before 1520, as in that year Domenica purchased a house
    next door to the convent for the confessor's use. Callahan, 'The Confessor's House at a
    Renaissance Convent'.

Io l'ebbi per la mattina che io vi avevo promesso. Pero ora non mi paretirei senza licenzia; non ci essendo il Padre non la posso avere; ma facciamo di visitarci spiritualmente, perche quando voi avessi veduto me, avresti veduto un sacco di fieno.[44]

> (I had it for the morning that I had promised to you. But now I would not leave without permission, since my [spiritual] Father [Francesco] is not here I can't have it, but let's have a spiritual visit, because if you had seen me, you would have seen a sack of straw).

'Sack of straw' was a term she frequently used to disparage her body, always inferior to the soul in her eyes. Domenica ended by exhorting the nuns: 'siate come buon cavaliere, che mai si ferma e sempre fortemente va' (be like good knights, never stopping and always going [ahead] strongly).[45]

Domenica's letters replaced her presence when she could not physically get to convents. She made her excuses in letters, as in this undated one to a group of anonymous nuns:

have[n]domi voi ma[n]dato a dire piu volte che mi vorreste vedere, io non ho mai potuto. no[n] vi curate di vedere ne me ne altri, che qua[n]do voi av[r]este veduto me, haresti veduto un sacho di fieno. ma facciamo di vederci spirtualmente e desiderano di vederci nella gloria di vita eterna.[46]

> (having sent me word many times that you would like to see me, I never could. Don't worry about seeing neither me nor others, because when you would have seen me, you would have seen a sack of straw, but let's see each other spiritually and desire to see each other in the glory of eternal life).

By seeing each other 'spiritually', Domenica may have meant joining in prayer or meditation at a certain time of day. Prayer was both solitary and communal, as nuns prayed alone in their cells or together in the choir, during the liturgy of the hours. Nuns (and friars and monks) also embarked on 'virtual pilgrimages' together to the Holy Land, using maps, images, texts, and silent prayer to achieve a deeper *imitatio Christi*.[47] The idea of coming together mentally and spiritually would have been familiar to anyone living in a convent. One wonders what exactly the nuns had requested of Domenica, as she chided them for what they had written in their latest letter, saying that 'parmi che voi siate

---

44 BDSMN, AMC, MS 7 Epistole Morali, letter no. 129, Domenica dal Paradiso, *Scritti spirituali*, ed. by Antignani, p. 172, no. 56.

45 BDSMN, AMC, MS 7 Epistole Morali, letter no. 129, Domenica dal Paradiso, *Scritti spirituali*, ed. by Antignani, p. 172, no. 56.

46 Florence, BDSMN, AMC, MS 7 Epistole Morali, letter no. 33 'Epistola exhoratoria ma[n] data ad alcune religiose'. See also Domenica dal Paradiso, *Scritti spirituali*, ed. by Antignani, p. 173, no. 57.

47 Rudy, *Virtual Pilgrimages in the Convent*. Rudy examines religious women of the Low Countries but also surveys wider European practices in Chapter IV.

un poco troppe curiouse e che voi pe[n]siate troppo nell'infinito' (it seems to me you are a little too curious and you think too much about eternity).[48]

These women who lived behind convent walls wanted to physically see Domenica. As a 'living saint', Domenica carried a connection to the divine, which she could share with others. They may have been hopeful she would be lifted into ecstasy during a visit or spontaneously begin to prophesy — having the chance to interact with Domenica by talking with her or touching her would allow them to get even closer to God. They may even have been called to testify if she were to be made a saint after her death. Being a witness to sanctity was an important part of Christianity, especially for women, who may have identified with Mary Magdalene, the first follower to see Christ's resurrection (though Domenica probably would have reminded them of Christ's admonition to St Thomas). But to share in such an experience with Domenica, the nuns were dependent on her coming to them. The nuns could not leave their convent, but they clearly knew of Domenica and heard news about the mystic.

Sick nuns who wanted to partake of Domenica's healing abilities were also dependent on the mystic's physical presence. In 1516 Suor Eugenia, who lived in the Savonarolan convent of S. Vincenzo in Prato, and her mother Cosa, requested a visit from Domenica.[49] It is not clear if Cosa also lived in S. Vincenzo; some women joined convents once widowed, and although there were rules limiting the number of family members in the same convent, they were often disregarded.[50] The location in Prato and a reference in the letter suggests that Suor Eugenia was related to Domenica's first follower, Mona Margherita di Lorenzo di Bartholomeo Cimatore da Prato, and her sisters Oretta and Constantia.[51] Mona Margherita had lived with Domenica since 1501 in Giovanni da Sanminiato's house, and her sisters joined them there in 1506.[52] In 1515 Oretta changed her name to Suor Michelangela when she

---

48 Florence, BDSMN, AMC, MS 7 Epistole Morali, letter no. 33. See also Domenica dal Paradiso, *Scritti spirituali*, ed. by Antignani, p. 173, no. 57.

49 Florence, BDSMN, AMC, Originali di lettere missive della BMSD, Filza E 5a, 'A diverse persone religiose', letter no. 13. See also Domenica dal Paradiso, *Scritti spirituali*, ed. by Antignani, pp. 176–77 no. 61, from Florence, BDSMN, AMC, MS 7 Epistole Morali, letter no. 84. S. Vincenzo was a Savonarolan convent that would later host St Caterina de' Ricci, the niece of Federigo de' Ricci.

50 In 1517 the archbishop of Florence decreed that no more than two sisters could be in the same convent, but this rule was frequently broken. Brown, 'Everyday Life, Longevity, Nuns in Early Modern Florence', p. 121 n. 29.

51 Margherita could have been a widow as she is referred to as Mona Margherita di Lorenzo di Bartolomeo Cimatore da Prato. Florence, BDSMN, AMC, unnumbered MS, Libretto delle monache, 1ʳ. The two letters share the same date of 6 April 1516, but were copied out separately according to Antignani's transcription, see Domenica dal Paradiso, *Scritti spirituali*, ed. by Antignani, pp. 176–78 no. 62.

52 Their sister, Costantia di Lorenzo Cimatore da Prato, joined on the same day as Oretta, but died before she became a nun. Florence, BDMSN, AMC, unnumbered MS, Libretto delle monache, 2ʳ, records Constantia and Oretta arriving 26 May 1506.

became a nun at La Crocetta, but Constantia died before she could profess.[53] The letter reveals that Cosa was sick in Prato, and Suor Eugenia asked both Suor Domenica and Mona Margherita to come to see her. Eugenia and Cosa could have heard about Domenica's curative talents from Mona Margherita, the wider Savonarolan network, or from others in Florence, where she may also have once lived.

Domenica told the women that Gammaro had said she could not leave La Crocetta except to go to the communal oven or to go around Florence begging, though his letter does not say that was all she could do.[54] Nor, according to Domenica, could Margherita go to Prato, as only the *fattoressa* (factor, or convent agent) and the *converse* (servant nuns) could leave the convent, and not those who 'said the Divine Office', who could only see their close relatives once a year and only through the grate.[55] This was disingenuous, as while Mona Margherita may have said the Divine Office like a choir nun, like Domenica, Margherita would not take full vows to become a nun until the year she died.[56] Domenica did not go to Prato, but as shown in their letter, Eugenia and Cosa believed it was a possibility. Domenica may have interpreted Gammaro's directive as not being able to leave Florence, or she may not have wanted to make the long walk to Prato.

Though unwilling to impart her healing touch in Prato, Domenica attempted to provide some 'spiritual solace' via letter. She reassured Mona Cosa's troubled soul that since the illness was a gift and a 'kiss from the Lord', Cosa should be thankful for it.[57] Mona Cosa should prepare herself to

---

53 Florence, BDSMN, AMC, unnumbered MS, Libretto della monache, 2[r]. Constantia died 26 March 1509.

54 Florence, BDSMN, AMC, Box A, Originali di lettere missive della BMSD, Filza E 5a, 'A diverse persone religiose', letter no. 13, see also Domenica dal Paradiso, *Scritti spirituali*, ed. by Antignani, p. 176, no. 61, letter dated 6 April 1516.

55 Florence, BDSMN, AMC, Box A, Originali di lettere missive della BMSD, Filza E 5a, 'A diverse persone religiose', letter no. 13 (the transcription mine) 'Mona Margherita no[n] puo venire chostagu [costà giù?] perche non usiamo dandare fuora senon accattare quelle che sono fattoresse e converse, le suore che dicono lufittjo non escono maj fuora et dalle gratte non si vegono seno una volta lanno et da parentti stretti conforattela da nostra pertte et ditte che noi lavisitjamo con molte orattjone. Rachomandomj lanostra madre priora i pregasse el signore che la disponga a governare perche lasene ride et dice che non vuol fare nulla che io o afare io che o fatto almonasterio ecosi dicono tutte lealtre, et pero vi priego che voi mi aiutasse'. This letter is not written in Francesco da Castiglione's hand, but the note that states this letter was to Suor Eugenia in S. Vincenzo in Prato appears to be in the confessor's hand. See also Domenica dal Paradiso, *Scritti spirituali*, ed. by Antignani, p. 176, no. 61, where he paraphrased the letter.

56 Mona Margherita only professed and was vested on her deathbed in 1540, and Suor Domenica waited until 1552, the year before she died.

57 Domenica dal Paradiso, *Scritti spirituali*, ed. by Antignani, pp. 176, 177–78, no. 62. The two letters share the same date and were copied out separately according to Antignani's transcription. Antignani noted that Francesco da Castiglione later had to defend Domenica from another cleric's censure for her phrase 'un bacio d'amore', citing 'Defensione' in codices J and H, which I have not seen in the archives.

meet the Lord and be joyful, yet still fearful of him. Here Domenica echoed generally Savonarola's thoughts on death in a sermon given in Florence on 2 November 1496, later printed as *Predica dell'arte del ben morire*, which may have been inspired by the earlier *Ars moriendi*.[58] Dying a 'good death' had become important to Florentines in the fifteenth and sixteenth centuries. Mona Cosa was probably a *conversa*, who had joined the convent without paying the typical nuns' dowry, and she may have been worried this would count against her in heaven. Domenica reassured her that the illness was the dowry furnished by God to meet her spouse, because she was low and poor.[59] Domenica noted that she and her *figliuole* (spiritual daughters) would help with prayers, but they could not visit, or assist, in any other way.[60] With her letter, Domenica wanted to make sure Cosa was adequately prepared for death, assisted by the prayers of the nuns of La Crocetta.

Crocetta nuns exchanged this benefit of group prayer with other nuns. In a letter of 1519, Domenica addressed Suor Samaritana of the Benedictine convent of S. Antonio in Polesine in Ferrara and thanked the nuns for including them in their *collegio*. Domenica appreciated a 'great present' that she had received from their spiritual father.[61] The letter offers no details of the gift; perhaps it was some of the miraculous liquid said to drip from a stone formerly on the tomb of the blessed Beatrice II d'Este (*c.* 1230–1262).[62]

Domenica also noted in this letter that Suor Samaritana had requested a sermon from Domenica in 1519.[63] Though technically Domenica does not provide them with a sermon, the letter is so long, and so full of advice, that it may as well have been a sermon. Why Benedictine nuns would be interested in a sermon from a Dominican tertiary might be explained by the convent's location in Ferrara. Savonarola's hometown had become a major centre for promotion of his movement after his death in 1498, and the duke of Ferrara, Ercole d'Este (1431–1505), welcomed Florentine *piagnoni* escaping persecution.[64]

---

58   On the sermon and its impact see Polizzotto, 'Dell'arte del ben morire', pp. 27–87.

59   Domenica dal Paradiso, *Scritti spirituali*, ed. by Antignani, p. 178, no. 63 'Lui fa per dotarvi che siate poverina e lui vole la sua sposa con qualche poco di dota, et essendo voi vile et povera è giusto che portiate qualche coselina. Se lui vi dota con la infermità ripiegate le donora con la pazienzia'.

60   Domenica dal Paradiso, *Scritti spirituali*, ed. by Antignani, p. 178 no. 63 'Noi vi aiutiamo con le oratione, non vi possiamo aituare né visitare con altro'.

61   Florence, BDSMN, AMC, Box A, Originali di lettere missive della BMSD, Filza E 5a, letter no. 16, A diverse persone religiose, letter no. 15; Domenica dal Paradiso, *Scritti spirituali*, ed. by Antignani, pp. 187–88, no. 69. The convent was dedicated to St Anthony Abbott. Antignani often copied out summaries on the back of letters by the seventeenth-century confessor Ignazio del Nente. This seems to be in Francesco da Castiglione's hand.

62   Rinaldi, *Vita della Beata Beatrice Seconda d'Este*, p. 17. See also *Memorie istoriche delle Chiese di Ferrara*, 275, 283.

63   Florence, BDSMN, AMC, Box A, Originali di lettere missive della BMSD, Filza E 5a, A diverse persone religiose, letter no. 15.

64   Herzig, *Savonarola's Women*, pp. 73–75.

There may have been Savonarolans among the Benedictine nuns who were interested in keeping the friar's message alive through contact with Domenica. Her reputation probably extended to Ferrara via the Savonarolan friars Jacopo da Sicilia and Fra Tommaso Caiani, who knew Domenica and Ercole's prized prophet Lucia Brocadelli (1476–1554).[65] Though both Jacopo da Sicilia and Caiani had split with Domenica after 1506, they may have spoken favourably about her in earlier years, or the Benedictine nuns may have thought that the Florentine mystic sounded interesting, despite negative reports from the friars. Convent networks crossed walls and orders, as female relatives and friends did not always join the same order.

Despite the gift from the Benedictines, Domenica refused their request for a sermon with some rhetorical modesty, saying 'mihavete fatta vergognare che io habbia a scrivere e insegnare a voi: confortovi a leggere e sermoni della vostra Regola e cosi confortate tutte costeste madre' (You embarrassed me [saying] that I should write and teach you. Take comfort in reading the sermons of your own rule and in this way, you will comfort all of your mothers).[66] She also explained why she had not written before, telling them:

> Non vi maravigliate ch'io non abbia risposto prima. Ho tante le occu-pazione che non ho tempo nè agio di scrivere et anche non uso troppo di rispondere alle lettere che mi sono mandate, perchè sarebbe troppo disagio et perdimento di tempo di me e d'altri. Io non so nè leggere nè scrivere, ingegniomi di rispondere colle orazione, benchè sono debole.'[67]

> (Don't be surprised that I haven't responded earlier. I am so busy that I don't have the time nor the ease to write and also I don't often respond to letters that are sent to me, because it would be too inconvenient and a waste of time for me and others. I don't know how to read or write, I figure out ways to respond with prayers, even if they are weak).

Domenica's reluctance to send a sermon to Ferrara may have been encouraged by Francesco, given the change in fortunes of the Savonarolan Brocadelli after Ercole d'Este's death in 1505. Brocadelli's Savonarolan opinion of Pope Alexander VI did not sit well with the pope's daughter Lucrezia Borgia, who

---

65 Fra Jacopo da Sicilia was one of Domenica's first confessors when she came to Florence, though he later turned against her. Tommaso Caiani instead supported Dorothea of Lanciuole, a competing mystic ultimately discredited by Domenica after she secured a confession of false fasting by Dorothea. See Polizzotto, 'When Saints Fall Out'; Callahan, 'Suor Domenica da Paradiso as "alter Christus"', p. 330; Herzig, *Savonarola's Women*, p. 75, notes Jacopo and Tommaso's ties to Lucia.

66 Florence, BDSMN, AMC, Box A, Originali di lettere missive della BMSD, Filza E 5a, A diverse persone religiose, letter no. 15. See also Domenica dal Paradiso, *Scritti spirituali*, ed. by Antignani, pp. 187–88 no. 69.

67 Florence, BDSMN, AMC, Box A, Originali di lettere missive della BMSD, Filza E 5a, A diverse persone religiose, letter no. 15. See also Domenica dal Paradiso, *Scritti spirituali*, ed. by Antignani, pp. 187–88 no. 69.

had married Ercole's son Alfonso in 1502, and then taken Tommaso Caiani as her confessor.[68] When Lucrezia and Alfonso came to power, Brocadelli was made to profess as a nun, and her confessor was removed in 1506.[69]

The request for a sermon proves Domenica's reputation for preaching extended beyond the immediate confines of her group, and she nourished and developed this reputation through letters and word of mouth. Domenica knew that St Paul had spoken against women preaching publicly but claimed he had come to her in a vision to reassure her that he did not really mean it.[70] Domenica knew it was risky to put her sermons into writing and send them out, given the restrictions against women preaching and the crackdown against Savonarolans, but Francesco recorded them and may have distributed them.[71]

Although few letters to Domenica survive, responses like this suggest she received many. It is not surprising that she claims to not have had time to write, as Domenica ran the convent, worked on her (auto)biography with Francesco da Castiglione, and re-enacted the Passion every Friday when the pain of her stigmata activated, and she fell into ecstasy.[72] On feast days and occasional Sundays, Domenica preached. Although she could not be seen behind the curtain that separated the inner, nuns' church from the outer, public church, Domenica could be heard as her voice crossed the grate to her lay followers.[73] While Domenica was fully aware of the prohibition against women preaching, she nonetheless gave sermons, and I have suggested elsewhere that one of the reasons Domenica founded the convent was as a protected environment in which to preach.[74] If she had been a man, Domenica could have reached many people through giving public sermons, but the restrictions on women preaching, combined with the political ramifications of being a Savonarolan in Florence, meant that she had to limit her audience to those who could be trusted to hear her prophetic utterances and not turn her over to the authorities. Domenica also had to be careful that her sermons did not cause strife among her followers, should anyone become swept away by her words and want to leave their family. She ensured that women who wanted to join the convent were making informed decisions.

In 1515, Mona Fiametta di Francesco Gambi and Mona Lucretia di Niccolò Lapi were inspired to leave their husbands and children and join Domenica at

---

68 Herzig, *Savonarola's Women*, pp. 133, 135 notes it was Lucrezia who ensured Brocadelli's activities were severely curtailed. Zarri, *La religione di Lucrezia Borgia*.

69 Herzig, *Savonarola's Women*, pp. 136, 138–39. These are only a few of the decrees noted, for the full account see Herzig, *Savonarola's Women*, pp. 140–42.

70 Callahan, 'Preaching in a Poor Space', pp. 225–27.

71 See Librandi and Valerio, *I Sermoni di Domenica da Paradiso*.

72 See Callahan, 'Suor Domenica da Paradiso as "alter Christus"'. See also Muessig, *The Stigmata in Medieval and Early Modern Europe*, pp. 106, 115 n. 102, 240 n. 100.

73 Callahan, 'Preaching in a Poor Space'.

74 Callahan, 'Preaching in a Poor Space'.

La Crocetta.[75] But she dissuaded them, writing in a letter dated 27 April that they should not leave their families to become nuns.[76] Domenica warned the women that while the idea of living behind cloistered walls and serving God might initially seem appealing, Fiametta and Lucretia would soon find that:

> Non sono i panni, figliuole mie, che faccino santo il Monaco, ma bisogna che il Monaco faccia santi i panni. Mai abito alcuno ha fatto i miracoli, ma hanno fatto i miracoli l'opera di quelli che li hanno portati. Iddio non opera nei panni, ma in quelli che servono a lui e si'innamorano di lui e diventatano nemici di loro medesimi[77]

> (It's not the clothes, my daughters, that make the monk holy, but it is the monk who needs to make the clothes holy. No habit has ever performed miracles, but the work of those who have worn it has performed miracles. God does not work though clothes, but in those who serve him and fall in love with him and become enemies to themselves).

Domenica cautioned the women that they might also find the life of a nun unexpectedly hard compared to the relative freedom they enjoyed as seculars. As Domenica reminded them, the two women were no longer young.[78] They would have to be prepared to reject everything they knew, from husbands and children to servants, and most importantly, their own freedom. If they entered La Crocetta, then regretted their choice and walked the halls weeping and sighing, they could damage the delicate construction that was convent life.[79]

---

75 The documents consistently used 'Fiametta' instead of the more typical spelling 'Fiammetta' and I have followed this throughout.

76 Florence, BDSMN, AMC, Originali di lettere missive della BMSD, Filza E 5a, A diverse persone religiose. See also letter no. 2, which also discusses a Fiametta, [sic] who might be the same person, 'La m[ad]re Sor Domenica al Rxdo Pre Fr. Giuliano Mazzei domenicano in ripoli Dice cheuna donna allogata voleva andare al suo mon[aste]rio. Per farsi monaca, il che lei non consente, e non approva. Eche se è suo ordine falli la cosa tornare in dietro' (The Madre Suor Domenica to the reverend Father Giuliano Mazzei Domincian in Ripoli (S. Jacopo di Ripoli) says that a woman lodger wanted to go to her monastery to become a nun, which she does not consent to nor approves. And if it is his order to reverse it). See also Domenica dal Paradiso, *Scritti spirituali*, ed. by Antignani, pp. 230–35, no. 105. While I have found no other record of Francesco Gambi in the Crocetta documents, various members of the Lapi family were connected to Domenica, including Lucretia's husband Niccolò di Girolamo Lapi, and Mona Dianora di Piero di Silvestro Lapi. See BDSMN, AMC, unnumbered MS Ricordanza, 6ʳ. Lapi (if it is the same person) was probably of the artisanal class. See Shaw and Welch, *Making and Marketing Medicine in Renaissance Florence*, pp. 206, 226, n. 128, 130. He is also mentioned as a syndic and procurator of the Compagnia dell'Annuziata in a land deal of 1512 in which Clarice de' Medici's garden was sold. See Elam, 'Lorenzo de' Medici's Sculpture Garden', p. 82.

77 Domenica dal Paradiso, *Scritti spirituali*, ed. by Antignani, p. 232, no. 105.

78 Domenica dal Paradiso, *Scritti spirituali*, ed. by Antignani, p. 232, no. 105 'ciascuna di voi è più che a mezza via un pezzo'.

79 Domenica dal Paradiso, *Scritti spirituali*, ed. by Antignani, p. 232, no. 105 'perchè porterebbe

As Domenica had learned (and rebelled against as a younger woman during a short stint at the convent of Le Candeli), a woman's time was not her own when she lived in a convent:[80]

> Quando vorreste andare a dormire si ha andare all'orazione, quando credereste andare a mensa sarà andare a lodare Iddio e non avete a intendere quell che si dà a mensa dal convento. Alle volte avrete cotti mal salati e mal conditi e pane secco e vino non molto buono, e se sarete negligenti, tutte queste cose vi parranono piu cattive che non saranno, ma se sarete ferventi vi parrano più condite e più saporite di quelle del secolo.[81]

> (When you would like to go to sleep, you have to go to prayers, when you think you would like to go eat, it will be time to go praise the Lord, and you don't have any idea of what they give for food at a convent. Sometimes you will have poorly salted and badly-flavoured roasts, and dry bread and not very good wine, and if you are negligent, all of these things will seem worse to you than they are).

Of course, if they managed to hang on to their fervent faith, the food would taste wonderful. But the women had to remember that becoming a nun did not mean putting up with poor food for a few hours, but for one's entire life. And every day and every night they would have to return to the same routine: prayer, discipline, and penitence.[82]

And what of their poor husbands? Domenica reminded the women that if they were to leave their husbands, the men would be left as if in a desert.[83] They had already been battling temptation for the past thirty or forty years with the help of their wives. The only way it could possibly work would be if the men also joined a religious order, as then each spouse would be in a safe place. But, as Domenica noted, this was very uncommon in Florence.[84] It was far better for the women to stay in the world and do the Lord's work there.

Domenica's convent had only been running for four years when she advised the women against joining. Domenica was well aware of Christ's words 'if anyone comes to me and does not hate father and mother, wife and

---

pericolo di non rovinare l'edificio, perchè se voi veniste qua e noi vi andassimo vezzando e piaggiando, porteremmo pericolo'.

80 See Callahan, 'The Politics of Architecture', pp. 48–51.

81 Domenica dal Paradiso, *Scritti spirituali*, ed. by Antignani, p. 233, no. 105.

82 Domenica dal Paradiso, *Scritti spirituali*, ed. by Antignani, p. 233, no. 105 'Ogni dì e ogni notte si ha a tornare a quell medesimo: orazione, disciplina, e penitenza'.

83 Domenica dal Paradiso, *Scritti spirituali*, ed. by Antignani, p. 233, no. 105.

84 Domenica must have known that the Savonarolan Camilla Bartolini Rucellai founded S. Caterina da Siena in Piazza San Marco in 1500, after she ended her marriage to Ridolfo Rucellai when he was vested as a Dominican friar at S. Marco in 1494. See Vasoli, 'Camilla Bartolini Rucellai'. See also Callahan, 'The Politics of Architecture', p. 206, citing Fantozzi Micali and Roselli, *Le soppressioni dei conventi a Firenze*, p. 99; Richa, *Notizie storiche delle chiese fiorentine*, pp. 278–84, and Polizzotto, 'When Saints Fall Out', p. 512.

children, brothers and sisters, yes, even their own life — such a person cannot be my disciple'.[85] But she knew if married women decided to abandon their families to become nuns at La Crocetta, this could create problems within the convent, and among her secular followers. The women might bring too much of the secular world into the convent or regret their choices, as she had suggested to Fiametta and Lucretia. The men and children might begin to resent Domenica for breaking up their families if wives and mothers left them to live in La Crocetta. It would be much better for Domenica (and her finances) to keep her followers' families intact. Her strategy paid off, as relations remained good enough for Niccolò Lapi to later act as Domenica's *procuratore* for some land purchases, and he even loaned her money to pay for real estate.[86] Domenica's ability to consistently raise money from her followers indicates she had a finely tuned sense of how to manage people and maintain support.

It was easier for Domenica to support widows' choices to enter convents. While many young widows were urged by their families to remarry in order to forge new alliances and family connections, those who had been married, provided an heir, and received their dowries back from their in-laws could have a bit more freedom. In a letter dated 19 April 1517 from Domenica to Ginevra Tiepolo, Domenica congratulated Ginevra on her entry into a convent (S. Pietro al Luco in Borgo San Lorenzo), assuring Ginevra that she had done the right thing 'a fuggire el mondo et correre drieto a Jesu Cristo et pigliarlo per Vostro sposo' (by escaping the world and running straight to Jesus Christ to take him for your husband).[87] She encouraged Ginevra to persevere despite the misfortunes that she had experienced over the past years, and provided St Bridget as an example of a widow who found peace after taking Christ as her second husband. Domenica noted that Christ would not abandon Ginevra to widowhood, as her earthly husband had done.

Ginevra's husband had been Giovanni Sforza, who married her and died in the same year, 1510. He could not have been an easy spouse, and was excommunicated by Pope Alexander VI for spreading rumours of incest about his first wife, the pope's daughter Lucrezia Borgia.[88] Domenica noted in her letter that Ginevra's 'earthly husband' was 'mancato et era un pezo di carne cogli occhi, era prigione, era ragazzo di quello el quale avete preso ora' (he

---

85 Luke 14. 26.

86 Florence, BDSMN, AMC, unnumbered MS Ricordanza, 4ᵛ–5ʳ, purchase of the house next door from the convent on Domenica's behalf from Lorenzo Marochi on 20 December 1518, see also Florence, ASF, CRSGF 107, filza 97 Filza d'Istrumenti Antichi 1511–1581, 49ᵛ–50ʳ.

87 Domenica dal Paradiso, *Scritti spirituali*, ed. by Antignani, pp. 178–79 no. 63. The letter refers to the Camaldolese convent in Luco; this must have been S. Pietro al Luco in Borgo San Lorenzo, near Florence, though not mentioned in the letter. 'Donna Ginevra daughter of Matteo Tiepolo, Patrizio Veneto, former consort of Giovanni Sforza Signore e Principe di Pesaro, flourished in 1513 in the mirror of sanctity' at this convent, see Farulli, *Istoria Cronologica del nobile, ed antico Monastero degli Angioli di Firenze*, p. 251.

88 Tamalio, 'Lucrezia Borgia'.

was a failure and was a piece of flesh with eyes, he was a prison, he was a boy compared to that one that you have chosen now).[89] Ginevra and Giovanni's son Giovanni Maria, known as Costanzo II, died at the age of two in 1512.

The loss of a child would have been very difficult, and Ginevra may have been pressured to remarry. But unlike Mona Fiametta di Francesco Gambi and Mona Lucretia di Niccolò Lapi, Ginevra's husband was also dead, and it was therefore much easier for her to espouse Jesus. In memory of her son, Ginevra commissioned Girolamo da Cotignola (also known as Girolamo Marchesi) for a painting of the Immaculate Conception of the Virgin Mary with Sts Augustine, Catherine of Alexandria, Jerome, and Anne, with a portrait of Costanzo II, for the high altar of S. Maria delle Grazie in Pesaro (Figure 2.3).[90] The inclusion of St Jerome probably refers to Ginevra's religious name.[91] Given Ginevra's previously unknown connection to Suor Domenica, I believe her choice of name suggests Ginevra was a Savonarolan.

Giovanni Sforza's majordomo Cesare Alberti noted that Ginevra left Pesaro 'on 27 April 1513 for La Verna, and she became a nun in a convent 16 miles outside Florence'.[92] It seems she was still there in 1519, though later she joined the Poor Clares at S. Chiara in Murano.[93] She probably returned to the lagoon because of her roots in the patrician Tiepolo family of Venice, but it is unclear how or why Ginevra arrived near Florence. It may have been because she was linked to the Medici family through her husband's first cousin once removed, Caterina Sforza. The wife of Giovanni de' Medici il Popolano and mother of Giovanni delle Bande Nere, Caterina was tangentially connected to Domenica through Francesco da Castiglione, who had been the tutor to her husband's nephew Pierfrancesco di Lorenzo de' Medici the Younger (1487–1525).[94] Medici ties were crucial in Florence, as the family had been

89 Domenica dal Paradiso, *Scritti spirituali*, ed. by Antignani, pp. 178–79, no. 63. It seems there was some difficulty in arranging the marriage, as Giovanni had asked the Republic of Venice to make a decision regarding his marriage to Ginevra. Lazzarini, *Catalogo delle pitture che si conservano nelle chiese di Pesaro*, pp. 13–14.

90 Donati, *Girolamo Marchesi da Cotignola*, p. 142 n. 17. Oil on panel transferred to canvas, 315 × 180 cm, signed HIERONIM<VS> |COTTIGNOLO<ENSIS>, MCCCCCXIII, Milan, Brera, Reg. Cron. 1272, provenance: Pesaro, Church of S. Maria delle Grazie, high altar, 1513; London, Collezione di Lord Ashburton, second half of nineteenth century; sold by London dealer to Brera in 1909.

91 Zama, *Girolamo Marchesi da Cotignola*, p. 113. Zama did not provide an exact citation in her catalogue entry, but see Lazzarini, *Catalogo delle pitture che si conservano nelle chiese di Pesaro*, pp. 11–13.

92 Cited in Lazzarini, *Catalogo delle pitture che si conservano nelle chiese di Pesaro*, p. 12. Lazzarini records that this information came from notes made by Giovanni Battista Almerici. I thank Heather Hess for help with the translation of majordomo.

93 Farulli, *Istoria Cronologica del nobile, ed antico Monastero degli Angioli di Firenze*, p. 251, Lazzarini, *Catalogo delle pitture che si conservano nelle chiese di Pesaro*, pp. 11–13.

94 On Caterina Sforza see Breisach, *Caterina Sforza*. Francesco was a witness (among other S. Lorenzo canons) when Archbishop Orsini gave Caterina Sforza permission to build an oratory and a portable altar on 31 December 1505. BDSMN, AMC, Box C Marked 'Brevi e

Figure 2.3. Girolamo da Cotignola (also known as Girolamo Marchesi), *Immaculate Conception of the Virgin Mary with Saints Augustine, Catherine of Alexandria, Jerome, and Anne with Costanzo II Sforza*, Milan, Museo del Brera. 1513. With permission of Museo del Brera, Milan.

de facto rulers of the city since the early 1400s. Partly due to pro-Savonarola sentiments and partly to Piero de' Medici's disastrous dealings with the French king, the family was exiled after 1494, but returned to power in 1512 when Giovanni de' Medici was elected Pope Leo X. Domenica knew the importance of keeping the powerful Medici family on her side, and it was valuable to cultivate elite contacts, such as Ginevra Tiepolo, who were connected to them, even indirectly.[95]

The duchess of Camerino, Caterina Cibo (1501–1557), and her daughter Giulia (1523–1547) were two women directly connected with the Medici who assisted Domenica.[96] Caterina Cibo, the daughter of Maddalena de' Medici (1473–1519) and the niece of Pope Leo X, loaned Domenica money for her building projects and visited her at La Crocetta.[97] Caterina moved to Florence in 1535 after her duchy of Camerino was placed under papal interdict; she had known the mystic since at least 1533 when she requested a sermon, as evidenced by a letter of 2 October 1533, in which Caterina sent word to La Crocetta 'che voleva venire la Domenica venente a comunicarsi qui con esso ni, et starve tutto '[i]l giorno et udire qualcosa di spirituale' (that we wanted to come the following Sunday to have communion and to be [there] all day and listen to something spiritual).[98] Camerino is about 225 kilometres from Florence and it would have taken several days travelling on horseback to get there, so this trip would have to have been planned in advance. The two women must have communicated frequently; a witness for Domenica's beatification later noted that there were many letters in the convent of S. Marta in Florence that Domenica had written to Caterina Cibo, but 'disgraziatamente si sono brugiate [sic]' (unfortunately they were burnt).[99]

Francesco da Castiglione noted that throughout 1533–1534, Caterina Cibo often came to the convent to listen to Suor Domenica's sermons, which she delivered to the nuns on feast days. Caterina would then remain in the convent all day.[100] He recorded that Domenica was doing this to help him, as she thought

Libri di Brevi, Pergamanee e folie'. Though attempts have been made to tie this document from the convent archive and Caterina Sforza to Domenica, there is no evidence that Caterina Sforza, who died in 1509, ever funded or knew Domenica. It is more likely that this document made its way to La Crocetta via Francesco.

95   McLean, *The Art of the Network*, notes throughout how Florentines used even tangential ties to request favours and patronage.

96   Domenica dal Paradiso, *Scritti spirituali*, ed. by Antignani, pp. 220–30 for letters to Giulia (no. 101) and to Caterina (nos 102, 103, and 104). See also Valerio, 'Caterina Cibo', pp. 141–54.

97   Callahan, 'Preaching in a Poor Space', pp. 222–23.

98   Callahan, 'Preaching in a Poor Space', p. 222; Valerio, 'Caterina Cibo', p. 147. Valerio quoted this passage without a reference, but earlier referenced a note from 2 October 1533, which was a letter or sermon by Francesco.

99   *Sacra Rituum*, part I, p. 138. testis XII n. 10. They were probably burnt when Caterina was placed under investigation by the Inquisition because of her relationship with Bernardino Ochino.

100 Florence, BDSMN, AMC, MS 1 Francesco Onesti da Castiglione, *Ephemeris*, 425'. Hoc anno

he was old and deserved a break from giving sermons on feast days (though Domenica was sixty years old herself). During these visits, Domenica and Caterina also 'would pray and decipher the Gospel together'.[101] Though left unsaid by Francesco, the two women were skirting dangerously close to the Protestant practice of interpreting the Bible without a priest.

Caterina had long been looking for spiritual succour and an outlet for her matronage; she had been involved since the 1520s with the new order of the Franciscan Capuchins.[102] She would later slip into what would be deemed dangerous radicalism when she befriended the preacher Bernardino Ochino (1487–1564), who became the general of the Capuchin order in 1538. Some felt Ochino's reform was too close to Protestantism, and he was called to the Vatican in 1542 to account for his sermons. Instead of going to Rome, Bernardino escaped to Switzerland, abandoning his Franciscan habit at the Palazzo Pazzi, where Caterina Cibo's brother Lorenzo lived.[103] Caterina would later be investigated by the Inquisition, and declared 'a heretic, a follower of heretics and a teacher of heretics'.[104]

Domenica had previously warned Caterina against Bernardino in a letter of 21 January 1540.[105] After thanking the duchess for a box of dried figs and excusing herself for not having written earlier due to a five-month long sickness that prevented her even from 'going to the grate', Domenica urged the duchess to pay attention to the 'true lessons' of the Lord. The mystic believed that 'Quelli che imparono et studiano senza l'amore di Cristo chiamo che egli imparono gran muffa. Perchè è la muffa in loro et non si destono alla doctrina celestiale, e la doctrina vera è il magnio Dio (those who learn and study without the love of Christ, I say that they are learning a great pile of mould, because the mould is within them and it doesn't bring them to celestial doctrine, and the true doctrine is the great God).[106] From Domenica's letter,

---

frequenter sermonis huit n[ost]ra ve[nerabi]lis m[ate]r ad moniales suas, in diebi festis, Ad Ducissam Camerini d[o]nam Catarinam Cibo pulchrim sermonem huit i[n]suo monasterio cum ipsa D[on]na Catarina venisse ad eam visitandam remaneret quam in monasterio totam diem'.

101 Florence, BDSMN, AMC, MS 1 Francesco Onesti da Castiglione, *Ephemeris*, 425ᵛ. 'orassit ut dichoriret sibi Evangelium'.

102 Valone, 'Architecture as a Public Voice for Women', pp. 304–06.

103 Felicangeli noted that it was not clear if Caterina remained in the Pazzi house the whole time she was in Florence; on 18 February 1537, she was recorded taking cover in the Fortezza da Basso because of public riots. After Margherita d'Austria left Florence in July 1537, Caterina is recorded renting a house on via Ghibellina until 1549, when her brother Lorenzo died and she received usufruct of the house on Canto dei Pazzi. Felicangeli, *Notizie e documenti sulla vita di Caterina Cibo-Varano*, pp. 206–07.

104 Robin, *Publishing Women*, p. 193, p. 326 n. 105, citing Petrucci. 'haeretica, sectatrix haereticorum et doctrix monialium haereticarum'.

105 Domenica dal Paradiso, *Scritti spirituali*, ed. by Antignani, pp. 224–26, no. 103; Valerio, 'Caterina Cibo', pp. 152–53.

106 Domenica dal Paradiso, *Scritti spirituali*, ed. by Antignani, p. 225, no. 103.

it appears the duchess was studying Church doctrine, and Domenica wanted her to be careful to do so with humility.

In her letter to Caterina, Domenica wondered at the hubris of those who wanted 'misurare et intendere al circuito del cielo, et io dico che San Paulo che fu ratto al 3 cielo non ne parlò, perchè non trovò riscontro nè sillibe nè sentenzie a potere scrivere con lingua umana' (to measure and understand the size of heaven, and I say that St Paul who was brought to the third heaven didn't talk about it, because he couldn't find a reply, nor syllables, nor sentences to be able to write with the human language).[107] Domenica was paraphrasing II Corinthians 12. 1, in which Paul refers to a man in Christ (often interpreted as Paul himself) who was raised to the third heaven.[108] 'Measuring heaven' demonstrates the lasting influence of the philosopher Pythagoras (sixth century BCE), who Nicomachus credited with using arithmetic to determine the size of the universe.[109] Though no writings were credited to Pythagoras, his theories were incorporated in the works of later Christian authors such as Sts Augustine, Jerome, and Thomas Aquinas, and he was often included in depictions of the Seven Liberal Arts, as in Andrea da Firenze's 1366 fresco of *The Triumph of Thomas Aquinas*, in the chapter room of the Dominicans at S. Maria Novella in Florence.[110]

Domenica continued that only 'Quelle che saranno innamorati et che aranno gustato Dio et dispregiato el mondo et loro medesimi, quelli saranno che vedranno gli abitanti Padre, Figlio et Spirito Sancto e i circuiti de' cieli (those who will be in love with and who will taste the Lord and despise the world and themselves will see the inhabitants [of heaven] the Father, Son and Holy Ghost and the circumference of Heaven).[111] Sts Francis, Dominic, Augustine, and many other saints had tried to understand the above-mentioned principles (i.e. measuring heaven), and 'dì et nocte contemplarono quelli' (day and night they contemplated them).[112] St Francis learned the 'true

---

107 Domenica dal Paradiso, *Scritti spirituali*, ed. by Antignani, p. 225, no. 103.
108 II Corinthians 12.1–5: 1. 'I must boast; there is nothing to be gained by it, but I will go on to visions and revelations of the Lord. 2. I know a man in Christ who fourteen years ago was caught up to the third heaven — whether in the body or out of the body I do not know, God knows. 3. And I know that this man was caught up into Paradise — whether in the body or out of the body I do not know, God knows — 4. and he heard things that cannot be told, which man may not utter. 5. On behalf of this man I will boast, but on my own behalf I will not boast, except of my weaknesses'.
109 Joost-Gaugier, *Measuring Heaven*, pp. 2, 259.
110 Joost-Gaugier, *Measuring Heaven*, p. 133. Pythagoras has been associated with the figure seated below Arithmetic, but he could just as easily be the figure seated with hammer and anvil, beating out perfect octaves as described by Nicomachus and later cited by Boethius. Joost-Gaugier, *Measuring Heaven*, p. 200, for Pythagoras as the figure below Arithmetic. She notes (36) Nicomachus' story of the hammer and anvils but does not tie it to the figure in the fresco, probably because of Giorgio Vasari's identification of the figure with hammer and anvil as Tubulcain in his Life of Taddeo Gaddi.
111 Domenica dal Paradiso, *Scritti spirituali*, ed. by Antignani, p. 225, no. 103.
112 Domenica dal Paradiso, *Scritti spirituali*, ed. by Antignani, p. 225, no. 103.

doctrine' after going to a garden to meditate and having the Lord come to him and teach him,

> E cosi san Domenico e gli altri sancti andavono alla scuola et udivono el maestro. Udito che avevono la vera leczione, egli andovono tucti innamorati alleggere agli altri et a quel modo studiavono et furno tucti doctorate et imparorno le 7 scienzie, intesono et imparorno la vera doctrina et andarono alla partita loro a trovare el vero Principe et viddonno le richezze eterne e le misure de' cieli.[113]

>> (And in this way St Dominic and the other saints went to school and listened to the teacher. Having heard the true lesson, he went all in love to read to the others and in that way, they studied and all became doctors, and learned the seven sciences, they understood and learned the true doctrine and they went to their meeting to find the true Prince and they saw the eternal riches and the size of heaven).

Domenica's references to Pythagorean theories and the seven sciences demonstrate that she was much less 'simple' than she claimed and had either been taught by Francesco or absorbed classical references from listening to books, sermons, or discussions.[114] She may also have been flattering Caterina Cibo's own knowledge, as the duchess was highly educated and knew Greek, Latin, and Hebrew.[115] Domenica also was aligning herself with both Franciscan and Dominican strains of thought. While she often went to the garden to contemplate the Lord in the same way St Francis did, she believed in the importance of scholarship, as promoted by St Dominic, to be able to better advise Caterina Cibo. Francesco da Castiglione (or others writing for Domenica) may have inserted such references, but Francesco was very often insistent in the biographies and recorded sermons that he had faithfully recorded Domenica's words.

Domenica stressed that none of these saints could have reached their knowledge of 'true doctrine' without love for the Lord. If Caterina Cibo wanted to share in that knowledge, she needed to have the same love for the Lord. Caterina had to be 'prudente e usate la prudenzia in ogni cosa. Levate e pericoli et le occasione del mormorare et abbiate sempre dinanzi agli occhi David et state con timore (prudent and use prudence in everything. Take away dangers and the occasion for gossip and always keep David before your eyes and be in a state of fear [of the Lord])'.[116] Domenica may have been concerned because she received news that Fra Bernardino and the duchess

---

113   Domenica dal Paradiso, *Scritti spirituali*, ed. by Antignani, p. 225, no. 103.
114   Francesco owned a copy of Boethius, as well as other books. Callahan, 'The Confessor's House at a Renaissance Convent', p. 23 n. 38.
115   Medici, 'Caterina Cibo — duchessa di Camerino'.
116   Domenica dal Paradiso, *Scritti spirituali*, ed. by Antignani, p. 226, no. 103. The reference is to Psalm 34, attributed to King David, verse 9 'O fear the Lord, ye his saints, for there is no want

had become friends.[117] But prudence would also have been advisable because Caterina's daughter Giulia had recently ceded Camerino to Ottavio Farnese, the nephew of Pope Paul III, to remove a sentence of excommunication. To ensure the sentence remained lifted, the Cibo women had to tread carefully.

On 13 November 1542, Domenica addressed these concerns directly and wrote to both Caterina Cibo and Fra Bernardino.[118] She told Caterina that she had already warned her about becoming too close to Fra Bernardino, as he was suspected of preaching against the holy Catholic faith. Domenica reminded the duchess that when she told her to be careful and that Bernardino was causing scandals, Caterina had responded that lords and ladies were friends with him and that she did not know enough herself to expound on the Gospels.[119] Domenica replied that 'el Sigiore disse a discepoli che gli andassino a predicare gli evangelij a tucto il mondo' (the Lord told the disciples that they should go preach the Gospels to the whole world).[120]

Domenica next directly addressed Fra Bernardino, no doubt relying on Caterina to deliver her message.[121] Already aware that he had left Italy, Domenica urged Bernardino to return home, stop hiding, and ask for help from omnipotent God. Domenica must have heard from the friar or about his new life, as she wrote 'Voi dite che siate in una città che vi si predica et provedevisi a poveri, ma non vi si dice messa. È come essere nel inferno, chè chi si priva de' sancti sacramenti et del celebrare l'ordine della Sancta Chiesa è in tenebre' (You say that you are in a city where you preach and take care of the poor, but you don't say Mass. It is like being in hell, whoever is denied the holy sacraments and to celebrate the order of the Holy Church is in darkness).[122] Like St Catherine of Siena, Domenica did not often hesitate to directly address powerful men such as popes, but in this missive the mystic used the letter to Caterina Cibo as a conduit to address the friar, perhaps in fear that she would be accused of directly communicating with a heretic.

---

to them that fear him', and 11 'Come, ye children, hearken unto me I will teach you the fear of the Lord'.

117 Valerio, 'Caterina Cibo', p. 153.

118 Domenica dal Paradiso, *Scritti spirituali*, ed. by Antignani, pp. 227–30, no. 83 n. 1, notes that he was not sure if this is Bernardino Ochino, as the letter is only addressed to 'Fra Bernardino, frate francescano', but the contents of the letter and the fact that it is addressed to Caterina Cibo suggest it is Ochino. Since Antignani's biographies are hagiographic, he was probably trying to avoid accusations that Domenica communicated with a known heretic.

119 Domenica dal Paradiso, *Scritti spirituali*, ed. by Antignani, p. 227, no. 104, 'Quando venisti qua sapete che dissi alla V. S. che mincresceva di voi che essendo el Padre fra Bernardino tanto usato in casa vostra e scoprendosi testè contro alla fede di J. C., io vi dissi che voi navessi cura et che voi lo ammonissi dello scandolo che faceva nella chiesa di Dio, et voi mi dicesti che Signori e Signiore avevono sua amicizia et che non eri sufficiente voi a dichiarare gli evangellij'.

120 Domenica dal Paradiso, *Scritti spirituali*, ed. by Antignani, p. 227, no. 104.

121 Valerio, 'Caterina Cibo', p. 153. For the letter see Domenica dal Paradiso, *Scritti spirituali*, ed. by Antignani, pp. 227–30, no. 104.

122 Domenica dal Paradiso, *Scritti spirituali*, ed. by Antignani, p. 229, no 104.

Domenica had herself been accused of heresy in 1501, so was well aware of the need for caution. Early modern letters were seldom private. They were dictated to scribes, delivered by intermediaries, and read aloud to recipients. Domenica knew that her words could be widely disseminated, but also misinterpreted. Her desire to be heard, and to spread what she believed was the message of the Lord overrode the recognized danger of her actions, though she was always careful to tread cautiously. Domenica and her followers' confidence that God granted her visions and prophecies allowed her to cross the boundaries of class, culture, and even the walls of convents through letters and sermons. Her caution and careful judgement about what she put into writing allowed her to survive at a time when other post-Savonarolan reformers, such as Pietro Bernardo, were exiled and killed.[123] While her low profile and status as a lower-class woman led to Domenica being largely forgotten by history, her skill at becoming the nexus of a community of individuals tied variously by faith, kinship, and politics ultimately enabled her to build the convent of La Crocetta as a place in which to continue and refine Savonarola's vision for a New Jerusalem.

---

123   Denunciatory anonymous letters were important in the exile and capture of Pietro Bernardo, see Tognetti, 'Pietro Bernardo'. Pietro Bernardo was also known as Pietro Bernardino, Bernardino de' Unti and Fra Bernardino. See Polizzotto, *Children of the Promise*, pp. 120–21; Callahan, 'Preaching in a Poor Space', p. 227 n. 62 for further citations.

Works Cited

Manuscripts and Archival Sources

Florence, Archivio di Ospedale degli Innocenti di Firenze (AOIF)
    Estranei
Florence, Archivio di Stato di Firenze (ASF)
    Corporazioni Religiose Soppresse dal Governo Francese, (CRSGF)
    ——, 107 (La Crocetta di Firenze)
Florence, Biblioteca Domenicana di S. Maria Novella Jacopo Passavanti (BDSMN)
    Archivio di Monastero della Crocetta (AMC)
    ——, Box A labelled Originali di lettere missive della BMSD [Beata Madre
        Suor Domenica]
    ——, Box C labelled Brevi e Libri di Brevi, Pergamanee e folie
    ——, MS 1 Francesco Onesti da Castiglione, *Ephemeris seu Diarius Vitae
        B.M. Sororis Domenica dal Paradiso*, segnato C
    ——, MS 4 Libro di Miracoli della nostra B. Madre sor. Domenica etc. scritti
        da Suor Michelangiola Bettini etc. in fol. segnato colla lett. G
    ——, MS 7 Epistole Morali dettate dalla B. M e Sposa di Iesu Christo S. Dom.
        ca dal paradiso per instrutt[e] delle sue figle, e figli spirituali, e scritte per
        mano di diverse Monache sue coetanee
    ——, MS H Epistole della Ven.l. Mre S.r Dom.ca Fondatrice et dotatrice del
        Monast.° della Croce di Firenze, dll'[sic] ordine di S. Dom.co
    ——, Unnumbered MS, Libretto delle monache
    ——, Unnumbered MS, Libro dei Partiti
    ——, Unnumbered MS, Ricordanza

Primary Sources

Borghigiani, Benedetto Maria, *Intera narrazione della vita, costumi, e intelligenze
    spirituali della venerabile sposa di Gesù Suor Domenica dal Paradiso fondatrice del
    Monastero della Croce di Firenze, composta, e divisa in tre parti e dedicata a Maria
    Vergine Madre di Dio* (Florence: Michele Nestenus all'Insegna del Nome di
    Gesù, 1719)
Corbinelli, Jean, *Histoire genealogique de la maison de Gondi* (Paris: Jean-Baptiste
    Coignard, 1705)
Domenica dal Paradiso, *Scritti spirituali*, vol. 1, ed. by G. Antignani, (Poggibonsi:
    Edizioni Tipolito Arti Grafiche Nencini, 1984)
Farulli, Don Gregorio, *Istoria cronologica del nobile, ed antico Monastero degli Angioli
    di Firenze del Sacro Ordine Camaldoese dal principio della sua fondazione fino al
    presente giorno, con la serie de' Beati, de' Vescovi, de' Generali, degli Abbati, e degli
    Uomini insigni nelle Lettere, che quivi fiorirono;co' loro gloriosi fatti, ed Azioni, e
    di tutti I Nobili, che in esso si dedicarono a Dio con le loro Dignità, e Gradi, Col
    racconto di molte cose notabili ad esso appartenenti; Raccolta dale Scritture, che
    sono in detto Archivio* (Lucca: Pellegrino Frediani, 1710)

Lazzarini, Giovanni Andrea, *Catalogo delle pitture che si conservano nelle chiese di Pesaro* (Pesaro: Casa Gavelli, 1783)

Mainardi, Fra Vincenzo, 'Epistolario di Fra Vincenzo Mainardi da San Gimignano Domenicano 1481–1521', ed. by A. F. Verde and E. Giaconi, *Memorie Domenicane*, 23 (1992), Centro Riviste della Provincia Romana, i, ii

Memorie istoriche delle Chiese di Ferrara e de' suoi borghi (Ferrara: Carlo Coatti, 1723)

Richa, Giuseppe, *Notizie istoriche delle chiese fiorentine divise ne' suoi quartieri* (Florence: 1758, facsimile edition, Rome, 1972)

Rinaldi, Giuseppe, *Vita della Beata Beatrice Seconda d'Este, fondatrice dell'insigne Monastero di S. Antonio in Ferrara della Regola di S. Benedetto* (Ferrara: Giuseppe Rinaldi, 1777)

Sacra Rituum Congregatione Emo & Rmo. Dno. Card. Guadagni Florentina Beatificationis & Canonizationis Ven. Ancillae Dei Sor. Dominicae a' paradiso. Monialis Professae & Fundatricis Monasterii SSmae. Crucis Florentiae Ordinis S. Dominici. Positio super Dubio, etc (Rome: Typographia Rev. Camerae Apostolicae, 1755)

Savonarola, Girolamo, *La semplicità della vita cristiana*, ed. and trans. by P. Tito S. Centi, O. P. (Milan: Edizioni Ares, 1996)

Scalabrini, G. A., *Memorie istoriche delle chiese di Ferrara e de' suoi borghi* (Ferrara: Carlo Coatti, 1723)

Strozzi, Alessandra Macinghi, *Selected Letters of Alessandra Strozzi*, ed and trans. by Heather Gregory (Berkeley: University of California Press, 1997)

——, *Letters to her Sons (1447–1470)*, ed. and trans. by Judith Bryce, The Other Voice in Early Modern Europe: The Toronto Series, 46 Medieval and Renaissance Texts and Studies, vol. 493 (Toronto: Iter, Arizona Center for Medieval and Renaissance Studies, 2016)

Tarabotti, Arcangela, *Semplicità ingannta — Paternal Tyranny*, ed. and trans. by Letizia Panizza (Chicago: University of Chicago Press, 2004)

——, *Lettere familiari e di complimento*, ed. by Meredith Ray and Lynn Westwater (Turin: Rosenberg and Sellier, 2005)

Vasari, Giorgio, *Le vite de' più eccellenti pittori scultori ed architettori*, ed by Rosanna Bettarini and Paola Barocchi (Florence: Sansoni, 1987)

Secondary Works

Antignani, Gerardo, *Vicende e tempi di Suor Domenica dal Paradiso* (Siena: Edizioni Cantagalli, 1983)

——, *La Crocetta di Firenze* (Poggibonsi: Edizioni Tipolito Arti Grafiche Nencini, 1994)

Breisach, Ernst, *Caterina Sforza: A Renaissance Virago* (Chicago: University of Chicago Press, 1967)

Brown, Judith, 'Everyday Life, Longevity, and Nuns in Early Modern Florence', in *Renaissance Culture and the Everyday*, ed. by Patricia Fumerton and Simon Hunt (Philadelphia: University of Pennsylvania Press, 1998), pp. 115–38

Callahan, Meghan, 'The Politics of Architecture: Suor Domenica da Paradiso and her convent of la Crocetta in Post-Savonarolan Florence', (unpublished doctoral thesis, Rutgers University, 2005)

——,'"In her name and with her money", Suor Domenica da Paradiso's Convent of la Crocetta in Florence', in *Italian Art, Society and Politics: A Festschrift for Rab Hatfield*, ed. by Barbara Deimling, Jonathan K. Nelson, and Gary Radke (New York: Syracuse University Press, 2007), pp. 117–27

——, 'Suor Domenica da Paradiso as "alter Christus": Portraits of a Renaissance Mystic', *The Sixteenth Century Journal*, 43.2 (2012), 323–50

——, 'Preaching in a Poor Space: Savonarolan Influence at Sister Domenica's Convent of La Crocetta in Renaissance Florence', in *Patronage, Gender & the Arts in Early Modern Italy: Essays in Honor of Carolyn Valone*, ed. by Katherine A. McIver and Cynthia Stollhans (New York: Italica, 2015), pp. 211–30

——, 'The Confessor's House at a Renaissance Convent: The Canon Francesco da Castiglione's Bequest and Inventory', in *Encountering the Renaissance: Celebrating Gary Radke and 50 Years of the Syracuse University Graduate Program in Renaissance Art*, ed. by A. Victor Coonin and Molly Bourne (New Jersey: WAPAAC & Zephyr Scholarly Publications, 2016), pp. 223–34

Calvi, Giulia, *Histories of a Plague Year: The Social and the Imaginary in Baroque Florence*, trans. by Dario Biocca and Bryant T. Ragan Jr. (Berkeley: University of California Press, 1989)

Camillocci, Daniela Solfaroli, 'La monaca esemplare. Lettere spirituali di madre Battistina Vernazza (1497–1587)', in *Per lettera. La scrittura epistolare femminile tra archivio e tipografia secoli XV–XVII*, ed. by Gabriella Zarri (Rome: Viella, 1999), pp. 235–62

Catholic Church, Congregatio de Causis Sanctorum, *Index ac Status Causarum* (Città del Vaticano: Congregatio de Causis Sanctorum, 1999)

Donati, Andrea, *Girolamo Marchesi da Cotignola* (San Marino: Asset Banca Spa Repubblica di San Marino, 2007)

Dunn, Marilyn, 'Nuns, Agents and Agency: Art Patronage in the post-Tridentine Convent', in *Patronage, Gender & the Arts in Early Modern Italy: Essays in Honor of Carolyn Valone*, ed. by Katherine A. McIver and Cynthia Stollhans (New York: Italica, 2015), pp. 127–51

Edler, Florence, *Glossary of Mediaeval Terms of Business: Italian Series 1200–1600* (Cambridge, MA: Harvard University Press, 1934), reprinted 1970

Elam, Carolyn, 'Lorenzo de' Medici's Sculpture Garden', *Mitteilungen des Kunsthistorischen Institutes in Florenz*, 36 (1992), 41–84

Fantozzi Micali, Osanna, and Piero Roselli, *Le soppressioni dei conventi a Firenze: riuso e trasformazioni dal sec. XVIII in poi* (Florence: L. E. F., 1980)

Felicangeli, Bernardino, *Notizie e documenti sulla vita di Caterina Cibo-Varano, Duchessa di Camerino* (Camerino: Tipografia Savini, 1801)

Gagliardi, Isabella, *Sola con Dio: la missione di Domenica da Paradiso nella Firenze del primo cinquecento* (Florence: SISMEL: 2007)

Hayum, Andrée, 'A Renaissance Audience Considered: The Nuns at S. Apollonia and Castagno's "Last Supper"', *The Art Bulletin*, 88 (June 2006), 243–66

Herzig, Tamar, *Savonarola's Women: Visions and Reform in Renaissance Italy* (Chicago: University of Chicago Press, 2007)

Joost-Gaugier, Christiane, *Measuring Heaven: Pythagoras and His Influence on Thought and Art in Antiquity and the Middle Ages* (Ithaca: Cornell University Press, 2006)

Librandi, Rita, and Adriana Valerio, *I sermoni di Domenica da Paradiso. Studi e testo critico* (Florence: SISMEL, 1999)

McLean, Paul, *The Art of the Network: Strategic Interaction and Patronage in Renaissance Florence* (Durham, NC: Duke University Press, 2007)

Medici, Catherine, 'Using Network Analysis to Understand Early Modern Women', *Early Modern Women: An Interdisciplinary Journal*, 13 (Fall 2018), 153–62

Medici, Maria Teresa Guerra, 'Caterina Cibo — duchessa di Camerino', Enciclopedia delle donne, http://www.enciclopediadelledonne.it/biografie/caterina-cybo-duchessa-di-camerino/ [accessed: 15 September 2019]

Monson, Craig, ed., *The Crannied Wall: Women, Religion and the Arts in Early Modern Europe* (Ann Arbor: University of Michigan Press, 1992)

Muessig, Carolyn, *The Stigmata in Medieval and Early Modern Europe* (Oxford: Oxford University Press, 2020)

Petrucci, Franca, 'Caterina Cibo', *Dizionario Biografico degli Italiani*, 25 (1981) http://www.treccani.it/enciclopedia/caterina-cibo_Dizionario-Biografico [accessed 15 September 2019]

Polizzotto, Lorenzo, '*Dell'arte del ben morire*: The Piagnone Way of Death, 1494–1545', *I Tatti Studies in the Italian Renaissance*, 3 (1989), 27–87

——, 'When Saints Fall Out: Women and the Savonarolan Reform in Early Sixteenth-Century Florence', *Renaissance Quarterly*, 46 (1993), 486–525

——, *The Elect Nation: The Savonarolan Movement in Florence 1494–1545* (Oxford: Oxford Clarendon Press,1994)

——, *Children of the Promise: The Confraternity of the Purification and the Socialization of Youths in Florence, 1427–1785* (Oxford: Oxford University Press, 2004)

Radke, Gary, 'Nuns and their Art: The Case of San Zaccaria in Renaissance Venice', *Renaissance Quarterly*, 54 (Summer 2001), 430–59

Robin, Diana, *Publishing Women: Salons, The Presses, and the Counter-Reformation in Sixteenth-Century Italy*, Women in Culture and Society, edited by Catharine R. Stimpson (Chicago: University of Chicago Press, 2007)

de Roover, Raymond, 'A Florentine Firm of Cloth Manufacturers', *Speculum*, 16 (January 1941), 3–33

Rudy, Kathryn M., *Virtual Pilgrimages in the Convent: Imagining Jerusalem in the Late Middle Ages*, Disciplina Monastica, 8. (Turnhout: Brepols, 2011)

Shaw, James, and Evelyn Welch, *Making and Marketing Medicine in Renaissance Florence*, The Wellcome Series in the History of Medicine, Clio Medica, 89 (Amsterdam: Rodopi, 2011)

Strocchia, Sharon T., *Nuns and Nunneries in Renaissance Florence* (Baltimore: The Johns Hopkins University Press, 2009)

Tamalio, Raffaelle, 'Lucrezia Borgia', *Dizionario Biografico degli Italiani*, 66 (Rome: Treccani, 2006) http://www.treccani.it/enciclopedia/ricerca/Lucrezia-Borgia/ [accessed 15 September 2019]

Thomas, Anabel, *Art and Piety in the Female Religious Communities of Renaissance Italy* (Cambridge: Cambridge University Press, 2003)

Toccafondi Fantappie, Diana, 'Marco del Nero', *Dizionario Biografico degli Italiani*, 38 (Rome: Treccani, 1990) http://www.treccani.it/enciclopedia/marco-del-nero_%28Dizionario-Biografico%29 [accessed 15 September 2019]

Tognetti, Giampaolo, 'Pietro Bernardo', *Dizionario Biografico degli Italiani*,
    9 (Rome: Treccani, 1967) http://www.treccani.it/enciclopedia/pietro-
    bernardo_%28Dizionario-Biografico%29/ [accessed 15 September 2019]

Valerio, Adriana, *Domenica da Paradiso profezia e politica in una mistica del
    Rinascimento* (Spoleto: Fondazione di Centro Italiano di Studi sull'Alto
    Medioevo, 1992)

——, '"Et io expongo le scripture": Domenica da Paradiso e l'Interpretazione
    Biblica. Un documento inedito nella crisi del rinascimento fiorentino', *Rivista
    di Storia e letteratura religiosa*, 3 (1994), 499–534

——, 'Caterina Cibo e la spiritualità savonaroliana attraverso il magistero profetico
    di Domenica da Paradiso', in *Munera Parva, Studi in onore di Boris Ulianich*,
    ed. by G. Luongo, II, (Naples: Federiciana Editrice Universitaria 1999),
    pp. 141–54

Valone, Carolyn, 'Architecture as a Public Voice for Women in Sixteenth-Century
    Rome', *Renaissance Studies*, 15 (2001), 301–23

Vasoli, Cesare, 'Camilla Bartolini Rucellai', *Dizionario Biografico degli Italiani*,
    6 (Rome: Treccani, 1964) http://www.treccani.it/enciclopedia/camilla-
    bartolini-rucellai_(Dizionario-Biografico) [accessed 15 September 2019]

Weddle, Saundra, 'Women in Wolves' Mouths: Nuns' Reputations and
    Architecture at the Convent of Le Murate', in *Architecture and the Politics of
    Gender in Early Modern Europe*, ed. by Helen Hills (Burlington: Ashgate,
    2003), pp. 115–29

Weinstein, Donald, *Savonarola: The Rise and Fall of a Renaissance Prophet* (New
    Haven: Yale University Press, 2011)

Zama, Raffaella, *Girolamo Marchesi da Cotignola. Pittore. Catalogo Generale*
    (Rimini: Luise' Editore, 2007)

Zarri, Gabriella, *Le sante vive. Profezie di corte e devozione femminile tra '400 e '500*
    (Turin: Rossenberg & Sellier, 1990)

——, *La religione di Lucrezia Borgia: le lettere inedite del confessore* (Comitato
    nazionale incontri di studio per il V centenario del pontificato di Alessandro VI
    (1492–1503) (Rome: Associazione Roma nel Rinascimento, 2006)

CATHERINE TURRILL LUPI*

Pursuing a Savonarolan Thread

Patrons, Painters, and Piagnoni
at S. Caterina in Cafaggio

Among the numerous connecting threads that helped define the networks of female Dominican convents in Florence and its environs in the 1500s, one of the most interesting — and, in its day, provocative — was the veneration of Girolamo Savonarola as prophet and martyr. An inspiring preacher and energetic reformer during his lifetime (1452–1498), this Dominican friar continued to be revered by members of the lay and religious communities long after his death, and in the face of sustained opposition by political and ecclesiastic authorities.[1] Several Tuscan Dominican convents that had been founded or restructured with Savonarola's assistance in the late 1400s continued to nourish his cult during the sixteenth century. The nuns in these communities preserved the friar's relics, transcribed or acquired compilations of his purported miracles, and commissioned images that presented him in the guise of a saint or martyr. All of these activities flourished at the Florentine convent of S. Caterina in Cafaggio, the subject of this essay. They also are documented at several other Dominican houses connected to it, notably the neighbouring convent of S. Lucia on via San Gallo and the convent of S. Vincenzo in Prato. These three convents were linked by other factors as well, such as the shared oversight by the friary of S. Marco and the presence of nuns from Florentine families who were related by blood or marriage. In this essay, I will examine ways in which these and other points of intersection were reflected in three works of art commissioned for S. Caterina in Cafaggio

* I would like to express my sincere gratitude to Dottoressa Oliva Rucellai for her hospitality when I consulted the Archivio Rucellai in Florence, and to California State University's Emeritus and Retired Faculty Association for its generous financial support.

1 Savonarola and two of the friars closest to him, Domenico Buonvicini and Silvestro Maruffi, were arrested and summarily tried before their public execution in Florence's Piazza della Signoria on 23 May 1498. For a concise discussion of the development of Savonarola's cult in the years that followed, see Dall'Aglio, 'Everyone Worships Fra Girolamo as a Saint'.

Catherine Turrill Lupi (turrillc@csus.edu), professor of Art History, retired from California State University, Sacramento in 2016. The primary focus of her scholarship is the sixteenth-century Florentine painter, Plautilla Nelli.

Convent Networks In Early Modern Italy, ed. by Marilyn Dunn and Saundra Weddle, ES 25 (Turnhout: Brepols, 2020) pp. 85–114   BREPOLS ✤ PUBLISHERS   DOI 10.1484/M.ES-EB.5.119514

during the 1520s and 1570s. The patrons were two women, Alessandra Bonsi del Pugliese and Marietta Sernigi Carnesecchi. Although separated by several decades, they were connected with each other, and with the convent they served, by their veneration of Girolamo Savonarola. The artistic projects they sponsored had counterparts in other Tuscan Dominican convents that were affiliated with S. Caterina in Cafaggio, offering tangible evidence of the network connecting these religious communities.

As related in the convent's chronicle and later histories based on it, the origins of S. Caterina in Cafaggio (also known as S. Caterina da Siena) go back to May 1496 when Ridolfo di Filippo Rucellai and his wife, Camilla di Domenico di Neri Bartolini, agreed to end their twelve-year marriage so that they could devote their lives to religion.[2] Their decision to join the Dominican order is said to have been a direct response to Savonarola's inspirational presence and preaching in Florence. As prior of S. Marco, he presided over their vestition ceremonies, in which Camilla took the name of Lucia, and her former husband became Teofilo. Savonarola also facilitated the establishment of a new community of Dominican tertiaries under Suor Lucia's leadership. At first these women shared a house on via del Cocomero (now via Ricasoli). It apparently was intended as a temporary residence from the beginning. One of Lucia's first companions, Suor Caterina da Cutigliano, later reported that Savonarola had given her instructions for the building of a convent dedicated to St Catherine of Siena prior to his execution in 1498.[3] Two years later, on 30 September 1500 (significantly, the feast day of Savonarola's name-saint, Jerome), the cornerstone of the new edifice was laid on a site across the square from the friary of S. Marco, whose brothers were charged with the administration of the convent.[4] Construction continued for the next several years.

Suor Lucia and her companions made their formal entry into the convent's church on 8 May 1506, the tenth anniversary of her vestition.[5] The crowd processing with them from their residence on via del Cocomero is said to have included not only women from the Rucellai family, but also other noble matrons from the first ranks of Florentine society, many of whom shared kinship ties to the Rucellai and/or were from families whose members were numbered among the so-called *piagnoni* ('big weepers', the

---

2   Richa, *Notizie istoriche delle chiese fiorentine*, p. 278. The divorce and two vestitions occurred on the same day (8 May 1496). This date also was reported in the convent chronicle excerpts that later were transcribed for the Rucellai family. See Florence, AR, Serie 1.8, Misc. Massai 32.3, c. 2; and Florence, BNCF, LF 72, fol. 112ᵛ.

3   That information appears in a copy of the Pseudo-Burlamacchi *Vita di Savonarola* that was owned by Suor Caterina Eletta Rosselli, one of the artist-nuns at S. Caterina in the late sixteenth century. It is now in the John Rylands Library, Manchester (Italian MS 13). See Herzig, *Savonarola's Women*, p. 34.

4   Florence, BNCF, LF 72, fol. 128ᵛ.

5   Florence, BCNF, LF 72, fol. 130ʳ. The names of the women participating in the procession are listed on fols 135ʳ–138ʳ.

pejorative nickname given to Savonarola's followers). Their Savonarolan sympathies can be inferred in part from the fact that the surnames of the husbands and fathers of many of the women who walked in the procession appear in the list of 503 signatures on the 1497 petition to Pope Alexander VI, asking him to lift his excommunication of Savonarola.[6] Several of the names also appear in the documents compiled during the friar's trial the following year, specifically those identifying the laymen who were counted among his friends, or who were said to have visited him at S. Marco.[7] Members of the same families willingly supported S. Caterina in Cafaggio, which stayed true to its Savonarolan origins throughout the 1500s. By 1513, a third of the nuns at the new convent might have been considered *piagnoni*, either because their fathers had signed the 1497 petition, or because they themselves are known to have been followers of Savonarola.[8]

Among the 'nobili matrone' participating in the 1506 procession was Lucrezia di Cristofano Spinelli, the second wife of Domenico Bonsi and the stepmother of his daughter Alessandra, the first important art patron associated with S. Caterina in Cafaggio.[9] With Alessandra Bonsi's marriage to Francesco di Filippo del Pugliese fifteen years earlier, two of the city's most prominent families had been united.[10] Domenico, a member of the 'della Ruota' branch of the Bonsi family, had been educated in law and held multiple political offices in Florence from the 1460s until his death in 1501; Francesco was a wealthy wool merchant and enthusiastic art patron.[11] Like other Florentines connected to S. Caterina in Cafaggio, the two men shared Savonarolan sympathies. Both Domenico and Francesco were said to have visited the friar at S. Marco in the late 1400s and were described as his friends by contemporary witnesses.[12] They also had signed the 1497 petition mentioned above.

Francesco's confirmed status as a *piagnone* is further documented by his involvement with several Dominican friaries and convents associated with Savonarola. For services rendered to S. Marco, to which he proposed to bequeath his country estate and its chapel,[13] he was given two paintings by Fra

---

6 For the signatories of the 1497 subscription list, see Polizzotto, *The Elect Nation*, pp. 446–61.

7 For the 1498 trial documents, see Villari, *La storia di Girolamo Savonarola*, vol. 2, pp. ccxlix–cd.

8 According to Polizzotto, '*Dell'arte del ben morire*', p. 48, twelve of the fifty-five nuns had fathers who were signatories, and another six of the women 'were Savonarolan followers in their own right'.

9 Florence, BNCF, LF 72, fol. 137[v].

10 The Bonsi and Del Pugliese families were included in Benedetto Dei's late fifteenth-century list of the two hundred oldest, richest, and noblest families of Florence. See Zambrano and Nelson, *Filippino Lippi*, pp. 80–81.

11 According to Geronimus, *Piero di Cosimo*, p. 124, Francesco was 'one of the most active patron-collectors in Florence' in the late 1400s and early 1500s.

12 Villari, *La storia di Girolamo Savonarola*, vol. 2, p. cccix (Del Pugliese) and p. cccxxxvii (Bonsi).

13 This proposed legacy is described in Francesco's second will, drafted in 1503 and published in its entirety by Polizzotto, '*Dell'arte del ben morire*', pp. 69–80.

Bartolomeo della Porta, the friary's foremost artist in the early 1500s.[14] He had personal ties to the nearby convent of S. Lucia in via San Gallo, described by Lorenzo Polizzotto as one of Florence's 'two most important centres of female Savonarolan spirituality' — the other convent being S. Caterina in Cafaggio.[15] His sister Caterina took the veil at S. Lucia after her husband's death in 1486.[16] Francesco later proposed to dower two of his female servants should they choose to become nuns at S. Lucia, and also promised a legacy to the convent itself.[17] According to Polizzotto, even the way in which Francesco formulated his wills reflected a *piagnone* outlook.[18] A similar attitude was expressed by his wife Alessandra, who became an occasional pensioner (*commessa* or, in English, corrodian) at the convent of S. Caterina starting in 1517 and who promised an endowment to S. Lucia the following year.[19] She owned a book of Savonarola's sermons and other objects associated with him.[20] As explained below, her reverence for the friar also seems to be reflected in the art work that she financed for the church of S. Caterina.

Given their reputations as Savonarolan foundations, either S. Lucia or S. Caterina would have been an appropriate destination for Alessandra when she decided to become a *commessa*. Her choice of the latter convent may have been motivated by the fact that both the Bonsi and the Del Pugliese families were connected to the Rucellai family, and therefore to the convent's founder Lucia, who was popularly regarded as a living saint at the time. Alessandra's paternal uncle was married to a Rucellai woman.[21] Through her sister-in-law's marriage into the Ginori family, Alessandra also was related to Lorenza di

---

14   Assonitis, 'Fra Bartolomeo della Porta', pp. 441–42. The two paintings given to Del Pugliese were the *Crucifixion* and *Saint George and the Dragon*. Both images are lost.

15   Polizzotto, *The Elect Nation*, p. 189. In his article 'When Saints Fall Out', p. 491, Polizzotto stated that S. Lucia and S. Caterina were two of five Dominican female convents 'controlled by Savonarolans', the other three being S. Croce (called La Crocetta), S. Vincenzo (called Annalena), and S. Maria degli Angeli (called Angiolini).

16   In her testament, drawn up on 24 July 1495 by Ser Bartolomeo Bindi, Caterina del Pugliese is identified as Suor Maria Maddalena, a nun at S. Lucia. See Florence, ASF, Notarile Antecosimiano 2874, filza 1, n. 18, c. 58ʳ. Her late husband, Giovanni di Francesco Ginori, also is mentioned. According to Passerini, he died in 1486. See Passerini, *Genealogia e storia*, tav. IV.

17   In his second will (1503), Francesco said he would dower his Circassian servant named Magdalena at S. Lucia or any other convent. He also promised a legacy of 200 florins to S. Lucia 'per l'amore di Dio' (Polizzotto, *'Dell'arte del ben morire'*, pp. 70 and 79). For the other servant, Lucia, see n. 27.

18   Polizzotto, *'Dell'arte del ben morire'*, pp. 63–64.

19   The paperwork for Alessandra's 1518 endowment is one of several legal documents cited by Polizzotto as an expression of a 'Savonarolan ideology'. He also includes her among the *piagnoni*. See Polizzotto, *'Dell'arte del ben morire'*, p. 60. For the document itself, drafted by Ser Filippo Cioni, see Florence, ASF, Notarile Antecosimiano 5439, fol. 137ʳ.

20   Alessandra's ownership of the book and other objects (unspecified) is mentioned in several versions of the pseudo-Burlamacchi biography of the friar. Among others, see *Vita del p. f. Girolamo Savonarola*, p. 174.

21   Bernardo di Baldassare Bonsi was married to Cleofe di Francesco Rucellai. Like his brother

Leonardo Ginori, the wife of Paolo di Pandolfo Rucellai and one of Lucia's closest friends.[22]

Suor Lucia still was alive when Alessandra met with a Savonarolan notary, Ser Filippo Cioni, to finalize her arrangement with the convent.[23] According to the terms of the contract drafted in July 1517 and recorded in the convent archive, Alessandra was conceded a furnished room at S. Caterina to which she could retreat now and then, whether for her solace ('consolazione') or so that she could attend convent solemnities.[24] A similar arrangement had been made a few years earlier for one of her kinswomen, Argentina Soderini, who was a *commessa* at another Florentine convent, S. Maria dell'Annunziata (known as Le Murate).[25]

Alessandra's initial phase as S. Caterina's *commessa* lasted just under three years. When Francesco del Pugliese dictated his fourth and last will in June 1519, he stated that his wife was then ('hodie') in the convent of S. Caterina but could enter S. Lucia or another convent after his demise.[26] However, even though both her sister-in-law and a former family servant were nuns at S. Lucia by the time she was widowed, Alessandra decided to extend her existing arrangement with S. Caterina and remain there as a boarder.[27] In April 1520, a few months after Francesco's death, the terms of her tenancy were renegotiated and a new contract was drafted by yet another Savonarolan notary, Ser Lorenzo Violi.[28] In addition to a furnished room that met her specifications ('una stanza a suo piacemento'), Alessandra was provided with an annual allowance drawn from an endowment of 525 florins.[29] She maintained

---

Domenico — Alessandra's father — he was among the *piagnoni* who signed the 1497 petition. For the list of names, see Polizzotto, *The Elect Nation*, p. 448.

22 Lorenza's father, Leonardo Ginori, was the brother of Caterina del Pugliese's husband Giovanni Ginori (both were sons of Francesco di Piero Ginori). For this line of the Ginori family, see Passerini, *Genealogia e storia*, tav. IV. On p. 45, Passerini discusses both Lorenza's close friendship with Suor Lucia and her involvement with the foundation of the convent.

23 Described by Polizzotto, *The Elect Nation*, p. 83, as a 'staunch Savonarolan notary', Cioni had worked for both Alessandra (see n. 19) and S. Caterina (see n. 32) on other occasions.

24 Florence, ASF, CRSGF 106, vol. 30, fol. 192ʳ. The contract was drawn up on 28 July 1517.

25 For the agreement between Argentina Malaspina Soderini and Le Murate, see Lowe, *Nuns' Chronicles and Convent Culture*, p. 181; and Strocchia, 'Taken into Custody', p. 187. Alessandra's brother Roberto was married to Lisabetta di Tommaso Soderini, Argentina's great-niece. Perhaps Alessandra's acquaintance with the Soderini contributed to her decision to become a *commessa*.

26 Polizzotto, 'Dell'arte del ben morire', p. 86.

27 Lucia de Barberia da Tripoli, identified as both a *serva* (servant) and *schiava* (slave) in Francesco's 1519 will, was accepted into S. Lucia on 27 February 1518/1519. Note that the Florentine year began on 25 March; here, 1518 reflects the Florentine style of dating, while 1519 reflects the modern style. Henceforth, this notation will be used for dates from January through to 24 March. See Florence, ASF, CRSGF 111, vol. 40, fols 51/li.

28 Violi transcribed several of the sermons Savonarola delivered in Florence between 1495–1498. He also drafted the last three wills of Francesco del Pugliese (1503, 1512, and 1519).

29 Florence, ASF, CRSGF 106, vol. 30, fol. 193ʳ.

her lay status at the convent for four more years, not taking the veil as Suor Antonina until 1524, according to the convent chronicle.[30] Shortly before her death the following year (18 April 1525), she made her solemn profession into the hands of the prioress, Suor Arcangiola de' Buonamici.[31]

Given her family wealth and the timing of her arrival at S. Caterina, Alessandra del Pugliese was well-positioned to play a significant role in the decoration of both the public church and the nuns' choir. When she became the convent's *commessa* in 1517, the last phase of the building project was underway, and she would have been a first-hand witness to its progress. According to entries in the convent chronicle that later were transcribed for the Rucellai family, a revised set of plans for the church and nuns' choir was drawn up during the priorate of Suor Domenica di Francesco da Santa Maria Impruneta (1510–1513), the church foundations were laid during the first priorate of Suor Arcangiola de' Buonamici (1513–1515), the church vault was completed during the priorate of Suor Maria Magdalena di Neri Rinuccini (1515–1519), and the nuns' choir was finished during the second priorate of Suor Arcangiola (1519–1522).[32] The new church also was re-consecrated during this last two-year period, at least according to one version of the chronicle, which implied that two ceremonies may have been involved: one on the feast of St Jerome (30 September, the same day the foundations of the convent were begun, two decades before) and the other on 3 February, the day of the original consecration in 1506.[33] The latter date was the one celebrated at S. Caterina in the following centuries.[34]

As recorded in a plan drawn up in about 1810, shortly after the convent was suppressed, the public church of S. Caterina had three altars, two against the side walls (for which Suor Plautilla Nelli produced the two paintings that Vasari first recorded in the 1560s) and one against the wall facing the entrance

---

30 Florence, AR, Serie 1.8, Misc. Massai 32.3, fol. 54. According to her obituary, Alessandra had been a nun for just over a year when she died in 1525.

31 Florence, AR, Serie 1.8, Misc. Massai 32.3, fol. 54. Although nuns typically made their solemn profession a year after taking the veil, the entry indicates that Antonina also was in failing health at the time.

32 In January 1513, the nuns at S. Caterina came to a final decision about the location of the entrance to the public church (on via Larga, now called via Cavour). This resulted in a new set of plans and a complete rebuilding of the church. For the 1513 meeting, recorded by the notary Ser Filippo Cioni, see Polizzotto, 'When Saints Fall Out', p. 513, n. 106; and Florence, ASF, CRSGF 106, vol. 71, filza 2. For the sequence of building projects, as recorded in the two sets of excerpts from the chronicle, see: Florence, AR, Serie 1.8, Misc. Massai 32.3, fols 4–6; and Florence, BNCF, LF 72, fols 94ᵛ–95ʳ.

33 Florence, AR, Serie 1.8, Misc. Massai 32.3, fol. 6. A note about the church consecration, referencing both 'el giorno di S. hieronimo' and 3 February, was inserted into the upper left margin of this page, next to the entry for the second priorate of Arcangiola de' Buonamici (1519–1522). The specific year is not reported. For the 3 February 1506 consecration date, see Richa, *Notizie istoriche delle chiese fiorentine*, p. 283.

34 Francesconi, *Firenze sacra*, p. 30.

from via Larga (now via Cavour), the *altare maggiore* (Figure 3.1).[35] The nuns' choir was on the other side of this wall. Its altar, recorded in the convent chronicle and mentioned in the early literature, is not indicated in the nineteenth-century plan.[36] According to the chronicle, the high altar of the public church and the altar in the nuns' choir were both decorated during the priorate of Suor Cecilia Michelozzi (1522–1524), in a two-phase project sponsored by Alessandra del Pugliese.[37] The first phase, launched several months before she took the veil, resulted in the altarpiece for the nuns' choir ('la Tavola dell'Altare del Coro').[38] Shortly after Alessandra became Suor Antonina, funds from her revenues ('entrate') were used to pay for the main altarpiece in the convent's public church ('la Tavola dell'Altare Maggiore di Chiesa').[39] During the same period, predellas for both altarpieces, the frames from which

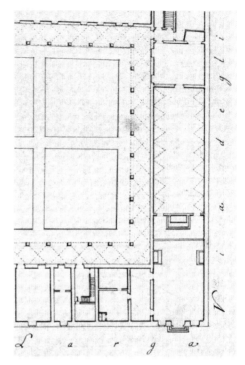

Figure 3.1. Detail of the ground floor plan of S. Caterina in Cafaggio. Florence, Archivio Storico Comunale, amfce. 0306 (cass.8, ins. B). About 1810. Reproduced with permission of the Archivio Storico Comunale.

35 Florence, ASC, amfce. 0306 (cass. 8, ins. B). For the full set of plans, prepared before the convent's conversion to an academy, see the ASC's website (ArchiDis, Fondo disegni tecnici). For the locations of Nelli's two altarpieces in the public church, the *Lamentation* (right altar; now in the S. Marco Museum) and the *Adoration of the Magi* (left altar; current location unknown), see Richa, *Notizie istoriche delle chiese fiorentine*, p. 283. Both altarpieces probably were painted before Nelli became prioress for the first time in 1563. See Turrill, 'Nuns' Stories', p. 13.

36 Because the nuns were fully cloistered by the late 1500s, restricting public access to their choir, there is very little information about that space in the literature. Richa said only that an altarpiece by the 'Frate' (Fra Bartolomeo) was installed there. By contrast, he was able to describe the subject of the church altarpiece in some detail. See Richa, *Notizie istoriche delle chiese fiorentine*, p. 284.

37 Florence, AR, Serie 1.8, Misc. Massai 32.3, fol. 6. For a concise summary of expenses incurred in the completion of this project, see Florence, ASF, CRSGF 106, vol. 30, fol. 97 (8 December 1524).

38 In the excerpts from the convent chronicle, the phrase 'sue entrate' is used twice to describe the source of funding. In the section about the priores (fol. 6), the 'entrate' are connected only to the church altarpiece; in Alessandra's obituary (which is more abbreviated), the 'entrate' are said to have been used to pay for both paintings (fol. 54). See n. 37.

39 Florence, AR, Serie 1.8, Misc. Massai 32.3, fol. 6.

Figure 3.2. Fra Paolino da Pistoia, *Madonna and Child Enthroned with Saints*, Florence, Museo di S. Marco. About 1524. Reproduced with permission of the Gabinetto Fotografico delle Gallerie degli Uffizi, Florence.

the altar curtains were suspended, the predellas of the church's minor altars, the *prie-dieux*, and other church furnishings were made at the convent's expense. The chronicler's use of the phrase 'ci fece la tavola' (made the panel for us) when referring to Alessandra's sponsorship of each of the altarpieces produced in the 1520s suggests that she may have had a personal involvement in the two projects. This seems to be reflected as well in specific details of the two paintings, both of which were found in the convent when it was suppressed in the early 1800s, and which have been preserved to this day.

The altarpiece from the nuns' choir, identified as the work of Fra Paolino da Pistoia in the convent chronicle, is now in the S. Marco Museum in Florence (Figure 3.2).[40] The altarpiece from the public church, generally attributed to Antonio del Ceraiolo on stylistic grounds, has been in the Bombeni Chapel in S. Trinita in Florence since 1957 (Figure 3.3).[41] The two artists were natural choices for the commissions. Fra Paolino had assumed the position of leading painter at S. Marco a few years before, after the death of Fra Bartolomeo della Porta (1517). As a result, he was frequently employed by other members of the order. Although a lay artist, Ceraiolo also had established multiple connections within the Dominican community, both personal and professional, before working for S. Caterina. His sister Elisabetta took the veil at S. Lucia in 1518, the same year that he received a commission for an altarpiece from yet another Florentine Dominican convent enjoying *piagnone* support, La Crocetta.[42] Two years later, in 1520, he produced a painting for the new choir of S. Lucia.[43] Finally, Ceraiolo was affiliated with a number of artists who had ties with Savonarola and/or with S. Marco. His teacher, Lorenzo di Credi, was close to members of Savonarola's circle and had a niece at La Crocetta (a possible contributing factor to Ceraiolo's employment by that convent).[44] His next master, Ridolfo del Ghirlandaio, and several of his peers belonged to the so-called 'Scuola di S. Marco', a group of Florentine artists who were trained or influenced by Fra Bartolomeo.[45] Any of these accomplishments

---

40 Once thought to be the work of Fra Bartolomeo, the choir altarpiece was reassigned to Fra Paolino on stylistic grounds in the 1880s. For a concise summary of its attributions and provenance after 1810, see Muzzi, 'Fra' Paolino: *Matrimonio mistico di Santa Caterina e Santi*', p. 253.

41 Gamba, 'Ridolfo e Michele', pp. 545–46, was the first scholar to assign the painting to Ceraiolo. The attribution was reaffirmed by Zeri, 'Antonio del Ceraiolo', p. 146.

42 For the record of Elisabetta's vestition as Suor Vittoria at S. Lucia, see Florence, ASF, CRSGF 111, vol. 40, fols 50/l and 165. For Ceraiolo's altarpiece commission from La Crocetta, see Callahan, 'Antonio del Ceraiolo at La Crocetta', pp. 8–9 and 11.

43 Florence, ASF, CRSGF 111, vol. 40, fols 167/clxvii.

44 For Lorenzo di Credi's connection to Savonarola, which was first mentioned by Vasari, see Kent, 'Lorenzo di Credi', p. 540. For his niece's presence at La Crocetta (documented in 1517–1521), see Callahan, 'Antonio del Ceraiolo at La Crocetta', p. 11.

45 In particular, Ceraiolo was associated with Giovanni Antonio Sogliani (born 1492) and Michele Tosini (born 1503), both of whom also had been pupils of Lorenzo di Credi. The son of a wax-modeler (*ceraiuolo*) named Arcangelo di Giuliano, he was born in the

Figure 3.3. Antonio del Ceraiolo, *Mystic Marriage of Saint Catherine of Siena*, Florence, S. Trinita. About 1524. Photo courtesy of Archivi Alinari, Florence.

and associations may have recommended Ceraiolo not only to the nuns of
S. Caterina, but also to Alessandra del Pugliese, whose sister-in-law, a nun at
S. Lucia, would have known the artist's sister and possibly his work as well.[46]

After the two altarpieces, the last components mentioned in the chronicle
and convent records are the predella panels. They were not listed with the
altarpieces in the inventory composed after the convent's suppression and may
have been separated from them before 1810. As discussed later, it is very likely
that one or more of the predella panels now in the Museo dell'Accademia Etrusca
in Cortona may have belonged to the altarpieces. No artist is mentioned in the
convent records for the project and for many years the panels were thought to
be the work of Ceraiolo's colleague, Michele Tosini.[47] Like the painting now
in S. Trinita, they were first attributed to Ceraiolo in the 1900s. They include
a pair of panels depicting the Annunciate Angel and the Annunciate Virgin;
a pair of panels that each depict two male saints and a devout angel (Figures
3.4 and 3.5); and a single long panel depicting nine martyr saints.

As several scholars have recognized, the composition of Fra Paolino's
painting, *Madonna and Child with Saints* (Figure 3.2), closely follows that of
Fra Bartolomeo della Porta's altarpiece for S. Marco, now in the Louvre (*Mystic
Marriage of Saint Catherine of Siena*; 1511). Fra Paolino would have been able
to follow the execution of the S. Marco painting, which occurred while he
was in Florence.[48] However, by the time he received the commission from
the nuns at S. Caterina, Fra Bartolomeo's altarpiece had been in France for
nearly a decade. He must have referred instead to the preliminary drawings,
many of which were included in the workshop materials that he had inherited
following Fra Bartolomeo's death in 1517.[49] Fra Paolino's access to these sketches
helps explain the strong resemblance between the figures of the Madonna,
the Christ Child, St Catherine of Siena, and St Catherine of Alexandria in
the two altarpieces. Indeed, his painting follows the older master's work so
closely that it usually is described as a depiction of the same subject, despite
the fact that the infant Christ is not shown offering a ring to St Catherine
of Siena. Instead, he is pointing toward a heart that she holds close to her
breast, his right index finger almost grazing its surface. The exact nature of
this interaction is not fully defined. Neither of the two episodes described

---

S. Michele Visdomini parish in April 1497 (Florence, OSMF, Registri Battesimali, Reg. 6,
fol. 173).

46 Suor Maria Maddalena (Caterina Pugliese Ginori) was still at S. Lucia in 1518, as recorded in
a document drafted for Alessandra Bonsi in May of that year (see n. 19).

47 For Tosini (also known as Michele di Ridolfo del Ghirlandaio), see n. 45. For the provenance
and attributions of the Cortona predella panels, see Speranza, 'Antonio del Ceraiolo:
Predella raff.', pp. 155–59.

48 This point also was made by Muzzi, 'Fra' Paolino: *Matrimonio mistico di Santa Caterina e
Santi*', p. 254.

49 Several of Fra Bartolomeo's preliminary drawings for the Louvre altarpiece are discussed and
illustrated by Fischer, *Fra Bartolommeo*, pp. 189–217.

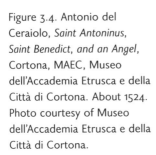

Figure 3.4. Antonio del Ceraiolo, *Saint Antoninus, Saint Benedict, and an Angel*, Cortona, MAEC, Museo dell'Accademia Etrusca e della Città di Cortona. About 1524. Photo courtesy of Museo dell'Accademia Etrusca e della Città di Cortona.

in the *Legenda maior*, Raymond of Capua's biography of St Catherine — the removal of her heart or its replacement with Christ's heart — is represented here. Nor can we be sure that the saint is shown offering her heart to Christ, as some scholars have argued.[50] The ambiguity of the gestures suggests that the heart may have been intended more as an attribute, one deliberately selected for its symbolism of the profound, intimate, and loving nature of the bond between the saint and Christ.[51]

Such an image would have resonated strongly with the altarpiece's primary audience, and in fact was repeated in a very similar painting made for a sister convent in Pistoia, also dedicated to St Catherine of Siena. Its history was intertwined with that of S. Caterina in Cafaggio. One of the first women to join Suor Lucia Rucellai when she started assembling her community in

50 Pieraccini, *Guida della R. Galleria*, p. 85; Bianchi and Giunta, *Iconografia di S. Caterina da Siena*, p. 271.

51 The heart serves as St Catherine's attribute in other images from this period. A Dominican processional was illustrated with a woodcut that showed her holding a banner emblazoned with a heart and the word AMOR. See Bianchi and Giunta, *Iconografia di S. Caterina da Siena*, p. 170.

1496 was a nun from the Pistoian house.[52] Thirty years later, two nuns from
the Florentine convent were assigned to administrative posts at S. Caterina
in Pistoia, one as prioress (Suor Paola di Domenico Pescioni) and the other
as novice mistress (Suor Margherita di Cristofano del Cittadino).[53] After
four years, they reversed roles, and in 1530 Suor Margherita became prioress
of S. Caterina in Pistoia. She then commissioned Fra Paolino to produce a
painting for the high altar of the nuns' choir there.[54] Having been a nun at
S. Caterina in Cafaggio from 1513 to 1526, she may have known Alessandra
del Pugliese well. She certainly would have been familiar with Fra Paolino's
painting, completed about two years before she went to Pistoia. The work that
resulted from her commission closely resembles the Florentine one.[55] Most

---

52   Suor Caterina da Cutigliano, also known as Caterina d'Andrea da Pistoia. See n. 3.
53   See Giaconi, *Il monastero domenicano di Santa Caterina a Pistoia*, pp. 228–33.
54   According to the convent chronicle, Suor Margherita commissioned the altarpiece from Fra
     Paolino during her first priorate (1530–1534) and made the final payments during her second
     priorate (1536–1538). See Giaconi, *Il monastero domenicano di Santa Caterina a Pistoia*,
     pp. 228–33 and 240.
55   Fra Paolino's Pistoia altarpiece was relocated to the sacristy of S. Domenico, Pistoia. See

Figure 3.5. Antonio del Ceraiolo, *An Angel, Saint Augustine, and Saint Thomas Aquinas*, Cortona, MAEC, Museo dell'Accademia Etrusca e della Città di Cortona. About 1524. Photo courtesy of Museo dell'Accademia Etrusca e della Città di Cortona.

importantly, the central tableau is repeated with the Madonna, Christ, and St Catherine of Siena holding poses almost identical to those of their counterparts in the earlier painting. As a result, the extraordinary bond between Christ and Catherine also provides the core of the Pistoia altarpiece's composition. Of all the *sacre conversazioni* produced by Fra Paolino between 1525 and his death in 1547, the one commissioned by Suor Margherita del Cittadino is the most similar to the altarpiece from S. Caterina in Cafaggio. It demonstrates the degree to which these two Dominican convents were impacted by the shared histories, interests, and personnel that linked them in the 1500s.

St Mary Magdalene, who was regarded as St Catherine's spiritual mother, has been given the same position (but not quite the same pose) in the foreground of both paintings. The standing saints in the middle ground of each work include some of the same individuals, although they are more easily identified in the Pistoia altarpiece. In the Florentine painting, the two female martyr saints are Catherine of Alexandria (on the right: identifiable by the wheel fragment in the lower right corner of the painting) and, very possibly,

Muzzi, 'Fra' Paolino: *Matrimonio mistico di Santa Caterina fra i santi*', p. 206.

Apollonia of Alexandria (on the left). She holds a palm frond and book but not the traditional pincers, unlike her counterpart in Pistoia.[56] However, despite the lack of Apollonia's most typical attribute, this identification could be justified both by tradition (the two Alexandrian martyr saints often were paired in *sacre conversazioni*), and by the implicit allusion to the given name of the patron, Alessandra. In the later painting, where St Catherine of Alexandria has been replaced by St Agnes, the conventional attribute was more necessary.

Two male Dominican saints are depicted in the Pistoia altarpiece: Dominic, holding a book and a stalk of lilies, and Peter Martyr, with the traditional head wound and palm frond. In a preliminary phase, the Florentine altarpiece also had just two male saints, Dominic on the left (holding the same set of attributes as in Pistoia), and, on the right, Peter Martyr. Although St Peter holds a book instead of a martyr's palm frond (unlike his counterpart in the Pistoia altarpiece), he can be identified from the faint streaks of blood on his tonsure. Well into the Florentine project, Fra Paolino inserted a third male

---

56 Several white roses are scattered on the pavement below this female saint. Unlike the book or the pincers, they are not usually associated with Apollonia. Their meaning is unclear.

Dominican into the group of saints, upsetting its original symmetry. This friar is barely indicated in a gridded drawing for the entire composition.[57] However, even in the shadowy recess of the apse, the painted figure is easily identified as Antoninus Pierozzi, thanks to his distinctive profile. The addition of this revered Florentine friar must have been prompted by his canonization on 10 May 1523. That event, the culmination of a process initiated the year before Alessandra became a *commessa* at S. Caterina, probably led her to select the name Antonina when she took the veil in 1524.[58]

Executed shortly after Alessandra's vestition, Antonio del Ceraiolo's painting illustrates the *Mystic Marriage of Saint Catherine of Siena* (Figure 3.3). This was a typical subject for altarpieces in Dominican convent churches in the 1500s, especially those connected with Savonarola.[59] It also appealed to Dominican nuns generally because they could identify with St Catherine's experience, having themselves been symbolically wedded to Christ during their profession ceremony.[60] However, Ceraiolo has presented the scene in an unusual way that gives greater emphasis to the role of the Madonna, and which may have been prompted by a recent development at S. Caterina. During the first quarter of the century, the prioress took charge of two important rituals that previously had been conducted by the friar from S. Marco who served as the convent's Father Confessor. It was into the hands of the prioress, not those of the friar, that the new nuns made their profession. She also presided over each nun's veiling the previous year. Judging from the brief descriptions of entry rituals in the excerpts from the convent chronicle, this procedural change was introduced at S. Caterina in about 1514, ten years before Alessandra took the veil.[61]

Considered in relationship to its likely compositional source, Ceraiolo's altarpiece shows a similar role reversal by assigning a man's role to a woman. He has modified a figure grouping that had been used by Raphael and other artists in depictions of the marriage of the Virgin. Where they showed the high priest conducting the ritual, Ceraiolo shows the Virgin Mary. Standing between Christ and Catherine, her gaze directed downward, she carefully clasps their right wrists to better guide their hands in the ring ceremony. The priest in Raphael's Brera altarpiece has the same pose. The resemblance between

57 Morgan Library & Museum, New York (I, 29). This preliminary sketch is discussed by Muzzi, 'Fra' Paolino: *Matrimonio mistico di Santa Caterina e Santi*', p. 156; and D'Apuzzo, 'Le monache di Savonarola', p. 140.

58 For discussions of the canonization process, see Polizzotto, 'The Making of a Saint', pp. 353–81; and Cornelison, *Art and the Relic Cult of St. Antoninus*, pp. 22–29.

59 Fortunati, 'Ruolo e funzione delle immagini', p. 14.

60 Many scholars have discussed the parallels between Dominican nuns' profession ceremonies and the mystic marriage between St Catherine of Siena and Christ. Among others, see Roberts, *Dominican Women and Renaissance Art*, pp. 75–77.

61 From 1496 until 1513, S. Marco friars presided over both ceremonies. For two chronicle excerpts describing the rituals as they were conducted before and after the change, see Florence, AR, Serie 1.8, Misc. Massai 32.3, fols 37 (1511) and 39 (1517).

Figure 3.6. Anonymous Florentine artist, *Portrait of Savonarola*, London, National Gallery. About 1500–1540. © The National Gallery, London.

Ceraiolo's trio and that in paintings of the marriage of the Virgin is further reinforced by his insertion of the long stalk of lilies into Catherine's left hand. They are her usual attribute, but in this particular context they also recall the flowering rod held at much the same angle by Joseph in Raphael's painting.

The Virgin Mary's centrality and her physical control of the ceremony also distinguish Ceraiolo's depiction from Raymond of Capua's description of the event. According to the *Legenda maior*, the Virgin held St Catherine's hand only, not that of Christ.[62] In several other respects, however, Ceraiolo's *Mystic Marriage* does conform to the medieval account. The *Legenda maior* was the likely source for his depiction of Christ as an adult, as well as for his inclusion of four male witnesses to the event: St Paul the Apostle, St John the Evangelist, the Prophet David with his harp, and St Dominic with his book and stalk of white lilies. In the painting, this last figure is of particular interest for his facial features, which are unmistakably those of Girolamo Savonarola.[63] The aquiline nose, pronounced chin, and strongly defined

62   Raymond of Capua, *The Life of Saint Catherine of Siena*, p. 107.
63   Zeri, 'Antonio del Ceraiolo', pp. 147–48, was the first to recognize Savonarola in the painting.

jawline also appear in early sixteenth-century portraits of the friar, such as an anonymous painting in London (Figure 3.6) and a polychrome terracotta relief in Lille that has been attributed to Fra Ambrogio della Robbia.[64] Finally, although bust-length portraits of Savonarola were not unusual by the 1520s, Ceraiolo may have been the first artist to depict him as a full-length figure in the guise of a Dominican saint.[65] Such a flattering depiction is likely to have met with the approval of the *piagnoni* who attended services in the public church at S. Caterina in Cafaggio. It also may have been sanctioned by Suor Antonina, who held Savonarola in high regard, judging from her possession of the aforementioned book of sermons and other objects associated with him.[66]

The two paintings that Alessandra/Antonina had made for the altars in S. Caterina's church and choir complemented one another in both subject and style. The predella panels that originally accompanied the two altarpieces may have reinforced the connection between them. Of the panels preserved in Cortona, the two sections with saints and angels seem the most likely candidate for the predella to Ceraiolo's altarpiece (Figures 3.4 and 3.5).[67] As Laura Speranza first suggested, they may have framed a central niche used for the ciborium (later replaced by the small arched door cut into the base of the painting).[68] That arrangement explains the devout poses of the two angels, who would have faced either side of the niche in the original configuration. Two male saints are depicted with each angel. St Antoninus is shown in his archbishop's regalia on the far left, and St Thomas Aquinas, the sun blazing on his breast, is on the far right. Each Dominican is paired with another saint revered by the monastic orders: St Antoninus with St Benedict, who holds a book and wears a black mantle over his cope (Figure 3.4), and St Thomas

64 Sebregondi, *Iconografia di Savonarola*, pp. 25–26, suggests that the Lille relief (Palais des Beaux-Arts, Pl. 1920) may have been the source used by the artist of the two-sided portrait in the National Gallery in London (NG 1301). Perhaps Ceraiolo referred to it as well.

65 This precedes Fra Paolino's portrayal of Savonarola as St Peter Martyr in the painting made for the high altar of S. Domenico in Pistoia (finished in 1528). For that work and its documentation, see Muzzi, 'Fra Paolino da Pistoia: *Sacra Conversazione*', pp. 198–200.

66 See n. 20. Zambrano and Nelson, *Filippino Lippi*, p. 488 and Burke, *Changing Patrons*, p. 180 both cite Alessandra's book in conjunction with two paintings by Filippino Lippi that were mentioned in her husband's second testament (*Christ and the Samaritan Woman at the Well* and *Noli me Tangere*; Manfrediana, Venice). On the basis of that evidence, the two scholars suggest Alessandra may have had a say in the selection of the subjects of Lippi's paintings.

67 Zeri and other scholars suggested that the long panel with nine martyr saints may have been the predella for Ceraiolo's *Christ in the House of Mary and Martha* (1524), which was found at S. Lucia in 1810 and is now in the Gemäldegalerie, Berlin. However, perhaps it was intended instead for Fra Paolino's altarpiece, as Paatz first suggested, the discrepancies in their measurements notwithstanding (the altarpiece is 218 cm. wide, and the predella is 285 cm. long). See Paatz, *Die Kirchen von Florenz*, vol. 1, p. 436; and Zeri, 'Antonio del Ceraiolo', pp. 143–44.

68 Speranza, 'Antonio del Ceraiolo: Predella raff.', p. 159. She also suggested that the two panels may have served as 'una sorta di gradino d'altare', rather than as a conventional predella. Tamborino, 'Considerazioni sull'attività', p. 120, n. 30, later agreed that these two panels might have served as the predella for Ceraiolo's altarpiece.

Aquinas with St Augustine, who holds a flaming heart (Figure 3.5). In the Cortona predella, as in Fra Paolino's altarpiece, the depiction of St Antoninus relates both to his recent canonization and to Alessandra's decision to take the name Antonina when she became a nun.

Judging from its resemblance to altarpieces later commissioned for two convents in Prato, S. Niccolò and S. Caterina da Siena, Ceraiolo's altarpiece did not go unnoticed in Dominican circles outside Florence. In the case of S. Niccolò, the presence of several Florentine nuns, including women from the Strozzi family (for which Ceraiolo had worked in the early 1520s), may have been a contributing factor to his receiving a commission that resulted in a painting almost identical to the one he had made for S. Caterina in Cafaggio.[69] The slight stylistic and compositional differences between it and the Florentine painting suggest that another artist may have been called in to finish the project, possibly as a result of Ceraiolo's death in 1527.[70] About forty years later, the basic composition was repeated in a painting executed by Giovan Battista Naldini and Giovanni Balducci for S. Caterina da Siena in Prato.[71] Naldini's sister had the altarpiece made for her convent's church on the occasion of her vestition there in 1568.[72] She even may have directed her brother to use Ceraiolo's painting of the *Mystic Marriage* as a model, imitating it in 'modo et forma' (manner and form), a clause often used in art contracts during the Renaissance. All of the protagonists from the earlier painting are present in Naldini's altarpiece, and all occupy the same places in the composition. However, there is a significant difference between the two Prato altarpieces and the one in Florence: they each portray St Dominic with generic facial features, rather than those of Savonarola. Either the Prato nuns did not share the *piagnoni* sentiments of the Florentine nuns, or they were more prudent about expressing them openly in the art commissioned for their churches during these years.

Indeed, six years after Naldini died, the Master General of the Dominican order, Fra Sisto Fabbri da Lucca, formally banned the possession of any portraits or images of Savonarola (5 April 1585).[73] His proclamation, directed

---

69   According to Stevenson, 'Conventual Life', p. 111, six Strozzi women were nuns at S. Niccolò in the late 1520s. In 1521, Selvaggia Gianfigliazzi Strozzi, the second wife of Filippo di Matteo Strozzi, had Ceraiolo paint an altarpiece for a church near Lastra a Signa. For this project and its documentation, see Bonavoglia and Parrini, *Mecenati e artisti in villa*, pp. 2–4, 10–11, and 69–70.

70   Ceraiolo's death in 1527 is documented in the archive of S. Lucia (Florence, ASF, CRSGF 111, vol. 40, fols 143/ccxxxxiii). This record of a legacy to his sister, Suor Vittoria, was first published by Callahan ('Antonio del Ceraiuolo', p. 11).

71   Now in the Museo di Palazzo Pretorio, Prato.

72   The S. Caterina altarpiece, begun by Naldini (to whom the 'archaic' composition is attributed, according to Mannini), was finished after his death in 1591 by his pupil, Giovanni Balducci. The reason for the delay is unknown. Mannini suggests that this altarpiece was inspired by the work in S. Niccolò but does not indicate if the portrait of St Dominic was painted (or altered) by Balducci. See Mannini, 'Giovan Battista Naldini', p. 152 (cat. no. 38).

73   For the text of the 1585 decree, see Gherardi, *Nuovi documenti*, pp. 234–35.

specifically to the members of the Dominican community, was preceded by two letters from Archbishop Alessandro de' Medici to Grand Duke Francesco I de' Medici that expressed strong concern about the flourishing cult of Savonarola in Florence and its environs.[74] In the first letter the archbishop fulminated against members of the religious orders who preserved relics of Savonarola or had portraits made of him, with specific reference to the Florentine friaries of S. Marco and S. Maria Novella (26 August 1583).[75] In the second letter, written two months later (20 October), he observed that the nuns at S. Vincenzo in Prato also had collected 'cose del Frate' (things of the Friar).[76] He easily could have levelled these accusations against the nuns at S. Caterina in Cafaggio. By the early 1580s, the Florentine nuns owned not only relics and writings of Savonarola but also two recent images that presented him openly in the company of his fellow martyrs, Domenico Buonvicini and Silvestro Maruffi.[77] The first of these paintings was commissioned by Marietta Carnesecchi, the next documented art patron at S. Caterina in Cafaggio after Alessandra del Pugliese. Over fifty years later in date than the church altarpiece made at Alessandra's behest, the Carnesecchi altarpiece is evidence of the lasting hold that Savonarola's memory had on the convent and the lay community that supported it. Despite the periodic opposition of the authorities, the *piagnone* spirit endured.[78]

Alessandra Bonsi and Francesco del Pugliese belonged to the first generation of *piagnoni*, those who had reached adulthood by the 1490s and who knew Savonarola personally. Marietta di Andrea Sernigi and her husband Girolamo di Alessandro Carnesecchi might be considered members of the second generation of Savonarolans. Like Alessandra del Pugliese, Marietta both came from, and married into, a family whose men had supported Savonarola in the late 1400s, and which maintained connections with Savonarolan convents and friaries through the 1500s. The Carnesecchi surname appears six times in the 1497 petition to Pope Alexander VI.[79] Two of Girolamo Carnesecchi's siblings, Piero and Alessandra, joined the Dominican order in the first quarter of the 1500s. Piero became a friar at S. Marco and Alessandra entered S. Caterina in

---

74 For transcriptions of the two letters, see Capponi, *L'officio proprio*, pp. 26–30, n. 24.

75 Capponi, *L'officio proprio*, pp. 26–27. See also Macey, 'Lauda', pp. 449–50; and Dall'Aglio, 'Everyone Worships Fra Girolamo as a Saint', pp. 343–44.

76 Capponi, *L'officio proprio*, p. 29; Macey, 'Lauda', p. 450, n. 42.

77 Relics and other objects associated with Savonarola that were recorded at S. Caterina prior to 1580 include a piece of his heart, a fragment of wood from the gallows from which he was hanged, an old tunic, and several manuscript books, among them Suor Petronilla Nelli's transcription of the Pseudo-Burlamacchi *Vita* (before April 1560; now in the Biblioteca Moreniana, Florence). The first two relics are recorded in the Rucellai chronicle (Florence, AR, Serie 1.8, Misc. Massai 32.3, fols 18 and 82); the third in the *Vita del p. f. Girolamo Savonarola*, p. 164.

78 Summarizing the situation in the second half of the 1500s, Dall'Aglio, *Savonarola*, p. 140, refers to 'close relationships and tight networks of *piagnone* activity'.

79 Polizzotto, *The Elect Nation*, p. 450.

Cafaggio, the second woman of the Carnesecchi family to do so.[80] Marietta's brother, Cipriano di Andrea Sernigi, was a lay administrator at S. Caterina in the mid-1570s, a decade after his daughter, also named Marietta, took the veil there.[81]

In November 1540, after her husband's death, Marietta Carnesecchi started renting a house on via Larga that belonged to the convent and was located just two doors away.[82] Twenty-three years later, the rental agreement was reconfirmed. According to its terms, the nuns agreed to look after the widow in both sickness and health, whether at her house or inside the convent.[83] As was perhaps anticipated, Marietta did fall ill and was placed under the personal care of Suor Faustina Gondi for the last part of her life.[84] During this period, she is likely to have become acquainted with the convent pharmacist, Suor Giovanna Ginori, and one of her apprentices, Suor Raffaella Gondi (Faustina's younger sister). Their relationship grew closer in the literal sense of the word in the early 1570s, when the nuns' pharmacy was moved to the ground floor rooms of the building located between Marietta's house and the convent.[85] Ten months before her death, Marietta wrote down a short list of legatees that included the names of all three nuns (1 January 1577/1578). She also set aside a sum to cover the cost of a panel painting that she described simply as 'la tavola dei martiri' (the panel with the martyrs), without indicating the artist or destination.[86] Successive convent records and chronicle entries make it clear that Suor Plautilla Nelli, the convent's *Madre Pittora*, was commissioned to produce the painting, and that it was installed over the altar in the corridor leading to the ground floor infirmary.[87] When pieced together, the different archival entries also confirm the subject of the altarpiece: Christ, the Madonna, and the 'three martyrs' — that is, Savonarola and the two friars executed with him, Buonvicini and Maruffi (variously identified as 'martiri' or 'compagni' in the literature of the period).[88]

---

80 Alessandra was preceded at the convent by a woman from another branch of the Carnesecchi family, Colomba di Zanobi Carnesecchi (vestition in 1504). Alessandra died in 1519, four years after her vestition, but Suor Colomba (died 1555) still was alive when Marietta began her tenancy. For these two nuns, see Florence, AR, Serie 1.8, Misc. Massai 32.3, fols 32 and 39.

81 For Cipriano Sernigi, see Florence, AR, Serie 1.8, Misc. Massai 32.3, fol. 16. For his daughter's vestition in 1564, see Florence, ASF, CRSGF 106, vol. 53, fol. 27ʳ.

82 Florence, ASF, CRSGF 106, vol. 31, fol. 94.

83 Florence, ASF, CRSGF 106, vol. 35, fol. 205 (19 March 1563/1564).

84 For Suor Faustina Gondi's assignment as Marietta's care-giver, see Florence, AR, Serie 1.8, Misc. Massai 32.3, fol. 81; and Florence, BNCF, LF 72, fol. 225ᵛ.

85 Florence, AR, Serie 1.8, Misc. Massai 32.3, fol. 14. For the new pharmacy, see also Strocchia, 'The Nun Apothecaries', p. 632.

86 Florence, ASF, CRSGF 106, vol. 162, filza 9.

87 In her signed statement, dated 4 February 1578/1579, Plautilla acknowledged receipt of 20 florins 'per fare una Tavola nell'androne della nostra infermeria'. Florence, ASF, CRSGF 106, vol. 162, filza 9, fol. 2ᵛ. Elsewhere the space is referred to as the 'andito'.

88 Florence, AR, Serie 1.8, Misc. Massai 32.3, fol. 20 ('Giesù, la Vergine, e li 3 martiri'). Two

Figure 3.7. Plautilla Nelli, *Madonna, Christ, and Three Dominican Martyrs*, Fiesole, Convento di S. Domenico. About 1579. Reproduced with permission of the Gabinetto Fotografico delle Gallerie degli Uffizi, Florence.

Marietta Carnesecchi's selection of this theme at this particular time may have been influenced in part by her acquaintance with Suor Giovanna Ginori, one of four daughters of Simone di Giuliano Ginori, all of whom were nuns at Dominican convents closely associated with the cult of Savonarola. Suor Giovanna and Suor Maddalena Ginori were at S. Caterina in Cafaggio, while Suor Obbedienza and Suor Prudenza Ginori were at S. Vincenzo in Prato.[89] Between October 1529 and March 1530/1531, Obbedienza had been healed from a crippling illness after being touched by a relic of Savonarola that was borrowed from the Florentine convent of S. Lucia in via San Gallo. Her miraculous cure was said to have been facilitated by her sister Prudenza's long-standing devotion to all three of the martyrs.[90] Forty years later, Prudenza Ginori was involved in an effort to secure a portrait of Savonarola for the convent of S. Vincenzo. She also sought advice on how all three martyrs should be portrayed on a veil that was intended to cover the finished painting.[91] This project, closely followed by Obbedienza's death in 1576, could have provided some impetus to Marietta's decision to commission a painting of a related subject for S. Caterina in Cafaggio in 1578.[92] She also may have been motivated by local events. Savonarola and his companions were attributed with miraculous cures at both S. Caterina in Cafaggio and S. Lucia during the 1500s.[93] In 1543, three years after Marietta had settled into the house on via Larga, a *conversa* (lay sister) at S. Caterina named Marta di Neri da Vaglia, who was 'greatly devoted' to Savonarola, was cured of a tumour after praying devoutly to all three martyrs.[94] Another case of miraculous or divine intervention occurred in the following decade. In January 1558, a fire broke out in the ground floor infirmary, ravaging both it and the dormitory rooms above. According to the chronicles, it was only thanks to the mercy of God that no one was killed or seriously injured.[95] Afterwards the nuns' neighbours and families rallied to their support, financing the repair and refurnishing of the damaged rooms. The

other chronicle entries refer to the painting as 'Giesù con i tre martiri' (Florence, AR, Serie 1.8, Misc. Massai 32.3, fol. 81; Florence, BNCF, LF 72, fol. 226ʳ). In the convent records, the same painting is variously described as 'la tavola della Madonna' (Florence, ASF, CRSGF 106, vol. 35, fol. 111) and 'la tavola dei martiri' (Florence, ASF, CRSGF 106, vol. 162, filza 9).

89 Passerini, *Genealogia e storia*, p. 34.

90 Obbedienza confirmed the details of the miracle in April 1566. See *Vita del p. f. Girolamo Savonarola*, pp. 206–10.

91 The two projects are recorded in St Caterina de' Ricci's correspondence with Lorenzo Capponi, a close Florentine friend (considered one of her 'figli spirituali') who was negotiating with the painter on the nuns' behalf. See Di Agresti, *Santa Caterina de' Ricci: Epistolario*, letters 429–31 (December 1572), 440 (February 1573), 464 (August 1573), and 501 (March 1574); and Sebregondi, 'Savonarola: Un percorso', p. 503.

92 For the year of Obbedienza Ginori's death, see Passerini, *Genealogia e storia*, p. 34.

93 *Vita del p. f. Girolamo Savonarola*, pp. 197–98.

94 Florence, AR, Serie 1.8, Misc. Massai 32.3, fols 81–82.

95 Florence, AR, Serie 1.8, Misc. Massai 32.3, fol. 9.

new altar for which Marietta Carnesecchi's 'tavola dei martiri' was intended may have been part of a later phase of that project.

It is very likely that the altarpiece Plautilla Nelli agreed to paint in 1579 is the same as a large panel painting that turned up in the Florence area in the mid-1800s, a few decades after the suppression of the convent.[96] It is now located at S. Domenico in Fiesole (Figure 3.7). No other sixteenth-century Florentine altarpiece featuring the Madonna, Christ, and the three Dominican martyrs is known. The presentation of Savonarola and his companions as mediators between the city of Florence (depicted in the middle ground), the Madonna, and Christ was very timely, given the proliferation of reports about miracles attributed to the three friars.[97] The smoke that seems to billow forth from buildings near S. Marco could be a reference to the fire that had devastated S. Caterina's ground floor infirmary, the space for which the painting was made.[98] The style also supports an attribution to Plautilla Nelli. The treatment of the figures, fabrics, and landscape is consistent with her work, taking into consideration the development that would have occurred in the decade separating this project from the paintings recorded by Vasari.[99]

The Fiesole painting also documents the impact of ecclesiastic opposition to images that glorified the three friars or honoured them as martyrs. At some later date, halos were painted over the rays that had identified the men as beatified, and the names and attributes of Dominican saints were added. Savonarola became St Dominic, the central friar (Buonvicini) became St Peter Martyr, and the friar on the right (Maruffi) became St Thomas Aquinas.[100] These visible alterations, a likely response to Sisto Fabbri's strict ban on the possession of images of Savonarola by members of the Dominican order, provide further justification for the identification of the Fiesole painting with the Carnesecchi altarpiece. The painting must have been made for a group of Florentine Dominicans who had a strong allegiance to Savonarola and who

---

96 Artists proposed as authors of the Fiesole painting include Fra Paolino da Pistoia (Steinberg), Zanobi Poggini (Muzzi), Giovanni Antonio Sogliani (Scudieri), and Plautilla Nelli (Traversi). In my first catalogue of Nelli's paintings (2000) I attributed it to her, but later had second thoughts and removed it from the list (2008). See Steinberg, *Fra Girolamo Savonarola*, pp. 174–75; Muzzi, 'Zanobi Poggini', 259–61; Scudieri, *Savonarola e le sue 'reliquie' a San Marco*, p. 73; Traversi, 'Episodi volterrani', pp. 254–55; Turrill, 'Preliminary Catalogue of Suor Plautilla Nelli's Paintings', p. 103; and Turrill, 'List of Paintings Attributed to Nelli', p. 128.

97 The additional miracle narratives appear in copies of the Pseudo-Burlamacchi *Vita* dating from the 1550s and 1560s, including the aforementioned manuscript by Suor Petronilla Nelli, Plautilla's older sister (see n. 77). For other copies of the treatise, see Benavent, 'El Tratado de Milagros de fra Girolamo Savonarola'.

98 Both Mancini, 'Pitture Savonaroliane a Lucca e a Prato', p. 402 and Sebregondi, *Iconografia di Savonarola*, p. 104 assert that the smoke is emanating from S. Marco. Mancini relates this to the siege that occurred the day before Savonarola and his companions were arrested.

99 For the phases of Nelli's artistic career and their connection to Vasari's account (probably composed during Nelli's first term as prioress, 1563–1565), see Turrill, 'Nuns' Stories', 13–14.

100 For the tentative identifications of the two companions, see Sebregondi, *Iconografia di Savonarola*, p. 104.

were willing to commission a painting expressing that sentiment, but who were later compelled to acknowledge the Master General's prohibition.[101] The hint of resistance implicit in the incomplete effacement of the friars' true identities — Savonarola is unmistakably himself, and each of his fellow martyrs holds a conspicuous palm frond — also would be expected of the Florentine nuns. In 1575, under the leadership of their prioress, Ippolita Arrighetti, they had openly disputed the forced implementation of enclosure at their convent, even while yielding to the authorities' demands.[102] Suor Ippolita, who also had been prioress in 1566 when the papal bull imposing *clausura* was announced, was re-elected to that office for the sixth time in 1585, the same year that Fra Sisto Fabbri issued his proclamation.[103] Possibly the painting was altered at her request.

Two more art projects will serve to round out this overview of *piagnoni* patronage at S. Caterina in Cafaggio in the 1500s. Both projects also tapped into kinship networks, as they involved contributions by men whose sisters were nuns at the convent. The first was the altarpiece for the new upstairs infirmary. According to the chronicle entry, it was acquired in 1573 with a legacy from a prominent *piagnone* banker named Giovambattista de' Servi, one of St Caterina de' Ricci's 'spiritual sons'.[104] The work featured a painting of the *Agony in the Garden* by Bartolomeo di Mariano Traballesi and a predella (subject unknown) by Plautilla Nelli.[105] Its production coincided with the vestition of Bartolomeo's sister Camilla, the third of five sisters to enter the convent.[106] Several years later, their brother Felice, a sculptor and goldsmith known for his devotion to the memory of Savonarola, donated a large, gilded wooden reliquary to the convent (1579–1580).[107] It was adorned with a painting of the Madonna, the Christ Child, and the three martyrs.[108] No artist is named in the chronicle entry for this project, but Felice's sister Agata, the nun who handled one of his payments, was a protégé of Plautilla Nelli and later held

---

101 For Fra Sisto Fabbri's 1585 order, see n. 73.

102 Evangelisti, '"We do not have it"', pp. 693–99. For the succession of papal bulls and apostolic orders that imposed and reinforced enclosure generally in convents during this period, see Evangelisti, 'Art and the Advent of *Clausura*', pp. 76–78.

103 Florence, AR, Serie 1.8, Misc. Massai 32.3, fols 10 (1566 bull) and 26 (Ippolita Arrighetti's sixth term as prioress).

104 In addition to sustaining a long correspondence with Caterina de' Ricci from 1546–1556, Giovambattista gave her some relics of Savonarola. See Sebregondi, *Iconografia di Savonarola*, p. 91.

105 Florence, AR, Serie 1.8, Misc. Massai 32.3, fol. 15. Traballesi is said to have given the nuns the painting 'per l'amor di Dio'. This altarpiece is unknown and unpublished.

106 For Suor Camilla's vestition record, see Florence, ASF, CRSGF 106, vol. 35, fol. 209.

107 For Felice Traballesi's reputation as a Savonarolan artist, see Sebregondi, *Iconografia di Savonarola*, p. 95.

108 Florence, AR, Serie 1.8, Misc. Massai 32.3, fol. 18. Like the above-mentioned altarpiece, this reliquary is unknown and unpublished. Among other relics, it contained a piece of Savonarola's heart that had been given to the convent by Costanza Michelozzi Micceri, the mother of three nuns and the sister of two others.

the office of *Madre Pittora* at the convent.[109] Perhaps Suor Agata's involvement with the reliquary project extended to the execution of this lost painting.

Alessandra Bonsi del Pugliese and Marietta Sernigi Carnesecchi, two Florentine matrons who enjoyed special relationships with S. Caterina in Cafaggio, expressed their gratitude to the nuns by commissioning altarpieces for important public and private spaces at the convent. Each woman may have been drawn to S. Caterina partly because of its Savonarolan origins and, especially in the case of Marietta, because of the nuns' steadfast regard for Girolamo Savonarola as a prophet, saint, and martyr. The altarpieces these women commissioned reflect this exalted view of the friar. The three paintings also share a common ground and many aspects with art produced for several of S. Caterina's sister convents in Florence, Pistoia, and Prato. They are both an expression and a consequence of the complex network linking these female Dominican communities in the 1500s.

---

109   Florence, ASF, CRSGF 102, Appendix, fols 23/xxiii. On 17 June 1580, Suor Agata handled a payment from Felice that was connected to this project. For her reputation as a painter, see Turrill, 'Nuns' Stories', p. 18.

Works Cited

Manuscripts and Archival Sources

Florence, Archivio Rucellai (AR)
    Serie 1.8, Miscellanea Massai (Misc. Massai) 32.3
Florence, Archivio di Stato di Firenze (ASF)
    Corporazioni religiose soppresse dal governo francese (CRSGF)
        ——, 102 (S. Maria Novella)
        ——, 106 (S. Caterina in Cafaggio)
        ——, 111 (S. Lucia in via San Gallo)
    Notarile Antecosimiano
Florence, Archivio Storico Comunale (ASC)
    ArchiDis – Fondo disegni tecnici del Comune di Firenze
Florence, Biblioteca Nazionale Centrale (BNCF)
    Landau-Finaly (LF) 72
Florence, Opera di Santa Maria del Fiore (OSMF)
    Archivio storico delle fedi di battesimo
        ——, Registri Battesimali

Primary Sources

Di Agresti, Domenico Guglielmo M., *Santa Caterina de' Ricci: Cronache, diplomatica, lettere varie* (Florence: Olschki, 1969)
——, *Santa Caterina de' Ricci: Epistolario*, vol. 3, *1564–1577* (Florence: Olschki, 1974)
Francesconi, P. Maurizio, *Firenze sacra, ovvero feste, devozioni, e indulgenze che sono nelle chiese della città di Firenze, distribuite in ciascun giorno dell'anno* (Florence: Stamperia Granducale, 1739)
Gherardi, Alessandro, ed., *Nuovi documenti e studi intorno a Girolamo Savonarola* (Florence: G. Carnesecchi e figli, 1876)
Giaconi, Elettra, ed., *Il monastero domenicano di Santa Caterina a Pistoia dalla fondazione alla soppressione (1477–1783): Cronaca e Documenti* (Florence: Nerbini, 2007)
Raymond of Capua, *The Life of Saint Catherine of Siena*, trans. by Conleth Kearns (Wilmington: Michael Glazier, 1980)
Vita del p. f. Girolamo Savonarola dell'Ordine de' Predicatori, scritta già dal p. f. Pacifico Burlamacchi Lucchese … riveduta ed aggiunta dal p. f. Timoteo Botonio (Lucca: Vincenzo Giuntini, 1761)

Secondary Works

Assonitis, Alessio, 'Fra Bartolomeo della Porta: Patronage and Clientelism at San Marco in the Early Cinquecento', *Memorie Domenicane*, 42 (2011), 423–37

Benavent, Júlia, 'El Tratado de Milagros de fra Girolamo Savonarola: El códice de Valencia y la tradición manuscrita', *Memorie domenicane*, 28 (1997), 5–146

Bianchi, Lidia, and Diego Giunta, ed., *Iconografia di S. Caterina da Siena*, vol. 1: *L'immagine* (Rome: Città nuova editrice, 1988)

Bonavoglia, Sara, and Francesca Parrini, *Mecenati e artisti in villa. Un patrimonio nascosto a Lastra a Signa* (Florence: Rotary Club Bisenzio, 1999)

Burke, Jill, *Changing Patrons: Social Identity & the Visual Arts in Renaissance Florence* (University Park: Pennsylvania State University Press, 2004)

Callahan, Meghan, 'Antonio del Ceraiuolo at La Crocetta and a Note on Lorenzo di Credi's Niece', *Burlington Magazine*, 152 (January 2010), 7–11

Capponi, Carlo, *L'Officio proprio per Girolamo Savonarola e i suoi compagni* (Prato: Guasti, 1863)

Cornelison, Sally J., *Art and the Relic Cult of St. Antoninus in Renaissance Florence* (Burlington: Ashgate, 2012)

Dall'Aglio, Stefano, *Savonarola and Savonarolism* (Toronto: Centre for Reformation and Renaissance Studies, 2010)

——, '"Everyone Worships Fra Girolamo as a Saint": Savonarola's Presumed Sanctity in Sixteenth-Century Manuscripts and Prints', in *The Saint Between Manuscript and Print in Italy, 1400–1600*, ed. by Alison K. Frazier (Toronto: Centre for Reformation and Renaissance Studies, 2015), pp. 331–49

D'Apuzzo, Mark Gregory, 'Le monache di Savonarola tra arte e committenza', in *Vita artistica nel monastero femminile: Exempla*, ed. by Vera Fortunati (Bologna: Compositori, 2002), pp. 131–45

Evangelisti, Silvia, 'Art and the Advent of *Clausura*: The Convent of Santa Caterina in Tridentine Florence', in *Suor Plautilla Nelli (1523–1588): The First Woman Painter of Florence*, ed. by Jonathan K. Nelson (Fiesole: Cadmo, 2000), pp. 67–82

——, '"We do not have it, and we do not want it": Women, Power, and Convent Reform in Florence', *Sixteenth Century Journal*, 34 (2003), 677–700

Fischer, Chris, *Fra Bartolommeo: Master Draughtsman of the High Renaissance* (Rotterdam: Museum Boymans-Van Beuningen, 1990)

Fortunati, Vera, 'Ruolo e funzione delle immagini nei monasteri femminili', in *Vita artistica nel monastero femminile: Exempla*, ed. by Vera Fortunati (Bologna: Compositori, 2002), pp. 11–41

Gamba, Carlo, 'Ridolfo e Michele di Ridolfo del Ghirlandaio', *Dedalo*, 9 (1928–1929), 544–61

Geronimus, Dennis, *Piero di Cosimo: Visions Beautiful and Strange* (New Haven: Yale University Press, 2006)

Herzig, Tamar, *Savonarola's Women: Vision and Reform in Renaissance Italy* (Chicago: University of Chicago Press, 2008)

Kent, F. W., 'Lorenzo di Credi, his Patron Iacopo Bongianni and Savonarola', *The Burlington Magazine*, 125 (1983), 538–41

Lowe, K. J. P., *Nuns' Chronicles and Convent Culture in Renaissance and Counter-Reformation Italy* (Cambridge: Cambridge University Press, 2003)

Macey, Patrick, 'The Lauda and the Cult of Savonarola', *Renaissance Quarterly*, 45 (1992), 439–83

Mancini, Augusto, 'Pitture Savonaroliane a Lucca e a Prato', *Memorie Domenicane*, 47 (1930), 401–13

Mannini, Maria Pia, 'Giovan Battista Naldini e Giovanni Balducci: *Sposalizio mistico di santa Caterina da Siena*', in *Museo di Palazzo Pretorio a Prato*, ed. by Cristina Gnoni Mavarelli and Maria Pia Mannini (Florence: Giunti, 2015), p. 152

Muzzi, Andrea, 'Fra' Paolino: *Matrimonio mistico di Santa Caterina e Santi*', in *L'Età di Savonarola: Fra Bartolomeo e la scuola di San Marco*, ed. by Serena Padovani (Venice: Marsilio, 1996), pp. 253–56

——, 'Fra' Paolino: *Matrimonio mistico di Santa Caterina fra i Santi Maddalena, Apollonia, Domenico, Pietro Martire e Agnese*' in *L'Età di Savonarola: Fra' Paolino e la pittura a Pistoia nel primo '500*, ed. by Chiara d'Afflitto, Franca Falletti, and Andrea Muzzi (Venice: Marsilio, 1996), pp. 205–07

——, 'Fra' Paolino: *Sacra Conversazione*' in *L'Età di Savonarola: Fra' Paolino e la pittura a Pistoia nel primo '500*, ed. by Chiara d'Afflitto, Franca Falletti, and Andrea Muzzi (Venice: Marsilio, 1996), pp. 198–200

——, 'Zanobi Poggini: *Savonarola chiede alla Madonna d'intercedere presso Cristo affinché protegga la città di Firenze*' in *Fra Bartolomeo e la scuola di San Marco: L'Età di Savonarola*, ed. by Serena Padovani (Venice: Marsilio, 1996), pp. 259–62

Paatz, Walter, and Elizabeth Paatz, *Die Kirchen von Florenz: ein kunstgeschichtliches Handbuch* (Frankfurt am Main: Klostermann, 1955), vol. 1

Passerini, Luigi, *Genealogia e storia della famiglia Ginori* (Florence: Cellini, 1876)

Pieraccini, Eugenio, *Guida della R. Galleria Antica e Moderna e Tribuna del David*, 5th edn (Florence: Tipografia cooperativa, 1883)

Polizzotto, Lorenzo, '*Dell'arte del ben morire*: The Piagnone Way of Death, 1494–1545', *I Tatti Studies in the Italian Renaissance*, 3 (1989), pp. 27–87

——, 'The Making of a Saint: The Canonization of S. Antonino, 1516–1523', *The Journal of Medieval and Renaissance Studies*, 22 (1992), 353–81

——, 'When Saints Fall Out: Women and the Savonarolan Reform in Early Sixteenth-Century Florence', *Renaissance Quarterly*, 46 (Autumn 1993), 486–525

——, *The Elect Nation: The Savonarolan Movement in Florence, 1494–1545* (Oxford: Clarendon Press, 1994)

Richa, Giuseppe, *Notizie istoriche delle chiese fiorentine divise ne' suoi quartieri* (Florence: Pietro Gaetano Viviani, 1759), vol. 8

Roberts, Ann, *Dominican Women and Renaissance Art: The Convent of San Domenico of Pisa* (Burlington: Ashgate, 2008)

Scudieri, Magnolia, ed., *Savonarola e le sue 'reliquie' a San Marco* (Prato: Giunti, 1998)

Sebrogondi, Ludovica, 'Savonarola: Un percorso per immagini', in *Una città e il suo profeta: Firenze di fronte al Savonarola*, ed. by Gian Carlo Garfagnini (Florence: SISMEL, 2001), pp. 497–512

——, *Iconografia di Savonarola 1495–1998* (Florence: SISMEL, 2004)

Speranza, Laura, 'Antonio del Ceraiolo: Predella raff.: *Nove Santi Martiri*', '2 parti di gradino d'altare raff. *Due Santi e un Angelo* (ciascuna)' and 'Due tavolette raffiguranti: *Annunciazione*', in *Il Museo dell'Accademia etrusca di Cortona*, ed. by Piera Bocci Pacini and Anna Maria Maetzke (Florence: Arti grafiche Giorgi & Gambi, 1992), pp. 155–59

Steinberg, Ronald, *Fra Girolamo Savonarola: Florentine Art and Renaissance Historiography* (Athens: Ohio University Press, 1977)

Stevenson, Jane B., 'Conventual Life in Renaissance Italy: The Latin Poetry of Suor Laurentia Strozzi (1514–1591)', in *Women Writing Latin, from Roman Antiquity to Early Modern Europe*, vol. 3: *Early Modern Women Writing Latin* ed. by Laurie J. Churchill, Phyllis R. Brown, and Jane E. Jeffrey (New York: Routledge 2002), pp. 109–32

Strocchia, Sharon, 'Taken into Custody: Girls and Convent Guardianship in Renaissance Florence', *Renaissance Studies*, 17 (2003), 177–200

——, 'Savonarolan Witnesses: The Nuns of San Jacopo and the Piagnone Movement in Sixteenth-Century Florence', *The Sixteenth Century Journal*, 38 (2007), 393–418

——, 'The Nun Apothecaries of Renaissance Florence: Marketing Medicines in the Convent', *Renaissance Studies*, 25 (2011), 627–47

Tamborino, Alessandra, 'Considerazioni sull'attività di Antonio del Ceraiolo e proposte al suo catalogo', *Proporzioni*, 2–3 (2001–2002), 104–22

Traversi, Francesco, 'Episodi volterrani: considerazioni intorno ad alcuni artisti della cerchia del Sodoma (Vincenzo Tamagni e Marco Bigio) e della Scuola di San Marco (Leonardo Malatesta, Suor Plautilla e Zanobi Poggini), pittori del cinquecento', *Rassegna volterrana*, 91 (2014), 243–67

Turrill, Catherine, 'Preliminary Catalogue of Suor Plautilla Nelli's Paintings', in *Suor Plautilla Nelli (1523–1588): The First Woman Painter of Florence*, ed. by Jonathan K. Nelson (Fiesole: Cadmo, 2000), pp. 103–10

——, 'Nuns' Stories: Suor Plautilla Nelli, *Madre Pittora*, and Her *Compagne* in the Convent of Santa Caterina da Siena' in *Plautilla Nelli (1524–1588): The Painter-Prioress of Renaissance Florence*, ed. by Jonathan K. Nelson (Florence: S.E.I., 2008), pp. 9–27

——, 'List of Paintings Attributed to Nelli' in *Plautilla Nelli (1524–1588): The Painter-Prioress of Renaissance Florence*, ed. by Jonathan K. Nelson (Florence: S.E.I., 2008), pp. 118–30

Villari, Pasquale, *La storia di Girolamo Savonarola e de' suoi tempi* (Florence: Le Monnier, 1882), vol. 2

Weaver, Elissa, *Convent Theater in Early Modern Italy: Spiritual Fun and Learning for Women* (Cambridge: Cambridge University Press, 2002)

Zambrano, Patrizia, and Jonathan Katz Nelson, *Filippino Lippi* (Milan: Electa, 2004)

Zeri, Federico, 'Antonio del Ceraiolo', *Gazette des beaux-arts*, 70 (1967), 139–54

LAURA LLEWELLYN*

Botticini's *Saint Monica* Altarpiece and the Augustinian Network of Florence's Oltrarno

Today, Francesco Botticini's altarpiece depicting *Saint Monica Enthroned with Women of the Augustinian Order* stands in the Bini chapel in the left transept of S. Spirito, the church of the Augustinian hermit friars located in Florence's Oltrarno (Figure 4.1). Though almost certainly painted for this church, it has been relocated internally several times throughout its history, and thus severed from its intended context. It depicts St Monica clothed in the habit of the order of Hermits of St Augustine, seated on an elegant marble throne in a walled garden. She is surrounded by fourteen kneeling women, two of whom are visible only by the crown of their heads, all wearing the same blue-black mantle. Two female children, dressed in white, kneel directly in front of the throne. Monica balances a closed book on her left knee. Her head is tilted to her right and her eyes are cast down as she hands a bound scroll to one of her kneeling company. In the predella, scenes from the life of St Monica flank an image of the Virgin and St Augustine at the tomb with Christ as Man of Sorrows. The altarpiece, and specifically the community of women depicted, bear witness to a complex network of Augustinian relationships, later dissipated by Tridentine reforms, which was once a prominent feature of the religious landscape of the Oltrarno neighbourhood.

The painting's imagery belongs to a type of iconography that enjoyed popularity with monastic audiences from the fourteenth century onward, depicting the founder issuing the rule to members of the order. Highly unusual in this instance, perhaps even unique (at least in terms of its survival into modern times), the altarpiece depicts a community of religious women but originates from the public area of the church of male mendicants. Despite this, scholarly investigation to date has tended to consider the altarpiece

* Material for this essay was developed from my doctoral thesis (The Courtauld Institute of Art, London, 2016) and therefore owes much to numerous individuals acknowledged there in full. Here, I would like to note my inestimable debt to my PhD supervisor, Scott Nethersole, and to express my gratitude to my examiners, Alison Wright and Donal Cooper, for their generous guidance. My sincere thanks also to the editors of this volume, Marilyn Dunn and Saundra Weddle, whose consistently scrupulous feedback on earlier drafts has improved my contribution immeasurably.

Laura Llewellyn (Laura.Llewellyn@ng-london.org.uk) is Associate Curator of Renaissance Painting at the National Gallery, London.

Convent Networks In Early Modern Italy, ed. by Marilyn Dunn and Saundra Weddle, ES 25 (Turnhout: Brepols, 2020) pp. 115–151   BREPOLS ❧ PUBLISHERS   DOI 10.1484/M.ES-EB.5.119515

Figure 4.1. Francesco Botticini, *Saint Monica Enthroned with Women of the Augustinian Order*, Florence, S. Spirito, Bini Chapel. *c.* 1485. © Gabinetto Fotografico, Uffizi, Firenze.

as having been conceived exclusively as an object of devotional focus for a community of Augustinian women. The following study proposes a reappraisal of this traditional assumption and suggests instead that the altarpiece is best understood as a point of intersection for a network of communities that together characterized the spiritual life of the neighbourhood of S. Spirito, as it played out both within the church and beyond its walls.

In her study of the role of neighbourhood and network in family patronage in the Oltrarno district of the late fifteenth century, Jill Burke characterized a publicly displayed work of art as a means with which a patron might position themselves in society.[1] Since identities are both reflected in and created by the

---

1   Burke, *Changing Patrons*.

visual arts, the commissioning and display of altarpieces for the family chapel necessarily plays out within a web of social, civic and religious concerns. This essay demonstrates that, in much the same way, the *Saint Monica* altarpiece was devised as a prominent visual nexus in a broad network of Augustinian interests. The chapel of St Monica where the panel first stood was contained within the public area of the church of the hermit friars and was under the *ius patronatus* of Augustinian women. Located in such a space, Botticini's panel was conceived to achieve multiple ends: in addition to serving the devotional needs of each branch of the order, it acted to proclaim the Augustinian cause to the lay public of the wider district — a campaign which had the women of the order at its very heart. Turning away from the traditional scholarly tendency to consider the altarpiece solely within the framework of a female religious viewership, I propose instead that the visual potency of the *Saint Monica* altarpiece was dependent upon its diverse spectatorship with an ever-shifting frame of reference.

The Augustinian Order: Friars, Nuns, *Mantellate*

The order of the Hermits of St Augustine was among the five mendicant orders founded in the thirteenth century that secured a strong and lasting foothold on the religious landscape of the Italian peninsula. The order was officially established by Pope Alexander IV in 1256. At the time, several groups of Tuscan hermits, who had joined together twelve years previously under the rule of St Augustine of Hippo, were united with other hermetic communities from central Italy. After this so-called 'Grand Union' of 1256, the friars abandoned their contemplative lives and, moving to the cities, devoted themselves to the ministry of souls and preaching. Their success during these founding years owed much to the recognition and active support of the papacy, thanks to which they survived the ruling of the Second Council of Lyons (1274) that all orders established since the Fourth Lateran Council (1215) should be suppressed.[2] Furthermore, in a bull of 1327 they were granted partial custody of the tomb of St Augustine in Pavia, which they shared with the Canons Regular of St Augustine.[3] This amounted to papal recognition of their status as rightful heirs to the legacy of St Augustine and was a culminating moment of a period of intense rivalry with the Canons Regular, who insisted that the hermits had no more special claim to the saint than any other group who followed his rule.[4] Such rivalry, which manifested in part as an endemic preoccupation with lineage, was not limited to the Augustinian canons, but extended to the other orders against whom the hermit friars were contending

---

2   Emery, 'The Second Council of Lyons'.
3   For papal bull (*Veneranda sanctorum patrum*) see Maiocchi and Casacca, *Codex Diplo-maticus*, pp. 13–19.
4   Warr, 'Hermits, Habits and History', p. 18.

for the alms and lay support that they needed to survive and flourish in their new urban surroundings.[5] Unlike the two largest and most prominent of the mendicant orders, the Franciscans and the Dominicans, the Augustinians had neither the visionary founder of the former, nor the united mission (the eradication of heresy) of the latter. The hermit friars were therefore concerned from the outset with crafting, and then solidifying, their corporate identity. In a campaign conducted through both literary and visual channels, they sought to propagate the myth that they had been founded by St Augustine himself. Accordingly, images of Augustine bestowing his rule upon the hermit friars were popular with the order from the late thirteenth century onward.[6] Furthermore, priority was given to disseminating the legend that the habit of the hermit friars — with its distinguishing features of the black cowl and leather belt — had been donned by Augustine following his baptism. Thus, the habit became an important visual mechanism by which members of the order asserted their legitimacy as the direct heirs of the saint from Hippo.[7]

The history of the women of the order is not clear-cut. St Augustine himself had taken a direct interest in female monastic living. Among the texts that are understood to have formed the basis for Augustine's rule is a letter (epistula 211), which he wrote to admonish the nuns formerly governed by his sister, Perpetua.[8] However, the early history of second order nuns associated with the Augustinian order is difficult to characterize, since initially many female monastic institutions, founded under the auspices of a local religious authority, followed the rule of St Augustine without any formal association with the order of the Hermits. Later, during the course of the fourteenth century, the *cura monialium* of the hermit friars was increasingly formalized and groups of nuns, previously without official affiliation, developed into second order Augustinian communities.[9]

Papal permission for the establishment of Augustinian confraternities, made up of both sexes, was only granted under Eugenius IV in a bull of 14 August 1439. However, confraternities associated with the order, with both male and female members, seem to have existed by the early fourteenth century.[10] The tertiary branch of the order, comprising women exclusively,

---

5   On the mendicant orders' concern with their origins, see Jotischky, *The Carmelites and Antiquity*, pp. 261–330.

6   The earliest example is probably a fresco in the Augustinian church in Fabriano dated *c.* 1280; see Blume and Hansen, 'Agostino *pater et praeceptor*', p. 77. For further examples see also Andrews, *The Other Friars*, pp. 159–62. Variations in the iconography also existed for groups that were associated with the order but did not follow the Rule. An early Florentine example is found in a *laudario* commissioned by a *laudesi* confraternity based at S. Spirito in *c.* 1310–1315 depicting St Augustine enthroned surrounded by friars and lay devotees. See Sciacca, 'Reconstructing the Laudario of Sant' Agnese', pp. 221–22.

7   Warr, 'Hermits, Habits and History'.

8   Piatti, *Il movimento femminile agostiniano*, p. 43.

9   Piatti, *Il movimento femminile agostiniano*, pp. 135–44. Gutierrez, *The Augustinians*, pp. 193–200.

10 This is evidenced by the *laudesi* community at S. Spirito (see n. 6 above).

was formally approved a few decades earlier, in 1399, when 'maidens, matrons and widows' were granted permission to don the habit of the order by Pope Bonifice IX.[11] Such groups, known as *mantellate* ('wearers of the mantle'), flourished over the course of the next two centuries, until communities of non-cloistered women were compelled to adopt enclosure in the wake of the Council of Trent.[12]

The addition of these various regular, semi-regular and non-regular branches to the Augustinian corporation during the course of the fourteenth century meant that the order now had direct engagement with the full cross-section of society and therefore helped to secure its position in the new urban settings. Moreover, the fierce rivalry between the various mendicant orders had diminished somewhat by the fifteenth century with the *Concordia* signed by the superiors of four mendicant orders in 1435, and renewed in 1458 and 1474, which pledged mutual cooperation.[13] Even so, the Augustinians experienced a period of internal instability in the early Quattrocento, when Observance threatened to rupture their congregation.[14] At this time, Monica, Augustine's mother, became a touchstone in efforts to fortify a sense of common Augustinian identity.[15] The Augustinians undertook several initiatives during the course of the fifteenth century in order to raise her profile. Her feast day (4 May) was inserted into the official events of the order's calendar and a decree was introduced that every Augustinian church should contain her image.[16]

The figure of Augustine's mother held dual significance for members of the order.[17] For the friars, she was an eyewitness to the ancient origins of the hermit friars and, therefore, at once the mother of their founder and the ancestor of their order. Given their preoccupation with lineage, St Monica's perceived capacity to authenticate the order's origins in the ministry of St Augustine himself made propagation of her cult a priority.[18] To the Augustinian women, whether second order nuns, tertiaries or members of lay confraternities, Monica was also their spiritual exemplar and founding saint. By the fifteenth century, all three groups wore the same habit as the friars, with its characteristic black mantel and leather belt.[19] According to a myth that gained traction around 1430 (and was ratified in a bull of 1439), Monica, seeking consolation in

11 Gutierrez, *The Augustinians*, p. 191. The bull of Boniface IX (*In sinu Sedis apostolicae*) is published in: *Bullarium ordinis eremitarum sancti Augustini*, ed. by Laurentius Orsacchi da Empoli, pp. 53–54.

12 See Evangelisti, '"We Do Not Have It"'; Evangelisti, *Nuns: A History of Convent Life*, p. 45.

13 Gutierrez, *The Augustinians*, pp. 178–79.

14 Walsh, 'The Observance'.

15 This came after a period in the previous century when Monica's role in Augustine's life, and by extension in the foundation myth of the order, had been actively downplayed with removal of references to her in official hagiographies. See Laferrière, 'The Doubting Augustine'.

16 Mazzon, 'La cappella di S. Monica', p. 223.

17 Webb, 'Eloquence and Education'.

18 Piatti, 'Il culto di santa Monica', p. xv.

19 In the papal bull of 1399, which gave sanction to the Augustinian tertiaries, a habit is

widowhood, asked the Virgin how she had dressed following the death of Joseph. Mary instructed Monica to don a black mantel and a black leather belt drawn in tightly above the hips, promising protection and consolation, not only to her but also to those who followed her. Monica later passed the belt to her son following his baptism.[20]

In addition to her individual standing with each branch of the order, Katherine Gill has suggested that Monica's relationship with her son presented 'a model of a certain kind of relationship between men and women'.[21] For though she contributed to the theological debates that often took place in his household, in her mastery of contemplation it was she who guided Augustine beyond words and intellect to divine truth. As such, Monica represented the ways in which various branches of the order could undertake their holy mission in partnership, as well as how they might operate effectively in service of one another.

The *Saint Monica* Altarpiece: Archival Records and Historiography

No known documents exist which relate to its commission and, consequently, in modern scholarship the *Saint Monica* panel has been the subject of debate at every turn. Whereas in the nineteenth century questions centred on attribution, the hand of Francesco Botticini is now widely accepted, while issues of date, setting, and patronal responsibly have come to the fore.[22]

Following the devastating fire which destroyed the old church of S. Spirito in March 1471, the newly built Brunelleschian church was in use by 1481, though construction work in its chapels continued for several years after that.[23] Like many of the other altarpieces painted for the new church, Botticini's panel, a *tavola quadrata* in an *all'antica* frame, shows the central protagonist enthroned before a garden wall surrounded by other figures. The homogeneity of the altarpieces strongly suggests that the *Opera di Santo Spirito* imposed a unifying programme on the patrons of the new chapels.[24] Its conformity with the other

---

mentioned but not described. (More, 'Dynamics of Regulation', p. 108.) On the habit of the Augustinian hermits see also Warr, 'Hermits, Habits and History'.

20 *Compendio dell'origine, miracoli, indulgenze, indulti, et privilegi*, p. 16.

21 Gill, 'Open Monasteries for Women', p. 33.

22 For attribution history, see Venturini, *Francesco Botticini*, cat. 24, p. 109. The attribution to Botticini was first advanced by Schmarshow, *Festschrift zu Ehren*, p. 88, and reaffirmed soon after by Berenson, *Italian Pictures of the Renaissance*, I, p. 40.

23 Florence, ASF, CRSGF 122, 67, fol. 280[r-v]. Botto, 'L'edificazione della Chiesa di Santo Spirito'.

24 There is a documented precedent for the schematisation of chapel furnishings in Brunelleschi's church of S. Lorenzo in the 1430s (Saalman, 'San Lorenzo: The 1434 Chapel Project') and visual evidence for a similar kind of programme at S. Maria Maddalena in Borgo Pinti. On homogeneity of the chapel altarpieces and *paliotti* at S. Spirito see Markowsky, 'Eine Gruppe bemalter Paliotti', p. 116; Burke, *Changing Patrons*, p. 77.

altarpieces in the neighbouring chapels whose production in the 1480s is documented, in addition to stylistic considerations, indicate a date of *c.* 1485. These visual characteristics make a date around the mid-1480s convincing even in the face of contradictory evidence provided by later archival sources, which imply that Botticini's *Saint Monica* panel predates the fire of 1471.[25] Despite the discrepancy among commentators with regards to chronology, there is broad, though not unanimous, scholarly agreement on two fronts. First, that the altarpiece was originally painted for the chapel dedicated to St Monica within the church of S. Spirito, and second, that this chapel was within the purview of the convent of S. Monaca, a local community of Augustinian nuns which existed under the jurisdiction of the friars of S. Spirito.

In the fresh analysis of the archival trail that follows, the former consensus is upheld while the latter is called into question. With the help of hitherto unpublished documents, the previously opaque history of the chapel of St Monica, from its formal bestowal in the late 1480s to its dismantling less than a century later, comes into focus. The clarification offered by this new evidence enables direct engagement with the two most recent interpretations of the altarpiece. First, it overturns Anabel Thomas's suggestion that the panel, whose 'enclosed nature' would have made it inappropriate for display in the public male church, originated inside the convent of S. Monaca.[26] Second, it enriches a hypothesis posited by Ian Holgate that there has been historic

---

25   In a *memoriale* of obligations, written in 1692 by Padre Andrea Arrighi, there are three references to the panel of St Monica, each of which state that it was transferred from the old church into the new church; see Busignani and Bencini, *Le Chiese di Firenze, Quartiere di Santo Spirito*, p. 82 and pp. 35–36. On the evidence of the Arrighi manuscript, Busignani, *Verrocchio*, pp. 14–15 and Padoa Rizzo, 'Per Francesco Botticini', p. 16 n. 20 argued that Botticini's panel predates the fire of 1471. Venturini, *Francesco Botticini*, pp. 48–49 later proposed that Botticini's altarpiece stood temporarily in the section of the burned-out church that was partially refitted so as to accommodate worshippers while the new church was still under construction. She did not provide any evidence to support her supposition that the old church was refitted and continued to be used during the construction of the new basilica. Blume, 'The Chapel of Santa Monica', p. 289 suggested that Botticini's panel replaced an altarpiece of the same subject which had stood in the earlier church, which could explain Arrighi's mistaken belief that it had survived the blaze. This hypothesis was reiterated by Holgate, 'The Cult of Saint Monica', p. 200. Stylistic comparisons are not wholly effective since so few of Botticini's works are fixed chronologically. However, regarding the question of whether the *Monica* panel pre- or postdates the fire, comparison with the securely-dated *Madonna and Child with Saints* (1471) today in Musée Jacquemart-André is enlightening. The *Monica* panel reveals a greater deftness in the treatment of the draperies and in the handling of pictorial space, which might indicate that it was produced at a later stage than the Jacquemart-André panel, and therefore after the fire. For the Jacquemart-André panel see Venturini, *Francesco Botticini*, cat. 20, pp. 106–07.

26   Thomas, *Art and Piety in the Female Religious Communities*, pp. 57–63. Thomas argued that the panel was possibly located on the high altar at S. Monaca, and was only brought to S. Spirito when the interior of the nunnery church was refurbished in the late sixteenth century.

confusion in the interpretation of the term '*mantellate*' in the documents in the S. Spirito archive.[27]

The first certain record for a chapel under the *ius patronatus* of Augustinian women at S. Spirito dates to 1487.[28] On 29 December of that year, the second chapel from the entrance in the left-hand aisle flanking the nave was conferred upon the 'donne amantalate di Santa Monicha' (mantle-wearing women of St Monica). Though this notice records the women's intention to install an altar and a window with their emblem in the chapel, no altarpiece, planned or existing, receives mention. Given that, stylistically, the *Saint Monica* altarpiece appears to have been painted in *c.* 1485, we can infer that it was produced specifically for the new chapel. However, until now the earliest known notice of the panel was found in a *memoriale* drawn up more than a century later in 1598, which lists the obligations associated with each of the chapels of S. Spirito. By that date the panel ('la Tavola di S. Monica') was standing in a chapel in the right transept belonging to the Capponi dell'Altopascio family.[29] This notice identifies the panel of St Monica located on the altar there:

> because of the presence of the above-mentioned panel there are many obligations to say Mass every day, for which we have [income from] the farm at Fraille. In addition, three times a week a Mass [is offered] for St Monica, and once a month a Mass [is offered] for St Augustine while there is a Mass or commemoration being performed in the choir, and Offices for the dead [are said] for Madonna Bartolomea di Rinier del Pace, widow of Luigi Sapiti, who left half a farm in Impruneta to our convent. And we must do an Office for all the Augustinian *mantellate*, for which the convent has an account of one hundred and fifty lire.[30]

Documents pertaining to the bequest of Bartolomea di Rinier del Pace survive in the S. Spirito account books. Drawn up in 1501, Bartolomea's will describes the donation of a *podere* in Impruneta to fund masses 'al'altare di S.ta Monica' and lists some of the same obligations cited in the *memoriale*: three masses a week at the altar of St Monica, a sung Mass once a month and an annual Office for the souls of Bartolomea, her mother, and all her relatives.[31] The cornerstone of Thomas's argument that Botticini's altarpiece never stood in the chapel of St Monica was the absence of any trace of the panel at S. Spirito prior to the record of obligations of 1598. This testamentary endowment

---

27 Holgate, 'The Cult of Saint Monica', p. 201.

28 Florence, ASF, CRSGF 122, 128, fol. 92ᵛ.

29 The Capponi dell'Altopascio were the branch of the Capponi family descended from Guglielmo Capponi, who had acquired the mastership of the Hospital of San Giacomo in Altopascio, near Lucca, in 1445; see McArdle, *Altopascio*, pp. 4–6.

30 Florence, ASF, CRSGF 122, 36, c. 23ᵛ.

31 Vulgate summary of will: Florence, ASF, CRSGF 122, 62, fol. 47ʳ n. 19. Full will in Latin: ASF, CRSGF 122, 77, fols 20ʳ–25ᵛ. Reference is also made to Bartolomea's bequest in: ASF, CRSGF 122, 67, fol. 180ᵛ.

provides a firm link between the altarpiece recorded in the Capponi chapel in the late sixteenth-century and an altar dedicated to St Monica which stood in the church, ninety-seven years earlier. Of course, technically the obligations were associated with the altar and not the altarpiece. However, the 1598 *memoriale* states that the obligations were owed 'due to the presence of the above-mentioned panel' ('Per esserci la sudetta tavola ci sono molti obblighi'), a strong reason to infer that the altar and its altarpiece were inextricably linked in the minds of the friars.[32]

Although all besides Thomas have assumed that the panel first stood in the chapel of St Monica, the motive for the panel's eventual transfer to the Capponi dell'Altopascio chapel has eluded commentators. More than once the choice of new location has been attributed to the Capponi clan's historic ties to the community of S. Monaca, and even taken as evidence of the family's possible role as patrons of the altarpiece in the fifteenth century. A series of new documents sheds important light on the date and circumstances of the altarpiece's relocation. We know from the 1487 record of the chapel's conferral upon the *mantellate* that it was the second on the left-hand aisle.[33] However, in the *memoriale* of 1598, this same chapel was assigned to the Riccio Nuovo family, indicating a change of patronal rights in the intervening decades.[34] Activity associated with this change of ownership is traceable in three documents drawn up in the second half of the 1570s. A *promissio* drafted by the Florentine notary Frosino Ruffoli on 6 November 1575 confirms del Riccio's acquisition of the rights to this chapel.[35] On 4 August of the following year the expenditure records in the S. Spirito archive log the receipt of 600 *scudi* 'left in memory of Guglielmo del Riccio for the endowment of the chapel in our church which is currently under the title of Sta. Monacha'.[36] Finally, the most revealing new source documents the fate of the *Saint Monica* altarpiece following the change of patronal rights in this chapel: a *memoria* of 8 May 1578 written by a certain Fra Egidio Bonsi.[37] It confirms that the S. Spirito chapter had voted on a motion to ask the Capponi family if the friars might place the altar and altarpiece of St Monica in their chapel in the transept. The community supported this motion and agreed that, if it failed to secure the approval of the Capponi family, it would instead ask the Ridolfi family, proprietors of the chapel of the Epiphany. This was not necessary since the Capponi family agreed, at least until they or one of their heirs decided to commission another altarpiece for the space. Fra Egidio's memo further undermines Thomas's

---

32 See n. 30.

33 Florence, ASF, CRSGF 122, 128, fol. 92[v].

34 Florence, ASF, CRSGF 122, 37.

35 Florence, ASF, Notarile Moderno, Protocolli 259–69, 266, fols 109[v]–110[v].

36 Florence, ASF, CRSGF 122, 68, fol. 77[v].

37 Florence, ASF, CRSGF 122, 68, fol. 82[r]. Capretti, *The Building Complex of Santo Spirito*, p. 51, listed the date of 1578 for the transfer of the *Saint Monica* panel to the Capponi chapel. This would suggest that she had knowledge of Fra Egidio's memo, though she did not cite it.

suggestion that the altarpiece was originally in the convent of S. Monaca, an argument which was predicated on the absence of documents placing the Botticini panel in the friars' church prior to refurbishments carried out in the nuns' church in c. 1583. Not only does this document locate the *Saint Monica* altarpiece in the church twenty years earlier than the *memoriale* of 1598, but it also underscores the tradition of obligations associated with the altar and altarpiece ('a detto altare et ancona di santa Monaca') since the beginning of the century.[38]

The Second Order Nuns of S. Monaca

The connection between the nunnery of S. Monaca and the aisle chapel dedicated to St Monica in the friars' church has been called into question only once. In his study of the rise of the Augustinian tertiary movement in relation to the cult of St Monica in the fifteenth century, Holgate pointed out that the published documentary evidence actually offered no watertight links between the aisle chapel and the convent.[39] Though the following exploration of documents relating to the convent's early years reveals that this is not strictly true, it also gives cause for a revision of the traditional tendency among scholars to equate the 'donne amantalate di Santa Monicha' cited in the 1487 bestowal document with the nuns of S. Monaca exclusively. As will become evident, a more nuanced examination of the chapel space and the community it served is required.

A slim folder in the patchy surviving archival holdings of the nunnery of S. Monaca constitutes the bulk of our knowledge about the earliest years of this community. The founding history is recorded in a fifteenth-century chronicle written by Fra Francesco d'Antonio Mellini.[40] Other sources, also apparently in Mellini's hand, include a collection of payment records for initial construction work at the convent, as well as a list of the first nuns in the chapter with the dates of their veiling, profession, and eventual death.[41] Fra Mellini, known as 'il zoppo' (the lame), was an Augustinian doctor of theology at S. Spirito and the S. Monaca community's first guardian and legal representative ('sindaco e procuratore'). Mellini's assiduous sponsorship of S. Monaca constituted just one part of his wider promotion of the Augustinian

---

38 Fra Egidio also makes specific reference to funds from the farm in Impruneta (Florence, ASF, CRSGF 122, 68, fol. 82ʳ).

39 Holgate, 'The Cult of Saint Monica', pp. 197–203.

40 Florence, ASF, CRSGF 131, 92, seg. 'A', I, n. 1, fols 3ʳ–4ᵛ. For an early copy of this chronicle see Florence, BNCF, MS Magliabechiano, Cl. XXVII, 188: 'Notizie del Convento di Santa Monica di Firenze'). Mellini's account is transcribed, almost in full, by Richa, *Notizie istoriche*, IX, pp. 237–51).

41 A number of these records are published in Simari, 'Profilo storico-architettonico di un monastero fiorentino del quattrocento: Santa Monaca'.

order in the neighbourhood. Antonio Manetti, in his biography of Filippo Brunelleschi, claimed that Mellini commanded considerable respect among the influential citizens of the Oltrarno and that he could be credited with urging them to bring greater prestige to the area by funding the new basilica of S. Spirito.[42]

The nunnery had its origins in Castiglione near Miniato al Tedesco (modern day San Miniato) located between Pisa and Florence. In 1441, a community of Augustinian nuns, left fearful by the wars being waged by mercenary soldiers in the territories around their convent, travelled to Florence under the protection of certain residents of the Oltrarno neighbourhood.[43] The following year their nunnery, dedicated to the mother of Augustine (identified from the outset with the Tuscan vernacular spelling of Santa *Monaca*), was founded in a house on the via della Fogna del Carmine, present-day via Santa Monaca, 400 metres from the friary of S. Spirito. During the community's fledgling years, the expansion of the convent met with severe opposition from the Carmelite friars at the nearby S. Maria del Carmine, resulting in delays to the construction of the nuns' church and in the imposition of restrictive measures designed to curb frequentation of the church by local residents. Lay citizens were forbidden from making confession in the convent's church and from having tombs at the premises. The convent could only have one bell weighing no more than 100 *libbre* (34 kilograms). Mass could be said once a day in the church but was otherwise strictly regulated and, significantly, preaching was forbidden except on the convent's feast day or for the veiling or vesting of a sister. Given that the then archbishop, Antoninus Pierozzi, insisted upon the necessity of hearing regular sermons, we can assume that the women came out of the nunnery to hear preachers, most likely their brothers in the neighbouring church of S. Spirito.[44] This was certainly the case for their counterparts affiliated with the nearby Carmelites, who prior to the construction of their own nunnery church, heard masses and sermons in the friars' church.[45]

During these early years, the nuns of S. Monaca probably did not practice absolute monastic enclosure, either active or passive. There is now consensus among historians of female monasticism in quattrocento Florence that the observance of *clausura* was often more elastic than the stated intentions of

---

42 Manetti, *Vita di Filippo Brunelleschi*, pp. 120–21.
43 The abbess, Suor Jacopa di Gomberoni da Milano, travelled to Florence first under the protection Luca di Taddeo, a citizen from the parish of S. Felice in Piazza who had female relatives residing in the nunnery in Castiglione. Following her arrival in Florence, she soon won the support of Ubertino dei Bardi and his wife Caterina, who believed that the abbess's prayers had helped her to conceive a child. After this miracle, Ubertino, together with Luca di Taddeo and local acquaintances Giovanni di Cenni Ugolino (Luca's uncle) and Goro di Cristofano da Legnaia, purchased the house on via Santa Monaca for use as a convent for Suor Jacopa's community of nuns. Richa, *Notizie istoriche*, IX, pp. 238–40.
44 Howard, 'Preaching and Liturgy', p. 318.
45 On the early history of the Carmelite women of S. Maria degli Angeli see Catena, *Le Carmelitane*, pp. 169–71; Vasciaveo, *Una storia di donne*, pp. 20–25.

the convent constitutions and, in many cases, egress and ingress were heavily restricted, rather than forbidden outright.[46]

An unpublished manuscript originating from the nunnery of S. Monaca and probably dating to the last quarter of the fifteenth century, containing both the rule of St Augustine, adapted for nuns, and the convent constitutions, has recently come to light, having been held in an unknown private collection, unknown to scholars, since 1939.[47] The constitutions are based on those of the nearby nuns of S. Elisabetta delle Convertite, which are understood to be the earliest surviving constitutions for a community of second order Augustinians.[48] Given that both S. Monaca and the Convertite were in the *cura monialium* of the hermit friars of S. Spirito, the similarities between their constitutions are not surprising.[49] However, though many of the chapter headings are the same and whole sections are lifted verbatim, there are various notable differences too. In the S. Monaca manuscript the first four chapters of the constitutions appear in a different order, and four chapters that are found in the Convertite constitutions are not included in the S. Monaca manuscript. In addition, several chapters are extended in the S. Monaca manuscript. But for neither community, though any exchange with the world outside the convent was certainly strictly regulated, *clausura* was not in fact specified outright. This is in marked contrast to the nearby Observant Dominican nuns at S. Pier Martire, for example, who observed a special constitution, originally granted to their counterparts in Pisa by Pope Urban VI and later extended to this Florentine community, which stipulated the privilege of enclosure.[50] Further, the rule

---

46 For a useful overview see: Hiller, *Gendered Perceptions of Florentine Last Supper Frescoes*, pp. 145–47. In a chapter entitled 'Contesting the Boundaries of Enclosure', Strocchia, *Nuns and Nunneries in Renaissance Florence*, pp. 152–90 provides an important analysis of the varying degrees to which enclosure was observed in early fifteenth-century female monastic institutions in Florence and of a gradual reform in the second half of the century as the enforcement of *clausura* became a priority.

47 The manuscript was acquired by University of California, Los Angeles in 2016 from Les Eluminures (Paris, New York, Chicago), who put it up for sale in September 2015. It is currently held under MS 170/880 in the Bound Manuscripts Collection of the UCLA Library Special Collections. Prior to 1939 it was in the collection of Piero Ginori Conti (1865–1939), Prince of Trevignano, whose *ex libris* is pasted onto the inside front cover.

48 Piatti, *Il movimento femminile agostiniano*, p. 8 and p. 134. The fourteenth-century constitutions of the Convertite are known through an Italian language translation produced in the sixteenth century. This manuscript is apparently held at the Archivio di Stato di Firenze, though is currently untraceable because the modern archival inventory number is unknown. A copy of this manuscript's text was published in 1901, see Mattioli, *Fra Giovanni da Salerno*, pp. 142–63.

49 It is possible that the manuscript was produced for S. Monaca by the women of S. Gaggio, a third community of Augustinian second order nuns in the district (also in the *cura monialium* of S. Spirito) whose production of choral books for their sisters at S. Monaca, under the direction Fra Mellini, is documented in the 1440s. See Arthur, 'New Evidence for a Scribal-Nun's Art', pp. 274–75.

50 Duval, 'Mulieres religiosae and sorores clausae', pp. 4–5.

of enclosure is specified in the rule of St Clare of Assisi (chapter XI) and was observed by Observant communities of Poor Clares. In fact, at S. Monaca, though by no means free to come and go as they pleased, and with all forms of communication with the outside world strictly controlled, there were instances when the nuns were granted permission to leave. One particularly enlightening addition to the S. Monaca constitutions is included at the end of Chapter 14 entitled 'del chiamare le suore al parlatorio e alla ruoto' ('on calling the sisters to the parlatorium and to the turn'). It describes how servant nuns ('servigiale') who must go out of the convent on official business were to be selected by the abbess, according to her sagacity, and must not carry letters, messages, or presents to or from other sisters. Any nun contravening this rule was to be punished. Interestingly, the text expressly states that, if the woman was not professed, she was to be discharged from her post and sent away from the nunnery, but if she was professed, then she was to be held within the convent and no longer allowed out. Apparently even professed nuns did go out, albeit under strictly monitored circumstances.

Finally, it is noteworthy that, in the S. Monaca constitutions, a section about manual labour was added, with the annotation 'Nolite negligere' ('do not neglect') added in a different (perhaps later) hand in the margin. The nunnery was one of a number in the city that were engaged in the production of gold thread and this addition to their constitutions, which is not found in the earlier Convertite prototype, highlights the centrality of these activities in the daily life of the convent. The text stipulates that the nuns' abilities in sewing and embroidery must be put to worthy causes such as textiles for ecclesiastical use, rather than for the vanity and fancy of secular men and women. Such commercial ventures, vital for the community's survival, indicate that they were not completely enclosed since some interaction with suppliers and trading associates would have been necessary for their work.[51]

Despite the initial limitations imposed as a fallout of the Carmelites' complaints during the S. Monaca community's first two decades, by 1460, building works at the nunnery church were complete and, following papal intervention, the earlier constraints had been relaxed. A decree of December 1460 declared that more masses could be said inside their church, except on solemn feast days and special Carmelite feast days. Public preaching was now permitted inside the church, though not on days when preaching was taking place inside the Carmine.[52]

Such restrictions, resulting from spats between monastic communities, were not unusual in Florence during this period and they offer a potent reminder that religious communities were in constant competition with one another for the support of the lay community in their immediate neighbourhood.

51 Strocchia, *Nuns and Nunneries in Renaissance Florence*, pp. 121–22 and p. 143.
52 The changes were implemented following the intervention of Pope Pius II, as chronicled by Mellini (Richa, *Notizie istoriche*, IX, pp. 248–49).

The greater the density of religious institutions in any one area, the greater the choice citizens had when channelling their allegiance and so the greater the challenge for convents in obtaining vital income from burial rights, commemorative masses, alms and testamentary bequests.[53] As Anabel Thomas has aptly remarked, between the various orders 'there was clearly vigorous competition analogous to that between brands in contemporary markets'.[54]

The friars' commitment to say Mass in the nuns' church on a daily basis was renewed as part of a contract drawn up on 1 February 1477 between the Augustinian friars and the women of S. Monaca, a document which is key to understanding the nuns' various relationships with external institutions at this date.[55] The contract explains that the women of S. Monaca had a debt to the friars of S. Spirito amounting to 1200 florins, a sum which had been lent to them for the construction of their convent. At some earlier time, the nuns had committed to sew, repair, and clean all the vestments and furnishings of the sacristy — perhaps further evidence, incidentally, that the nuns were not completely enclosed — until such time that the friars had been duly compensated and the debt repaid in full. However, citing their growing numbers, the women had requested dispensation from their remaining dues, declaring that they did not have the means to repay them either through alms or labour. After considerable deliberation on the part of the friars and lay agents acting on behalf of the women, it was decided that the nuns would be released from their debt. Having set out these circumstances, the contract goes on to describe the conditions of this absolution. The nuns would entrust the government of their nunnery to the Augustinian friars in perpetuity, annually paying out one florin on the feast day of St Monica as a token of their submission to the authority and protection of the friars. For their part, the friars committed to say Mass daily in the women's church and also perform a sung Mass there on the feast day of St Monica as well as on the day after four major feast days: Easter, Christmas, Epiphany and Pentecost. Funds for these offices would be taken from the rental income of an apothecary shop located near the tavern called 'el Bucho'. These premises were managed by the Arte del Cambio, which had inherited it from a certain Luca del Serra. Luca had allocated its annual rental income of eighty lire in perpetuity to the 'infirm' ('infirmis') of S. Spirito. In the contract of 1477, the friars formally designated this income to fund regular masses inside the church of S. Monaca.

The S. Spirito *entrate e uscite* (incoming and outgoing funds) records for the period 1485–1495 show the terms of the contract being honoured. The

---

53   In 1440 there were two large mendicant friaries, an ancient Camaldolese monastery and six female convents as well as four parish churches in the Oltrarno distinct and its immediate environs. Five new nunneries, S. Monaca included, were founded in the district in the following two decades.

54   Thomas, *Art and Piety in the Female Religious Communities*, pp. 66–67.

55   Florence, ASF, CRSGF 131, 92, I, n. 15. For the transcription see Simari, 'Profilo storico-architettonico di un monastero fiorentino del quattrocento: Santa Monaca', doc. 11.

records reveal payments made every six months by the Arte del Cambio for offices for the 'chapel of the nunnery of S. Monica' ('cappella del monasterio di Sta. Monicha'), namely the church of S. Monaca.[56] The nuns also upheld their obligations with annual contributions of one large florin for other masses performed by the hermit friars on St Monica's feast day.[57] The payments are listed briefly, but wherever the incoming Arte del Cambio money is recorded, the location of the nunnery church of S. Monaca is specified. The site of the celebrations toward which the nuns made their donation is not listed. However, given that these are the friars' account books, we can assume that they took place at the friary church (just as the masses for other saints, for which various monetary contributions are logged, were). It follows that the friars' offices for St Monica would have centred on the altar that was dedicated to her within their church. Therefore, the annual payment of one florin faithfully handed over each year by the women of S. Monaca reveals that they were bound, financially at least, to the cult of St Monica as it was commemorated within the friars' church.

Richa singles out a number of important benefactors to the nunnery whose involvement post-dates the death of Fra Mellini and therefore is not recorded in the chronicle.[58] In the later part of the Quattrocento the Capponi replaced the Bardi as the nuns' main benefactors. This family's *stemma* (coat of arms), still visible on the façade of the church of S. Monaca above the oculus, survives as a testament to their legacy at the site. Despite this documented involvement at the nunnery, proposed links between the Capponi family and the chapel dedicated to St Monica in the friars' church stem from a misreading of the contract of 1477. Andrew Blume believed the contract to refer to a new loan but in fact it recorded the nuns' absolution from an earlier debt to the friars.[59] This is important because Blume supposed the Arte del Cambio payments for offices in the church of S. Monaca to be repayments of this debt. In fact, the contract makes clear that the two things were quite separate. The women were formally released from their debt on the understanding that they would give the friars one large florin each year as *censo*.[60] In the second part of the agreement the friars consented to say regular masses inside the church of S. Monaca which would be paid for by the Arte del Cambio. Given

56 Florence, ASF, CRSGF 122, 8, fols 11ʳ, 17ᵛ, 20ʳ, 31ᵛ, 34ᵛ, 44ᵛ, 48ʳ, 53ʳ, 58ʳ, 61ʳ, 120ᵛ, 122ʳ, 125ʳ. Records from this volume are not complete owing to considerable water damage in the lower part of many of the pages. The outgoing funds are also recorded in the Arte del Cambio ledgers: ASF, Arte del Cambio, 21, fols 164ᵛ, 180ʳ, 186ʳ. These same payments are traceable in the *Campione* of S. Spirito: ASF, CRSGF 122, 1, fols 129ᵛ–130ʳ.

57 Florence, ASF, CRSGF 122, 8, fols 6ᵛ, 13ᵛ, 17ᵛ, 19ᵛ, 24ᵛ, 26ᵛ, 30ʳ, 32ᵛ, 36ʳ, 43ᵛ, 48ʳ, 53ʳ, 55ʳ, 58r, 60ʳ, 119ʳ, 122ʳ.

58 Richa, *Notizie istoriche*, IX, p. 249.

59 Blume, 'The Chapel of Santa Monica', p. 290.

60 A 'censo' was a monetary tribute or offering given to a religious or civic authority by those subject to it. This word is used in the vulgate summary of the contract not the original Latin (see n. 31 above).

the involvement of the Arte del Cambio, Blume tentatively assigned fiscal responsibly for Botticini's altarpiece to the Capponi family, through their roles as senior members of that guild.[61] However, the contract shows that the income from the apothecary shop had already been allocated to the 'infirm' of S. Spirito by Luca del Serra and that these premises, with the incumbent obligations, were simply managed by the Arte del Cambio. As such, the guild may have been merely a conduit for the funds owed to the friary of S. Spirito via a pre-existing pledge. This being said, a Capponi connection cannot be discounted entirely because the original donor, Luca del Serra, was married to Margherita Capponi, who was a benefactor of the nunnery of S. Monaca.[62] Margherita's brother, Niccolò di Giovanni 'il Grasso' Capponi was a senior member of the Arte del Cambio.[63] It was Niccolò's heirs who had *ius patronatus* of the chapel in the right transept, where the *Saint Monica* panel was eventually moved. But whether Capponi money was used to fund Botticini's altarpiece cannot be negated or proved from the existing evidence. Either way, Fra Egidio's *memoria* undermines the notion that Botticini's panel made its way into the Capponi chapel because of that family's historic connections to S. Monaca. We recall that, failing the consent of the Capponi, the friars had planned to ask the Ridolfi family to house the altarpiece instead. The circumstances of the altarpiece's arrival in the Capponi chapel were, it seems, rather prosaic, the result of a timely availability of chapel space.[64]

Holgate's suggestion that there are no documented links between the aisle chapel and the nunnery of S. Monaca is refuted by their annual *censo* for masses in the friars' church at the altar of their patroness. Nonetheless it is also clear that from the late 1440s the nuns heard Mass on a daily basis inside their own church and just over a decade later they could also hear preachers there. This begs the question of how, if at all, the chapel in the left aisle of the friars' church served the community's needs. Were they in fact the intended audience of Botticini's altarpiece? In particular, Holgate's postulation that the space 'potentially hosted a variety of women — tertiaries (some or all of whom may have found permanent or occasional refuge at S. Monaca), and the nuns from S. Monaca', requires attention.[65]

---

61 The payment records of the Arte del Cambio (see n. 56 above) show that the funds were administered by Niccolò di Giovanni Capponi.

62 In 1476 Margherita bequeathed sixty lire a year towards masses inside the nunnery church (Simari, 'Profilo storico-architettonico di un monastero fiorentino del quattrocento: Santa Monaca', p. 150 n. 10).

63 See n. 56 above.

64 The question of who funded the altarpiece remains open. The scenes in the predella are divided by painted decorative devices. Two of these dividing motifs appear to be coats of arms, one with a rampant lion and the other with a rampant unicorn. These seem to have been painted over the top of the narrative scenes, which may indicate that they are later additions. Unfortunately, though perhaps easily recognizable to the 'period eye', the heraldic motifs are too generic to be identified.

65 Holgate, 'The Cult of Saint Monica'.

The Cult of St Monica inside the Friars' Church

In the fifteenth century, throughout the Italian peninsula, examples could be found of an area within the hermit friars' church dedicated to St Monica which served as a place of confluence for several interested parties. This wider trend in Augustinian churches provides a useful context for understanding the ways in which the aisle chapel at S. Spirito, and in turn Botticini's altarpiece, were experienced. They reveal that the space was used in different ways — liturgical, commemorative, institutional — by various parties. Just like the branches of the Augustinian network that the altars or chapels served, such activities did not exist in parallel, but were intertwined and interdependent.

In April 1430, Monica's remains were rediscovered in Ostia and transferred, apparently through the efforts of an 'unmarried, religious' woman, to the now-demolished Roman church of S. Trifone.[66] Very shortly thereafter, in June, the decree was issued that St Monica's image should be painted in every church of the order. At S. Trifone, a lay confraternity (or, more precisely, consorority given its exclusively female membership) was dedicated to overseeing the liturgical requirements associated with the tomb as well as undertaking charitable works in the neighbourhood.[67] These *mantellate* (as they are frequently referred to in the documents) not only maintained and decorated the tomb space but also promoted Monica's cult by organizing masses and processions with her relics.[68] Monica's remains were translated into the nearby Augustinian church of S. Agostino following its reconstruction in 1455. The confraternity of women transferred its supervision to this site, and several of them later were buried within the new church.[69] The translation and the new chapel of St Monica, with its lavish marble mausoleum and a gem-encrusted reliquary for the saint's head, was funded by the humanist poet Maffeo Vegio, who was subsequently entombed there.[70] Vegio had a profound personal devotion to Monica, whom he venerated as an ideal mother and on the subject of whom he wrote two *vitae*, as well as offices for her feast and a treatise on Christian education.[71] In Rome therefore, although women contributed to the chapel's upkeep and generously provided many of its furnishings, they did not own the patronal rights to it outright.[72] At this

---

66 Gill, 'Open Monasteries for Women', p. 29.

67 Esposito, 'I gruppi bizzocali a Roma nel'400'. Esposito provides an Appendix with transcriptions of key documents relating to the Roman *mantellate* in the fifteenth century, including notices regarding their confessors, reforms undertaken in the 1460s, and donations by members of the community.

68 Maroni Lumbroso and Martini, *Le confraternite romane*, p. 307.

69 Gill, 'Open Monasteries for Women', pp. 30–31, p. 46 n. 58.

70 Piatti, *Il movimento femminile agostiniano*, pp. 45–46. See also Holgate, 'The Cult of Saint Monica', pp. 186–87.

71 Clark, *Monica: An Ordinary Saint*, p. 169.

72 Gill, 'Open Monasteries for Women', p. 31 remarks that, 'as benefactors, such women take their place beside bishops, cardinals, priests, and important officials of the papal court. Their

site, their interests in St Monica — as their patron and spiritual exemplar — coexisted with those of the friars, whose commitment to the cult of St Monica was now an institutional requirement, as well as the interests of an individual patron, for whom St Monica was intercessor and guardian of his soul in death. Similarly, in Venice, the involvement of tertiary women at the altar of St Monica in the Augustinian church of S. Stefano is signalled by a communal tomb for the 'mantellate o terziarie agostiniane' recorded in the altar's vicinity. The altarpiece for that chapel, produced by Antonio Vivarini and Giovanni d'Alemagna, probably in the 1440s, may well have been commissioned by this group of tertiaries. Later in the century, in 1473, a testamentary bequest records sums of money entrusted to the 'done de lhabito [*sic*] de sancta monica' (the women of the habit of St Monica) to be distributed to the poor and to be used for decoration in the chapel of St Monica.[73] As in Rome, the Venetian tertiary women's commitment to St Monica comprised charitable works beyond the church as well as the upkeep of the chapel space. Furthermore, despite the women's active involvement at the chapel site, Holgate has also argued convincingly that the space and its altarpiece catered to the devotional needs of various interested parties within the hermits' church, in particular the friars themselves.[74]

In Prato, there also appears to have been a chapel dedicated to St Monica, located inside the friars' church, which was entrusted to the *mantellate*. In 1459, Neri di Bicci received a commission to produce 'una tavola quadra' (a square panel) for the 'amantellate di Prato' (*mantellate* of Prato) which was destined for the hermits' Pratese seat of S. Agostino. Neri described the painting in his *Ricordanze* as: 'a Saint Monica in the middle, seated, with some *mantellate* kneeling, Saint Augustine to one side and Saint Nicholas of Tolentino to the other, with the stories of Saint Monica in the predella'.[75]

Finally, the site of a chapel of St Monica as a place of confluence between Augustinian female devotees and their male protectors is also recorded at another Florentine Augustinian church, S. Maria in S. Gallo. This reputedly impressive edifice outside the gate of S. Gallo belonged to the Augustinian hermit friars of the Lombardy congregation, the Observant branch of the order. Antonia de' Pulci, the first prioress of the *suore* of S. Maria della Misericordia, received the Augustinian habit at S. Maria in S. Gallo. Though history does not relate where precisely within the church her vesting took place, we do know that Antonia was later buried inside the chapel of St Monica situated within that church.[76] Here then, as in Venice, we find the chapel of St Monica as a

donations indicate an intimate involvement in the ceremonial life of the church and insured an ongoing association with the liturgical functions and physical fabric of Sant'Agostino'.

73   Holgate, 'Santa Monica, Venice and the Vivarini', pp. 174–75.
74   Holgate, 'Santa Monica, Venice and the Vivarini', pp. 178–81.
75   Santi, *Neri di Bicci*, p. 119 n. 232 and p. 134 n. 261.
76   Richa, *Notizie istoriche*, V, p. 250. Antonia had lived as a *pinzochera* since her husband's death in 1487 but only took formal vows and withdrew into cloistered life in 1500. She died the

burial site for at least one, though quite possibly more than one, Augustinian tertiary. Moreover, we might reasonably assume that, as the burial site of their foundress, the women of S. Maria della Misericordia maintained an interest in the site and so probably continued to frequent, and perhaps contribute to the upkeep of, the chapel in the years following her death.

The Augustinian *Mantellate* of S. Spirito

A deeper trawl of the S. Spirito archive lays bare an historic confusion regarding the term *mantellate* in the interpretation of the documentary sources. As already indicated, prior to Holgate's suggestion, every commentator has assumed that the phrase 'donne amantalate di Santa Monicha' of the 1487 bestowal notice relates exclusively to the nuns of S. Monaca. This is problematic not least because nowhere in the primary documentary sources relating to the nuns of S. Monaca is the term *mantellate* used to described them. There are, however, several instances of *mantellata/e* in the S. Spirito records which instead refer to tertiary women. An unpublished will of 1430 refers to the tomb of the 'mantellate di sancto agostino' inside the church.[77] Such evidence of Augustinian *mantellate* residing in the Oltrarno in the earlier part of the century, prior to the arrival of the nuns from San Miniato, is limited. Precisely because of their unofficial status, documentation about the friars' responsibilities towards such non-regular groups of women is scarce.[78] Even so, the seventeenth-century historian of the order, Father Luigi Torelli, informs us that one group lived together in a *reclusario* in the neighbourhood near the friary; their first prioress, Suor Francia Sanese, was elected in 1432.[79] Torelli also relates that there were historic ties between the tertiary groups in Florence and Prato, since they were both initially established under the jurisdiction of Fra Cesare Orsini, the first rector of the consorority associated with the chapel of St Monica in S. Trifone in Rome.[80] These connections lend credence to the oft-mooted notion that Botticini possibly took Neri di Bicci's earlier altarpiece for the *mantellate* in Prato as a model, since the Pratese and Florentine *mantellate* may have hoped to proclaim their wider network by creating visual consistency between their chapels.[81]

---

following year. See Wyatt Cook and Collier Cook, *Antonia Pulci: Florentine Drama*; Weaver, *Antonia Pulci: Saints' Lives*.

77 Florence, ASF, CRSGF 122, 76, fols 143^r ^{v}. I am grateful to Alexander Röstel for first bringing this reference to my attention. A summary of the will is also found in ASF, CRSGF 122, 66, fol. 47^v n. 32.

78 Piatti, *Il movimento femminile agostiniano*, pp. 117–25.

79 Torelli, *Secoli Agostiniani*, VI, p. 639. The same page records a community of *mantellate* in Città di Castello.

80 Torelli, *Secoli Agostiniani*, VI, p. 670. See also Holgate, 'The Cult of Saint Monica', p. 200.

81 Thomas's suggestion that this now lost painting for the Prato *mantellate* may have provided

It is clear then that communities of tertiary women associated with the church of S. Spirito — called *mantellate* in the records — predate arrival of the S. Monaca nuns in Florence from Castiglione. Moreover, these groups did not cease to exist after the nuns' arrival. Several fifteenth-century documents signal their continued existence after the nunnery was founded. For example, an inventory of 1453 lists an ivory crucifix rosary, which, at the time it was drawn up, was in the possession of the prioress of the *mantellate*.[82] The use of the term 'priora' is significant since in the S. Monaca documents 'badessa' is employed exclusively, an indication that this reference relates to a separate community. Furthermore, in all of his entries in the S. Monaca expenditure records, as well as his chronicle, Fra Mellini refers to the nuns as 'monache' or 'suore' and never 'amantellate'. Indeed, the S. Monaca archive contains records which show that the two communities — the nuns of S. Monaca and the *mantellate* of St Augustine — were distinct from one another, though geographically close and with at least some interaction. There is a record of one nun who joined the chapter in 1445 having formerly been a *mantellata* in a nearby community in S. Felice in Piazza.[83] The following page logs a testamentary bequest from Mona Lisa de' Baroncelli ('amantellata dell ordine di Sancto Agostino stava nel popolo di San Felice in Piazza').

Unlike earlier records of *mantellate*, the 1487 record of the left aisle chapel's bestowal refers to the 'donne amantalate di Santa Monicha' rather than 'di sancto agostino'.[84] This, it appears, was because either an existing or a new group of tertiary or non-regular women had adopted Monica as their patroness,

---

the model for Botticini's version is attractive given that it was commissioned, and likely produced, during his tenure in Neri's shop (Thomas, *Art and Piety in the Female Religious Communities*, p. 70). Holgate also argued that Botticini's *Saint Monica* altarpiece was modelled on Neri's lost work, and that the Pratese panel in turn may have been modelled on the altarpiece which stood in the *mantellate* chapel at S. Spirito before the fire of 1471 (Holgate, 'The Cult of Saint Monica', p. 200). Such visual linkages between two altarpieces standing in associated, but geographically separate, sites led Michelle O'Malley to characterize Benozzo Gozzoli's altarpiece for the Purification Confraternity (National Gallery, London, 1461–1462, NG283) as a 'visible knot that ties together an invisible skein of relations', a concept which she borrowed from the anthropologist Alfred Gell's seminal essay entitled 'Art and Agency' (see O'Malley, 'Altarpieces and Agency').

82   Florence, ASF, CRSGF 122, 60, fol. 13ʳ: '…uno crucifixo davorio in me[z]o della vergine maria e di San Giovanni evangelista … davorio guasto. Allo la priora delle mantellate' ('an ivory crucifix flanked by the Virgin and St John the Evangelist … in damaged ivory. The prioress of the *mantellate* has it'). This reference is cited but not transcribed by Thomas, who slightly misinterpreted the entry as referring to an ivory crucifix which belonged the prioress of the *mantellate* (Thomas, *Art and Piety in the Female Religious Communities*, p. 348 n. 53). The object is listed under 'Rosario' and must therefore have been a rosary with an ivory crucifix on it. Moreover, 'allo' ('à lo') is an old form of 'lo ha', meaning 'she has it'. The entry directly beneath refers to another rosary with a small leather pouch containing a relic of St Monica 'un pezzo del capo di Santa Monaca'.

83   Florence, ASF, CRSGF 131, 92, 1, fol. 5ʳ.

84   See n. 30.

and does not indicate irrefutable affiliation with the nunnery of S. Monica. Records of *mantellate* in the S. Spirito archives continue, throughout the final quarter of the century and into the following, which confirm that such groups persisted as separate entities to the nuns of S. Monaca. These include the sale of property in the val d'Ambra on behalf of 'nostre amantellate' in 1475 as well as a notice of October 1480 relating to the pension of a certain Mona Pippa at the 'casa del collegio delle mantellate' situated in via San Giovanni, to the west of the friary.[85] In 1491, the ledgers of S. Spirito record payments made by the 'casa delle amantellate', and in 1494 the friars logged an annual payment by the Badia of S. Pancrazio 'alle amantellate nostre'.[86] Most tellingly, on the feast day of St Monica in 1493 the friars listed two incoming payments, one after another, the first 'dalle mantellate lire quatro' and the next 'dalla badessa di Sancta Monicha lire tredici', confirming that the two groups, though linked in more ways than one, were distinct from one another.[87]

The will of Bartolomea di Rinier del Pace, whose bequest of 1501 was cited both by Fra Egidio and in the late sixteenth-century *memoriale* of obligations, offers another clue for identifying the proprietors of the St Monica chapel.[88] It states that, following the death of her husband, Bartolomea had become an Augustinian *commessa* (pensioner) of S. Spirito. Not wishing to take solemn vows, she had dedicated her life to a state of widowhood and had professed simple vows as a member of the 'amantellate ordinis Sancti Augustinini de Florentia'. The documents do not indicate whether she lived communally with other tertiaries or alone, but the nunnery of S. Monaca is not mentioned. In fact, various women are listed in friars' records as 'nostra commessa' (our pensioner), but the nature of their relationship with S. Spirito itself remains unclear.[89] They should not be confused with servant nuns who are typically referred to as 'converse', as indeed they are in the S. Monaca constitutions. In short, the most substantial bequest for obligations at the altar of St Monica was made directly to the friars of S. Spirito, by a woman with no declared affiliation with the second order nuns S. Monaca.

The archival records, as well as the evidence from chapels dedicated to St Monica in other Augustinian churches, give cause for a revision of the traditional tendency among scholars to conflate the 'donne amantalate di Santa Monicha' cited in the 1487 chapel bestowal document with the nuns of S. Monaca. It is apparent that numerous communities of Augustinian women resided in the vicinity — the second order nuns of S. Monaca and also those

85 Florence, ASF, CRSGF 122, 67, fol. 115[r]; ASF, CRSGF 122, 67, fol. 129[r]. It is not clear whether Mona Filippa and Mona Pippa in these two records are one and the same woman.

86 Florence, ASF, CRSGF 122, 8, fol. 40[v]. S. Pancrazio payment is found at: ASF, CRSGF 122, 1, fol. 235[v]; ASF, CRSGF 122, 8, fols 57[r], 121[v], 126[v]; ASF, CRSGF 122, 66, fol. 46[r] n. 1 & fol. 47[v] n. 31.

87 Florence, ASF, CRSGF 122, 8, fol. 48[r].

88 See n. 31.

89 Florence, ASF, CRSGF 122, 66, 11[v], 12[r], 13[v]–14[r].

of S. Elisabetta delle Convertite as well as at least one, though probably several, communities of lay and tertiary women — all of which operated under the supervision of the friars in the motherhouse.[90] And although the tertiary 'amantalate' held patronal rights to the chapel, probably taking responsibility for its upkeep in addition to contributing funds towards masses held therein, the life of the chapel also relied on friars' commitment to the cult of St Monica as well as the monetary offerings of the nuns of S. Monaca. Clearly then, the chapel of St Monica was a place where the devotional activity and institutional agendas of the Augustinian friars, second order nuns, and tertiary and lay female communities coexisted and intermingled.[91]

Proclaiming the Augustinian Network: The Iconography of the *Saint Monica* Altarpiece in Context

How might we characterize these institutional agendas? This question is best explored by examining the choices Botticini made in conceiving the altarpiece's imagery. For, though the painting clearly relies on the established iconographic tradition of 'founder' images, it also departs from precedent in significant ways. Most obviously, it is Monica, and not Augustine, who issues the scroll. A late trecento fresco in the choir of the Augustinian nuns at S. Marta in Siena is an early example of an image depicting the bestowal of the rule on a group of Augustinians which includes women (Figure 4.2). In that case, Augustine is seated on a throne surrounded by members of the order, who are smaller in scale, and he hands an unravelled scroll with legible excerpts of the rule to a representative from each group.[92] A fresco in the Augustinian nunnery church in the Umbrian hill town of Cascia depicts Augustine handing his mother

---

90 Payment records for the Convertite for the *feste* of St Elisabeth, St Mary Magdalen and St Sebastian are found in ASF, CRSGF 122, 8, fols 12[r], 21[r], 36[r], 37[r], 43[r], 44[v], 51[r], 57[r], 59[r], 120[r], 125[r].

91 Tertiary life for women on the Italian peninsula in the pre-Tridentine period took countless forms. On the whole, the tertiary path was particularly attractive to urban widows or younger women who perhaps did not have the means for the dowry typically required to marry. These women, members of the Order of Penitence, followed the rule of the mendicant order with which they were associated, adapted to accord with their life in the world as opposed to inside the convent. They took the habit of that order, or a variation of it. In earlier centuries, they congregated for their devotions and charitable works, but lived at home. By the fifteenth century communal living was increasingly common among tertiary women. The extent to which they were connected with the official cooperation of the order, varied between orders and from community to community. Franciscan tertiaries, for example, typically had strong institutional affiliation, whereas Dominican tertiaries could be only loosely connected to the Order of Preachers, if at all (see Lehmijoki-Gardner, *Dominican Penitent Women*, p. 7). For a useful discussion of the complexity of characterizing tertiary life and the penitential movement in early modern Italy see Gill, 'Open Monasteries for Women', pp. 17–23 and Gill, *Penitents, Pinzochere and Mantellate*.

92 Corsi, *Gli affreschi medievali in Santa Marta*, p. 37. Corsi provides a bibliography for other images of St Augustine giving the rule (n. 39).

Figure 4.2. Martino di Bartolomeo (?), *Saint Augustine Giving the Rule*, Siena, former convent of S. Marta. Early fifteenth century. © Biblioteca comunale degli Intronati di Siena.

an unbound scroll with the opening lines of his rule: 'Ante omnia, sorores carissimae diligatur Deus, deinde pr[oximus]' (Before all else, beloved sisters, love God, and then your neighbour). St Monica acts as intermediary between her son and the community of women kneeling at her feet (Figure 4.3).[93] The above-mentioned constitutions of S. Monaca has a remarkable illuminated

93 The fresco was commissioned by the abbess of the nunnery in 1444. See Cascia, *La Chiesa di Sant'Agostino* (online publications in bibliography).

Figure 4.3. Unknown, *Saint Augustine Giving the Rule to Saint Monica and the Augustinian Nuns*, Cascia, S. Agostino. Mid-fifteenth century. Reproduced with the permission of Associazione dei Comuni della Valnerina Servizio Turistico Associato del Comprensorio della Valnerina.

Figure 4.4. *Saint Augustine Giving the Rule to Saint Monica and the Augustinian nuns*, Los Angeles, University of California MS 170/880, frontispiece. *c.* 1475–1500. Reproduced with permission Library Special Collections, Charles E. Young Research Library, UCLA.

frontispiece which shows the nuns kneeling to receive the rule and a blessing from the enthroned Augustine, with Monica standing behind them (Figure 4.4). Her left hand rests protectively on one of the nuns' shoulders, and with the other she makes a gesture as if presenting them to her son. The S. Marta fresco shows the women receiving the rule directly from Augustine, as does the S. Monaca manuscript but with St Monica as an intercessor, whereas in the Cascia fresco St Augustine hands the rule to St Monica to pass on to her daughters. In Botticini's altarpiece, St Monica has moved centre stage.

This privileging of St Monica reflects her newly elevated status following the active campaign to promote her within the order's hierarchy of saints and is discernible in other Augustinian churches.[94] In order to emphasize her status, Botticini seems to have consciously modelled his work on images of the enthroned Virgin, an association that would have been reinforced by a peppering of altarpieces depicting that subject in the nearby chapels at S. Spirito.[95] Enthroned in a *hortus conclusus*, Monica even rests her book on her knee in a comparable position to the placement of Christ in the other altarpieces. Parallels between Monica and the Virgin are also evident in the predella where the scenes of the *Marriage* and the *Death of Monica* draw on the traditional iconography of analogous scenes from the life of Mary. By casting Monica in the image of the Virgin, Botticini mirrors the way in which Monica had fashioned herself in the Virgin's image by adopting her widow's robes and belt. And since the clothes that Monica wears are also worn by her attendant devotees, then they too, through the conduit of Monica, are modelled in the Virgin's image.

In the fifteenth-century Florentine context, the (probably slightly later) panel of *Saint Catherine of Siena Giving the Rule to Members of the Second and Third Orders*, attributed to Cosimo Rosselli, offers an important point of comparison (Figure 4.5).[96] The similarities between Botticini's altarpiece and Rosselli's *Saint Catherine* panel are numerous. However, their differences prove especially useful in understanding how the two paintings were experienced as well as in clarifying represented distinctions between second and third orders.

First, St Monica's book and scroll are closed, while those of St Catherine are open. In the earlier frescoes depicting St Augustine in Siena and Cascia, the unravelled scroll containing legible excerpts was employed as an established iconographic motif that made visual reference to the rule, and to the

94 For example, Monica was also given special prominence in Benozzo Gozzoli's fresco cycle depicting episodes from the life of St Augustine (1464–1465) painted in the high chapel of the Augustinian church of S. Gimignano; see Cole Ahl, *Benozzo Gozzoli*, p. 122.

95 Similarities to images of the enthroned Virgin were also observed by Holgate, 'The Cult of Saint Monica', p. 203.

96 The provenance of this painting, now in the National Galleries of Scotland (NG 1030), is not known, but scholarly debates have centred on S. Domenico del Maglio and the Capitolo of S. Caterina in via Gualfondo (see Thomas, *Art and Piety in the Female Religious Communities*, pp. 254–69; Padoa Rizzo, 'Sulla iconografia', pp. 281–82).

Figure 4.5. Cosimo Rosselli, *Saint Catherine of Siena Giving the Rule to the Second and Third Orders of Saint Dominic*, Edinburgh, National Galleries of Scotland (Inv: 1030), 1490s(?). © National Galleries of Scotland.

community's commitment to it.[97] In Rosselli's panel too it seems likely that the script on the book and scroll were once legible. Indeed, Thomas, who argued that the book and the scroll symbolize the regulations and the rule

---

97   The long tradition of this iconographic motif in the female monastic context is demonstrated by an early trecento missal for the Benedictine nuns of S. Pier Maggiore. Benedict hands the nuns a scroll inscribed with the opening lines of his rule: 'ausculta o filii precepta magistri' ('Listen, O my child, to the teachings of the Master'). Florence, SAMF, MS 325, fol. 225ʳ; see Bertani, 'Codici del monastero benedettino femminile', p. 150.

respectively, has noted that in Rosselli's painting the texts were not only legible but that St Catherine also points to specific sections.[98] It has been suggested that the image may have been intended for the commemoration of, or as the backdrop to, a profession ceremony.[99] In contrast, the book and the scroll in Botticini's altarpiece are closed, thus specific reference to a particular text is removed. This might plausibly be explained by the fact that the altarpiece's intended audience did not follow the same set of guidelines for monastic living and so Botticini elected to make visual reference to their commitment to the authority of the order, in the person of St Monica, without the specificity engendered by inscriptions.

Second, except for the two diminutive figures in white that kneel in the foreground, Botticini's women all wear the same habit. Rosselli, on the other hand, depicted women in the distinctive habits of the second and third order as well as a young woman in secular dress, perhaps also a postulant. Given the historic significance of the habit as a means of asserting institutional identity, Botticini's careful depiction of the black habit, worn by both second and third order Augustinians, repeated fifteen times to varying degrees of visibility, amounts to an affirmation of the Augustinian corporation at large. In the 'sameness' of Monica and her company, Botticini's altarpiece can be associated with a tradition of self-fashioning as 'corporation' that was characteristic among male orders, such as earlier Dominican imagery, which Joanna Cannon has identified as a means of celebrating the order 'through an assembly of notable friars'.[100] These images, such as the panel by the Master of the Dominican Effigies, which gives the artist his sobriquet, 'offered a suitable method for expressing multiple aims and aspirations' of the order. Another example, itself a hybrid of the 'corporate' image and the 'founder' image, is the fresco by Neri di Bicci formerly in the cloister of the Vallombrosan community of S. Pancrazio, now in S. Trinita in Florence. In the tradition of 'founder' images, Giovanni Gualberto, who established the order, is enthroned at the centre with an open book inscribed with words from the rule. The image also nods to the 'corporate' image tradition because he is surrounded by saints and *beati* of the order as opposed to an anonymous Vallombrosan congregation. Such group images, where members are depicted with painstaking individuality but are homogenised by their shared habit, were intended to emphasise the kinship and corporate identity of the order. In Botticini's *Saint Monica* panel the proclamation of the Augustinian corporate identity is especially salient because all branches of the order wore the same readily identifiable black

---

98 Thomas, *Art and Piety in the Female Religious Communities*, pp. 263–64.

99 Padoa Rizzo suggested that the iconography of Rosselli's painting makes particular allusion to the charitable vocation of the Catherinian sisters and that it may have been commissioned to mark the profession of a certain sister at the convent. Padoa Rizzo, 'Sulla iconografia', p. 284.

100 Cannon, *Religious Poverty, Visual Riches*, p. 185.

habit with the tightly drawn in leather belt. Thus, the wearer — friar, nun, or tertiary — becomes a standard-bearer for the entire Augustinian entity.

Finally, Botticini appears to have taken certain measures to ensure that the ceremonial nature of the scene, detectable in Rosselli's work, is downplayed. He included no attendant saints and so the gathering is exclusively female. The absence of standing figures enabled him to wrap the congregation of women around Monica's throne more completely and to depict them in greater numbers. In Rosselli's painting the women's heads arrive at the height of Catherine's knees. This elevation of the central protagonist, in addition to the buttressing presence of the saints who flank her throne, introduces a strong sense of hierarchy as the kneeling devotees crane their necks to face their saintly founder.[101] In Botticini's panel, although Monica is raised above the nuns and also appears on a marginally larger scale than they do, there is nevertheless a quality of intimacy that sets it apart from Rosselli's painting. Monica is depicted as first among equals. The fact that so few of the women actually look at her heightens the relative informality of the scene. Botticini also made the unusual decision to mask three of the women's faces entirely. The impression is that the women have been captured in the midst not of a ceremony, but a community meeting, neither ritualistic nor intended to be witnessed or observed.

Certain aspects of Botticini's image seem to have been included so as indicate that this collective of Augustinian women represents, at least in part, second order nuns. The two young girls in the foreground are identifiable as postulants by their white attire and their hair, which is loose over their shoulders. Numerous comparisons lend weight to this reading. A similar, bareheaded figure is present among the women in the S. Marta fresco in Siena, who is presumably a postulant. Paolo Schiavo's fresco depicting the *Crucifixion with Nuns of the Order* at S. Apollonia in Florence also shows postulants clad in white with no veil. In the Florentine Augustinian context, there is further precedent for such figures both in the *Madonna della Misericordia* (c. 1380) which originates from the community of S. Maria dei Candeli and also an antiphonary from the nunnery of S. Gaggio, though in both of these examples, the young girls wear dark robes.[102] Such junior members are not typically found in images that represent tertiary or confraternal groups of devotees. And, even though the Augustinian tertiary order was described as

---

101 An earlier altarpiece produced by somebody in the workshop of Fra Filippo Lippi, perhaps Fra Diamante, showing *Saint Francis Giving the Rule to Tertiary Women*, today in the Gemäldegalerie, Berlin (inv: 1131) also has a hierarchical composition, similar to Rosselli's, with the enthroned St Francis and his flanking male saints painted on a larger scale than the women who kneel at their feet. (Pittaluga, *Filippo Lippi*, p. 199).

102 The Candeli *Madonna della Misericordia* is in the Galleria dell'Accademia in Florence (Inv. 1890, 8562). S. Gaggio, situated about a mile outside the city's southern gate, was also under the jurisdiction of S. Spirito (see n. 49). The antiphonary is now in the Museo di S. Marco in Florence (Inv. 1890, n. 10073, fol. 19ᵛ); see Kanter and Palladino, *Fra Angelico*, p. 229.

comprising 'maidens, matrons and widows' in the papal bull of 1399, records
from S. Spirito indicate that the *mantellate* groups were more typically made
up of widows or older unmarried women. Therefore, we might interpret the
young girls clad in white in Botticini's altarpiece as evidence that some of the
women wearing the habit represent professed nuns.

The depiction of different types of documents may also signal that the
community depicted comprises both second or third order women. Thomas's
observation that in Rosselli's *Saint Catherine* panel the scroll (handed to the
nun) represents the rule while the book (handed to the tertiaries) represents
the regulations or statutes, generally holds up in other 'founder' type images
of the fifteenth century. For example, in a fresco depicting *Saint Catherine of
Siena with Dominican Tertiary Women* in the friary of S. Domenico in Prato,
St Catherine holds a book, while in the Cascia and Siena frescoes, the nuns
are handed scrolls. Similarly, in a mid-quattrocento panel showing *Saint
Francis Giving the Rule to Tertiary Women*, today in Berlin, the tertiaries are
handed a book.[103] On occasion, nuns are depicted receiving a book, such as
in the S. Monaca frontispiece and also the antiphonary from S. Gaggio, but
the tertiaries and the confraternities are never, to my knowledge, shown
receiving the scroll. The fact that Botticini depicts St Monica with both the
book and the scroll may be an allusion to her role as patron of both regular
and non-regular Augustinian women, both of whom are to be found among
her company.

Members of the community of S. Monaca probably entered the church of
S. Spirito rarely, if at all, by the time Botticini's altarpiece was installed around
1487. However, the postulants and the scroll served as a subtle reminder to
others who did enter the church of the nuns' roles as benefactors to the site,
their presence within the neighbourhood and their close association with the
cult of St Monica. It also would have provided a conspicuous reminder to the
friars of their obligations regarding the nuns, as outlined in the contract of
1477. The aisle chapel, prominently located in the nave of the friars' church,
had a shared dedication with the nuns' church, and could thereby function
as an extension of the nunnery. Botticini's image 'placed' the nuns in the aisle
chapel, unmistakably Augustinian in their black mantles, thus allowing them to
be present alongside their tertiary sisters though physically absent.[104] Indeed,
Botticini may have employed the unusual device of concealing some of the
women's faces entirely to allude to the fact that the altarpiece is representative
of many more women and girls, both enclosed and non-enclosed, than the
sixteen depicted.

---

103   See n. 101.
104   A mid-sixteenth-century ceremonial originating from the nunnery of S. Monaca contains a
frontispiece depicting the enthroned Monica bestowing the rule upon the nuns, apparently
closely based on Botticini's earlier image. This implies that, at least by 1543 when the
manuscript was produced, the nuns felt some institutional affinity with the chapel in the
friars' church; Christies, *The Helmut N. Friedlaender Library Sale*, 23 April 2001, lot. 9.

The various fifteenth-century works explored here, and others besides, whose iconography is comparable to Botticini's *Saint Monica* panel — at least those for which the provenance is certain — tend to originate from the headquarters of the community depicted. Botticini's panel has always stood inside the friary church, a space that was associated with and maintained by the male brothers. The *Saint Catherine* fresco in S. Domenico in Prato is an important exception. This work shares the 'founder' image qualities of the *Monica* panel, with a central founder-saint holding a book and surrounded by members of the order who are dressed identically to her. The two differ, however, in their location and intended purpose, since the Prato work, a fresco not an altarpiece, once adorned the tertiaries' communal tomb in the friary cloister. Not only was its function primarily commemorative, but its location in the cloister limited its audience. At S. Spirito, Botticini's altarpiece does not appear to have marked the site of a tomb for Augustinian women. It is not impossible that tertiary women continued to be buried inside the friars' church after the fire of 1471, but there is no record of this. The nuns of Santa Monaca were entombed in the *chiesa vecchia* of their own convent.[105]

This is not to say that the altarpiece served no commemorative function. At least by 1453, S. Spirito possessed a relic of St Monica — 'un pezzo del capo di Santa Monaca' ('a piece of St Monica's head') — perhaps a fragment of her skull.[106] As already mentioned, the tomb chapel of St Monica in Rome housed the saint's remains and contained a precious reliquary for her head. If indeed the 'pezzo del capo' was a piece of St Monica's skull, we might deduce that the Florentine community had obtained its relic, which must have been tiny since it was kept in the pouch of a rosary, from their sister community in Rome.[107] It may be significant that by the sixteenth century at least, the chapel of St Monica in Rome contained a processional standard depicting the saint accompanied by two *sorelle*. This may be further evidence of Augustinian tertiaries in another city adopting similar iconographic schemes within their chapel of St Monica so as to create visual links that underscored their institutional ties.[108] Even so, while Botticini's altarpiece may have served to signal the presence of this relic and so to memorialize the cult of the saint, his carefully devised depiction of Monica and her company, clearly visible in the public area of the church, also functioned on a level beyond the purely commemorative. As we have seen, the artist deftly and meticulously combined and manipulated established iconographic precedents in order to celebrate not just Monica herself, modelled on the example of the Virgin, but also her daughters, who were cast in her image. While the authoritative figure of Monica enfolds the

---

105   Florence, ASF, CRSGF 131, 92, I, n. 1, fol. 5ʳ.
106   See n. 82.
107   Richa, *Notizie Istoriche*, pp. 39–45 does not mention the relic of St Monica in his description of the relics at S. Spirito, although he does highlight a few of the community's most significant examples.
108   Mazzon, 'La cappella di S. Monica', p. 222.

women into her ministry, they huddle around her like a protective shield.[109] As such, the altarpiece communicates a sense of the women's affiliation with, even possession of, St Monica rather than just their devotional zeal towards her. The image is a declaration of the women's custody of the chapel but also of their privileged position as the heirs to her legacy.

Conclusion

The documentary evidence, though fragmentary, makes it clear that the chapel in S. Spirito dedicated to St Monica was a place of confluence for different strands of the order within the district, a situation which belonged to a wider tradition in fifteenth-century Augustinian churches. The women's signature black habits, which would have been instantly recognisable as those worn by all members of the Order of Hermits, provided a visual reminder of their spiritual legitimacy as sanctioned by their holy patroness, St Monica. When the friars stood at the altar to perform Mass, the corporation would have been complete. Thus, the altarpiece served to promote the Augustinian network and strengthen its position within a neighbourhood where rival monastic organisations were jostling for the loyalty, and the alms, of the local lay public.

The great majority of chapels at S. Spirito were under the patronage of private families, and housed altarpieces designed to cater to their particular devotions as well as to reflect their public standing in the district. Botticini's altarpiece is usefully understood within the parameters of a tradition of family chapel patronage, in which the spiritual lives but also the secular interests of the patrons are tended to. As with the nearby altarpieces, rather than being conceived exclusively for the contemplation of the women, a broader audience was anticipated and accommodated in Botticini's design. The panel's prominent position in the public realm of the church, alongside the nave, meant that its iconography was devised both for the devotional needs of the Augustinian 'family' but also as a means of proclaiming its standing to the wider world. Far from having an 'enclosed nature', according to Thomas's characterization, its imagery was carefully conceived with a frequently changing and disparate audience in mind: regular visitors to the chapel — tertiaries, hermit friars, local lay women — and also more casual frequenters of the church space — visiting clergy, secular officials and the citizens of the Oltrarno neighbourhood. Even more ingenious, it operated in the service of those who were not present, the nuns of S. Monaca, by making them visible *in absentia*. Today, Botticini's altarpiece survives as a poignant vestige of the once thriving Augustinian network that underpinned the spiritual life of the local district.

---

109 A similar visual device can be observed in Cosimo Rosselli's fresco in the *Cappella del Miracolo* in S. Ambrogio where the nuns are shown clustered around the miraculous relic in an apparently conscious pictorial statement of proprietorship. See Holmes, *Fra Filippo Lippi*, p. 244.

Works Cited

Manuscripts and Archival Sources

Florence, Archivio di Stato di Firenze (ASF)
 Corporazioni Religiose Soppresse dal Governo Francese (CRSGF)
 ——, 122 (S. Spirito)
 ——, 131 (S. Monaca)
 Notarile Moderno
 ——, Protocolli 259–269
Florence, Biblioteca Nazionale di Firenze (BNCF)
 MS Magliabechiano, Cl. XXVII, 188
Florence, Seminario Arcivescovile Maggiore Fiorentino (SAMF)
 MS 325
Los Angeles, University of California (UCLA)
 MS 170/880

Primary Sources

Bullarium ordinis eremitarum sancti Augustini, ed. by Lorenzo Orsacchi da Empoli
 (Rome: Scuola tipografica salesiana, 1628)
*Compendio dell'origine, miracoli, indulgenze, indulti, et privilegi appostolici della Sacra
 Cintura … si ritrova anco in S. Eufemia di Verona* (Verona: B. Merlo, 1642)

Secondary Works

Acidini Luchinat, Cristina, ed., *La Chiesa e il Convento di Santo Spirito a Firenze*
 (Florence: Cassa di Risparmio di Firenze, 1996)
Andrews, Frances, *The Other Friars: The Carmelite, Augustinian, Sack and Pied
 Friars in the Middle Ages* (Woodbridge: Boydell, 2006)
Arthur, Kathleen G., 'New Evidence for a Scribal-Nun's Art: Maria di Ormanno
 degli Albizzi at San Gaggio', *Mitteilungen des Kunsthistorischen Institutes in
 Florenz*, 59.2 (2017), 271–80
Bacci, Pèleo, 'La cappella delle suore della penitenza detta la "Cappella delle volte
 in San Domenico di Siena" — ricerche sulle sue fasi costruttive', *Bullettino
 senese di storia patria*, ser. 3, 49 (1942), 3–21
Banker, James, and Kate Lowe, 'Female Voice, Male Authority: A Nun's Narrative
 of the Regularization of a Female Franciscan House in Borgo San Sepolcro in
 1500', *The Sixteenth Century Journal*, 40, no. 3 (Fall, 2009), 651–77
Benvenuti Papi, Anna, 'Donne religiose nella Firenze del due-trecento. Appunti
 per una ricerca in corso', in *Le Mouvement confraternel au moyen âge: France,
 Italie, Suisse* (Rome: École française de Rome, 1987), pp. 41–82
Berenson, Bernard, *Italian Pictures of the Renaissance: Florentine School*, 2 vols
 (London: Phaidon, 1962)

Bertani, L., 'Codici del monastero benedettino femminile di San Pier Maggiore, a Firenze', in, *Codici liturgici miniati dei Benedettini in Toscana*, ed. by Maria Grazia Ciardi Duprè Dal Poggetto (Florence: Centro d'Incontro della Cetosa di Firenze, 1982), pp. 141–60

Blume, Andrew C., 'The Chapel of Santa Monica in Santo Spirito and Francesco Botticini', *Arte cristiana*, 83 (1995), 289–92

Blume, Dieter, and Dorothee Hansen, 'Agostino *pater et praeceptor* di un nuovo ordine religioso: considerazioni sulla propaganda illustrata degli eremiti agostiniani' in *Arte e spiritualità nell'ordine agostiniano e il Convento San Nicola a Tolentino*, ed. by Centro Studi 'Agostino Trapè' (Rome: Argos, *c.* 1992), pp. 77–92

Botto, Carlo, 'L'edificazione della Chiesa di Santo Spirito in Firenze', *Rivista d'Arte*, 13, no. 4 (1931), 477–511

Burke, Jill, *Changing Patrons: Social Identity and the Visual Arts in Renaissance Florence* (University Park: Pennslyvania State University Press, 2004)

Busignani, Alberto, *Verrocchio* (Florence: Sadea/Sansoni Editore, 1966)

Busignani, Alberto, and Raffaello Bencini, *Le Chiese di Firenze, Quartiere di Santo Spirito* (Florence: Sansoni, 1974)

Cannon, Joanna, *Religious Poverty, Visual Riches: Art in the Dominican Churches of Central Italy in the Thirteenth and Fourteenth Centuries* (New Haven: Yale University Press, 2013)

Capretti, Elena, *The Building Complex of Santo Spirito* (Florence: 'Lo Studiolo' Cooperativa, 1991)

——, 'La Pinacoteca Sacra', in *La Chiesa e il Convento di Santo Spirito a Firenze*, ed. by Cristina Acidini Luchinat (Florence: Cassa di Risparmio di Firenze, 1996), pp. 239–301

Catena, Claudio, *Le Carmelitane: Storia e Spiritualità* (Rome: Institutum Carmelitanum, 1969)

Clark, Gillian, *Monica: An Ordinary Saint* (Oxford: Oxford University Press, 2015)

Cole Ahl, Diane, *Benozzo Gozzoli* (New Haven: Yale University Press, 1996)

Corsi, Maria, *Gli affreschi medievali in Santa Marta a Siena: studio iconografico* (Siena: Cantagalli, 2005)

Dunlop, Anne, 'Introduction: The Augustinians, the Mendicant Orders, and Early-Renaissance Art', in *Art and the Augustinian Order in Early Renaissance Italy*, ed. by Louise Bourdua and Anne Dunlop (Aldershot: Ashgate, 2007), pp. 1–15

Duval, Sylvie, 'Mulieres religiosae and sorores clausae', in *Mulieres religiosae: Shaping Female Spiritual Authority in the Medieval and Early Modern Period*, ed. by V. Fraeters and I. De Gier (Turnhout: Brepols, 2014), pp. 193–218

Emery, Richard W., 'The Second Council of Lyons and the Mendicant Orders', *The Catholic Historical Review*, 3 (Oct., 1953), 257–71

Esposito, Anna, 'I gruppi bizzocali a Roma nel'400 e le sorores de poenitentia agostiniane', in *Santa Monica nell'Urbe dalla tarda antichità, al Rinascimento. Storia, Agiografia, Arte. Atti del Convegno*, ed. by Maria Chiabò, Maurizio Gargano, and Rocco Ronzani (Rome: Centro culturale agostiniano, 2011), pp. 157–88

Evangelisti, Silvia, '"We Do Not Have It, and We Do Not Want It": Women, Power, and Convent Reform in Florence', *The Sixteenth Century Journal*, 34 (2003), 677–700

——, *Nuns: A History of Convent Life, 1450–1700* (Oxford: Oxford University Press, 2007)

Gill, Katherine, 'Open Monasteries for Women in Late Medieval and Early Modern Italy: Two Roman Examples' in *The Crannied Wall: Women, Religion, and the Arts in Early Modern Europe*, ed. by Craig Monson (Ann Arbor: University of Michigan Press, 1992), pp. 15–47

——, 'Penitents, Pinzochere and Mantellate: Varieties of Women's Religious Communities in Central Italy, c. 1300–1520' (unpublished doctoral dissertation, Princeton University, 1994)

Gutierrez, David, 'La Biblioteca di Santo Spirito in Firenze nella metà del secolo XV', *Analecta Augustiniana*, 25 (1962), 5–88

——, *The Augustinians in the Middle Ages, 1357–1517*, trans. by Thomas Martin (Villanova: Augustinian Historical Institute, 1983)

Hiller, Diana, *Gendered Perceptions of Florentine Last Supper Frescoes, c. 1350–1490* (Aldershot: Ashgate, 2014)

Holgate, Ian, 'The Cult of St Monica in Quattrocento Italy: Her Place in Augustinian Iconography, Devotion and Legend', *Papers of the British School at Rome*, 71 (2003), 181–206

——, 'Santa Monica, Venice and the Vivarini', in *Art and the Augustinian Order in Early Renaissance Italy*, ed. by Louise Bourdua and Anne Dunlop (Aldershot: Ashgate, 2007), pp. 163–81

Holmes, Megan, *Fra Filippo Lippi: The Carmelite Painter* (New Haven: Yale University Press, 1999)

Howard, Peter, 'Preaching and Liturgy in Renaissance Florence', in *Prédication et Liturgie Au Moyen Âge*, ed. by Nicole Bériou and Franco Morenzoni (Turnhout: Brepols, 2008), pp. 313–33

Jotischky, Andrew, *The Carmelites and Antiquity: Mendicants and Their Pasts in the Middle Ages* (Oxford: Oxford University Press, 2002)

Kanter, Laurence B., and Pia Palladino, *Fra Angelico* (New York: The Metropolitan Museum of Art, 2005)

Laferrière, Anik, 'The Doubting Augustine: The Deletion of Monica from Fourteenth-Century Vitae Augustini in the Augustinian Order of Hermits', *Studies in Church History*, 52 (2016), 150–63

Lehmijoki-Gardner, Maiju, *Dominican Penitent Women* (New Jersey: Paulist, 2005)

Maiocchi, Rodolfo, and Nazzareno Casacca, *Codex Diplomaticus Ordinis Erematarum S. Augustini Papiae*, vol. 1 (Papiae: Rossetti, 1902)

Manetti, Antonio, *Vita di Filippo Brunelleschi: preceduta da La novella del Grasso*, ed. by Domenico Di Robertis (Milan: Il polifilo, 1976)

Markowsky, Barbara, 'Eine Gruppe bemalter Paliotti in Florenz und der Toskana und ihre textilen Vorbilder', *Mitteilungen des Kunsthistorischen Institutes in Florenz*, 17 (1973), 105–40

Maroni Lumbroso, Matizia, and Antonio Martini, *Le confraternite romane nelle loro chiese* (Rome: Fondazione M. Besso, 1963)

Mattioli, Nicola, *Fra Giovanni da Salerno dell'Ordine romitano di S. Agostino del secolo XIV e le sue opere volgari inedite*, Antologia Agostiniana, vol. 3 (Rome, 1901)

Mazzon, Antonella, 'La cappella di S. Monica in S. Agostino. Riflessioni sulla documentazione dei secoli XV–XVI', in *Santa Monica nell'Urbe dalla tarda antichità, al Rinascimento. Storia, Agiografia, Arte. Atti del Convegno*, ed. by Maria Chiabò, Maurizio Gargano, and Rocco Ronzani (Rome: Centro culturale agostiniano, 2011), pp. 205–26

McArdle, Frank, *Altopascio: A Study in Tuscan Rural Society, 1587–1784* (Cambridge: Cambridge University Press, 2005)

More, Alison, 'Dynamics of Regulation, Innovation, and Invention' in *A Companion to Observant Reform in the Late Middle Ages and Beyond*, ed. by James D. Mixson and Bert Roest (Leiden: Brill, 2015), pp. 85–110

Nardinocchi, Elena, 'Arredi e Paramenti Sacri', in *La Chiesa e il Convento di Santo Spirito a Firenze*, ed. by Cristina Acidini Luchinat (Florence: Cassa di Risparmio di Firenze, 1996), pp. 373–87

O'Malley, Michelle, 'Altarpieces and Agency: The Altarpiece of the Society of the Purification and Its "Invisible Skein of Relations"', *Art History*, 28, no. 4 (2005), 416–41

Paatz, Walter, and Elisabeth Valentiner Paatz, *Die Kirchen von Florenz: ein kunstgeschichtliches Handbuch*, 6 vols (Frankfurt am Main: Vittorio Klostermann, 1940)

Padoa Rizzo, Anna, 'Per Francesco Botticini', *Antichità Viva*, 15, no. 5 (1976), 3–19

—— , 'Sulla iconografia e la destinazione di una importante tavola di Cosimo Rosselli', in *La Toscana al tempo di Lorenzo il Magnifico. Politica Economia Cultura Arte, Convegno di Studi promosso dalle Università di Firenze, Pisa e Siena, 5–8 novembre 1992*, ed. by Riccardo Fubini (Pisa: Pacini, 1996), pp. 277–88

Piatti, Pierantonio, *Il movimento femminile agostiniano nel Medioevo: momenti di storia dell'Ordine eremitano* (Rome: Città Nuova, 2007)

—— , 'Il culto di santa Monica e gli Eremitani di S. Agostino: una riflessione introduttiva', in *Santa Monica nell'Urbe dalla tarda antichità, al Rinascimento. Storia, Agiografia, Arte. Atti del Convegno*, ed. by Maria Chiabò, Maurizio Gargano, and Rocco Ronzani (Rome: Centro culturale agostiniano, 2011), pp. xi–xx

Pittaluga, Mary, *Filippo Lippi* (Florence: Del Turco, 1949)

Richa, Giuseppe, *Notizie istoriche delle chiese fiorentine, divise ne' suoi quartieri*, 10 vols (Florence: Viviani, 1754–1762)

Ruda, Jeffrey, 'A 1434 Building Programme for San Lorenzo in Florence', *The Burlington Magazine*, 120, no. 903 (June 1978), 358–61

—— , *Fra Filippo Lippi: Life and Work with a Complete Catalogue* (London: Phaidon, 1993)

Saalman, Howard, 'San Lorenzo: The 1434 Chapel Project', *The Burlington Magazine*, 120, no. 903 (June 1978), 361–64

Santi, Bruno, ed., *Neri di Bicci: Le ricordanze (10 marzo 1453–24 aprile 1475)* (Pisa: Marlin, 1976)

Schmarsow, August, *Festschrift zu Ehren des Kunsthistorischen Instituts in Florenz / dargebracht vom Kunsthistorischen Institut der Universität Leipzig* (Leipzig: A Liebeskind, 1897)

Sciacca, C., 'Reconstructing the Laudario of Sant'Agnese' in *Florence at the Dawn of the Renaissance: Painting and Illumination, 1300–1350*, ed. by Christine Sciacca (Los Angeles: J. Paul Getty Trust, 2012), pp. 219–35

Simari, Maria Matilde, 'Profilo storico-architettonico di un monastero fiorentino del quattrocento: Santa Monaca', *Rivista d'Arte*, 39 (1987), 147–90

Strocchia, Sharon T., *Nuns and Nunneries in Renaissance Florence* (Baltimore: Johns Hopkins University Press, 2009)

Thomas, Anabel, *Art and Piety in the Female Religious Communities of Renaissance Italy* (Cambridge: Cambridge University Press, 2003)

Torelli, Luigi, *Secoli Agostiniani overo Historia generale del sacro ordine eremitano del gran dottore di Santa Chiesa S. Aurelio Agostino vescovo d'Hippona*, 8 vols (Bologna: Monti, 1659–1686)

Vasciaveo, Chiara, *Una Storia di Donne: Il Carmelo Santa Maria degli Angeli e S. M. Maddalena de' Pazzi di Firenze* (Rome: Edizioni Carmelitane, 2013)

Venturini, Lisa, *Francesco Botticini* (Florence: Edifir, 1984)

Walsh, Katherine, 'The Observance: Sources for a History of the Observant Reform Movement in the Order of Augustinian Friars in the Fourteenth and Fifteenth Centuries', *Rivista di storia della chiesa in Italia*, 31 (1977), 40–67

Warr, Cordelia, 'Hermits, Habits and History: The Dress of the Augustinian Hermits', in *Art and the Augustinian Order in Early Renaissance Italy*, ed. by Louise Bourdua and Anne Dunlop (Aldershot: Ashgate, 2007), pp. 17–28

Weaver, Elissa B., ed., *Antonia Pulci: Saints' Lives and Bible Stories for the Stage, A Bilingual Edition*, trans. James Wyatt Cook (Toronto: Iter, 2010)

Webb, Diana, 'Eloquence and Education: A Humanist Approach to Hagiography', *Journal of Ecclesiastical History*, 31 (1980), 19–30

Wyatt Cook, James, and Barbara Collier Cook, eds, *Antonia Pulci: Florentine Drama for Convent and Festival: Seven Sacred Plays* (London: University of Chicago Press, 1996)

Online Publications

Cascia, La Chiesa di Sant'Agostino, Servizio Turistico Associato della Valnerina (2015) http://www.umbriaturismo.net/wp-content/uploads/2015/03/sant_agostino.pdf [accessed 01 August 2019]

SAUNDRA WEDDLE

Identity, Alliance, and Reform in Early Modern Venetian Convents

The sixteenth-century illustrated chronicle of the Augustinian convent of S. Maria delle Vergini in Venice refers to the great scandal caused at the convent by the patriarch of Venice, Antonio Contarini, and especially his vicar, Ottaviano Brittonio, whom the chronicler disparages as the 'son of a Jewish mother', an associate of witches, a simoniac, and a traitor to the Church.[1] The chronicler tells how, in 1519, Contarini and his entourage came to the convent uninvited, violating an ancient privilege stating that no one could occupy the *campo* (square) outside Le Vergini's walls without the abbess's permission.[2] But the patriarch's disregard for the abbess's control of the convent site was the least of Le Vergini's concerns, for Contarini had come to impose a severe reform designed to change completely the community's way of life. Contarini's reform, which was supported by Venice's civic council, known as the Council of Ten, and by Pope Leo X, centred on the introduction of strict Observant nuns into Conventual convents, that is, houses where norms for monastic rules were only loosely followed.[3] Once installed, the Observant nuns were to control the convent's finances and government, and one of them was to assume the role of abbess. Conventual nuns, meanwhile, were forbidden to admit any new members to their community, guaranteeing that their cohort would eventually die off. The reformers' aim, according to the chronicler, was to 'damage, destroy, and ruin' the convent, resulting in its 'degradation and disgrace'.[4] The scandal had both tangible and intangible consequences,

---

1   Venice, BMC, MS Correr 317, fols 57ᵛ, 62ʳ–63ʳ.
2   Venice, BMC, MS Correr 317, fol. 60ᵛ.
3   The history of the distinction between Conventuals and Observants is not well documented, but seems to originate with relaxed adherence to the Franciscan rule beginning almost immediately after Saint Francis's death in 1226, leading to a division between *fratres de communitate*, who came to be known as Conventuals, and more observant brothers. In 1415, the Holy See formally recognized the division of the order. See Robinson, 'Order of Friars Minor Conventuals'. The term is also applied to other orders.
4   Venice, BMC, MS Correr 317, fol. 61ʳ. Fassera, 'La vita monastica a San Zaccaria', p. 114 n. 33 cites ASVe, S. Anna di Castello, b. 1, Catastico, fols 153–59, which includes a copy of the Contarini reform, a brief from Pope Leo X, and other patriarchal decrees.

Saundra Weddle (sweddle@drury.edu) is Professor of Architectural and Urban History and Theory in the Hammons School of Architecture at Drury University, Springfield, Missouri.

Convent Networks In Early Modern Italy, ed. by Marilyn Dunn and Saundra Weddle, ES 25 (Turnhout: Brepols, 2020) pp. 153–191   BREPOLS PUBLISHERS   DOI 10.1484/M.ES-EB.5.119516

involving the built fabric of Le Vergini's complex, which separated the Observant and Conventual communities, but it also affected the convent's status and reputation. And Le Vergini's nuns were not alone.[5] Theirs was one of eight institutions targeted by civic and ecclesiastical authorities for reform; also included were the Benedictine houses of S. Zaccaria, SS. Biagio e Cataldo, S. Secondo, S. Anna, and S. Marta; the Franciscan house of S. Chiara; and the Cistercian house of S. Maria della Celestia.[6]

The 1519 reform itself is familiar to historians of Venetian convents, but this chapter sets the episode in new contexts, addressing not only civic and ecclesiastical authorities' consideration of the communities as a cohort, but also how the reformed institutions connected with one another in the midst of crisis.[7] Further, it examines how the reform inspired the development of new patronage patterns and networks, within the convents — amongst Observant nuns — and outside the enclosure — with lay benefactors. At the centre of this study is the 1519 reform's greatest novelty, indeed, a feature that may have been unique to Venice — its architectural expression, which, until now, has been almost completely neglected. The division of convents served as a tool of control for authorities who had given up on traditional means of reforming Conventuals, such as imposing new rules or re-education, instead, reinforcing differences between Conventuals and Observants through confinement. Over time, art and architecture at the targeted convents reflected and constructed identities and alliances, first when reform was imposed, then as lax practices faded with the elimination of Conventual communities and, finally, as renewed and rehabilitated convents asserted themselves within Venice's urban and patronage contexts.

A Conventual Cohort and Its Experiences with Reform

The principal characteristic shared by the targeted communities was their relaxed approach to norms of monastic decorum. This followed directly from their specific designation as Conventual, which practically institutionalized their lack of compliance with monastic vows, giving them a liminal identity in comparison with Venice's Observant convents.[8] Their status permitted Conventuals to move freely outside the enclosure, wear secular clothes, own

5   Although the women at Le Vergini did not profess solemn vows and were technically canonesses, I will refer to them as nuns, and to their house as a convent; for variations in nomenclature used at Le Vergini, see Lowe, *Nuns' Chronicles and Convent Culture*, p. 148.

6   S. Marta eventually accepted the Augustinian rule, which governed the nuns from S. Giuseppe who were introduced there as a result of the reform.

7   Pedani, 'L'Osservanza imposta'; Sperling, *Convents and the Body Politic*; Lowe, *Nuns' Chronicles and Convent Culture*; Laven, *Virgins of Venice*; and Fassera, *Tentativi di riforma*.

8   All eight reformed houses were identified in the reform as Conventual, but it is not clear how this designation was formalized through constitutions or vows except at Le Vergini, where, according to the chronicle, the nuns never professed solemn vows. Venice, BMC, MS Correr 317, fol. 58^r.

private property, and take other liberties not available to nuns who professed solemn vows of poverty, chastity, and obedience. They also enjoyed less strict and less local supervision.

These communities shared other attributes as well. They numbered among Venice's oldest houses; all were founded before 1315.[9] Many also ranked among the city's wealthiest houses, and their communities were populated predominately by women from patrician families.[10] With this background of privilege came an expectation of comfort, if not luxury, that might have led to further relaxation of monastic practices.

Also conspicuous is the number of convents named in the 1519 reform with a history of sexual promiscuity. Three of them appear on Guido Ruggiero's list of houses most frequently cited during the fourteenth and fifteenth centuries as sites of sex crimes (most commonly a layman's fornication with a nun): Le Vergini saw fifteen prosecutions, SS. Biagio e Cataldo saw sixteen prosecutions, while La Celestia saw nineteen, and, although it did not rank among the top offenders, S. Zaccaria was the site of at least one sex crime prosecution.[11] These activities sometimes even led to births within the convent: Ruggiero reports that one birth was recorded at La Celestia, and five were recorded at Le Vergini.[12]

These facts caught the attention of civic and ecclesiastical authorities, leading them to treat the communities as a cohort even before the 1519 reform, an important point that previous accounts of the reform have not noted. In 1501, the Venetian Senate had asked Pope Alexander VI to return these same eight houses to strict observance of enclosure regulations by revoking licences allowing egress.[13] It is somewhat surprising that these civic leaders expected the pope to be amenable to their request given that he had only recently issued a brief allowing the nuns of at least one of these houses — S. Zaccaria — to leave their convent and circulate within the city.[14] But the pontiff not only agreed, he gave specific instructions to Patriarch Tommaso Donà (r. 1492–1504) that clearly forecast the shape of the 1519 reform.[15] The pope ordered the patriarch to inspect each of the convents, introduce observant practices, and attempt to persuade Conventual nuns to embrace them. To those who refused to reform, the patriarch was to offer a choice. The Conventuals' first option was to move

---

9 Foundation dates: S. Zaccaria, 827; S. Secondo in Isola 1034; S. Maria delle Vergini 1224; SS. Biagio e Cataldo 1222; S. Chiara di Venezia 1236; S. Maria della Celestia 1237; S. Anna 1297; S. Marta 1315. Sperling, *Convents and the Body Politic*, pp. 248–49.

10 Sperling, *Convents and the Body Politic*, pp. 250–56.

11 Ruggiero, *Boundaries of Eros*, p. 78.

12 Ruggiero, *Boundaries of Eros*, p. 78.

13 Fassera, 'La vita monastica a San Zaccaria', p. 114.

14 Fassera, 'La vita monastica a San Zaccaria', p. 114, cites Venice, ASVe, Compilazione delle leggi, b. 288; and ASVe, Senato Terra, reg. 14, c. 6.

15 Venice, BMC, MS Cicogna 2570, fols 68–70. See also Fassera, *Tentativi di riforma*, p. 103, citing Venice, ASPV, Diversorum F, fol. 157.

to a designated area of their convent complex, separated from the Observants, which would then serve as an enclosure within the enclosure; their privileges permitting egress would be revoked. These tenacious Conventuals would receive a stipend for their maintenance, but they could not admit any new applicants, effectively limiting their income and ensuring their community's demise. Their other option was to move to another religious house willing to admit them. In January 1503/1504, Donà and three companions responded to this order, focusing on securing enclosures by restricting contact between religious and laypersons, and retracting the privilege allowing nuns at these eight convents to leave the enclosure.[16] Curiously (and perhaps uniquely), Le Vergini's nuns each declared a position on Donà's programme, either supporting or rejecting it. While the abbess at the time, Angela Marcello (1490–1503/1504), expressed support, three community members dissented. The identities of these protestors are noteworthy because each went on to become abbess — Leona Lion (1503/1504–1505), Margarita Badoer (1504/1505–1513), and Chiara Donato (1513–1523). Their rebellious act may have secured support for their later abbacies, and certainly expressed the spirit of bold determination and resistance that came to characterize Le Vergini once the Contarini reform was enacted.[17] Indeed, only two of Le Vergini's thirty-seven sisters followed their abbess's lead: Peregrina Lezze and Peregrina Venier.[18] Donà returned to inspect Le Vergini almost a month later, focusing on the physical enclosure, identifying four 'suspect' doors that needed to be walled up within a matter of fifteen days: one to the vineyard, one from the sacristy to the 'abbess's small garden', one from the sacristy to a courtyard, and one to the infirmary of the *converse* (servant nuns or lay sisters).[19] In addition, the patriarch called for the removal of secular women living in the convent, and ordered the replacement of some convent office holders. In short, Donà attempted to rein in some of the convent's privileges and practices, but failed to advance the scale of reform proposed by the pope. According to diarist Girolamo Priuli, the blame for inaction could be laid at the feet of the nuns' kinsmen in powerful civic positions:

> none of [the reforms] was executed and this is because these nuns have great favour in the Venetian councils and colleges, because many of those who govern the Venetian Republic have daughters, sisters, and relatives in these bordello-like convents, and they will be happy to have [their kinswomen] as public prostitutes.[20]

---

16   Venice, BMC, MS Cicogna 2570, fols 68–69. The date 1504 reflects modern dating, which marks the new year on 1 January. The cited document recorded the *more veneto* (abbreviated henceforth *as m.v.*), in which the new year began on 1 March.

17   Venice, ASPV, Visite pastorali b.1 (S. Maria delle Vergini), unfoliated, dated 23 January 1504 *m.v.*. No known documentation from pastoral visits to the other houses indicates that other communities passed judgment on the reform.

18   Venice, ASPV, Visite pastorali b.1 (S. Maria delle Vergini), unfoliated, dated 23 January 1504.

19   Venice, BMC, MS Cicogna 2570, fol. 69.

20   Fassera, *Tentativi di riforma*, p. 251 citing Priuli, *I diarii*, pp. 195–96; the translation is my own.

The lack of traction for reform campaigns was a familiar problem: authorities had had an imperfect record with past efforts, even when they transferred Observant nuns to problematic houses to impose order and stoke the fire of religious fervour where it had cooled or even been extinguished. A few examples pre-dating the 1519 reforms demonstrate common practices — some successful, some not — that bear this out. A case of successful reform through the integration of members of different communities dates to 1434, when three nuns from S. Croce della Giudecca were sent to reform S. Servolo, where, Flaminio Cornaro reports, the number of nuns grew from four 'inobservant' members to eighty Observants.[21] Sometimes, a particular individual's reforming talents were repeatedly called upon to return a community to observance: Marina Celsi served as abbess first at S. Matteo di Murano and then at S. Eufemia di Mazzorbo, but grew dissatisfied at both houses when the sisters spurned her attempts to establish a rigorous monastic way of life.[22] But she had better results elsewhere. In 1481, she helped found SS. Cosma e Damiano, located on Giudecca, and saw her convent's population rise to 100 by 1508.[23] Celsi's zeal was such that Contarini sent her to reform the convent of S. Secondo as part of his 1519 programme; she ultimately combined the S. Secondo community with that of SS. Cosma e Damiano, acquiring S. Secondo's revenue and privileges at the same time, a success story for both the reform and Celsi's community. By contrast, in 1437, S. Croce della Giudecca sent a group of nuns to S. Angelo di Contorta (better known as S. Angelo della Polvere) and, in that case, it is quite possible that the reformers were corrupted rather than the corrupted being reformed: during the Quattrocento, S. Angelo saw the prosecution of fifty-two sex crimes and the birth of at least four children.[24] Pope Sixtus IV suppressed S. Angelo in 1474, ordering its nuns to move to S. Croce, where the measure was contested by some nuns' families. In response to their objections, the pope permitted some of the women to stay at S. Angelo and, anticipating the approach taken in the 1501 and 1519 reforms, stipulated that no new nuns could be admitted to the community in an effort to starve the convent of members.[25] Interestingly, sex crimes and pregnancies continued, but by 1518 the last remaining nun died, marking the end of the convent of S. Angelo.

Perhaps such unreliable outcomes associated with earlier reform campaigns gave the Conventuals named in the 1519 programme the impression that they

Priuli's comment referred directly to Pope Alexander VI's bull, but predates Donà's visit to Le Vergini. I have found no evidence confirming or refuting Priuli's claim that Venetian patricians were indifferent to the promiscuity of their kinswomen in convents.

21 Cornaro, *Notizie storiche delle chiese e monasteri di Venezia*, p. 535.
22 Cornaro, *Notizie storiche delle chiese e monasteri di Venezia*, pp. 531–33.
23 Paul, *Nuns and Reform Art*.
24 Cornaro, *Notizie storiche delle chiese e monasteri di Venezia*, pp. 535–37; Ruggiero, *Boundaries of Eros*, p. 78.
25 Ruggiero, *Boundaries of Eros*, p. 83 and Cornaro, *Notizie storiche delle chiese e monasteri di Venezia*, p. 466.

(or their allies) could delay the proposed changes indefinitely, but there is also historical evidence that convents could resist reform by appealing to the pontiff. This was the case in the mid-fifteenth century when Le Vergini appealed successfully to Pope Nicholas V to reverse limits on the sisters' privileges.[26] The Conventuals would not give in to the 1519 reform without a fight.

The Reform's Implications for Networks Old and New

Diarist Marin Sanudo reported how the process of creating the physical divisions specified in the 1519 reform evolved at Le Vergini, one of the first to be transformed.[27] In June of that year, workers and their supervisors entered violently, breaking down doors, and then renovating the area that would be turned over to the Observants. In the months that followed, walls dividing Conventual and Observant nuns went up at all eight convents. Within days of the wall's construction at Le Vergini, the Conventuals either damaged or completely demolished it.[28] Reconstruction did not take long; Observant Augustinians from the nearby convent of S. Giustina moved in a few weeks later. The conflict did not end there, and the shared sense of purpose amongst the convents targeted for reform grew.

While civic and ecclesiastical authorities saw these convents as united in their decadence, the convents identified alliances amongst themselves, banding together to support their common cause, in protest and survival; the connections between these convents extended to their lay relatives outside the enclosure. Two years after dividing walls were installed, in August 1521, Le Vergini's Conventual abbess, Chiara Donato, along with the Conventual abbesses of S. Zaccaria, La Celestia, and S. Marta, relied on their allies to support their case, going with their patrician kinsmen to the Collegio (the government's executive branch) to advocate on behalf of all the reformed convents in the hope that the initiative would be reversed.[29]

The nuns and their relatives were taking advantage of a moment of regime change coinciding with the death of Doge Leonardo Loredan (doge 1501–1521), who had favoured the reform, and the start of Doge Antonio Grimani's tenure: Grimani (doge 1521–1523) was more sympathetic to the Conventuals, perhaps in part because his son, Cardinal Domenico Grimani,

---

26   Venice, BMC, MS Correr 317, fols 58ᵛ–62ʳ. The nuns tried the same strategy in response to the 1519 reform, appealing to Pope Leo X and his papal legate, but local authorities frustrated their efforts.

27   S. Anna was the first to be divided, on 17 May 1519. Sanudo, *I diarii*, 27. 301 and 321 for S. Anna and 27. 402 and 407 for Le Vergini. For Le Vergini's account of the event, see Venice, BMC, MS Correr 317, fols 62ʳ ᵛ.

28   Sanudo, *I diarii*, 27. 407: on 24 June 'the nuns of Le Vergini broke down the wall made to separate [the two communities]'. Venice, BMC, MS Correr 317, fol. 62ʳ.

29   Sanudo, *I diarii*, 31. 276–77.

was the procurator of S. Chiara.[30] Indeed, S. Chiara's Conventual abbess had preceded her colleagues' visit to the Collegio by a couple weeks, armed with a licence to leave her convent granted by the Cardinal-procurator, and complaining of mistreatment by the Observants at her house.[31] Whether the abbesses communicated with one another and with their relatives to organize their visit to the Collegio, or it was their kinsmen who initiated the effort is not known, but family connections were relevant to the composition of the group — many of the kinsmen who spoke in the Collegio are known to have previously held government posts reserved for patricians.[32] While the spectacle of nuns inside the Palazzo Ducale was unusual, even offensive to the officials, the nuns' kinsmen addressed members of the Collegio as equals and familiars, and their shared social and political position was central to their appeal.[33] Sanudo reports that, at this meeting, the Observant interlopers were called 'bastard Greeks and commoners', an indignity that any patrician would understand and appreciate, revealing the degree to which these houses were understood as enclaves for Venetian elites — the same political class represented in civic and ecclesiastical positions of power. In fact, various groups of kinsmen continued to advocate before the Collegio on the Conventuals' behalf during the weeks that followed, but their efforts backfired: on 10 September 1521, the patriarch announced his intention to excommunicate any person — lay or religious — who 'favoured or gave aid to Conventual nuns'.[34] Within a few days of this announcement, the Conventuals at La Celestia broke down their dividing wall to gain access to the Observants' granary for needed food. Less than a week after that, the government seems to have reached its limit of chaos and argument, and initiated a simplified and clarified process of communication and oversight by establishing the civic office of *Provveditori sopra i monasteri* (supervisors of monasteries) consisting of three *zentilhuomini* (gentlemen), to limit lay persons' transgression with respect to convents, to represent the government to the convent and vice versa, and to manage provisions for the nuns.[35] Understanding that family and business ties could compromise the officers' effectiveness and objectivity, the Council explicitly stipulated that no fathers, brothers, cousins, or uncles of any nuns — Conventual or Observant — and

---

30 Domenico Grimani was cardinal from 1505 to 1523. Sanudo, *Città Excelentissima*, p. 389.

31 Sanudo, *I diarii*, 31. 162.

32 See Sanudo, *I diarii*, 27. 301 and 407; 31. 340, 423, 424 noting that several advocates for the Conventuals had previously served as Avogadori de Comun.

33 Sanudo, *I diarii*, 31. 276–77.

34 Sanudo, *I diarii*, 31. 384–86.

35 Sanudo, *I diarii*, 31. 398–99; 31. 423–25; 31. 446. See also Fassera, *Tentativi di riforma*, pp. 304–05, which cites Venice, ASVe, Provveditori sopra i monasteri, b. 1, Capitolare I, fols 6ʳ ᵛ. Note that this office operated at the city-wide level; members of this commission should not be confused with procurators, who served individual convents and will be discussed below.

no one with business dealings with a convent could assume the post of *provveditore* (supervisor).[36]

This prohibition on the civic level must have responded to an established if informal practice of kinsmen serving individual convents in the role of procurator — an advocate who operated as an agent for nuns, extending the convent's interests into the public sphere, a practice in evidence in the protest against the 1519 reform. For example, one advocate before the Collegio was Alvise Loredan, whom Sanudo identified as a relative of some nuns at La Celestia, likely including the convent's last Conventual abbess, herself a Loredan.[37] At S. Zaccaria, the Conventual abbess was a Michiel, and that community's most vociferous advocate was her brother, Nicolò Michiel, who also had daughters there.[38]

Convents might also look beyond their nuns' kinsmen to identify procurators, official agents and advisors — thereby forming alliances with prominent Venetian men who served (for life) — and they, too, played an important role in the implementation of the 1519 reform.[39] The positions were often either inherited or maintained among different generations of a single family, and approved by the convent, rather than appointed by the patriarch.[40] An example is Francesco Zio, a procurator at Le Vergini. Zio's father, Benedetto, was procurator at the convent until his death in 1506, but even before that date, Francesco also served as procurator there, continuing after the 1519 reform was instituted.[41] He retained the position until his death in 1523, a sign that he was trusted to support the imposition of observance. Working with both Observants and Conventuals must have been a delicate situation, given his family's long-standing connection to the Conventuals, but

---

36 Venice, ASPV, Visite pastorali b. 1 (Santa Maria delle Vergini), unfoliated, dated 17 September 1521. Sanudo, *I diarii*, 31. 446 states that this was discussed by the council on 19 September 1521. See also Galeazzo, 'Entrepreneurship Beyond Convent Walls', in this volume.

37 Sanudo, *I diarii*, 28. 72. The position of *procuratore* originated in the thirteenth century.

38 Sanudo, *I diarii*, 31. 276–77.

39 On procurators and patronage, see Sherman, '"Soli Deo honor et gloria?"', 15–32. Regarding thirteenth-century procurators at Le Vergini, see Venice, BMC, MS Correr 317, fol. 33ʳ.

40 A possible example of this heredity can be found among Le Vergini's procurators in the mid-fifteenth century: Girolamo Badoer, Piero Badoer, Zuanne Contarini and Tommaso Contarini. It has not been confirmed that these shared surnames indicate direct family relations. Venice, BMC, MS Correr 317, fol. 45ᵛ. On the convent's election of its procurators, see for example Venice, BMC, MS Correr 317, fol. 52ʳ.

41 Both Benedetto and Francesco Zio are noted as procurators as early as March 1502. Venice, ASVe, S. Maria delle Vergini, b. 43, fasc. GG, fols 5ʳ and 7ʳ. These details verify that the position was not strictly inherited, that is, passed to a son after the death of his father, as has been suggested in Schmitter, '"Virtuous Riches"', p. 920. Apparently, Francesco's illegitimate son, Giacomo, also served as a procurator at the convent; Schulz, 'A Newly Discovered Work', p. 663 n. 43, citing Battilotti and Franco, 'Registri di committenti e dei primi collezionisti', p. 80. Patriarch Antonio Contarini confirmed Francesco's re-appointment on 27 June 1519: 'nunc vero Gastoldioni Monialium per dictas moniales acceptato & per nos confirmato'. Schulz, 'A Newly Discovered Work', p. 663.

it is clear that he tried to be even-handed: in 1521 he loaned 174 ducats expressly for the maintenance ('*el vivere*') of Le Vergini's Observant nuns in particular.[42] At the very least, the gesture indicates Francesco's acknowledgement of the diverse needs of two separate populations residing within the convent. He also provides an example for the ways in which the procurators continued their investment in and support for their convent-charges after their death. He designated Le Vergini as one of his beneficiaries, and his tomb, located on the church's left wall, drew the attention of sixteenth-century historian Francesco Sansovino, who described it as one of 'two beautiful marble sepulchres'.[43]

As Allison Sherman has shown, for the procurator himself, the position represented 'a valuable opportunity to establish a record of service and virtue, but also a justification for magnificence and display'.[44] For convents, it opened a new vein of patronage support: as procurators changed, new patrons emerged, and the convent could establish new connections, beyond the individual procurator to members of his family and allies. For reformers, the procurator could ensure continuity, clear lines of communication, and accountability, always important to the supervision of convents, but especially so during periods of reform, such as when convents were divided between Observants and Conventuals, and later, following the Council of Trent.

The Implications of Division and Reform during the Period of Transition

When convents called on these male advocates to amplify their protests against the 1519 reform, both the nuns and their patrons had history and investments to protect. Arguments against the reform centred on issues of historic privilege and status, shared amongst the Conventual communities. Sanudo's diary and archival evidence from a number of the reformed convents reveal that the division of convent complexes offended Conventuals on a number of scores: the workers entered their home without their permission and altered the architectural fabric in ways the community did not approve.[45] At S. Zaccaria

---

42 Venice, ASPV, Visite pastorali b. 1 (Santa Maria delle Vergini), unfoliated, dated 1521. The account specifically mentions that this was a loan ('imprestadi'), not a donation.

43 Sansovino and Martinioni, *Venetia città nobilissima*, p. 20. The location of the tomb, now lost, is described by Cicogna, *Delle inscrizioni veneziane*, p. 59, which provides an excerpt from Zio's testament, which calls for 'una sepoltura di pietra alta da terra colli stemmi della famiglia e lettere indicanti il nome e la famiglia, dirimpetto all'altar N. S. Gesù Cristo' (a stone tomb raised high above the ground, with the family crest and an inscription with the forenames and family name, opposite the altar [dedicated to] Our Lord Jesus Christ [known as Corpus Domini]). Schulz tentatively connects a sculpted triptych of Christ Man of Sorrows and angels, attributed to Giammaria Mosca, with Zio's tomb; 'A newly discovered work', pp. 656–64.

44 Sherman, '"Soli Deo honor et Gloria?"', p. 15.

45 Sanudo, *I diarii*, 31. 276.

and Le Vergini in particular, the convent division was said to have spoiled extensive and expensive building campaigns recently undertaken. In Le Vergini's case, a renovation had followed a fire in 1487, and was funded not only by a 2000-ducat donation from the Venetian government, but also by many of the nuns' patrician family members, including Francesco Marcello, Constantin Priuli, Andrea Bragadin, Matteo Loredan, Marin Contarini, Girolamo Donato, Alvise Marcello, Andrea Gradenigo, Domenico Venier, and others.[46] At S. Zaccaria, a significant programme of architecture, paintings, and choir stalls was completed only a few years before the reform, in 1515.[47] Nicolò Michiel, arguing before the Collegio on behalf of the Conventuals in late August 1521, recalled that 46,000 ducats had been spent at S. Zaccaria 'on the church and the convent and the beautiful refectory', and that the Conventuals were now deprived of access to these works and spaces.[48] Moveable objects were also of concern. Even as Conventuals were barred from some areas of their convents, they did what they could to retain portable items to prevent their belongings from ending up in the hands of Observants, as happened at S. Zaccaria, where the patriarch 'took the books and the silver and everything and gave them to the Observants'.[49] Many sent both personal and community possessions to their relatives for safe keeping and, at Le Vergini, where sisters damaged the dividing wall shortly after it was constructed, they sought to recover belongings that had found their way to the area occupied by the Observants.[50]

Artistic and architectural projects and convent possessions had meaning beyond the glorification of God and the enhancement of religious devotion. They expressed personal and communal identity, part of a discursive ensemble of prayers, financial support, and favours whose experiential, spatial, and semantic syntax the reform disrupted. As Gary Radke has pointed out, '[…] the nuns ingratiated themselves to a broad segment of Venetian society. At the same time, they expected reciprocity: public recognition and prestige on the one hand and minimal internal intervention and interference on the other'.[51] This tacit understanding was also supported, for example, through rituals that expressed convents' significance to the city of Venice. S. Zaccaria and Le Vergini enjoyed particular civic status. S. Zaccaria was the destination of a dogal procession each Easter, recalling both the abbess's gift to Doge Pietro Tradonico of a jewelled crown, the doge's first ceremonial hat, or *cornu*,

---

46   Venice, BMC, MS Correr 317, fol. 50ᵛ.

47   Radke, 'Nuns and Their Art', pp. 430–59; Goy, *Building Renaissance Venice*, pp. 167–89; Aikema, Mancini, and Modesti, ed., *'In centro et oculis'*.

48   Sanudo, *I diarii*, 31. 276–77.

49   Sanudo, *I diarii*, 28. 72.

50   Le Vergini's chronicler notes that the convent's silver cross, a large painting of Christo Passo (Man of Sorrows), a tabernacle with relics, and 'so many other things' were sent away from the convent, see Venice, BMC, MS Correr 317, fol. 61ʳ. For the attempted recovery of possessions, see Venice, BMC, MS Correr 317, fol. 62ʳ.

51   Radke, 'Nuns and Their Art', p. 432.

and the convent's donation of land for the construction of Venice's Palazzo Ducale.[52] At Le Vergini, newly elected abbesses participated in a symbolic marriage with the doge. The convents' significance was also promoted to and shared with foreigners: Sanudo named Le Vergini among the noteworthy sites to show important visitors to the city, and Le Vergini and S. Zaccaria were also well known for attracting visitors to hear the nuns' singing.[53] Although S. Zaccaria and Le Vergini were, in some sense, in a class by themselves within the group of convents targeted for reform, their experiences help explain a general perception that the changes imposed by Contarini disregarded and threatened the status of the Conventuals and, by extension, their associates.

Corresponding to this sentiment was convents' outrage over the violation of their long-established privileges — favours and concessions offered by Church authorities.[54] The implication and, for the convent that received them, hope were that these privileges would be permanent and irrevocable, but as has already been pointed out, even before the 1519 reform it was not unheard of for a pope to retract privileges conceded by his predecessors.[55] It is perhaps for this reason that privileges can regularly be found, meticulously recorded, in convent chronicles and other archival documents. Being subject to individuals with the power to alter their way of life, convents appealed to the historic record when arguing against the termination of concessions, the significance of which went beyond individual or communal benefits: they were understood simultaneously to augment and result from a convent's merits.[56]

Complaints also focused on the practicalities of the division, which resulted in limited or even denied access to resources (especially food), as the episode at La Celestia, described above, confirms. At S. Marta, the division and changing character of the populations had practical implications both for architecture and for daily life from the reform's beginning and for decades after. More than forty years after the convent's division, in 1564, the Observant abbess explained in a supplication to the doge that the number of Observant

---

52 Muir, *Civic Ritual*, pp. 221–23.

53 Noteworthy visitors to Le Vergini included Anne de Foix, future Queen of Hungary, Sanudo 4. 298; and the duke and duchess of Nicosia, Venice, BMC, MS Correr 317, fol. 42ᵛ. See also Sanudo, *De origine*, p. 62. For the 1469 visit of Emperor Frederick III to S. Zaccaria see Modesti, 'Le chiese e le monache', p. 125.

54 Boudinhon, 'Privilege'. Examples of privileges include exemptions from payment of certain taxes, indulgences, permission to eat meat, to own and sell property, to leave the convent on specific occasions, the right to live in extreme poverty, or even, as at Le Vergini, exemption from professing solemn vows.

55 A good general source for privileges and their re-confirmation or retraction is Cornaro, *Notizie storiche delle chiese e monasteri di Venezia*, pp. 94, 100, 113, 148, 153, 253, 277, 319, 382, 394, 396, 519, 523, 544, 591, and 594.

56 In addition to the complaint made by Le Vergini's chronicler, cited above, family members of S. Zaccaria's nuns attempted to have the patriarch cited in the papal court because of violation of what the convent understood as its sovereignty, but the patriarch and the Venetian ambassador in Rome worked to maintain the reform. Sanudo, *I diarii*, 27. 450 and 27. 473.

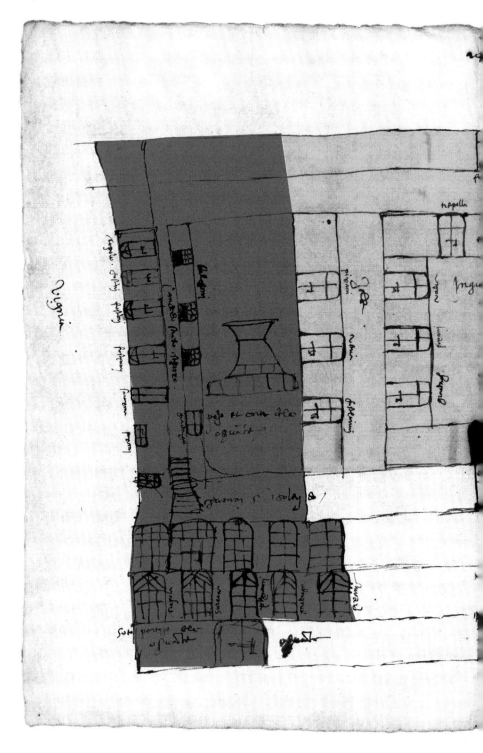

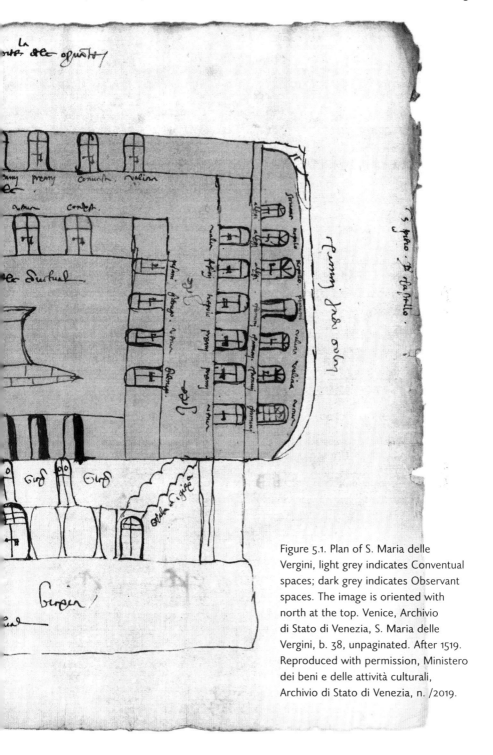

Figure 5.1. Plan of S. Maria delle Vergini, light grey indicates Conventual spaces; dark grey indicates Observant spaces. The image is oriented with north at the top. Venice, Archivio di Stato di Venezia, S. Maria delle Vergini, b. 38, unpaginated. After 1519. Reproduced with permission, Ministero dei beni e delle attività culturali, Archivio di Stato di Venezia, n. /2019.

nuns had grown to forty-six, including eight new nuns whose dowries were needed to pay debts and finance the community's everyday maintenance: as the community grew, so did its needs, and its resources were inadequate. Further, she reports that in 1519 the patriarch 'knew of our weakness' and had arranged for 'the monastery of San Zacaria [*sic*] [to give] help and support to both our Conventuals and our Observants', but at that time her community had been smaller — with only thirty nuns — and, by the time of her supplication, their resources were stretched thin.[57] Beyond these general needs, the abbess noted that the convent also required a new refectory, kitchen, dormitory, and granary, and had already spent 1400 ducats for repairs, seeing that the complex was 'a ruin'.[58] In addition to the stresses of the growing Observant community, co-existence with the Conventuals who still lived there, albeit separately, also presented challenges: that same year (1564), S. Marta's Conventuals complained not only that the Observants were withholding their share of food, but also that the promised provisions from the nuns of S. Zaccaria had stopped coming, so that they were practically starving.[59]

The exact physical and material character of the earliest dividing walls at these convents remains elusive. Sanudo describes the construction workers as 'masons'.[60] Supporting the idea that the divisions were masonry walls is the reference in Le Vergini's chronicle to a *muros* that divided the convent into two parts; to repair the damage done by the nuns, the author notes, more than twenty-five 'masons and demolition workers' brought stone, mortar, and sand to the site.[61] The cost of the division was not inconsiderable according to Sanudo, but no known records survive to document the quantity and precise cost of the material and construction.[62] Regardless of the form, material, and scale of the initial divisions, it is clear that permanent and large-scale architectural interventions followed.

One instructive (and perhaps unusual) example is a project for a courtyard, cistern, cells, and a refectory at Le Vergini. Definitive evidence that this building programme was initiated during the sixteenth-century comes from a sketch housed at the Venice State Archive, which adheres to a convention of representing both plan and elevation simultaneously (Figure 5.1).[63] It is significant not only because it documents the convent complex while the reform's transitional process was underway, but also because it is one of a small number of contemporary representations of the targeted convents,

57   Venice, ASVe, S. Marta. b. 7, insert 185.
58   Venice, ASVe, S. Marta. b. 7, insert 185.
59   Venice, ASVe, S. Marta, b. 7, inserts 167 and 185.
60   Sanudo, *I diarii*, 27. 402 uses the term *mureri*.
61   'Con li capitanei et tutti li officiali ... Et etiam più di 25 mureri et guastatori cum li burgi di piera, de calcina, de sabion, et arte cum tutte li mistieri et artegliorie come righiede de volte andar adar el guasto a una terra'.Venice, BMC, MS Correr 317, fol. 61ᵛ.
62   Sanudo, *I diarii*, 27. 473; 28. 73.
63   Venice, ASVe, S. Maria delle Vergini, b. 38, unfoliated.

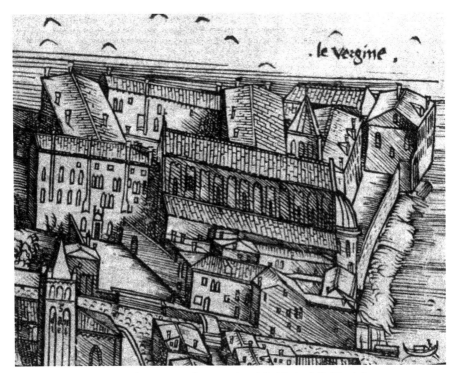

Figure 5.2. Jacopo de' Barbari, *View of Venice*, detail, S. Maria delle Vergini. 1500. Minneapolis Institute of Art, Minneapolis, MN, Duke Digital Repository, https://repository.duke.edu/catalog/duke:448098.

a research challenge that is exacerbated because Le Vergini and the other reformed convents are now either entirely demolished or were renovated after early nineteenth-century suppressions.[64] There can be no doubt that the drawing post-dates the convent's division because it identifies parts of the complex assigned to Conventuals and Observants respectively. It is also clear that it predates 1537, when the Conventual community definitively dissolved; given the large number of cells assigned to Conventual nuns recorded on the drawing, it likely captures a moment fairly near the Observants' introduction.[65]

---

64 All the convents were suppressed in the early nineteenth century, with the exception of S. Secondo, which had ceased to function as a convent in the mid-sixteenth century and was turned over to the preaching friars of S. Domenico di Castello. Of the eight reformed convents, only the churches of S. Anna, S. Zaccaria, and S. Marta survive; building fabric from the convents themselves still exists at S. Anna, La Celestia, and S. Zaccaria, but these spaces have been altered significantly and converted to other institutional or private uses. Galeazzo, 'Mapping Change and Motion', pp. 43–50.

65 There appear to have been twenty-nine cells assigned to Conventuals, including two Conventual lay sisters, and fifteen cells assigned to Observants. Note that in October 1521, there were twenty-two Conventuals and two Conventual lay sisters, with two Conventuals

Examining the drawing alongside two other representations — the earlier bird's-eye view of Venice by Jacopo de' Barbari from *c.* 1500, and the later Giovanni Casoni plan of Le Vergini from the nineteenth century — reveals how the convent complex accommodated the introduction of Observant nuns, and how it changed as the Conventual community dissolved and the Observants asserted their outright possession of the site (Figures 5.2 and 5.3).

Using the de' Barbari print as a pre-reform datum, two important changes to Le Vergini's architecture are indicated in the Archive drawing. One relates to the Observants' courtyard, bordered by nuns' cells. The drawing shows two courtyards: one, labelled 'in giostro e pozo delle conventuali' (the cloister and well of the Conventuals), adjacent to the church's north flank, corresponding to the large courtyard shown in the de' Barbari view; and a second, smaller courtyard, labelled 'pozo e chorte delle os[ser]va[n]ti' (well and courtyard of the Observants), which does not appear in the de' Barbari print. The Casoni plan confirms that, by the time of the convent's nineteenth-century suppression, that second, smaller courtyard 'of the Observants' had been built, just north and west of the church. A fraction of the size of the Conventual courtyard, it exemplifies the utilitarian nature of such spaces — the dimensions are large enough to accommodate a cistern and admit some light and air to the Observants' portion of the complex, satisfying essential needs for that community to function independently. This pragmatic quality is accentuated by the absence of a portico in the smaller courtyard space, a stark contrast with the one seen encircling the earlier, larger, and certainly more architecturally refined courtyard of the Conventuals.

It is significant that the Archive drawing represents the site at a moment when Observants were still outnumbered by Conventuals. The sketched plan appears to show fifteen cells for Observants, located on the second floor, identified by the stair at the end of their wing. The modesty of this wing is indicated by the 'andido streto e schuro' (narrow and dark hallway), lit somewhat by windows that were shuttered on the bottom, with what appears to be crown glass above. Beyond these was a balcony (or balconies) facing the courtyard, providing exposure to more light and air than would have been experienced on the courtyard's ground level. On the other side of the plan the capacious Conventual courtyard is surrounded by twenty-nine cells, including two for *converse* — lay servants; some appear to be on the ground floor — an undesirable, damp site in Venice — and others are on the second floor, suggested by the stair at the end of the wing, with those on the east side lining a double-loaded corridor, giving a very crowded impression.

The top of the Archive drawing is labelled 'reffetorio et chorte delle os[ser]va[n]ti' (the refectory and courtyard of the Observants); the refectory itself

---

living outside the convent, and eight Observants and six Observant lay sisters, so the plan must have been produced in the interim between 1519 and 1521. ASPV, Visite pastorali b. 1 (Santa Maria delle Vergini), unfoliated, dated 19 October 1521.

is not represented and, like the Observants' courtyard, it does not appear in the de' Barbari print. But the Casoni plan confirms its eventual construction, locating it to the north, beyond the two courtyards, in the same general area where the label appears on the Archive drawing.[66] The Observants' refectory, as shown in the Casoni plan, follows the norm for monastic dining spaces: an anteroom where ablutions could take place, followed by a wide and, probably, tall box-shaped room with a row of columns supporting the vaults. The Conventual refectory is not identified in any of these sources, but the Casoni plan includes a room with a refectory's spatial typology, mediating between the Conventuals' and Observants' courtyards; its location off the Conventuals' courtyard makes that area of the complex an independent, segregated unit.

Devotional practices, such as praying and singing in the choir, represented nuns' most fundamental and significant opportunity to enact and embody their monastic identity, communicating through their singing with the lay public gathered in the nave,[67] and even within and between the Conventual and Observant communities. These two groups entered the choir separately: a 'sotoportego delle os[ser]va[n]ti' (sottoportegho of the Observants) connected the Observants' courtyard to the choir by way of a door fitted with a sliding bolt lock; adjacent to the Conventuals' courtyard is another door leading to the church, also fitted with a lock.[68] Once in the choir, the two groups appear to have been separated by another door or perhaps an open gate — without a lock — Observants on one side, Conventuals on the other side, and apparently located in front of the Observants facing the main altar. Taken together, these documents confirm that significant building works were intended to truly separate the two communities at Le Vergini; however the precise dates of this construction are not known.

Even interventions as seemingly minor as inscriptions can offer insights about how the reform influenced patronage and identity over time. Transcriptions made by Emmanuele Cicogna during the nineteenth century prove invaluable, especially when they can be considered in relation to their original context. For example, at the 'refectory of the Observants' at Le Vergini, Observant nuns used their commissions to establish their own status and to bolster their resolve (Figure 5.4). The anteroom to their refectory was the site of a telling intervention: a basin meant to hold water for the customary ablutions before the meal; it has never been fully considered in the context of the Observant

66 It is possible that the refectory is hidden behind the convent church in the Barbari view, but this is unlikely given the evident scale of the refectory's building volume. It seems more probable that a land reclamation project preceded the construction, but no accounts for such an undertaking have been found.

67 Modesti, 'Le chiese e le monache', p. 144 n. 74 notes that the norm in Venetian convents was to locate the nuns' choir in a balcony above the church entry. See also Allen, 'The San Zaccaria Choir', pp. 169–72.

68 A sottoportego is a portico with at least one storey located above; it can be enclosed on one or two sides.

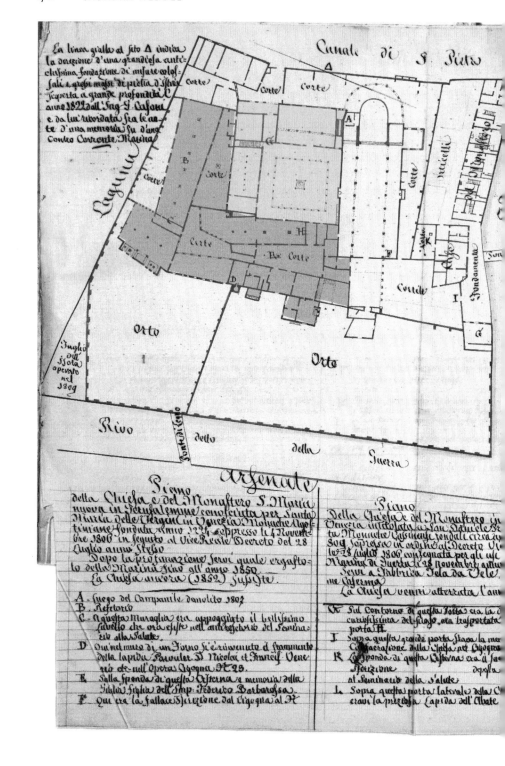

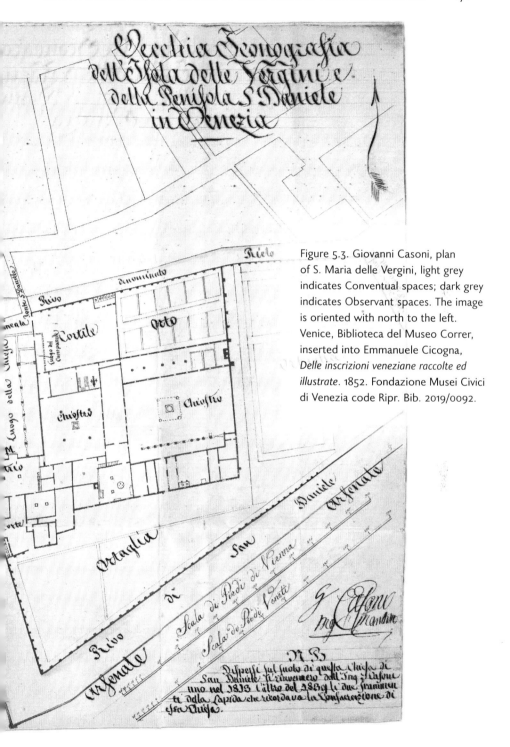

Figure 5.3. Giovanni Casoni, plan of S. Maria delle Vergini, light grey indicates Conventual spaces; dark grey indicates Observant spaces. The image is oriented with north to the left. Venice, Biblioteca del Museo Correr, inserted into Emmanuele Cicogna, *Delle inscrizioni veneziane raccolte ed illustrate*. 1852. Fondazione Musei Civici di Venezia code Ripr. Bib. 2019/0092.

Figure 5.4. Lavabo, originally at S. Maria delle Vergini. Venezia, Seminario Patriarcale. 1531. Reproduced with permission, Osvaldo Böhm Archive, Venice, Italy.

reform or Observant patronage.[69] Its materials, green porphyry, *verd antique*, and Verona marble were valuable, and the scale not insignificant, reflecting the wealth of its patrons. The ensemble includes a sculpture of the Madonna and Child, with two nuns — generally presumed to be abbesses — arms open in a gesture of offering, perhaps kneeling in the traditional pose adopted by donors, although their knees cannot be seen.[70] The inscription reads: 'CORPORIS MVNDITIA CONFORMIS SIT ANIME' (the body's cleanliness reflects the purity of the soul), perhaps recalling the Augustinian rule's reminder that the virtue and vow of chastity 'consisted in purity and cleanliness of the body and the mind'.[71] Not only does the inscription befit the basin's function, but it also expresses the mission of the Observants sent to purify the souls and discipline the bodies of Le Vergini's Conventual nuns. On the pilaster capitals, the initials S.P. and M.B. appear beside the main inscription; Cicogna was the first to suggest a likely reference to Sofia Pisani and Marina Barbaro, both elected Observant abbesses at Le Vergini while the convent was still divided.[72] The dark veils identify the abbesses with the reforming nuns from S. Giustina, who wore a grey habit until the entire community was united in observance, at which point they traded their old habit for the white one worn (from head to toe) during rituals at Le Vergini.[73] Unexamined in the scholarship to date are additional details: the inscriptions 'Abstine' (an order to abstain, forego, or refuse something, perhaps the obvious enticement of food, but also distraction, idle talk, or other temptations common to the convent refectory) and 'Sustine' (an order to pause, or wait, but perhaps also an instruction to be patient and

---

69   The sculptural ensemble has been housed at the Seminario Patriarcale since Le Vergini's suppression in 1806 and appears to be a pastiche rather than a cohesive ensemble. Leaving aside the fact that the lavabo was transported and reconstructed, evidence for this assessment will be discussed in the notes that follow. I would like to thank Anne Markham Schulz for confirming that she, too, considers this to be the case, although I wish to note that her assessment was based on a photo, not on inspection of the lavabo itself.

70   The two nun figures appear to have been added to either side of the Madonna and Child, who are depicted on a heavy base that projects from the plane of the lunette occupied by the nuns.

71   Regola di S. Agostino, p. 18. Although the cited document was intended for Augustinians at the convent of Le Vergini in Rome, the text would have been representative of the Augustinian rule followed in Venice as well. The inscription is not centered between the pilasters.

72   Note that the P and the M are on the inside face of the two pilasters. Barbaro formally assumed the post in 1524. Lowe, *Nuns' Chronicles and Convent Culture*, p. 380 reports that Barbaro commissioned a document of her consecration on 25 January 1524, now housed at the British Library. The verso of the document's first folio includes an engraving representing the raising of Lazarus; it is tempting to read this as an analogy to Le Vergini, being revived from the dead through the reforming zeal, faith, and devotion of the Observants. Pisani became abbess in 1528. Cicogna, *Delle inscrizioni veneziane*, p. 94.

73   Cornaro, *Notizie storiche delle chiese e monasteri di Venezia*, pp. 99–100; Lowe, *Nuns' Chronicles and Convent Culture*, pp. 210–12. That habits conveyed identity and status was made explicit when *converse* at Le Vergini adopted the white habit in the mid-sixteenth century, causing conflict within the convent. *Converse* were required to wear black habits by Pope Paul III. Venice, ASVe, S. Maria delle Vergini, Atti, b. 73, insert NN, fol. 5ʳ ᵛ.

exercise restraint) — a further reminder of the Observant nuns' commitment and the long and slow war of attrition they were waging against the hold-out Conventual nuns. These two words are punctuated with roundels — at either end of the inscription, with profile portraits of white-veiled nuns, and in the middle, with Christ wearing the crown of thorns, an inspiration for perseverance through suffering and a reminder of its rewards.[74] Finally, the date, 1531, confirms that the basin was commissioned during the period of division. This ensemble is an unequivocal statement of Observant identity, mission, and, given its material, scale, and status, served as a daily reminder of who was now in charge of the convent's artistic heritage.[75]

Other inscriptions reinforce the reformist message and the relationship between the physical body and the spirit. One on the parapet beside the stair step to the refectory read: 'LANIMA NON AVITA SEL CHORPO NON LACVISTA:' (the soul does not have life unless the body acquires it), possibly another reference from St Augustine's writings.[76] Still other inscriptions share the same admonishing spirit. One, carved into the floor in front of a room identified as the 'Chiesetta della Madonna'[77] emphasized obedience and the abbess's authority: 'PRIMA A DIO SI DA HORE. ET REVERENTIA/ET POI ALLA MADRE B. SVMA OBEDIENZA:' (First, give honor and reverence to God, and then give supreme obedience to the Mother Abbess), a reference

---

74 I wish to thank Marilyn Dunn for inspiring me to consider more deeply the differences between the dark grey veil worn by the larger figures shown in a three-quarter view in the lunette above, contrasting with the white veil worn by the figures represented without relief and in profile below. This may distinguish the Observant abbess-donors from the Conventual nuns they were sent to reform. The veil color as well as the scale and position of these two sets of figures suggest a significant power and status difference between the Observant abbesses and Conventual nuns.

75 First-hand examination of the lavabo in June 2018 raised questions regarding the upper basin, which seems incongruous with the rest of the ensemble. The stone and the carving technique differ significantly from the rest of object, and the features and details of the represented faces also seem out of place. The upper basin is at such a height that it was not possible to confirm how it is attached to the wall and integrated with the other parts of the lavabo. Although it seems unlikely that the upper basin is by the same hand as the other parts of the lavabo, it cannot be confirmed whether it is a fragment from some other time period and place, or when it might have been incorporated into the ensemble. At least one precedent for a double-basin lavabo exists in Venice, in the Frari sacristy. In that case, too, the basins are quite different. My thanks to Julia DeLancey for bringing this example to my attention. I would like to thank Dottoressa Silvia Marchiori for allowing me to view the lavabo at the Seminario Patriarcale di Venezia.

76 The inscription's location is noted in Cicogna, *Delle inscrizioni veneziane*, p. 95. Based on the opinion of Giovanni Casoni, the engineer who surveyed the convent after the 1806 suppression, Cicogna expressed the view that this inscription was contemporary with the nearby basin and the lunette, but because the inscription no longer exists, it is impossible to offer an opinion now.

77 It is not clear whether the Madonna in question is the Virgin Mary or whether this refers to the abbess's chapel, since she was sometimes referred to in archival documents as 'Madonna Badessa'.

to chapter ten of the Augustinian rule, on obedience.[78] A few steps beyond, another one: 'PAS[S]ATE CON LA PACE/CHE QVESTO A DIO PIACE S.PI'. (Pass with peace, because it pleases God).[79] Cicogna quite reasonably hypothesizes that S. PI refers again to Sofia Pisani, the abbess associated with the lavabo; the proximity of these last two inscriptions and the likely association with Pisani amplifies the Observant spirit noted in the refectory lavabo. Pisani's tenure as abbess was extraordinarily long, lasting fifty-four years, until her death in 1577, and the date when these inscriptions were carved cannot be verified. Pisani's longevity was perhaps an unexpected support for the establishment of the Observant community, and these inscriptions were doubtless intended to extend her influence for years to come. Interventions, even on this small scale, had the potential to communicate and reinforce a shared sense of mission.[80]

The nature of building works for the division of other targeted convents is not as well documented. Paola Modesti reports that at S. Zaccaria, by 1521, the 'convent, church, and bell tower had been structurally divided to allow Observant and Conventual nuns to use them independently, without even seeing each other', with Observants attending services in an upper choir and Conventuals below.[81] As for the living spaces, Gianmario Guidarelli has shown that a significant construction campaign, including the addition of a second cloister housing a dormitory and some cells, dates from the period between 1555 and 1561.[82] This is quite different from the Vergini example, however, in that it was not a means of accommodating the convent's division. By the mid-sixteenth century, the Conventual community at S. Zaccaria was much reduced: as early as 1521 only four Conventuals remained, and by 1566 there were only two, with the Observants already numbering more than sixty.[83]

---

78 Cicogna, *Delle inscrizioni veneziane*, p. 95. Marilyn Dunn has made the intriguing suggestion that this inscription could have been located at the chapter room, where nuns admitted their faults and received punishments. The chapter room's location has not been noted in any known plans of Le Vergini, so this possible connection cannot be confirmed.

79 Cicogna, *Delle inscrizioni veneziane*, p. 95.

80 Two additional inscriptions were noted by Cicogna but without enough detail to determine if they are coeval with those discussed here; as dicta, however, they are certainly in the same spirit as the others and are worth noting. One, over a washbasin, reminds nuns that 'AQUA MVNDIT OMNIA CRIMINA', (water purifies every crime); the other, which appears in the arch where the parlour was once located, reads: SANCTA MARIA VIRGO INTERCEDE PRO NOBIS' (Holy Virgin Mary intercede for us). Cicogna, *Delle inscrizioni veneziane*, p. 95.

81 Modesti, 'The Churches and Nuns of San Zaccaria'; see also Modesti, 'Le chiese e le monache', p. 144.

82 Guidarelli, 'L'architettura del monastero', pp. 261–66.

83 Modesti, 'Le chiese e le monache', p. 145 and Guidarelli, 'L'architettura del monastero', p. 361 n. 35; three other Conventuals survived in 1566, but they lived outside the convent. Ackerman, 'Appendix C', pp. 554–59 proposed that the second cloister at S. Zaccaria post-dated S. Zaccaria's division, and perhaps even resulted from it, but the numbers of Conventuals reported by Modesti and Guidarelli suggest that it was unlikely to be a response to reform simply because it would not have been necessary by the time of the cloister's construction.

Some surviving convent account books record smaller scale interventions as the reform progressed. At S. Marta, for example, ten years after the reform began, the convent received a licence from the patriarch to raise the height of its enclosure walls so that neighbours could not see into the complex.[84] At S. Anna, account books dating from the 1550s and into the 1560s record expenses for mundane materials and projects: nails, mortar, bricks, plaster, wood, stone, and metal tie brackets, all used for stairs, doors, windows, shutters, and hardware for grates and locks — elements that mark the liminal locations of transition, from one place or condition to another.[85] Similar interventions are found at S. Zaccaria and Le Vergini.[86] These kinds of expenses could have been part of routine maintenance, not necessarily a sign of heightened concerns about enclosure, privacy, or division.[87]

Given that the ratio of Observants to Conventuals within any given complex was regularly in flux, it is surprising that even one of the convents invested in significant building projects designed to accommodate two separate communities. Observants moved to Conventual convents and attracted new members; Conventuals became Observants, moved to other convents, died, left to live with lay family members, and accepted Conventuals from other convents.[88] The pragmatic challenges of accommodating and providing for

---

84 Venice, ASVe, S. Marta, b. 1, 22 March 1529.

85 Venice, ASVe, S. Anna di Castello, b. 4, unfoliated.

86 Venice, ASVe, S. Maria delle Vergini, b. 43, fasc. GG.

87 Sperling shows the percentage of expenditures spent on repairs at convents as of 1564; while S. Zaccaria, SS. Biagio and Cataldo, and S. Croce declared no expenditures on repairs to their convent, S. Chiara has the highest percentage of expenditures on repairs of all Venetian convents, with fourteen per cent. This predates the 1574 fire at S. Chiara, which destroyed the church and led to a significant rebuilding campaign there. Le Vergini ranks second among the reformed convents, with eight per cent of its expenditures spent on repairs. Sperling, *Convents and the Body Politic*, pp. 260–61.

88 Note that on 4 May 1519, the Council of Ten decided to permit Conventuals to transfer from one Conventual house to another, and that the new house would be obligated to accept them. Fassera, *Tentativi di riforma*, p. 392, citing Venice, ASVe, Provveditori sopra i monasteri, b. 1, Capitolare I, fol. 15ʳ. For examples of nuns moving between convents, see Sanudo, *I diarii*, 27. 301 and Cornaro, *Notizie storiche delle chiese e monasteri di Venezia*, p. 278; for nuns leaving the convent to live with relatives, see Venice, ASVe, S. Maria delle Vergini, b. 1, 23 January 1534 and 13 September 1536. For total numbers of Observant and Conventual nuns at these convents at various points in time, see Venice, ASPV, Visite pastorali b. 1 (Santa Maria delle Vergini) unfoliated, and Venice, BMC, MS Correr 317, fol. 54ᵛ. When the reform was initiated, twenty-two Observants from SS. Cosma e Damiano went to S. Secondo, where there were fourteen Conventuals at the time; Cornaro, *Notizie storiche delle chiese e monasteri di Venezia*, p. 278. Fourteen went from Ognissanti to SS. Biagio e Cataldo; Cornaro, *Notizie storiche delle chiese e monasteri di Venezia*, p. 529. Five women went to S. Marta from S. Giuseppe; Cornaro, *Notizie storiche delle chiese e monasteri di Venezia*, p. 510. An unknown number went from S. Croce and S. Sepolcro to S. Chiara, along with three from S. Maria dei Miracoli; Cornaro, *Notizie storiche delle chiese e monasteri di Venezia*, p. 649. By 1521, there were thirty Observants and only four Conventuals at SS. Biagio e Cataldo; Venice, ASPV, Visite pastorali b. 2 (SS. Biagio e Cataldo), fol. 3ᵛ. For counts of Observant nuns at S. Zaccaria

these parallel communities must have been considerable as the Observant community grew and the Conventual community declined and, eventually, dissolved. The period of conversion lasted decades. For example, in 1537, the last of Le Vergini's Conventual nuns, Suor Elena Pisani, Suor Diana Tiepolo, and Suor Pisana Pisani, joined the Observant community, thereby extinguishing for good the name 'Conventual' at Le Vergini.[89] At S. Chiara the convent remained divided until 1565 — almost fifty years after Contarini initiated the reform, and S. Marta was divided for a similar period of time.[90]

Approaches to building during the period of transition differed from convent to convent, and internal dynamics were not the only determinant of scale and scope. While convent identity and alliances were in flux, Venice itself was besieged by political and economic challenges that dampened patronage activity to some extent. But once the conversion to Observance was achieved, convent art and architecture once again became common vehicles of self- and communal expression.

Asserting Observant Identity through New Commissions

How did Observants assert their own identity through the nature, function, and patronage of convent architecture, sculpture, and painting?

The size of convent populations, nuns' family status, and their extended networks of allies all affected revenue streams, and all of these shifted after the transition to Observance was achieved. Data for pre-reform convent populations are spotty so it cannot be said with certainty that their numbers were comparable after conversion to Observance, but by 1564 all of the targeted convents were quite large: none had fewer than forty nuns and most had over fifty, Le Vergini being the largest with sixty-five.[91] These numbers translate into income not only in the form of convent dowries, but also from additional support offered by nuns and their families, who served as the core patrons for convent art and architecture. Mid-sixteenth-century estimates of net revenue and expenditures indicate that the reformed convents still ranked among

---

see Venice, ASPV, Visite pastorali b. 2 (San Zaccaria), fol. 579, and at La Celestia, see Venice, ASPV, Visite pastorali b. 2 (Santa Maria della Celestia), fol. 603ᵛ.

89 Venice, ASVe, S. Maria delle Vergini, b. 1, 28 December 1537.

90 For S. Chiara, see Cornaro, *Notizie storiche delle chiese e monasteri di Venezia*, p. 401. The exact date when S. Marta's division ended is not known, but must post-date the above-cited letter of 1564, which mentioned both Observants and Conventuals.

91 In 1564, S. Anna had a population of sixty, SS. Biagio e Cataldo fifty-four, S. Chiara fifty-six, S. Zaccaria forty, and La Celestia fifty-seven. S. Marta was not named in the 1564 document, but a petition from Venice, ASVe, Sopraintendenti alle Decime del Clero, b. 32, polizza 45 says that there were forty-six Observants. For the petition, see Sperling, *Convents and the Body Politic*, pp. 182 and 352 n. 47. Venice, BMC, MS Cicogna 3677 notes convent populations in 1593: S. Anna sixty-two, Le Vergini eighty, S. Zaccaria fifty-five, SS. Biagio e Cataldo fifty, La Celestia sixty, S. Chiara eighty-three, and S. Marta sixty-four.

Venice's wealthiest communities.[92] And they continued to attract members from the city's elite families, thereby benefiting from nuns' ties outside their convent. Significant building programmes occurred at many of these houses starting during the second half of the sixteenth century, but some began earlier.

It is perhaps not a coincidence that the scale of building projects at Le Vergini changed the very year (1537) when the last of its Conventuals joined the Observants. The new project focused on the church, including a new *barco* (elevated nuns' choir) and numerous architectural details, such as door frames, friezes, cornices, columns, arches, and brackets in the white Istrian limestone that was increasingly fashionable at the time, as well as floor paving in the red and white checkerboard pattern characteristic of Venetian churches.[93] The sizeable *barco* was added to the west of the pre-existing church façade, above a portico that extended into the *campo*. The Casoni plan represents this addition as a substantial building volume — the portico was open on the ground level, with two stone engaged columns, complete with bases and capitals, and six full columns, also made of stone, which supported the choir above.[94] The building process followed models produced by respected Bergamasco architect, Guglielmo Grigi, who served as *proto*, the architect of record, until his death in 1550.[95] Many of the contracts order the workers to follow the *proto*'s models exactly, adding that the work 'requires no additional stonecutting', as much a safeguard against surprise charges for unrequested embellishments as an indication of the desire for simplicity.[96]

This building campaign advanced rapidly following the death of the convent's most trusted procurator, Girolamo Giustinian. His name appears

---

92 Sperling, *Convents and the Body Politic*, pp. 258–59 and 260–61.

93 Venice, ASVe, S. Maria delle Vergini, b. 43, fasc. GG, fols 25ʳ and 36ʳ. Some of these contracts are also mentioned in Cicogna, *Delle inscrizioni veneziane*, pp. 13–15. For eighteenth-century drawings said to represent this church, see London, RIBA SB39[125]3; SB39[125]2; and SB39[125]1. These are attributed to Antonio Visentini or his assistants, although the identification with Le Vergini appears to be mistaken. Neither the plan nor the section corresponds to the building represented in the Casoni plan, and indeed these drawings more closely resemble the plan of the convent church of S. Daniele, which was located just across the canal to the south of Le Vergini. Further, RIBA drawing SB35[99]1, labelled as S. Daniele, bears no resemblance to Casoni's plan of S. Daniele. Bassi accepts the association of RIBA SB39[125]3; SB39[125]2; and SB39[125]1 with Le Vergini, *Tracce di chiese veneziane distrutte*, pp. 272–81. Additional questions about attributions to Visentini are discussed by Modesti, 'I disegni architettonici', pp. 191–202. See also Canaletto's *View of the Lagoon and the Church of Santa Maria delle Vergini from Campo San Pietro di Castello*.

94 See Venice, ASVe, S. Maria delle Vergini, b. 43, fasc. GG, fols 25ʳ⁻ᵛ for contracts are dated 12 January 1546 *m.v.* and 9 July 1547, and fol. 36ʳ, dated 20 November 1549, for a description of how this new structure met the existing church: 'Maistro Zuan Piero de Francesco del Bon must demolish the façade of the church and rebuild it, reinforcing the vaults and the roof, as ordered by Maistro Guielmo, proto'. In December 1562 sarcophagi were added below the choir. Venice, ASVe, S. Maria delle Vergini, b. 43, fasc. GG, fol. 60ʳ.

95 Venice, ASVe, S. Maria delle Vergini, b. 43, fasc. GG.

96 See, for example, Venice, ASVe, S. Maria delle Vergini, b. 43 fasc. GG, fol. 27ʳ.

in Le Vergini's accounts as early as 1523; he served the convent until his death in 1558 and was involved in most of its contracts written during his tenure.[97] In his testament, he named Le Vergini as beneficiary of 'tutto il suo residuo' (the surplus of his estate) on the condition that the nuns keep two candles burning in their church, one before the crucifix and one before the Madonna, with the nuns saying daily vespers and prayers for his soul.[98] His was the second of the 'beautiful' tombs mentioned by Sansovino along with Francesco Zio's, which had been placed nearby.[99]

The church and choir project were begun by Abbess Sofia Pisani and completed under her successor, Abbess Maria Eletta Benetti (r. 1578–1599). In addition to support from Giustinian and other associates of the convent, the project's progress may also have been helped at this time by a significant papal recognition: in 1548, Pope Paul III reconfirmed some of the convent's privileges, especially relating to its real estate possessions, perhaps leading to an influx of income.[100]

Le Vergini was not the only convent to see major interventions after the transition from Conventual to Observant community was complete. At the beginning of the seventeenth century, S. Anna's abbess also seemed to recognize an opportunity to capitalize on her convent's new, reformed identity. She wrote supplications to the Senate, stating it was 'a major miracle' that her convent did not crumble, just from the din of the nearby Arsenale.[101] Revealing that, despite their insularity, convent communities were informed about events outside the enclosure, she noted the government's assistance to the Gesuiti, Le Zitelle, and the convent of S. Croce, and she appealed for similar assistance to rebuild her convent's church.[102] In another request, she shrewdly reminded senators that S. Anna was fulfilling its duty as one of Venice's oldest convents, with over seventy of the city's 'nobles and citizens who pray continually to

---

97   Venice, ASVe, S. Maria delle Vergini, b. 1, unfoliated, 4 March 1523. Cicogna's transcription of the epigraph of Giustinian's tomb states that Giustinian had been procurator at the convent for twenty-three years when he died in 1558, thus indicating his term began in 1535. The document cited here suggests that he served in the post for thirty-five years. Lowe, *Nuns' Chronicles and Convent Culture*, pp. 85–88, speculates that the author of Le Vergini's chronicle may have been Francesca Giustinian; it cannot be confirmed whether she was related to Girolamo.

98   Venice, ASVe, S. Maria delle Vergini, b. 1, fol. 20 July 1558; and b. 2, fol. 107ʳ. Venice, ASVe, S. Maria delle Vergini, b. 1 and b. 2 include numerous entries regarding disputes with Giustinian's sons and widow, and with the nearby convent of S. Daniele, in relation to this bequest; see for example, Venice, ASVe, S. Maria delle Vergini, b. 2, fol. 188ʳ.

99   Sansovino and Martinioni, *Venetia città nobilissima*, p. 20.

100 Cicogna, *Delle inscrizioni veneziane*, p. 17. For the reconfirmation of privileges, see Venice, ASVe, S. Maria delle Vergini, b. 1, 20 August and 19 October 1548 and February 1564.

101 Venice, ASVe, S. Anna di Castello, b. 6, unfoliated.

102 Venice, ASVe, S. Anna di Castello, b. 6, unfoliated. Mention of Le Zitelle indicates that the document must at least date from after 1579, when construction began at the convent, and after 1583, when construction at S. Croce began according to a design by Antonio da Ponte, with the church being consecrated in 1600.

God for the Most Serene Republic', and yet, because of the 'decrepitude of its antiquity', the church should be demolished. The implication was that the senators should now do their duty and support S. Anna. The nuns' lives were in danger, she said, so she appealed to the Senate to help the convent avoid 'some miserable accident' by extending 'that same charity and kindness that they had [given] in similar cases', so that the nuns could maintain 'tranquility of soul' and renew their prayers for the 'conservation of this most excellent dominion' and for 'each one of you most illustrious *signori*'.[103] Additional requests followed: the nuns (figuratively) placed themselves 'at the officials' feet' because they had exhausted their own funds, supplicating for the ancient and ruined convent in which they were enclosed, where 'ruin threatened from every side' and, 'with every breeze that blows' they were 'constrained to retire to the cloister or the garden, because the walls were not secure', living constantly in fear of losing their lives.[104] New church construction began in 1634 following a design by Francesco Contin, and the building was consecrated in 1659.[105] According to a seventeenth-century edition of Sansovino's *Venezia città nobilissima*, the entire project was funded by donations, and plaques placed inside and outside the church commemorated a variety of donor groups and made their connections both visible and durable. For example, a tablet placed over the church's side door, dated 1659, explicitly named fifteen '*procuratori e massimi beneffatori*' (procurators and greatest benefactors).[106] Another, inside the church, identified the patrons of the main chapel — carpenters, caulkers, oarmakers, and sawyers from the Arsenale, who were perhaps drawn by the site's convenient proximity to their workplace, and vowed in 1630 to undertake the project in exchange for deliverance from the plague.[107] S. Anna also received funds from the apothecaries' *scuola*, which transferred its building from a site

---

103   Venice, ASVe, S. Anna di Castello, b. 6, unfoliated.

104   Venice, ASVe, S. Anna di Castello, b. 6, unfoliated.

105   Cornaro, *Notizie storiche delle chiese e monasteri di Venezia*, p. 108. A campanile was designed by Baldassare Longhena in the 1660s. Venice, ASVe, S. Anna di Castello, b. 6 and b. 12, with contracts for the campanile in b. 12, but no evidence that the campanile was ever built has been found. A plan in Venice, ASVe, S. Anna di Castello, b. 6 notes the 'luogo dove si voleva far il campanil' (the place where *they wanted* to build the bell tower) suggesting that it was never completed. No discussion of Longhena's work for S. Anna appears in Hopkins, *Baldassare Longhena*. A plan, a longitudinal section, and horizontal sections of S. Anna's church, which appear to correspond to the existing building, can be found at London, RIBA SB34[87]1; SB34[87]2; and SB34[87]3.

106   Sansovino, *Venezia città nobilissima*, p. 24. For the tablet inscription, see Oriundi, *La chiesa e convento di S. Anna*, p. 27. In addition to Abbess Gabriella Marcello, the inscription names her niece, Domina Barbara Marcello, as well as Doge Carlo Contarini, Antonio da Canal, Nicolo Querini, Andrea Duodo, Reverend Signor Giovanni Battista Falier, Don Giustinian Martinoni, Francesco Nichetti and his brothers, Tommaso Canal, Giovanni Maria Pulignol and his brothers, Vincenzo Trevisan, Giusto Albertini, Gaspara della Chiesa, and Suor Paula Bonardini. Oriundi, *La chiesa e convento di S. Anna*, p. 6 also notes support for the project from the Senate, dated to 21 June 1585, but does not provide documentation.

107   Oriundi, *La chiesa e convento di S. Anna*, pp. 21–25; pp. 22–23 transcribes the 1634

across the canal from the convent to a location adjacent to the church, and this relationship was commemorated with another plaque.[108] The patrons' piety, generosity, and connection to the convent were therefore made known to all — perhaps most significantly for those placed on exterior walls, where even those who did not enter the church could see the patrons' names. But these memorials also allowed the convent to formalize and make manifest its connections to its network of supporters, presenting the patrons as a cohort of individuals with shared interests.

Writing New Histories

This survey of post-reform projects demonstrates how convents worked with their patrons to communicate the transition to Observance: while convent building programmes, especially church construction, often projected identity and alliance into the public realm, as we have seen, such themes were no less important for commissions behind convent walls. But it is important to keep in mind that visual rhetoric and the agendas it served were dynamic: competing messages could and often did coincide or shift over time.

In this regard the tenure at Le Vergini of Abbess Maria Eletta Benetti, between 1577 and 1598, is noteworthy. On one hand, Benetti oversaw the completion in 1581 of the convent's church and choir — monumental in scale but restrained in their detailing, an assertion of Observant steadfastness. On the other, her abbacy marked a fascinating transition: a rehabilitation of Le Vergini's old (original) history. A possible reason for this could have been an emerging desire on the convent's part, some sixty to eighty years after the community's division, to assert Le Vergini's long-standing exceptionalism, its nobility, and the privileges and patronage that accompanied them; even after enduring the process of converting to an Observant institution, these associations would have been prized.

The best-known source for this late-sixteenth century revival of the convent's illustrious past would have been Le Vergini's illustrated chronicle, written after the 1519 reform was initiated. One of the chronicle's interesting but little-noticed features is its front matter, which establishes the convent's noble origins, supposedly established by Pope Alexander III, Emperor Frederick Barbarossa, and Doge Sebastiano Ziani. The chronicle begins with a list of names of the popes from Alexander III to Leo X, followed by a list of doges, from Sebastiano Ziani to Andrea Gritti. This is followed by a Tree of

---

commission, naming Abbess Gabriella Marcello, thirty-seven professed nuns, their procurator, Alvise Mocenigo, and the church's architect, 'Signor Francesco Contin Proto'.

108   For the *scuola's* support, see Oriundi, *La chiesa e convento di S. Anna*, p. 7; Tassini, *Edifici di Venezia*, p. 11, notes the 'Scuola dei Confettieri' at S. Anna; it moved to the site from its location across from the church in 1636. The *scuola* is noted in the plan from Venice, ASVe, S. Anna di Castello, b. 6, beside the church's main chapel.

Jesse, showing the ancestors of Jesus, and then a list of Le Vergini's abbesses, beginning with Giulia, daughter of Emperor Frederick Barbarossa, and ending with the last Conventual abbess at the time of the chronicle's writing, Chiara Donato (d. 1523).[109] The author thus asserted the legitimacy of Le Vergini's claim to historic status and privilege in the same way that other civic and religious institutions traditionally had: in other words, through lineage. These lineages helped set the stage and establish the narrative for Le Vergini's late sixteenth-century recovery of its pre-reform status and privileges, and this was perhaps explicitly articulated for the first time since the reform on a tablet located at the church's door, which commemorated that project's completion, and explicitly recalled to the lay persons who entered there the convent's papal, imperial, and dogal origins.[110] Through the inscription, these figures and their associated status were seemingly combined in the noble person of Abbess Giulia, and connected to then-Abbess Maria Eletta Benetti, who had overseen the church's completion.

These noble origins, and the status and privileges that seem to have resulted from them, were not only cultivated by Le Vergini's nuns after the Conventual community died off, but they were also acknowledged by religious authorities. In 1614, the papal nuncio granted an exceptional licence for the nuns to process out of their church and into the enclosed atrium outside (where the public door was closed to preserve the nuns' privacy) to see the body of Abbess Giulia, whom they considered a Beata, although no known evidence demonstrates that she was ever formally recognized as such.[111] Indeed, Le Vergini's chronicler seems to have anticipated the eventual desire to appeal to Abbess Giulia's devout past: an illustration in the chronicle shows Giulia, dressed in her all-white habit, recumbent in a kind of black catafalque

---

109 Numerous historians have pointed out inconsistencies with regard to the convent's foundation date. They say that the church was founded around 1224 during the Pietro Ziani dogate; they also point out that Giulia died in 1204, twenty years before, and may never have been to Venice. Further, Pope Alexander III died in 1181. Note that Venice, ASVe, S. Maria delle Vergini, b. 1, unfoliated, claims that the convent was founded in 1205.

110 TEMPLVM HOC AB ALEX. III PONT. FRIDERICO BARBAROSSA IMPER. SEBAS-TIANO ZIANO VENETO PRINCIPE MCLXXVII FUNDATVM A IVLIA EIVSDEM IMPERATORIS FILIA PRIMA ABBATISSA RECTVM MARIA ELECTA BENETTI PATRIT. VENET. ABBATISSA INSTAVRANDVM ET AMPLIFICANDVM MANDAVIT APPOLLONIO MASSA PHILOSOPHO, AC MONASTERII MEDICO, ET PROCVR CONSVLENTE ATQUE PROCVRANTE. MDLXXXI. KAL. AVGVSTI. (This temple was founded in 1177 by Pope Alexander III, Emperor Frederic Barbarossa, and Doge Sebastiano Ziano; Giulia, daughter of the emperor [was the] first abbess to govern; Abbess Maria Eletta Benetti, Venetian patrician, began and saw through the [building's] expansion; Apollonio Massa, philosopher, [was the] convent's doctor, counselor, and procurator. August 1581) Cicogna, *Delle inscrizioni veneziane*, p. 17.

111 Musolino and others, *Santi e beati Veneziani*. Two women from Le Vergini's earlier years were formally recognized as *beate*, Abbess Maria Ziani, who died in 1247, and Abbess Francesca Zorzi, who died in 1431.

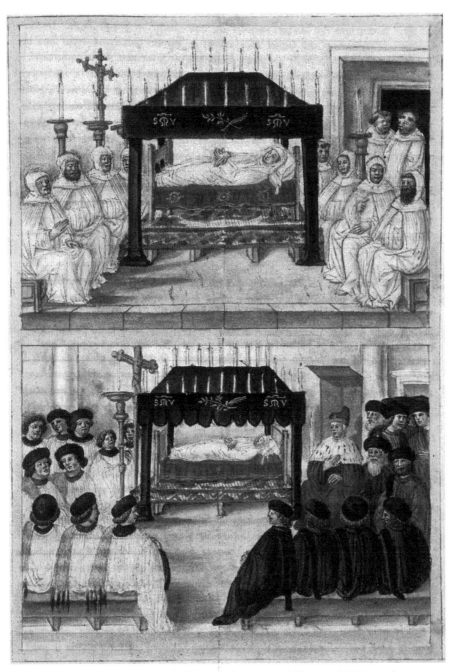

Figure 5.5. Detail of burial of Abbess Giulia, Venice, Biblioteca del Museo Correr, MS Correr 317, fol. 27ʳ. Fondazione Musei Civici di Venezia code Ripr. Bib. 2019/0092.

Figure 5.6. Antonio Zonca, *Doge's Pascal Visit to S. Zaccaria*, Venice, S. Zaccaria. 1684.
Photo: Didier Descouens. Wikimedia Commons, reproduced under Creative
Commons Attribution-Share Alike 4.0 International (https://creativecommons.org/
licenses/by-sa/4.0/).

inscribed with the convent's emblem: SMV (Figure 5.5).[112] In one frame, she is shown surrounded by tonsured monks, dressed in white, perhaps canons of S. Marco Evangelista di Mantova, with whom the convent was associated. In another, she is shown surrounded by laymen, some dressed in white tunics with fringed stoles, others in black, all with the *beretta* signifying their status as senators, except the doge, who sits enthroned, wearing the *cornu*, his ceremonial crown. This combination of religious and secular attendants is meant to show that Giulia's reputation for devotion was well known and widely admired — a kind of witnessing perhaps not unlike that required by the canonization process that follows beatification, something Le Vergini's chronicler seems to prepare for with the image's details.

While rituals like the nuns' procession to see Abbess Giulia's body were special occasions, inscriptions and paintings located within the enclosure served daily to fortify the nuns' sense of status through their connections to the convent's exalted beginnings. Cicogna noted a seventeenth-century inscription found on a cistern, which, like the lavabo discussed earlier, was a place of regular and mundane activity, elevated through text to a higher purpose: 'B.A GIVLIA FIGIAA D. FEDERICO IMPERATOR N.P. ABBADESSA' (Blessed Giulia, daughter of the Emperor Federico, our first Abbess), perhaps an appeal for intercession from the 'Beata', or just a reminder of the convent's origins.[113] Cicogna also notes that two paintings representing Le Vergini's foundation, depicting the pope, the emperor, and the doge, could be found at the church of Madonna dell'Orto after Le Vergini's suppression in 1806, but both are now lost.[114] Archival documents confirm that one of them was an enormous canvas by Antonio Molinari, dated to 1700, for which the convent paid 440 ducats; it was said to have been located in the nun's choir, another place where the nuns would receive a daily reminder of their history.[115]

In this, too, Le Vergini and S. Zaccaria were peers: in 1688 S. Zaccaria commissioned its painting of the doge's pascal visit to its convent from Antonio Zonca, but unlike Le Vergini's history painting, it was located in the public church, and would therefore have been directed toward a different audience, reminding laypersons of the convent's noble history and connections (Figure 5.6).[116] The value of these associations cannot be overestimated, and their revival once the Conventual community disappeared must be acknowledged as a conscious choice that served to reinforce the perceived legitimacy of

---

112 Venice, BMC, MS Correr 317, fol. 27ʳ.

113 Cicogna, *Delle inscrizioni veneziane*, p. 93.

114 Cicogna, *Delle inscrizioni veneziane*, pp. 8, 15, and 17.

115 Venice, ASVe, S. Maria delle Vergini, b. 2, fol. 14ᵛ, 1699.

116 Note that this painting by Zonca was just one of the history paintings produced for S. Zaccaria during the seventeenth and eighteenth centuries; see also Zonca's *Procession of the Relics of Saints Pancrazio and Sabina*, Antonio Fumiani's *The Visit of Emperor Otto III in 1001, accompanied by Doge Pietro Orseolo II*, and Daniel Heintz's *Doge Pietro Lando attending the Consecration of the Church in 1543 with Lucio Stofilio, Bishop of Sibenik*.

claims to status and privilege. Although some of the rigour imposed by the 1519 reform was never formally relaxed, and the Council of Trent's decrees represented a second wave of restriction in the late sixteenth century, some prerogatives returned.

References to ancient status and privileges began to be expressed ritual-istically as convent reputations were rehabilitated and the particular fervour associated with the 1519 reform faded, thereby allowing convents to express their identity in a performative way that could be witnessed by laypersons. In 1613, Le Vergini's nuns successfully appealed to Doge Marcantonio Memmo to resume the tradition by which the doge and senate processed to their church annually on 1 May, recalling a papal privilege whose original arrival at the convent happens to be recorded in great detail in the chronicle.[117] Meanwhile, other ritual privileges had already been reinstated: in 1599, Doge Marin Grimani participated in the investiture of Abbess Sofia Malipiero after she succeeded in having the convent's submission to the patriarch reversed by means of a bull from Pope Clement VIII, which also served to re-affirm the doge's *jus patronatus* at the convent.[118] While the chronicle's role in the efforts to regain privileges cannot be confirmed, it seems likely that Le Vergini's nuns referred to their archive to justify and legitimize their claims to have these prerogatives reinstated.[119] Indeed, if Cicogna is to be believed, it is possible that the chronicle itself played a decisive role in winning back the privileges its author wished to secure: the historian notes that on 7 July 1625, the Giudici del Piovego approved the construction of a *scuola* associated with Le Vergini, 'removing every impediment', after confirming the doge's *jus patronatus* through the 'historic chronicle of the convent'.[120]

Conclusion

Whatever similarities, alliances, and contacts were shared by reformed convents before their houses were divided, the authorities never again addressed them as a discrete group, even as efforts to control Venetian convents in general continued. Patriarchal visitation records from the late sixteenth and early seventeenth centuries — and even later — record countless transgressions, many no less shocking than those reported before 1519. Even if doors had been walled up or locked, windows shuttered, and thresholds guarded, every one

---

117 Battiston, *Tre monasteri scomparsi*, p. 25. The privilege came from Pope Boniface IX; Venice, BMC, MS Correr 317, fol. 42ᵛ.

118 Cicogna, *Delle inscrizioni veneziane*, p. 7.

119 Cicogna, *Delle inscrizioni veneziane*, p. 14.

120 Cicogna, *Delle inscrizioni veneziane*, p. 14. This status was also confirmed by Sanudo, who recorded the symbolic marriage of the Doge to Abbess Margarita Donado in 1506, *I diarii*, 6. 225; Sanudo, *I diarii*, 22. 464 expressly mentions the doge's *juspatronatus* at Le Vergini in his account of the doge's presence at the investiture of Chiara Donado.

of the reformed convents was later ordered to tighten their enclosure still more. Despite all the commotion it caused, then, the 1519 reform had only limited and uneven success. These conflicts were only resolved definitively in the nineteenth century, when sparsely populated convents were closed, and nuns who observed the same monastic rule would be integrated, condensed in a few convents while the rest of the convents were suppressed, bringing the struggle to control Venetian convents to an end.

These case studies reveal that, despite efforts to weaken their efficacy, Venetian convents resourcefully relied upon and fostered various kinds of networks and alliances. Networks existed within convents in various forms: among Observants and among Conventuals, as social cliques, collaborating on patronage projects or, as suggested by Le Vergini's 1504 rejection of an early reform, forming political voting blocks. Networks extended outside convents by relying upon family members, connecting and referring to other houses sympathetic to their aims, developing meaningful connections to procurators and other patrons, and finessing their communications with civic and religious authorities of various ranks. Works of art, architecture, and inscriptions expressed, reinforced, and recalled the meaning and value of the connections that resulted from various kinds of convent networks. In the absence of that built, designed, painted, and sculpted evidence, the written records, which were so critical to nuns who tried to communicate, maintain, and shape their own identities and networks, continue to serve their purpose.

Works Cited

Manuscripts and Archival Sources

London, Royal Institute of British Architects Library and Collections (RIBA)
    Visentini, Antonio (1688–1782)
    ——, Chiesa di Sant'Anna di Castello, Venice SB34[87]
    ——, Chiesa di Santa Maria delle Vergini, Venice SB39[125]
    ——, Chiesa di San Daniele, Venice SB35[99]
Venice, Archivio di Stato di Venezia (ASVe)
    S. Anna di Castello
    S. Maria delle Vergini
    S. Marta
    Sopraintendenti alle Decime del Clero
Venice, Archivio Storico Patriarcale di Venezia (ASPV)
    Visite pastorali a monasteri femminili
Venice, Biblioteca del Museo Correr (BMC)
    MS Correr 317
    MS Cicogna 2570
    MS Cicogna 3677

Primary Sources

Priuli, Girolamo, *I diarii*, ed. by Arturo Segre and Roberto Cessi, Rerum Italicarum
    Scriptores XXIV/III/2 (Città di Castello-Bologna: S. Lapi, 1912–1933)
Regola di S. Agostino per le Monache di Santa Maria Vergini (Rome: 1613) no
    author identified (https://books.google.com/books?id=pNgW_xop5ecC&
    newbks=1&newbks_redir=0&printsec=frontcover#v=onepage&q&f=false)
Sansovino, Francesco, and Don Giustiniano Martinioni, *Venetia città nobilissima et*
    singolare (Venice: Stefano Curti, 1653)
Sanudo, Marino, *I diarii di Marino Sanudo (MCCCCXCVI–MDXXXIII)*
    dall'autografo Marciano ital. cl. VII codd. CDIX–CDLXXVII, ed. by Rinaldo
    Fulin, and others, 58 vols (Venice: Visentini, 1879–1902)

Secondary Works

Ackerman, James, 'Appendix C: The Cloisters of S. Zaccaria', in *Venetian*
    Architecture of the Early Renaissance, ed. by John McAndrew (Cambridge, MA:
    MIT Press, 1980), pp. 554–59
Aikema, Bernard, Massimo Mancini, and Paola Modesti, ed., *'In centro et oculis*
    urbis nostre': la chiesa e il monastero di San Zaccaria (Venice: Marcianum, 2016)
Allen, Joanne, 'The San Zaccaria Choir in Context', in *'In centro et oculis urbis*
    nostre': la chiesa e il monastero di San Zaccaria, ed. by Bernard Aikema,
    Massimo Mancini, and Paola Modesti (Venice: Marcianum, 2016), pp. 151–73

Bassi, Elena, *Tracce di chiese veneziane distrutte. Ricostruzioni dai disegni di Antonio Visentini* (Venice: Istituto Veneto di scienze, lettere ed arti, 1997)

Battilotti, Donata, and Maria Teresa Franco, 'Registri di committenti e dei primi collezionisti di Giorgione', *Antichità viva*, 17 (1978), 58–86

Battiston, Odilla, *Tre monasteri scomparsi a Venezia, sestiere di Castello (S. Daniele, S. M. delle Vergini, S. Anna)* (Venice: Filippi, 1991)

——, *Un piccolo regno teocratico nel cuore di Venezia: il monastero di San Lorenzo* (Venice: Filippi, 1993)

Boudinhon, Auguste, 'Privilege', in *The Catholic Encylcopedia* (New York: Robert Appelton Company, 1911) http://www.newadvent.org/cathen/12436b.htm. [accessed 1 July 2016]

Cicogna, Emmanuele, *Delle inscrizioni veneziane raccolta ed illustrate*, vol. 5 (Venice: Giuseppe Molinari, 1842)

Cornaro, Flaminio, *Notizie storiche delle chiese e monasteri di Venezia e Torcello* (Venice: Giovanni Manfrè, 1758)

Fassera, Mario L. Paolo, *Tentativi di riforma dei monasteri femminili di Venezia prima del Concilio di Trento*, series Italia Benedetta, 38 (Cesena: Badia di Santa Maria del Monte, 2014)

——, 'La vita monastica a San Zaccaria nei secoli XV–XVI', in *'In centro et oculis urbis nostre': la chiesa e il monastero di San Zaccaria*, ed. by Bernard Aikema, Massimo Mancini, and Paola Modesti (Venice: Marcianum, 2016), pp. 95–119

Fontana, Vincenzo, 'Modelli per la laguna di Venezia nel cinquecento', in *Il Paesaggio*, ed. by Ludovico Zorzi (Venice: Fondazione Giorgio Cini, 1999), pp. 179–92

Galeazzo, Ludovica, 'Mapping Change and Motion in the Lagoon: The Island of San Secondo', in *Visualizing Venice: Mapping and Modeling Time and Change in a City*, ed. by Kristin L. Huffman, Andrea Giordano, and Caroline Bruzelius (London: Routledge, 2017), pp. 43–50

Giuliani, Innocenzo, 'Genesi e primo secolo di vita del magistrato sopra monasteri, Venezia 1519–1620', *Le venezie francescane*, 28 (1961), 42–68 and 160–69

Goy, Richard John, *Building Renaissance Venice: Patrons, Architects and Builders, c. 1430–1500* (New Haven: Yale University Press, 2006)

Guidarelli, Gianmario, 'L'architettura del monastero di San Zaccaria (IX–XVIII secolo)', in *'In centro et oculis urbis nostrae'. La chiesa e il monastero di San Zaccaria*, ed. by Bernard Aikema, Massimo Mancini, and Paola Modesti (Venice: Marcianum Press, 2016), pp. 243–66

Hopkins, Andrew, *Baldassare Longhena and Venetian Baroque Architecture* (New Haven: Yale University Press, 2012)

Laven, Mary, *Virgins of Venice: Broken Vows and Cloistered Lives in the Renaissance Convent* (New York: Viking, 2003)

Lowe, K. J. P., *Nuns' Chronicles and Convent Culture in Renaissance and Counter-Reformation Italy* (Cambridge: Cambridge University Press, 2003)

Modesti, Paola, 'I disegni architettonici di Antonio Visentini (1688–1782): un corpus inedito e una produzione con un'etichetta da riconsiderare', in *Porre un limite all'infinito errore: Studio di storia dell'architettura dedicati a Christ of Thoenes*, ed. by Alessandro Brodini and Giovanni Curcio, Saggi di Storia dell'Arte (Collana: Campisano, 2012), pp. 191–202

——, 'The Churches and Nuns of San Zaccaria in Fifteenth- and Sixteenth-Century Venice', presented at Renaissance Society of America Annual Meeting, March 2015, reproduced on academia.edu, https://independent. academia.edu/PaolaModesti [accessed 5 September 2018]

——, 'Le chiese e le monache di San Zaccaria (XV–XVII secolo)', in *'In centro et oculis urbis nostre': la chiesa e il monastero di San Zaccaria*, ed. by Bernard Aikema, Massimo Mancini, and Paola Modesti, Chiese di Venezia 4 (Venice: Marcianum, 2016), pp. 121–49

Muir, Edward, *Civic Ritual in Renaissance Venice* (Princeton: Princeton University Press, 1981)

Musolino, Giovanni, Antonio Niero, and Silvio Tramontin, *Santi e beati Veneziani* (Venice: Edizioni Studium Cattolico Veneziano, 1963)

Oriundi, Federico Paleologo, *La chiesa e convento di S. Anna in Venezia ora Ospedale della Regia Marina* (Venice: Carlo Ferrari, 1914)

Paul, Benjamin, *Nuns and Reform Art in Early Modern Venice: The Architecture of Santi Cosma e Damiano and its Decoration from Tintoretto to Tiepolo* (Farnham: Ashgate, 2012)

Pedani, Maria Pia, 'Monasteri agostiniane a Venezia', *Archivio Veneto*, series 5, 125 (1985) 35–78

——, 'L'Osservanza imposta: I monasteri conventuali femminili a Venezia nei primi anni del cinquecento', *Archivio Veneto*, 5 (1995), 113–25

Radke, Gary, 'Nuns and Their Art: The Case of San Zaccaria in Renaissance Venice', *Renaissance Quarterly*, 54 (2001), 430–59

Robinson, Paschal, 'Order of Friars Minor Conventuals', *Catholic Encyclopedia*, vol. 4 (New York: Robert Appleton Company, 1908) http://www.newadvent. org/cathen/04344a.htm [accessed 1 August 2018]

Ruggiero, Guido, *Boundaries of Eros: Sex Crime and Sexuality in Renaissance Venice* (Oxford: Oxford University Press, 1989)

Sanudo, Marin, *Città Excelentissima: Selections from the Renaissance Diaries of Marin Sanudo*, ed. by Patricia Labalme and Laura Sanguineti White (Baltimore: Johns Hopkins University Press, 2008)

Sanudo, Marino, *De origine, situ et magistratibus Urbis venetae ovvero la città di Venetia (1493–1530)*, ed. by Angela Caracciolo Aricò (Milan: Collana di Testi Inediti e Rari, 1980)

Schmitter, Monika, '"Virtuous Riches": The Bricolage of Cittadini Identities in Early-Sixteenth-Century Venice', *Renaissance Quarterly*, 57 (2004), 908–69

Schulz, Anne Markham, 'A Newly Discovered Work by Giammaria Mosca called Padovano', *The Burlington Magazine*, 146 (2004), 656–64

Sherman, Allison, '"Soli Deo honor et gloria"? Cittadino Lay Procurator Patronage and the Art of Identity Formation in Renaissance Venice', in *Architecture, Art and Identity in Venice and its Territories, 1450–1750: Essays in Honour of Deborah Howard*, ed. by Naby Avcioğlu and Emma Jones (Aldershot: Ashgate , 2013), pp. 15–32

Sperling, Jutta Gisela, *Convents and the Body Politic in Late Renaissance Venice* (Chicago: University of Chicago Press, 1999)

Tassini, Giuseppe D., *Edifici di Venezia distrutti o volti ad uso diverso da quello a cui furono in origine destinati* (Venice: Giovanni Cecchini, 1885)

LUDOVICA GALEAZZO

Entrepreneurship Beyond Convent Walls

The Augustinian Nuns of S. Caterina dei Sacchi in Venice

At the turn of the seventeenth century the modest and peripheral convent of S. Caterina dei Sacchi was in great turmoil. The community of Augustinian nuns, relegated to the northern edges of Venice, found itself — deliberately or not — at the centre of the spiritual and institutional storm that for almost a century had been stirring in the city. The post-Tridentine renewal of Catholicism in Venice had aggravated the long-standing conflict between the Roman Curia and the Venetian government, which culminated in the second papal interdict (1606).[1] Among many concerns, the heart of the argument was jurisdiction over monastic institutions and, more specifically, the question of the extent to which the authority of the Serenissima might prevail over that of the Holy See.

The establishment in 1521 of the *Provveditori sopra monasteri* — the new office for affairs relating to convents in the city and its surrounding lagoon — undoubtedly represented a turning point.[2] However, over the course of the century the dispute was fuelled by a series of laws passed by urban authorities in order to curb the disproportionate growth of Church patrimonies, subjecting existing possessions to secular taxation.[3] Since the first half of the fourteenth century, the Republic imposed restrictions on

---

1 Bouwsma, *Venice and the Defense of Republican Liberty*, pp. 95–115.
2 Instituted to obviate recurring scandalous episodes in sacred places, the state magistracy consisted in three noblemen elected by the Senate to serve as overseers of all Venetian convents. Their jurisdiction encompassed any outsider (lay or clerical) who transgressed the laws relating to enclosed nunneries, excluding female religious themselves who were subject to the Patriarch for their transgressions. See Giuliani, 'Genesi e primo secolo di vita del magistrato sopra monasteri'.
3 Pious donations and bequests were a great concern for the Republic. Mortmain possessions of ecclesiastical and charitable foundations, in fact, could not be alienated and this had a disastrous effect on the Venetian market by freezing sales of land and buildings. On this, see the still-compelling analysis by Stella, 'La proprietà ecclesiastica nella Repubblica di Venezia'.

Ludovica Galeazzo (ludovica.galeazzo@gmail.com) is an architectural and urban historian and she currently works as Digital Humanities Research Associate at I Tatti, The Harvard University Center for Italian Renaissance Studies.

Convent Networks In Early Modern Italy, ed. by Marilyn Dunn and Saundra Weddle, ES 25 (Turnhout: Brepols, 2020) pp. 193–229   BREPOLS ❧ PUBLISHERS   DOI 10.1484/M.ES-EB.5.119517

real estate belonging to ecclesiastical institutions, tightening mortmain laws. In 1333, the Great Council prohibited pious bequests or donations (*pie cause*) of landed property for longer than ten years, while expressly permitting the foundation of new churches and hospitals in the city.[4] In 1536, the Venetian Senate reiterated the decree and ruled that no real estate located in the city could be bequeathed, bestowed, or permanently leased to ecclesiastical institutions for more than two years.[5] Ultimately, in 1605, this regulation was extended to the entire Dogado (the Venetian dukedom).[6]

These measures coincided, on the one side, with Patriarch Antonio Contarini's reform of Conventual convents,[7] and on the other side with the stiffening of sumptuary legislation and the gradual implementation of directives concerning *clausura*.[8] Amidst these conditions, beginning in 1602 and covering almost two decades, the Republic issued additional rules to impose upper limits to spiritual dowries with the intent of standardizing monachization fees and transforming them into lifelong annuities.[9]

Not surprisingly, of the profound changes that convent communities underwent after the monastic reform, regulations on dowries received the most frenzied attention. Capping a maximum threshold for spiritual dowries was anathema to nunneries since these tax-exempt endowments constituted the largest part of convents' cash income. In fact, all these hard-line resolutions had a twofold meaning: on the one hand, they were designed to limit dramatically the increase of convents' finances. On the other hand, the state's efforts sought to implement strict enclosure through the promotion of convents as self-sufficient entities and, by extension, the disengagement of nuns from external support or ties with other people, including natal families.

Against this backdrop many ecclesiastical communities became more vocal about their position, and S. Caterina was among those that most fiercely resisted government actions.[10] Besides determinedly disregarding

4   After ten years, ecclesiastical institutions had to return the properties to the market and the accumulated capital had to be invested in government bonds. See Penco and Trolese, *Monastica et humanistica*, pp. 395–97.

5   Venice, ASVe, Senato, Terra, Deliberazioni, reg. 29, fols 83^v–84^r (22 December 1536). While the office of tax collectors, the Dieci savi alle decime in Rialto, was in charge of selling properties returned by ecclesiastical institutions, the Procurators of St Mark had to administer the money belonging to them. See Sperling, *Convents and the Body Politic*, pp. 195–98.

6   Venice, ASVe, Senato, Terra, Deliberazioni, reg. 75, fol. 19$^{r\ v}$ (26 March 1605).

7   See the essay by Saundra Weddle in this volume.

8   Laven, *Virgins of Venice*, pp. 79–98.

9   Following the Patriarch Lorenzo Priuli's dowry decree of 1593, the Senate issued new dowry laws in 1602, 1603, 1610, and again in 1620. Mantioni, *Monacazioni forzate*, pp. 30–42.

10   It should be noted that S. Caterina had proven to be a driving force in the religious reform movement beginning in the fifteenth century. In 1478 the Augustinian nuns were in charge of reforming the convent of S. Giacomo di Murano, while two sisters from its cloister founded

regulations by increasing their personal possessions, the Augustinian nuns also publicly aired their dissent. Along with the sisters of S. Lorenzo, they repeatedly defied the state legislative authority's establishment of a ceiling for dowry payments at 1200 ducats.[11] The case reached a climax in 1610 when the nuns threatened to close the doors of their convent to applicants rather than admitting thirty-seven *novizze* (novices) at a reduced rate,[12] a menace that would have had serious consequences for the Republic, which was engaged in a dispute with the pope related to its authority over the city's convents. Indeed, the Venetian government's unconditional surrender to the nuns' desire would have weakened the State's convent-reform policy and, consequently, its sovereignty claim to the Holy See. The episode soon moved beyond the walls of the convent, turning into a more complex affair. The Senate, in fact, asked for the intervention of Patriarch Francesco Vendramin to discourage the nuns' disobedience. The skillful patriarch found a way to satisfy the letter of the law while also circumventing it, by secretly persuading the girls' parents to pay the legal amount, while disbursing the outstanding balance as an offer for the religious house. Providing evidence of the complexity of civic and ecclesiastical interests, which sometimes conflicted in Venice, the patriarch's dubious plan met surprisingly strong resistance from future Doge Nicolò Contarini, an important patron who counted several relatives at S. Caterina, and who would therefore have been expected to support the subterfuge.[13] But Contarini was one of the city's most fervently anticlerical patricians,[14] and was more concerned about avoiding a conflict between the nuns and the Venetian government. To that end, he attempted in vain to convince the Senate of the principle of the convent's financial independence and its rights regarding spiritual dowries. Instead, the *querelle* reached its conclusion in 1615 with the one-sided victory in the nuns' favour: all the families tacitly assented to Vendramin's suggestion, paying the authorized sum of 1200 ducats but offering the remaining amount to the nunnery as alms.[15]

If the event serves as an example of the ineffectiveness of the government's convent-reform programme, it also represents a valuable mirror that reflects the power of nunneries as political and social structures within the city. Moreover, it helps to indicate the extensive relationship between 'virgin colonies' and

---

as many communities in the Venice lagoon: Maria Carolo established the complex of Spirito Santo (1483), while Maria Merlini founded the convent of S. Martino in Murano (1501). See Pedani, 'Monasteri di agostiniane a Venezia', pp. 50, 52, and 56.

11 Sperling, *Convents and the Body Politic*, pp. 221–24.
12 The arrangements between nuns and patrician families suggested the payment of 2500 ducats for each novice admitted. Venice, ASVe, Senato, Deliberazioni, Roma Ordinaria, reg. 18 (1610–1612), fasc. 33 (3 May 1610).
13 Sperling, *Convents and the Body Politic*, pp. 221–22.
14 On Contarini, see Cozzi, *Il Doge Nicolò Contarini*. On his role in the dispute between the convent of S. Caterina and the Senate see pp. 68–69.
15 Città del Vaticano, ASV, Nunziature di Venezia, reg. 42c, fol. 344[r] (28 November 1615).

the upper echelons of Venetian society. As argued by Jutta Gisela Sperling, the open dissent of S. Caterina and S. Lorenzo was consistent with the views of advocates for civic liberty — such as Paolo Sarpi, Fulgentio Micanzio, and Nicolò Contarini himself, leaders with whom the two communities maintained close connections, complementing the kinship ties that bound the nuns to the most elite and prestigious patrician families.[16]

Despite several allegations made against the religious women, accused of opposing the city's public interest, their unwavering dissent reveals the desire for more self-empowerment. Apart from the economic outcomes the Republic's fiscal burdens would have had on the convent's capital, there was much more at stake. Nuns not only sought to defend their financial and institutional independence but above all, and *clausura* notwithstanding, they protected the multifaceted network of lucrative relationships that extended behind the walls of their complex.

From the most prominent politicians of the Republic to sisters of neighbouring communities, from the Serenissima's highest offices to expert master-builders, from the wealthiest Venetian merchants to peasants on the Venetian controlled mainland: a wide spectrum of intertwined connections informed the rich life of this seemingly enclosed community. By retracing the intricate weaving of these stories, we realize the engagement of S. Caterina in the physical, social, and cultural growth of the northern rim of the city. This must have been quite apparent to contemporaries. Flaminio Cornaro, in his description of the convent, extolled it for 'the increase of its income, the "nobility" of its nuns, and even more for its spiritual treasures'.[17] These three salient features have truly been the hallmark of the nunnery over the course of its entire history.

A Patrician Community at the Outer Margins of the City

Located on the western tip of the Fondamente Nuove, the old convent of S. Caterina stands in what is today widely regarded as the periphery of the city, an area almost neglected by tourists and Venetians alike. A thick brick wall surrounds the whole perimeter of the present-day Liceo Convitto Marco Foscarini, while a series of round-headed windows and two portals emerging along the Fondamenta di S. Caterina are the limited vestiges of its sacred church. The modest scale of the complex, its position at the edges of the city, as well as the utter simplicity of its architecture do not reflect the significance

16   Despite Contarini's position in relation to the protest of S. Caterina, his contribution — along-side people from the circle around Paolo Sarpi — played a significant role in the convents' development as a political force. See Sperling, *Convents and the Body Politic*, pp. 225–26.

17   Cornaro, *Notizie storiche delle chiese e monasteri di Venezia*, p. 334.

of this female house in early modern Venice nor the role of its residents as relevant players in the political and economic strategies of the Republic.

Scholars have not given much consideration to the community's history.[18] Accounts about the convent's origins mainly rely upon Flaminio Corner's description (1758)[19] and a copy of Giustinian and Gussoni's chronicles (fifteenth century).[20] These sources narrate histories about the earliest inhabitants of the area, the mendicant friars — Sacchini (or Sacchiti), also known as the Sack Friars because of the indigence of their habit. Officially recognized in 1251, the order was short lived, and was disbanded by the second Council of Lyon in 1274.[21] Following this measure, on 8 June 1288 Pope Nicholas IV, along with the bishop of Castello, Bartolomeo Querini, sold the complex to the wealthy merchant Giovanni Bianco. In the following year, the Venetian nobleman decided to bestow his newly acquired property to the young patrician lady Bortolotta Giustinian[22] so that she could found a renewed institution entrusted to a group of Augustinian nuns.[23]

According to chronicles, soon after Bortolotta's investiture as first abbess of the convent under the protection of St Catherine, the newcomers erected their own lavish church and improved the complex's buildings.[24] The praiseworthy management of the nunnery elevated the small peripheral community to one of the most prestigious female institutions of the city, one that persisted until the arrival of French troops, and the convent's suppression by Napoleon in June 1806. Following suppression, the nuns were transferred to the community of S. Alvise, while all their possessions were requisitioned by the State. After a fitful history of building reconversions, the old convent is today used as a boarding school, whereas the church serves as temporary premises for exhibitions.[25]

---

18 Besides the significant but succinct article by Moschini Marconi, 'Note per la chiesa di Santa Caterina', the only comprehensive study on this convent community is Toffolo's unpublished dissertation, 'Art and the Conventual Life'.

19 Cornaro, *Notizie storiche delle chiese e monasteri di Venezia*, pp. 332–34.

20 Venice, ASVe, SCdS, b. 21, proc. A, fols 1ʳ–3ʳ.

21 On this order see Andrews, *The Other Friars*, pp. 175–223.

22 Bortolotta came from the convent of S. Adriano di Costanziaco and was the daughter of Nicolò Giustinian, a well-known monk who was forced to renounce the Benedictine habit to prevent his family line's extinction. See, Gennari, *Notizie spettanti al beato Nicolò Giustinian*.

23 The nuns' choice to join the Augustinian order is likely explained in part by an Augustinian revival already underway in Venice in the twelfth century. This led to the establishment of a raft of female houses under the rule of St Augustine both on the northern side of the city and on nearby islands. See Pedani, 'Monasteri di agostiniane a Venezia', pp. 37–38.

24 Venice, ASVe, SCdS, b. 1/2, preface (eighteenth century).

25 The convent was transformed into a Liceo Convitto and the church into its oratory; both underwent radical alterations in the process. During World War I the complex was temporarily used as a Red Cross hospital and the church as a storage room. At the end of the conflict, the main buildings were then converted into a boarding school while the church remained closed until the thirties, when the Soprintendenza oversaw its renovation. Between 1957 and 1960, a most invasive restoration revived the church's alleged ancient

In looking for an explanation for S. Caterina's ability to maintain its powerful position within a city that counted more than ninety sacred buildings in the sixteenth century, one cannot help but consider the importance and selectivity of the patrician families to which its nuns belonged. The practice of coerced monachization was a distinctive feature of S. Caterina throughout its history and, to some extent, always cast a pall over it. From the mid-sixteenth century, the number of women within its cloister steadily increased. Whereas in 1564 there were sixty-five women in the community, by the second decade of the seventeenth century the population of nuns had impressively reached 120, in contrast to the average of approximately eighty nuns recorded in other Venetian convents.[26] The trend coincided with the peak of patrician monachization in Venice. This was the result of noble families' strategies geared towards the preservation of the patrician patrimony and, above all, the insurance of its pure blood. The explosion of the monachization of noblewomen had important implications for Venetian social and religious life. It happened that, in 1553, the Council of Ten felt compelled to abrogate the rule that prohibited patricians whose female relatives were nuns from being appointed as *Provveditori sopra monasteri*. Given the difficulty of finding a pool of candidates that fitted this requirement, the office had to enlarge the number of eligible applicants, but it banned office holders from taking decisions about communities hosting their kin.[27]

Nevertheless, the practice of coerced monachization was certainly mutually rewarding for Venetian families and ecclesiastical institutions. The visitation of Patriarch Giovanni Trevisan to the convent of S. Caterina in 1565 attests to the community's determination to maintain aristocratic standards. As the patriarch disapprovingly observed, the nuns deliberately admitted only noblewomen. On the first day of September he wrote vigorously to protest the convent's custom and to exhort it to adhere to Christian and Republican values that tolerated and even encouraged diversity of status, under threat of excommunication.[28] Yet, the patriarchal rebuke did not succeed, and the practice of rejecting non-patrician women continued unabated.

Sharp critiques not only came from the higher echelons of the Venetian Curia. Complaints emerged even from socially inferior spheres, as can be seen in the harsh criticism of the Augustinians by Agostino Enzo. Involved at the end of the sixteenth century in a border dispute with the convent, his claim for compensation was rejected by the Council of Forty, the Supreme Court for criminal and civil cases. Determined not to give up, he wrote to the judges questioning their neutrality, having pointed out their family relationships with numerous religious women at S. Caterina. Although his

---

Gothic features through the construction of a pointed-arch colonnade. On Christmas morning 1977, a devastating fire almost completely consumed the wooden ceiling and the vault over the presbytery.

26   Sperling, *Convents and the Body Politic*, pp. 244–45 table A1.

27   Venice, ASVe, Provveditori sopra monasteri, Capitolari, reg. 1, fol. 26ʳ (12 April 1553).

28   Venice, ASPV, Visite pastorali a monasteri femminili, b. 2, fols 17ʳ–19ʳ (1 September 1565).

allegation was not acknowledged, defence of the convent was consistent with numerous similar situations within other Venetian convents.[29] Thus, the counteroffensive itself reveals the extent to which patrician monachization was a firmly-rooted phenomenon.

Indeed, less than twenty years later, Patriarch Francesco Vendramin again encountered an exclusively aristocratic institution. In 1616, all but one of S. Caterina's one hundred nuns was a noblewoman. Among these, the Contarini clan headed the list with fourteen nuns, followed at a distance by the Venier family counting six nuns, and the Foscarini, Loredan, and Vallaresso families with five nuns each.[30]

The increasing enclosure of patrician women inside convent walls had important ramifications for S. Caterina's history. Kinship ties provided the foundation of an ecclesiastical elite that could count on an extensive network of influential relationships. In addition, this led to the establishment of a cluster of learned, refined, and skillful women. While nuns projected the public face of the 'poor virgins', they participated in patronage networks and developed qualities that were considered valuable for the administration of the convent. Indeed, in the running of their community, the nuns wielded truly exceptional skills. This is particularly seen in S. Caterina's private documentation; its robust archive contains numerous records related exclusively to property, including accounts of land sales or acquisitions, contracts for building works and artistic commissions, rental agreements, interest-bearing investments, and endless accounts of land reclamation processes.

Dynamics of Urban Growth

Located on the northern limit of the city, overlooking the mainland, in a settlement physically on the edge of land and water, the history of the convent of S. Caterina hinges on the spatial maturation process undertaken by Venetian ecclesiastical institutions upon the physical 'creation' of the city (Figure 6.1). From the early thirteenth century, religious communities began vast operations of land reclamation even on the scale of entire quarters.[31] These pioneering campaigns were an effort to rectify the still frayed and irregular margins of the city, and to enhance urban areas dominated by empty lands, swamps, and marshes. During this slow colonization process, the original founding intentions, which centred on spiritual motivations, were no longer the driving force of the religious orders' actions, but rather the convent was

---

29 Venice, ASVe, SCdS, b. 21, proc. 8, reg. A, fols 1ʳ–4ᵛ (15 April 1599).
30 Venice, ASPV, Visite pastorali a monasteri femminili, b. 4 (1616).
31 The subject of Venice's urban expansion during the medieval period has been masterfully studied by Élisabeth Crouzet-Pavan in 'La conquista e l'organizzazione dello spazio', and 'La maturazione dello spazio urbano'.

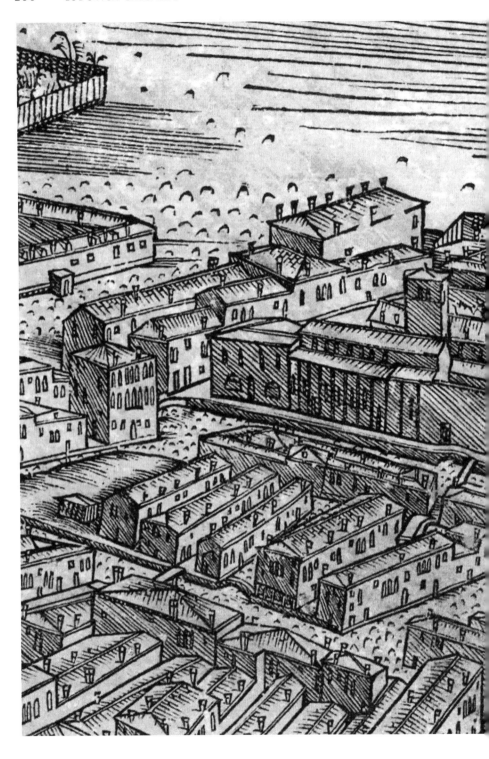

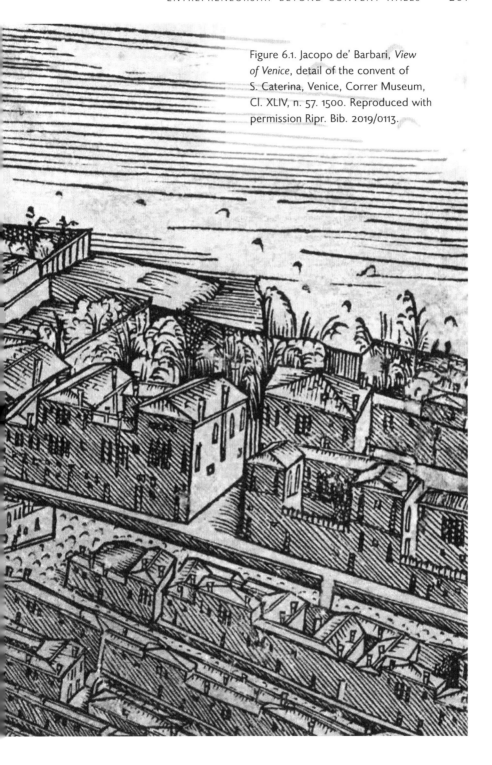

Figure 6.1. Jacopo de' Barbari, *View of Venice*, detail of the convent of S. Caterina, Venice, Correr Museum, Cl. XLIV, n. 57. 1500. Reproduced with permission Ripr. Bib. 2019/0113.

driven by a sort of 'space hunger' combined with aesthetic needs, as well as a desire for profitable investments.[32]

This approach is unequivocally reflected in the growth of S. Caterina's real estate. Thanks to inheritances and bequests but, above all, through a strategically calculated financial policy, the Augustinian nuns gradually gained control of all the properties around their convent, persistently extending their possessions even beyond the civic borders. Two precious sources help in charting this slow but spectacular progression. The first one, a *catastico* crafted by the lay procurator Domenico Prezzato beginning in 1771, minutely records all the wills, bills of sale, and private loan agreements (*livelli*) acquired by the thirteenth century.[33] The second is a prospectus of the convent's revenues and expenses in which all the economic transactions are schematically reported in relation to property owners in the year 1797.[34] As these documents elucidate, nuns carried on a massive and hectic property-purchase initiative that would have equally included land and water, following Giovanni Bianco's donation and in contravention with mortmain legislation.

Between 1294 and 1388, the advance involved the parishes of S. Sofia and S. Felice, where the nuns of S. Caterina bought numerous urban dwellings and lands from both private citizens and the Procurators of St Mark.[35] The last of these economic transactions, concluded on 1 November 1388 between the Crociferi — the twelfth-century friars set up on the other side of the *insula* — and their neighbour sisters, reflects just how complex neighbourhood relationships could be.[36] On that occasion, the friars conceded to the nuns four of their properties, which encompassed *case da sazenti* (rental residences), courtyards, vineyards, but also 'the church and the convent of S. Caterina and the houses behind [them]'. It is not easy to give an indisputable explanation for this apparent concession to the nuns of their own church and convent. As Silvia Lunardon has pointed out, the most reasonable hypothesis is that the nuns had earlier transferred the land to the Crociferi.[37] While it is impossible to assert whether the friars had held the property at *livello* from the time of the Sacchiti, the event offers evidence of the close contacts between the two religious communities, which had been sharing not only a common space but also cross-cultural experiences.

A second wave of purchases took place almost a century later, between the 1460s and 1480s, allowing the nuns to entrench their local power. In 1466 they obtained a house with land along the rio della Misericordia from the *Provveditori di comun*; eight years later they bought from Vettor Bragadin the adjacent building where they established and rented out a small workshop to

---

32 See Crouzet-Pavan, *Venice Triumphant*, pp. 9–18.
33 Venice, ASVe, SCdS, b. 1/2.
34 Venice, ASVe, SCdS, b. 5, fasc. 1 (17 August 1797).
35 On these acquisitions see Galeazzo, 'Dinamiche di crescita', p. 583 n. 244.
36 Venice, ASVe, SCdS, b. 20, proc. 5, fols 11r–13v (1 November 1388).
37 Lunardon, 'L'ospedale dei Crociferi', p. 78 n. 33.

grind pigments; in 1486 they finally acquired from the *Magistrato alle cazude* (the office responsible for exacting arrears of taxation with a ten per cent penalty) a series of residences equipped with courtyards and cisterns, located along the Fondamenta di S. Caterina.[38] Thus, from one side of the *insula* to the other, the contours of the Augustinian convent's real estate holdings grew with rapid pace.

As the island's unbuilt space started to diminish, the nuns rapidly turned their attention to extending their property assets over the marshlands surrounding the religious walls. Their enterprise soon confronted the general hydrological policy of the Republic, which had been engaged in re-establishing its jurisdiction on the lagoon environment. The alarming rise in the number and proportion of illegal reclamations had forced the Venetian authorities to strengthen their control programme through the curtailment of the procedure of *gratiae* (recorded land licences),[39] as well as the introduction of systematic surveys, which were conducted in 1485, 1503, and 1556.[40] Every square foot of unauthorized reclaimed land was assigned a standard value according to the area's location. Despite the increased efforts and the strict surveillance, the government proved unable to impose obedience, and urban regulations were brazenly contravened.[41]

Regarding abuses, the convent of S. Caterina was, once again, noteworthy. A *fascicolo* (a small register) within the archive extraordinarily illustrates the force of the nuns' strategy in wrenching — both legally and illegally — land from the waters. The register neatly gathers the complete documentation related to 'water business' carried on by different abbesses between 1502 and 1595.[42] It includes extracted copies of technical reports, land measurements, as well as ordinances compiled by the *Savi ed esecutori alle acque*.[43] Appended to this dossier are three drawings recalling interventions made just north of the convent. These are two sketches along with a watercolour map on parchment, which visually describe the gradual maturation of the urban space. Whereas the first drawing only delineates the perimeter of recent acquisitions, the second map focuses on the area's urban development by representing new public infrastructure and facilities.[44] The final map brings the two urban practices together. Precious paper material, design quality, and colour variations seem to suggest its function

---

38 Records of these acquisitions acquirements are in Venice, ASVe, SCdS, b. 26, fol. 30ʳ (11 September 1466); fol. 30ʳ (30 April 1474); fol. 22ʳ (4 April 1486).

39 In 1463, land permits that authorized citizens in their landfill operations were entirely diverted to the responsibility of the Senate and *Collegio delle Acque*. Venice, ASVe, Savi ed esecutori alle acque, reg. 330, fol. 62ʳ⁻ᵛ (14 September 1463).

40 See Pavanini, 'Venezia verso la pianificazione?', pp. 485–88, and Piasentini, 'Aspetti della Venezia d'acqua'.

41 Svalduz, 'Al servizio del magistrato', pp. 257–58.

42 Venice, ASVe, SCdS, b. 20, proc. 7.

43 Established in 1501, the office oversaw the hydrological welfare of the waterways and the lagoon.

44 The first sketch was likely made by the *proto* (master builder) Cristoforo Sabbadino in 1556. By contrast, the date and author of the second drawing are unknown. This represents

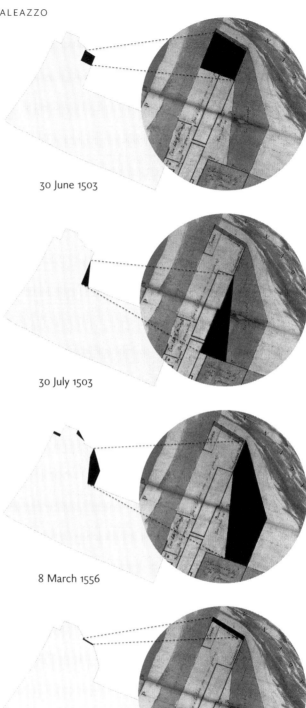

30 June 1503

30 July 1503

Figure 6.2. Digital
reconstruction of the
nuns' reclamation
activities based on the
survey by Giovanni
Alvise Galesi. Venice,
ASVe, SCdS, b. 20,
proc. 7, fol. 21ʳ. 1594.
Drawing by the author.

8 March 1556

26 June 1594

as a presentation piece. The inscription 'ad istantia delle Reverende Madre Monache' ('conducted at the behest of Reverend Mother Nuns') corroborates this interpretation. Most likely, the drawing, signed by Giovanni Alvise Galesi as member of the *Provveditori sopra beni inculti*,[45] was commissioned by the nuns and was intended as a 'graphic history' — a kind of visual inventory — of their achievements. Therefore, this iconographic representation must be read in parallel with the set of written documents in order to reconstruct the chronology of the nuns' engagement with business and building practices, as well as the administrative structures of their day (Figure 6.2).

The first intervention began on 30 June 1503 and consisted of 126 square feet of illegally reclaimed land (more than 200 square metres), which is represented as a square box in the upper part of the drawing. The following month the nuns arranged to completely fill the triangular area on the right side of their convent. The ensuing intervention was recorded only fifty years later, on 8 March 1556.[46] In charge of measurements was the famous Venetian engineer Cristoforo Sabbadino. His calculations revealed an expansion of more than 405 Venetian square feet (approximately 700 square metres), which was assessed at 101 ducats and ten *grossi*.[47]

Not even the government fiscal amnesty stopped the nuns' unabated march. On 26 June 1594, a last on-site inspection by Giovanni Alvise Galesi revealed a small reclamation (16 square feet) at the far north end of the area. Confiscated for one year, the site was then sold to the convent for two ducats per square foot — according to its right of first refusal.[48] The recent land acquisition may seem to be one of the numerous accomplishments achieved by the female community, but it is important to note that the timing of this last intervention would be connected to the future, and historically significant, construction of the Fondamente Nuove (1590–1610), which came to define the northern extremity of the city.

The nuns' attitude toward real estate acquisition serves as a barometer of common qualities shared with their relatives who sat in the councils of the Venetian State. Theoretically, according to *clausura* regulations, both administrative and managerial work should have been considered alien to them; as a matter of fact, the above events testify to the fact that regular speculative dealings and profitable ventures were normal practice for the convent's chapter. Abbesses, prioresses, and *camerlenghe* (treasurers) were not only direct spokespeople, but also initiators in the massive programme of urban redevelopment for this zone of the city.

---

the design for a series of new buildings, as well as walkways and two cisterns visible on the bottom part of the sketch.

45 The office was charged with supervising the reclamation of uncultivated land, irrigation, and drainage.
46 Venice, ASVe, SCdS, b. 20, proc. 7, fols 7ʳ–8ʳ (8 March 1556).
47 Venice, ASVe, SCdS, b. 20, proc. 7, fol. 10ʳ (19 August 1556).
48 Venice, ASVe, SCdS, b. 20, proc. 7, fol. 22ʳ (15 November 1594).

Therefore, it is not a surprise to discover the nuns' engagement with two leading characters of the Venetian economic world, such as Benetto Tiepolo and Giacomo Ragazzoni. Both rented from the convent newly reclaimed lands to establish their agricultural or proto-industrial activities. It makes sense to examine these two figures together since they influenced the sisters' managerial strategy over their possessions. The former (1524–1587), son of the notorious statesman Stefano Tiepolo, is remembered as one of the wealthiest Venetian merchants of timber and iron.[49] In 1561, he took a lease on a piece of land called *paluo* (swamp) located on the northern tip of the convent's property. Given the area's proximity to the Sacca della Misericordia — the water basin where timber coming from the mainland was stored — he decided to construct a series of wooden warehouses for his lucrative activities.[50] The second renter, Giacomo Ragazzoni (1528–1610), was one of the most talented traders that the Republic could boast.[51] In the aftermath of a long career spent between England and the Levant, he came back to Venice where he built on numerous land-oriented enterprises. Among others, in the area located in front of his house near S. Caterina, he introduced manufacturing activities connected to his old trades in soap, raisins, sugar, wax, and leather.[52] In 1580, he rented for 180 ducats a year a *casa da statio* (a patrician-status residence) along with a vegetable garden and a patch of land where he established a site for bleaching waxes as well as storing grain, timber, and other goods.[53] In addition, the twenty-year contract allowed him to build a sugar refinery.[54]

From a micro to a macro scale: these economic choices capitalized on the nuns' renters' needs and, by extension, those of the nuns, but they also responded to the exigencies of a city that was slowly moving from a mercantile vocation to a productive investment economy. Thus, the solid soil recently acquired served to secure industrial and agricultural needs.

Urban Development Processes

By the mid-sixteenth century the movement of the city's borders toward the lagoon became particularly intense. A series of motivations drove new leaps of expansion: the explosion in population,[55] the necessity of draining the mud from the excavations of canals, as well as the government's need to define a

---

49 Venice, ASVe, Miscellanea Codici, Storia veneta, Genealogie Barbaro, vol. VII, b. 23, fol. 84.
50 Venice, ASVe, SCdS, b. 19, proc. V (1565).
51 De Maria, *Becoming Venetian*, pp. 33–35, 159–69, and 219–28.
52 Galeazzo, *Venezia e i margini urbani*, pp. 178–86.
53 Venice, ASVe, SCdS, b. 30, proc. A (3 August 1580).
54 While nuns would have covered the cost up to 1200 ducats, he should contribute six per cent of the total amount along with expenses for future maintenance, though the property belonged to the nuns.
55 Between 1530 and 1580 the number of houses in Venice grew from 13,789 to 19,546, while,

regular boundary for the urban settlement. Despite the many physical and financial efforts undertaken by the Republic, the city appeared more and more as a prisoner of its surrounding water. Against repeated abuses and contraventions, the urban authorities arrived at a broad state-controlled plan. This led to the construction of the Fondamente Nuove, the long, paved quay that solidifies the city's northern border, from S. Giustina to the Sacca della Misericordia. The 'great addition' defined a new permanent margin for the city's northern margin and brought the nuns' march to an end. However, it did not weaken their ambitious growth plan.

As Manfredo Tafuri and Elena Svalduz have demonstrated, the construction of the Fondamente Nuove proceeded slowly with numerous setbacks, extending over a period of twenty years.[56] Despite practical impediments, the Republic did impose a stepped approach in order to enable magistrates to push forward the work only as eastern sections were completed.[57] This strategy was, therefore, adopted for the urbanization process. Once filled — or partially filled — new lands were divided into lots (*prese*) and gradually sold at auction by the *Savi ed esecutori alle acque* through specific contracts called *instrumenti*.[58] This real estate speculation avoided bidding that would inflate the market but it also allowed the Venetian Republic to obtain necessary revenue to carry on the public intervention because it required urban infrastructure and facilities to fall entirely on individual citizens.[59]

The comparison between the *instrumenti* and the private ecclesiastical sources enables the evaluation of dates, procedures, and especially the purchasers of the new land market. This indicates that about sixty per cent of the 8700 square metres of land sold went to religious communities: eighty per cent of these lands were acquired by the Augustinian nuns for more than 2600 ducats, while the remaining forty per cent was transferred to private owners. Once more, archival sources reveal just how S. Caterina had a vested interest in capitalizing in unused water and land spaces transforming them into lucrative investments, extending its presence into the urban realm.[60]

Certainly, the State's choice to sell the new lots of land also to Church institutions, thus contravening its own regulation on ecclesiastical real estate possessions, might seem, at least, peculiar. However, it must be tied to the wider political situation on Venice at the end of the sixteenth century. By the time the project of the Fondamente Nuove materialized, the Most Serene Republic was facing a delicate political and economic juncture due to the

---

before the plague of 1575–1577, the population reckoned as nearly 180,000 citizens. See Favero and others, 'Le anime dei demografi', pp, 28–31.

56 Tafuri, 'Documenti sulle Fondamenta Nuove', and Svalduz, 'Procedure materiali'.

57 This explains why, in 1594, Giovanni Galesi was asked to inspect and take measurements of S. Caterina's small land abuse.

58 Venice, ASVe, Savi ed esecutori alle acque, reg. 323.

59 Svalduz, 'Procedure materiali', pp. 564–74.

60 Galeazzo, *Venezia e i margini urbani*, pp. 81–83.

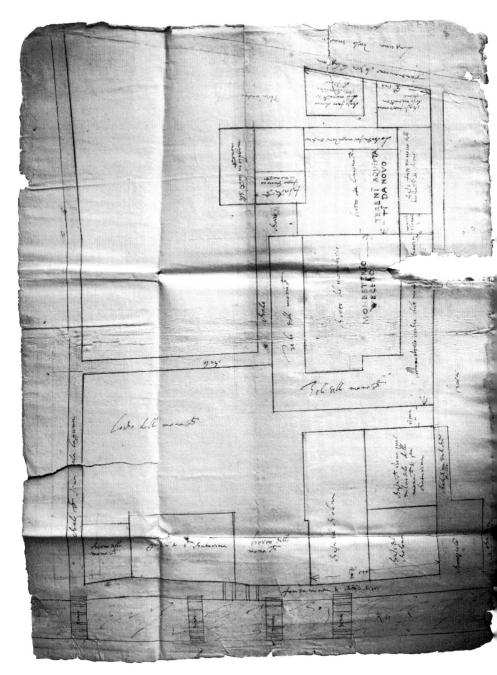

Figure 6.3. Survey of the convent of S. Caterina and design for the new buildings to be constructed, Venice, Archivio Storico del Patriarcato di Venezia, Parrocchia di San Felice, Santa Sofia, Atti generali, fasc. 4. First half of the sixteenth century. Reproduced with permission PROT. 11.19.2417.

agricultural crises of the 1560s and 1570s, the Turkish invasion of Cyprus (1570), and the devastating plague epidemic of 1576–1577. The Republic's initiative should likely be tallied as an effort to provide new revenue. But the State's hopes were not completely fulfilled. As the *instrumenti* elucidate, the sale processes for the entire new stone quay took several calls to ensure a buyer and this could therefore have pushed the government to sell the new lands also to ecclesiastical institutions.[61]

The subsequent urbanization process followed this strategic manoeuvre. While from an urban perspective the recent enlargement did not create a major transformation of the urban pattern,[62] from an economic point of view the expansion initiated a profound change in the site's purpose and the intended use of its structures. As a result of their latest acquisitions, nuns began speculative operations in order to realize substantial profits.[63] Their intervention aimed to exploit fully the urban fabric, reserving a limited space for public areas (such as *calli* and *campielli*) or for those industrial production activities that needed empty lots. The nuns' choice followed the general speculative nature of the expansions, as well as the intensive exploitation of the new urban space.[64] However, what is striking is the extension of their investment programme. Quite significantly, among 3000 square metres of new consolidated soil, none was converted into spaces for the convent's needs. Unlike early land reclamation interventions, the nuns and their current renters did not engage in agricultural or industrial activities. On the contrary, they intensified their investment in real estate. All the properties were transformed into buildings to be rented out, as clearly elucidated in a map preserved in the Archivio Patriarcale in Venice (Figure 6.3).[65] In a sketch-like wireframe visualization, newly designed buildings are indicated as 'chase fatte da novo dale monache da fitar' (new houses to rent out) and 'locho da far magazine da fitar' (place to rent out as warehouse).

As a close analysis of the tax records from 1564 to 1661 shows, the nuns increased their real estate possessions by sixty per cent as their urban dwellings grew from seventeen to forty buildings. Consequently, annual urban revenues

61 See Svalduz, 'Procedure materiali', pp. 570–79. In particular, for the *insula*, consider Venice, ASVe, Savi ed esecutori alle acque, reg. 323, fols 36ʳ–37ᵛ (7 September 1602 — buyer: Marin Tressa, after four calls); fol. 38ʳ⁻ᵛ (24 November 1603 — buyer: nuns of S. Caterina, at the first call); fols 61ʳ–62ᵛ (7 June 1606 — buyers: brothers Andrici, Virginio Tonelli, Domenico Buglio, after three calls); fols 70ʳ–71ᵛ (4 June 1609 — buyer: Giovan Battista Appiano, after five calls).

62 The sequence of parallel and straight spits of land that extend towards the lagoon persisted and the new lands fit as a natural continuation of the medieval urban design.

63 Sale invoices and material accounts give evidence of the nun's involvement even in the construction of the new buildings. A contract with Giacomo Ragazzoni testifies to the agreement for the supply of clay bricks, lime, and roof tiles produced in his furnace in Noventa, near Padua. Venice, ASVe, SCdS, b. 31, proc. C (6 July 1609).

64 Chauvard, *La circulation des biens*, pp. 127–36 and 491–516.

65 Venice, ASPV, Parrocchia di San Felice, Santa Sofia, Atti generali, fasc. 4.

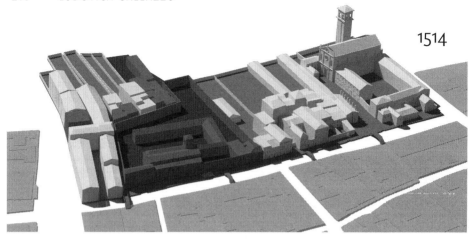

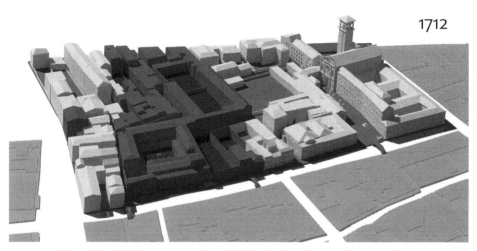

Figure 6.4. Digital reconstruction of S. Caterina's real estate in 1514 and 1712. Drawing by the author.

rose from 547 to 1256 ducats.[66] Tax revenues also helped in shaping the quality of the new properties. These were mostly warehouses, residential buildings, and low-cost houses built on two or three stories.[67] Renters belonged mainly to the upper-middle class and, in particular, to the manual workers' world. Against the Republic's expectations (repeatedly stated in the magistrates'

66 Venice, ASVe, Sopraintendenti alle decime del clero, b. 32, cond. 83 (1564) and ASVe, Dieci savi alle decime in Rialto, b. 421 (1661).
67 Annual rentals ranged from forty to seventy ducats. Only a few houses located along the Fondamente Nuove reached 160 ducats.

reports), the expansion did not bring far-reaching residential investments or innovative architectural projects (Figure 6.4).

Once more, to identify the reasons lying behind these acquisitions, it is necessary to take a look at the economic and political framework of seventeenth-century Venice. The nuns' entrepreneurial strategy, just like the general approach of laypersons who owned property, appears strictly tied to the gradual decline of Venice as a major international centre of trade, as well as to its conversion toward a real estate-based economy. It also reveals how urban space began to be prioritized as an economic opportunity for investing in property, rather than to be considered as fulfilling a basic need.

The minor but repeated efforts carried out by the nuns were instrumental in securing for the convent vast and significant real estate holdings, but they also can be seen as a sort of exercise in the Augustinians' future network formation and exploitation. As part of the 'collective enterprise' that developed the area's expansion, nuns' action was, in fact, strongly involved in the social construction of the urban site. Besides significant consequences for the *insula's* development, this led to the convent's integration into the urban fabric and neighbourhood. Moreover, it provided the nuns long-term connections with magistrates, architects, engineers, master-builders, as well as private citizens who were all together involved in the 'production' of space.

Economic Investments on the Mainland

From its very inception, the investment policy of the convent also encompassed the Venetian *terraferma*. If the Augustinian nuns noticeably showed their entrepreneurial skills within the dolphin-shaped contours of the city, they carried on an even greater enterprise in extending their rural real estate holdings in the Venetian territory. The economic business of S. Caterina can safely be associated with the land-oriented politics of the largest Venetian religious complexes.[68] Although *clausura* presented serious challenges to distant landholding management, this did not prevent nuns from acquiring possessions in remote areas, stretching them as far as the Veronese area and Polesine.

To a large extent, the *pars dominica* (rural real estate) was the result of a long raft of purchases and donations established during the thirteenth century. However, the convent's deals steadily continued over the next three centuries. The first acquisition dates to September 1290. On that occasion, the nuns secured from Alberico da Treviso two *mansi* (plots of land) in Bonisiol, near Treviso, to be used as both woodland and grassland.[69] This area was strategically important for Venice because of the demands for firewood

68   See Sperling, *Convents and the Body Politic*, pp. 270–71 table A12.
69   Venice, ASVe, SCdS, b. 30, proc. A, fol. 1ʳ (8 September 1290).

and the transit of flocks of sheep. However, it seems also to have appealed to the convent, which engaged in a long string of acquisitions. Between 1333 and 1370 the nuns purchased farmlands, and several houses and warehouses from the Zanin and della Seda families, which also counted kinswomen in the convent.[70] In 1400 they extended their property over a portion of woods belonging to the Nascimben, whereas almost thirty years later they obtained a large plot from Albertino da Bonisiol as a spiritual dowry. Ultimately, in 1516, the *Ufficio del Sopragastaldo* (the office in charge of execution of civil sentences of all Venetian magistracies) ceded to them some warehouses and barns belonging to Batta Antonioli as compensation for his agricultural debts to the convent.[71]

At the same time, nuns' interests had been focused on a broad scope of rural patrimonies. Over the fourteenth century, they acquired several fields and agricultural buildings in Zerman, along with woody areas in Casale sul Sile, Villa d'Arzere and Povegliano, all in the area south of Treviso that specialized in viticulture.[72] Beginning in the fifteenth century, nuns also extended their real estate on farmlands in Villa del Conte (Padua) and in Crea (near Mestre), while in 1599 they bought 400 *valli* (fish basins) from Almorò Dolfin, President of the Ritratto delle Valli in Lendinara (Rovigo).[73]

In defiance of mortmain laws, which were repeatedly issued, S. Caterina went further than simply accumulating a series of new real estate possessions and lands. On 10 September 1680, the convent purchased a whole fiefdom worth 45,100 silver ducats. This was located in Villa d'Orti — today known as a minor district of Bonavigo, in the southern countryside of Verona. It belonged to the monastery of S. Giorgio in Braida and was sold at auction after the suppression of the Benedictine order in 1668.[74] The event is largely reflective of the convent's liquidity and, moreover, it is a tell-tale sign of its accumulated wealth.[75]

The expansive growth was extremely lively, although records give us only an approximate account. The difficulties arise from the very nature of conventual registers, which rarely report the extent of the area of acquired

---

70 Toffolo, 'Art and the Conventual Life', p. 105.
71 See, respectively: Venice, ASVe, SCdS, b. 30, proc. A, fols 38ʳ–44ᵛ (1333–1339) and 133ʳ–139ᵛ (1365–1370); fols 174ʳ–191ʳ (7 June 1400); fol. 189ʳ (29 November 1427); fol. 194ʳ (17 September 1516).
72 Venice, ASVe, SCdS, b. 30, proc. A, fols 16ʳ–19ʳ (17 January 1321 *m.v.*); fols 56ʳ–58ᵛ (28 May 1346); fols 160ʳ–165ʳ (2 March 1395). The abbreviation *m.v.* refers to *more veneto*, the Venetian convention of beginning the new year on 1 March.
73 Following the purchase, the nuns rented out all the basins to Almorò Dolfin himself in the typical form of a *livello*. Acting as president of the area, he was in charge of the land reclamation of all the properties. Venice, ASVe, SCdS, b. 37 (7 September 1600).
74 Venice, ASVe, SCdS, b. 5, fasc. 7, fol. 1ʳ. See Biancolini, *Notizie storiche delle chiese di Verona*, p. 486 where the estimated cost is 47,000 ducats.
75 It is interesting to note that, after this purchase, in the archival documents all abbesses are also addressed as 'contesse' (countess) of Villa d'Orti, a title typically associated with laywomen.

lands, merely indicating them in terms of plots, vineyards, or woods. Problems also result from the paucity of archival documentation, definitely biased toward the eighteenth century, and also because nuns were required to declare their estimated possessions only to the ecclesiastical tithe.[76] Fragmented data, the common use of income in kind (foremost wheat, wine, chickens, and cheese), and the dizzying fluctuation of the Venetian monetary system make it impossible to produce a detailed picture of the distribution of the convent's rural properties.

Regardless of quantitative data, one characteristic of these acquisitions clearly emerges from archival descriptions. In a surprisingly large number of cases, lands were located near rivers or canals whose water was used for both water milling and manufacturing activities. From the fifteenth century, the control of waterways and related infrastructures was a matter of great interest for both private citizens and the State, which was strongly committed to the capital city's food supply. The Augustinian nuns directed their energies toward this field too. On 20 February 1679, the *Provveditori sopra beni inculti* allowed them to construct at their expense, a two-wheeled mill in Bonisiol, on the Zero river.[77] As for Villa d'Orti — which was located near the Adige River and the Canale del Terrazzo — water was used to irrigate the extensive paddy fields. The 1797-account book reports an annual income of 18,722 pounds of rice that was only partially used for the convent's internal consumption. For the most part it was dried and sold for a net revenue of more than 500 ducats.[78]

Like their metropolitan counterparts, mainland contracts prove that, although facilitated by male agents, nuns managed the convent's affairs by themselves, including drawing up lease contracts, collecting income, handling revenues, and overseeing farmlands. A colourful example provides evidence of the nuns' inveterate freedom of mobility. In 1405 the nobleman Marco Cavalli gave the convent twenty-five ducats per year to be paid to his daughter Elisabetta as a pension. Only one condition was imposed: his daughter could not 'go to town, nor could she go out from the house [convent] more than usual'.[79] This precise instruction is highly indicative of the nuns' urban custom that extended to retreats in the countryside. As the documentation about the management of the fiefdom in Villa d'Orti distinctly reveals, the nuns' inclination did not change over time, even after reforms instituted both by the Venetian government and by the Council of Trent, of which nuns carefully kept copies in their archive.[80] Abbesses, along with their prioresses,

76 According to these tax records, the increase of revenues from landholdings between 1564 and 1769 was extremely high, increasing to 2621 per cent.
77 See the drawing by the *perito* (expert) Sebastiano Alberti in ASVe, Provveditori sopra beni inculti, Disegni, Treviso-Friuli, rotolo 433, mazzo 25/B, drawing 7 (15 April 1678).
78 Venice, ASVe, SCdS, b. 5, fasc. 7 (17 August 1797).
79 Venice, ASVe, SCdS, b. 11, fol. 1ʳ (18 October 1405).
80 Venice, ASVe, SCdS, b. 31, proc. C.

Figure 6.5. Interior of the church of S. Caterina, Venice, Università
Iuav di Venezia, Archivio Progetti, fondo Egle Renata Trincanato.

After 1957 and before 1977. Reproduced with permission
Ripr. 226 VFE 25/11/2019.

camerlenghe, and the convent's procurator, used to make regular visits to their possessions as if they were ordinary landowners.[81]

Art and Architecture Patronage

While engaged in increasing their fixed assets within and outside the metropolitan city, by the second half of the sixteenth century the Augustinian nuns carried out a programmatic campaign of artistic and architectural initiatives for embellishing their church and convent, which also gave expression to their networks, which included patrons and artists alike. Even though there is little archival evidence about these works, guidebook descriptions provide important details about the appearance of the interiors, the nature of their decoration, and specifics about the location, authorship, and sometimes patronage of individual works of art.[82] These were commissioned both by the nuns themselves and families connected to the convent through family ties, or social interests. The amount and quality of the works of art enjoyed by the nuns give us a sense of the impressive artistic wealth of the nunnery, which boasted paintings by each of the great Renaissance triumvirate: a Titian (1488/1490–1576) — probably commissioned by the Bembo family —,[83] six canvases by Tintoretto (1518/1519–1594), and a Veronese (1528–1588), all painted under the tenure of Abbess Teodosia Donà, who headed the convent between 1567 and 1592. They also disclose a sort of 'planned' agenda of the nuns for artistic works, which entails a decorative programme almost solely devoted to the convent's Alexandrine patron saint.

If externally the bare shape of the church of S. Caterina assimilates it to many Gothic religious buildings, it was in the lavishly decorated interior that one could find the clearest indication of the nunnery's high profile. The general plan of the church followed the classic pattern of thirteenth-century structures consisting of a rectangular building entered via an atrium. A nave with two shallow side aisles and no transepts was rhythmically articulated with two rows of columns supporting pointed arches. The central nave was covered with a polychromatic wooden ship's-keel ceiling, while the lateral aisles had flat ceilings enriched with truss ornamental patterns (Figure 6.5). On the counter façade, a wood-beamed nuns' choir suspended upon two columns embodied the image of the religious women's *clausura*. At the opposite side, two square-shaped chapels flanked the chancel that featured the high altar.

Like a *crescendo*, a panoply of altarpieces, paintings, and statues devoted to St Catherine decorated the walls of both aisles to climax with Veronese's

---

81   See the documentation preserved in Venice, ASVe, SCdS, b. 30, proc. A.

82   The principal sources are Martinioni, *Venetia città nobilissima*, p. 173; Boschini, *Le minere della pittura*, pp. 428–32; Moschini, *Guida per la città*, I, pp. 673–80.

83   See the following section *The Church of Santa Caterina as a Neighbourhood Pantheon*.

altarpiece depicting the *Mystical Marriage of Saint Catherine* (1570–1575).[84] This was metaphorically enclosed by Tintoretto's cycle of the life of the saint, located on the side walls of the main chapel and probably begun in 1582. Six canvases — now preserved at the patriarchal palace in Venice — represented as many episodes of St Catherine's life from the *Refusal to Adore Pagan Idols* to the *Martyrdom*.[85] To this iconographic programme, in 1613, nuns added four paintings by an aged Jacopo Palma il Giovane (1548/1550–1628) who was almost at the end of his career, after the 'long marathon' of works executed for the nearby church, the sacristy, and the *ospedaletto* of the Crociferi. While his *Consultation with Saint Catherine's Mother* was located on the north side wall of the chancel, the remaining paintings depicting episodes from the life of the martyr were placed in the left aisle of the church, including the *Transportation of Saint Catherine's Body to Mt. Sinai* that was destroyed by fire in 1977. On the same wall, a lay confraternity (*scuola piccola*) dedicated to St Catherine[86] had established an altar devoted to the patron, which included a wooden statue of the saint, later replaced by a marble copy. Furthermore, the confraternity's inventory reported a variety of altar furnishings embellished with the representation of St Catherine, used in both the church and their *albergo*, which seem to have fostered a sort of monopoly on the image of the patron saint.[87]

Along with these major works of art, a large group of lesser-studied artists contributed to the decoration of the church's interior space:[88] among others, Antonio Vassilacchi known as l'Aliense (1556–1629), Pietro Vecchia (1603–1678),[89] Pietro Ricchi (1606–1675), and Sebastiano Mazzoni (1611–1678).[90] The clerestory was completely covered with an early seventeenth-century cycle by Andrea Vicentino (*c*. 1542–1617); it encompassed fourteen paintings depicting Sibyls and stories from the Old Testament.[91] Despite the lack of written evidence, study of the works of art reveals the initiative that nuns took to select the iconographic design, artists, and subject matters for their church. Moreover, these works are the tangible sign of their taste for innovation and quality that is most clearly reflected in the selection of Paolo Veronese, a favourite painter of the patriciate.

---

84 The painting was transferred in 1915 to the Gallerie dell'Accademia. On this masterpiece, see Salomon, *Veronese*, pp. 131–34 and cat. 23, p. 256.

85 See Caputo, ed., *Tintoretto: il ciclo di Santa Caterina*.

86 The devotional guild was founded in 1337 and had its meeting house in a two-floor building located in front of the church's atrium. See Vio, *Le Scuole Piccole*, pp. 561–68.

87 The observance of the patronal feast, regularly organized and financed by the *scuola* on 25 November, would compete with the wealthiest Venetian nunneries. See Toffolo, 'Art and the Conventual Life', pp. 123–24.

88 Galeazzo, *Venezia e i margini urbani*, pp. 287–92.

89 See Bisceglia, *Pietro Vecchia nell'ambiente veneto del '600*.

90 See Caburlotto, ed., *Sebastiano Mazzoni*.

91 Moschini Marconi, 'Note per la chiesa di Santa Caterina', p. 36.

At the turn of the eighteenth century, a second phase of commissions began, this time primarily involving architectural structures and the renovation of extant buildings. The initiative summoned the most prominent architects of the Venetian Settecento. Above all, the nuns' chose the architect Domenico Rossi (1657–1737) who, at the time, was working on the other side of the *insula*, at the church of S. Maria Assunta dei Gesuiti. He was also particularly well known in the area for having been the *proto* (master builder) of the Zane family of the parish of S. Stin, whose members owned an extensive parcel of land, located right behind the convent, for storing and working timber.[92] The architect was first in charge of the construction of a new dormitory (1711) and then, between 1723 and 1727, of the renovation of the main chapel along with the erection of the high altar, under the supervision — perhaps not accidentally — of the Abbess Celeste Zane.[93]

The chancel was elevated with the construction of a high dome-on-pendentives, while a thermal window was opened on the south wall with the express purpose of allowing light to come inside and highlight Veronese's masterpiece.[94] The dome frescoes depicting St Catherine in Glory and the four Virtues in the pendentives were assigned to the artist Gerolamo Brusaferro (1677–1745).[95] Walls were decorated with stuccoes modelled by Abbondio Stazio (1665–1745), whose activity would cross paths with Domenico Rossi in the nearby Jesuits' church some years later. During the eighteenth-century restoration, the two lunettes with *Agony in the Garden* and *Resurrection of Christ* by Antonio Foller (1536–1616) were renovated, remodelled, and placed in the high chapel.[96]

In the following years, the architect Paolo Tremignon, the son of the best-known Alessandro, along with Andrea Tirali (1657–1737) was commissioned to restore the sacristy (1727) and some conventual buildings.[97] In 1753, the young Bernardino Maccaruzzi (1728–1800) was asked to renovate the chapel of Madonna del Rosario dedicated to the Virgin (on that occasion the space was also redecorated with a Marian programme), while fifteen years later he replaced the Romanesque bell tower with the still extant bell-cote.[98]

The availability of archival documents surviving from the eighteenth century clarifies and solidifies the nuns' intimate involvement in artistic decisions.

92 The Zane family sold its land and buildings in 1663, two years before beginning the construction of the magnificent façade of the palace along the Grand Canal. Galeazzo, *Venezia e i margini urbani*, pp. 186–94.

93 He was commissioned to design entablatures, cornices, mouldings, bases, and capitals. Venice, ASVe, SCdS, b. 18.

94 Zanetti, *Rinnovazione delle Ricche minere*, p. 386.

95 Venice, ASVe, SCdS, b. 18 (1727).

96 While the lunette with the *Resurrection* was located on the high dome, the canvas depicting the *Agony* was squared and placed above the cycle of Jacopo Palma il Giovane. Both paintings were destroyed by the fire in 1977.

97 Venice, ASVe, SCdS, b. 18.

98 Venice, ASVe, SCdS, b. 34, fasc. V (12 August 1767).

From the quality of the materials to the model's design to the final cost: abbesses committed themselves to the comprehensive building and artistic processes. The nuns' artistic and architectural endeavours, as well as their determination to pursue an artistically refined patronage agenda, eloquently reflect both the ambition and power of this community of religious women. Through their commissions and investments, the Augustinians were able to imprint their aesthetic and stylistic choices but, above all, to strengthen their network of cultural and social interactions with the most prominent figures of the Venetian artistic world. The artefacts that enriched the church of S. Caterina serve as evidence of the place of the community within the city's life, which bring it widely and well beyond the convent walls, but they also present the public face of the enclosed women in the convent to the broader secular-social world of Venice.

Due to the lack of substantive supporting archival evidences, it is difficult to ascertain how much the nuns' actions might have been influenced directly by their natal families' taste and, by contrast, how much it was the result of personal and autonomous ideas. However, an intricate pattern of relationships and friendships between the nuns' family networks and prominent artists clearly emerge from different kind of sources. For example, tax assessments help in shedding light on the relationship between the Zen family and Paolo Veronese. According to Vincenzo Zen's submitted tax declaration, by 1582 the painter lived in the mezzanine floor of his palace along the Fondamenta di S. Caterina.[99] In the same period, Marietta and Gioconda Zen, daughters of Carlo Zen and nieces of Vincenzo, were both nuns in S. Caterina and they might have contributed to the choice of Veronese for the main chapel's altarpiece.[100] The Zen family could also have epitomized the social bond with another important figure for the decoration programme of the church's chancel. Indeed, a young Tintoretto is mentioned as assistant of Andrea Schiavone (c. 1510 –1563) for the exterior fresco cycle of the Zen Palace, now almost completely lost.[101] Moreover, in his mature age, the artist painted the superb portrait of Vincenzo Zen (c. 1560), today preserved in the Galleria Palatina of Palazzo Pitti in Florence. It is worth recalling that Tintoretto was also responsible for another remarkable portrait of a figure intimately bound both by economic and social interests in Persia and by blood to the Zen family[102] and also, as it will be soon explained, to the convent of S. Caterina itself: the Procurator of St Mark, Nicolò Priuli. The nobleman was portrayed by Tintoretto in 1545 in a manner consistent with the office, even before his

---

99   Venice, ASVe, Dieci savi alle decime in Rialto, 1582, b. 120, cond. 1848.
100 Venice, ASVe, SCdS, b. 21, fasc. A, fol. 58ʳ (1596).
101 See Ridolfi, *Le maraviglie dell'arte*, II, pp. 15–16.
102 Nicolò Priuli married one of the nieces of the emperor of Trebizond and was uncle to the Caterina Cornaro. He was connected to the Zen family through his mother Lucrezia Crispo, sister of Violante, the wife of Caterino Zen known as 'il Cavaliere'. He is also mentioned as testamentary executor for Pietro Zen. See Concina, *Dell'arabico*, pp. 27–56.

election to the position, one of the highest of the Venetian state. Priuli died just four years later, but his remains still rest with those of many of his family in the tomb that was constructed for them at the turn of the fifteenth century in the church, just in front of the Tintoretto cycle.

The Church of S. Caterina as a Neighbourhood Pantheon

Along with the nuns' commissions, the church served in fact as a 'pantheon' for many citizens who lived near the convent and belonged to very different social backgrounds.[103] In particular three families maintained residences located on the other side of the canal: the above-mentioned patrician Priuli, the *cittadini* Ragazzoni, and the *popolani* De Nasi. The three status conditions, the Venetian trifold social hierarchy of the Republic, however, did not reflect a similar variety among the inhabitants of S. Caterina's sacred walls.[104]

Reflecting a privileged hierarchy, the Priuli of the da S. Felice branch were conferred the more dignified burial site in S. Caterina's church. The family was conceded a tomb in the chancel, which today is no longer visible due to the numerous re-fittings and radical restorations of the presbytery. The main chapel, along with the family's tomb, was in fact rebuilt sometime between the late fifteenth and early sixteenth centuries with the financial support of one of the female members of the family, Samaritana Priuli. In her second will (1494), the noblewoman bestowed a substantial amount of money to be invested for the construction of a new altar chapel.[105] Almost fifty years later, the grave served as the resting place for the most prominent figure of the family, the above-mentioned Nicolò Priuli. There is little evidence of the arrangement of his funeral, but as the still extant epitaph reads, his body rests

---

103 Venetian society was essentially divided into three social groups: the *nobili* (aristocrats), who were allowed to occupy the highest offices of the Serenissima; the *cittadini* (rich bourgeois), who were denied both the dignity of aristocracy and participation in the political government; and the *popolani* (commoners), who formed the majority of the population and covered a broad spectrum of individuals, from wealthy merchants to poor day labourers. It should be noted, however, that the caste-based system of the government was quite permeable and the three legal categories were not homogeneous. Remarkable families excluded from the nobility were designated as 'original' citizens and occupied a highly prestigious position in the society. Thus, well-educated and 'honourable' *cittadini* could occupy important bureaucratic positions in state government as well as in the administration of the Scuole Grandi or lay confraternities. Moreover, the tripartite system allowed citizens who had resided and paid taxes in Venice to become naturalized citizens. According to the time of residency and the privileges acquired they were called *cittadini de intus* or *de intus et extra*. In addition, in times of economic or social hardship, the government temporary opened both the patriciate and the *cittadini* status to people who were able to buy their own new social position. See Grubb, 'Elite Citizens', pp. 339–40.

104 Toffolo, 'Art and the Conventual Life', pp. 95–121.

105 Venice, ASVe, SCdS, b. 11, proc. 2, fol. 48ʳ (30 January 1493 *m.v.*). A description of the old chapel is provided by Sansovino, *Venetia città nobilissima*, p. 61.

in the prestigious space reserved for his family in the most exclusive burial location, directly in front of the high altar. Many Priuli family members asked to be buried in the church, including some nuns from the family. In particular, we are aware of the presence of Suor Graziosa (originally named Orsetta) Priuli, daughter of Nicolò, whose wishes are known through her will, which was drawn up together with Suor Francesca (originally named Caterina) Zen, daughter of Vincenzo Zen and Graziosa's distant relative.[106]

By contrast, the last desires of the ambitious Giacomo Ragazzoni are disclosed in the octogenarian's testimonial pages.[107] And yet, this documentation is more than a will or a post-mortem inventory; it offers a picture of an intense and fruitful life lived at the highest cultural and political levels of Venetian society.[108] This condition is only partially reflected in the burial monument he chose for his remains along with those of his wife and most of his thirteen sons. The modest architecture aligns with the family's social status and with the sober behaviour of the wealthy trader. His funerary monument is still visible, although quite altered, on the counter façade of the church, below the nuns' choir. It consisted of a marble bust of the patron (once preserved in his house),[109] the gravestone in front of the main door, as well as the marble portal that Giacomo donated to the nuns as thanks for the space granted within the sacred church of their 'patrician' nunnery.

Worthy of the position of patrician citizens was the burial site of Zuan Antonio De Nasi. He is an intriguing figure in Venetian history, and, as many scholars have lamented, deserving of greater analysis. Mentioned by Giuseppe Tassini as son of a fustian maker from Cremona, but most likely of Greek origins, he lived in the vast house that faced S. Caterina, near the Zanardi bridge.[110] Marin Sanudo identified him as a supervisor of works in

---

106 Venice, ASVe, SCdS, b. 11, proc. 4, fols 23^r–24^r (27 June 1642).

107 Venice, ASVe, Notarile, Testamenti, b. 784, n. 244 (7 May 1609).

108 As stated by Giuseppe Trebbi, he was the one who best represented what an intelligent and rich *cittadino* (citizen status) could do despite not being authorized to cross the boundary that separated him from the patriciate (Trebbi, 'La società veneziana', p. 177). As a diplomatic agent at the court of King Henry VIII and his daughter Mary I, Ragazzoni served as conduit of information between the Tudor family and the Papacy because his brother, Monsignor Vettor Ragazzoni, worked as secretary to Pope Julius III. In addition, he participated in the arrangement of Mary's marriage contract to King Philip II of Spain and, thus, the queen awarded him the privilege of adding the Tudor rose to the Ragazzoni coat of arms. In 1571, during the war of Cyprus, he was sent as an ambassador to Constantinople to assist the *bailo* (the resident Venetian ambassador in the city) Marco Antonio Barbaro in the negotiations with the Grand Vizier Sokollu Mehmed Pasha. Although the diplomatic mission was not successful, the Republic praised Giacomo for his professional appointment by giving him and his brothers the title of count of S. Odorico, a feudal seat near Sacile. See De Maria, *Becoming Venetian*, pp. 159–69 and Galeazzo, *Venezia e i margini urbani*, pp. 178–86.

109 The bust was replaced by a nineteenth-century copy that portrays a religious man wearing a mitre. Scholars have argued that it might depict his brother Girolamo, bishop of Famagusta and Bergamo. See Toffolo, 'Art and the Conventual Life', p. 109.

110 Venice, BMC, MS. P.D.c. 4, G. Tassini, *Cittadini veneziani*, III, fol. 276^r.

copper and tin (*sorastante di rami et stagni*) at the Fondaco dei Tedeschi[111] but, quite surprisingly, he was also remembered as a refined collector and owner of several paintings, including masterpieces by Titian and Giovanni Bellini.[112] In addition, he was a prominent character for the history of the nunnery to which he left, besides his remains, a variety of goods, as many of the *cittadini* from the upper echelons did.

On 25 March 1567, he drew up a will in which he outlined his funeral and entombment in great detail, in this way disclosing a certain familiarity with the Augustinian nuns.[113] He requested a grave for himself and his family members to be placed at the foot of the altar dedicated to the Archangel Raphael, the monument that he established on the right aisle of the church.[114] Among other objects, he also bequeathed to the church two precious paintings that belonged to his private house. One was the now-lost *Supper at Emmaus*, which was located on his altar. The second masterpiece has been identified as Giovanni Bellini's *Virgin and Child with Saints Catherine, Lucy, John, and Peter*, now in storage at the Metropolitan Museum of Art in New York City. According to his will, this was likely placed on the altar of the nuns' choir.[115]

De Nasi's last wish is particularly significant for a couple of reasons. First, it testifies to the easy accessibility of the church and its role as a site for wealthy families' patronage, regardless of social rank. In addition, it confirms the presence of another remarkable private commission within the church's walls. Beginning with the art critic Carlo Ridolfi (1648), guidebook descriptions recall that the altar was later decorated with Titian's painting of *Archangel Raphael and Tobias* (*c.* 1508),[116] today preserved in the Gallerie dell'Accademia in Venice.[117] Scholars have recently speculated about a possible commission by the Bembo family (in particular, by Bernardo) for this masterpiece.[118] In fact, the household coat of arms in the foreground would suggest such patronage. This assumption, although not completely corroborated by archival sources, is supported by the presence of a long line of female members of the family in chapter meetings at S. Caterina from 1374

111   Sanudo il Giovane, *I diarii*, LVIII, col. 392.

112   Hochmann, 'Le collezioni veneziane del Rinascimento', p. 16.

113   The testament is kept in ASVe, Notarile, Testamenti, b. 1259, n. 588 and a copy is in Venice, ASVe, SCdS, b. 11, proc. 3, fols 70ᵛ–81ᵛ. For a complete transcription, see Toffolo, 'Art and the Conventual Life', Appendix b, pp. 164–67.

114   The altar was also enriched with a magnificent *predella*. This is an alabaster triptych with scenes from the *Life of Saint Catherine* now on display at the Galleria Franchetti at the Ca' d'Oro. See Murat, 'Medieval English Alabaster Sculptures', pp. 403–05.

115   Toffolo, 'Art and the Conventual Life', pp. 117–18.

116   Paul Joannides, along with Peter Humfrey and Mauro Lucco, had suggested a later date for the painting, between 1511 to 1514. See Joannides, *Titian to 1518*, pp. 165–70; Humfrey, *Titian*, p. 65 n. 27; Lucco, *Tiziano e la nascita*, pp. 92–95 n. 13.

117   See Ridolfi, *Le maraviglie dell'arte*, I, pp. 152–53; Boschini, *Le minere della pittura*, p. 428; Moschini, *Guida per la città*, I, p. 674.

118   See Ferrari, 'Tiziano Vecellio' and related biography.

until 1554.[119] In addition, Patricia Fortini Brown has demonstrated that Marcella Marcello (1496–1555), niece of Cardinal Pietro Bembo and wife of the doge of Candia Giovanni Matteo Bembo, was also raised in the convent. Remembered as a well-educated and refined woman, shortly after her marriage when her husband was working as Venetian diplomat in the Holy Land, she served as a mediator between Pope Leo X and the convent of S. Caterina where her two sisters Maria and Giulia were nuns.[120] Her presence adds yet another piece of evidence to the enduring and extensive influence of wealthy and aristocratic families and their involvement with the nunnery's quotidian life.

Beyond Enclosure: A Glimpse into the Early Modern World

Despite the nuns' heroic resistance, the Venetian Curia eventually won its war, ensuring complete *clausura* and imposing severe limitations on secluded communities. But beyond the legislation, evidence suggests that nuns still maintained some control over what happened inside and outside their nunneries. As Kate Lowe has convincingly stated, convents should not be regarded simply as religious communities, but rather as distinctive institutions with undeniable social and political significance.[121]

As a long line of scholars has proven, S. Caterina certainly was not an anomalous case in Venetian history. Many religious institutions — first and foremost the convents of S. Zaccaria and S. Maria delle Vergini — were equally independent and active. Regarding S. Caterina, what is to some extent surprising, however, is not only the modest scale of the nunnery, but also the broad scope of ventures and enterprises that its nuns pursued. Their forward-thinking plans included urban expansion, land reclamation, urban development, real estate investment, building renovation, as well as art patronage. Certainly, the upper-class background of these 'brides of Christ' provided them with considerable business expertise and allowed them to manage unusually complex situations. Unfortunately, archival sources tend to be short on information about nuns' family networks and do not help in identifying precisely the specific branches of the families in question. This is due to the sisters' custom of changing their name after monachization, and also because of the absence of nuns' names in the genealogies compiled in the sixteenth century by Marco Barbaro.[122] However, sketchy and scattered

---

119   Catarucia Bembo and Marieta Bembo, Venice, ASVe, SCdS, b. 38 (5 July 1357) and b. 26, proc. M, fol. 26ʳ (26 November 1554).

120   Marcella Marcello was the daughter of Pietro Bembo's sister Antonia. On her contacts with Pope Leo X see Fortini Brown, 'Becoming a Man of Empire', pp. 231–49.

121   Lowe, 'Power and Institutional Identity', pp. 129–30.

122   Family trees drawn up by Marco Barbaro are in Venice, ASVe, Miscellanea Codici, Storia veneta, Genealogie Barbaro.

data nestled amongst lease contracts and economic transactions provide us of a solid overview of the high social and political level of the nuns' relatives.

A few additional examples from the second half of the sixteenth century demonstrate this status. The convent welcomed Giulia Foscarini, sister of Daniele Foscarini and sister-in-law of Giulia Pisani, the natural daughter of the Cardinal Francesco Pisani.[123] The prioress Anzola Basadonna and her cousin Cecilia were sister and niece of the Senator Piero Basadonna respectively.[124] Eugenia Donato was aunt of Zuanne Alvise, who was awarded the title of knight by the King of France Henri III.[125] Perpetua Bernardo was aunt of the Procurator of St Mark Giacomo Renier[126] and Elena and Laura Foscarini were sisters of Michiel, counsellor in the Council of Ten, and Gerolamo, superintendent in Zante.[127] In addition, a significant document preserved within the convent archive informs us of the presence, between 1566 and 1590, in the magistracy of the *Sopraintendenti alle decime del clero* of as many as sixteen noblemen who counted female relatives in the convent of S. Caterina.[128] The widespread kinship ties with patricians involved in the state government and, more specifically, in the management of the office that oversaw property taxes, which was of great importance to the nuns, might support the idea of the influence of nuns' natal families in the development of their entrepreneurial skills and policy-making capacities.

An additional emblematic figure was one of the last abbesses of the convent, the princess Maria Luigia Rezzonico, niece of Pope Clement XIII, the abbess to whom Gasparo Gozzi dedicated sumptuous words of praise.[129] She headed the nunnery for ten consecutive three-years periods, from 1762 to 1791, proving amazing skills in the efficient management of the convent's finances.[130]

---

123 For Daniele Foscarini see: Venice, ASVe, Miscellanea Codici, Storia veneta, Genealogie Barbaro, vol. III, b. 19, fol. 545.

124 For Piero Basadonna see: Venice, ASVe, Miscellanea Codici, Storia veneta, Genealogie Barbaro, vol. II, b. 18, fol. 258.

125 For Zuanne Alvise Donato see: Venice, ASVe, Miscellanea Codici, Storia veneta, Genealogie Barbaro, vol. III, b. 19, fol. 317.

126 For Giacomo Renier see: Venice, ASVe, Miscellanea Codici, Storia veneta, Genealogie Barbaro, vol. VI, b. 22, fol. 417.

127 For Michiel and Gerolamo Foscarini see: Venice, ASVe, Miscellanea Codici, Storia veneta, Genealogie Barbaro, vol. III, b. 19, fol. 537.

128 Venice, ASVe, SCdS, b. 21, proc. 8, fasc. B, fols 21ʳ–22ᵛ. The report lists the following names: Daniel Foscarini q. Sebastian; Bernardo Molin q. Francesco; Nicolò Tron q. Polo; Antonio Donato q. Zuan Battista; Vincenzo Correr q. Zuan Francesco; Vettor Correr q. Polo; Alessandro Contarini q. Pandolfo; Michiel Falier q. Zuanne; Bortolomanio Gradenigo q. Marco; Alessandro Trevisan q. Anzolo, Girolamo Dandolo q. Leonardo, Andrea Cappello q. Alvise; Giacomo Renier q. Andrea, Piero Bondimier q. Bernazzo; Piero Basadonna q. Alessandro; Lorenzo Cappello q. Piero.

129 Gozzi, *Opere scelte*, vol. 12, pp. 221–25.

130 Venice, ASVe, SCdS, bb. 34–36.

Knowledgeable, erudite, and ambitious: these 'women of means' were able to look well beyond the enclosure of the complex where they were — or were supposed to have been — segregated. Thanks to both their wide network of relationships established over the centuries and the development of their own autonomy, they became acquainted with, and, consequently, actively participated in, the social, economic, and political dynamics of Venice and its State.

Works Cited

Manuscript and Archival Sources

Città del Vaticano, Archivio Segreto del Vaticano (ASV)
    Nunziature di Venezia
Venice, Archivio di Stato di Venezia (ASVe)
    Dieci savi alle decime in Rialto
    Miscellanea Codici
    ——, Storia veneta
    Notarile, Testamenti
    Provveditori sopra beni inculti
    ——, Disegni
    ——, ——, Treviso-Friuli
    Provveditori sopra monasteri
    Santa Caterina dei Sacchi (SCdS)
    Savi ed esecutori alle acque
    Senato
    ——, Deliberazioni
    ——, ——, Roma Ordinaria
    ——, ——, Terra
    Sopraintendenti alle decime del clero
Venice, Archivio Storico del Patriarcato di Venezia (ASPV)
    Visite pastorali a monasteri femminili
    Parrocchia di San Felice
    ——, Santa Sofia
    ——, ——, Atti generali
Venice, Biblioteca del Museo Correr (BMC)
    MS. P.D.c. 4

Primary Sources

Biancolini, Giovanni Battista, *Notizie storiche delle chiese di Verona* (Verona:
    A. Scolari al Ponte delle Navi, 1749)
Boschini, Marco, *Le minere della pittura. Compendiosa informazione di Marco
    Boschini non solo delle pitture publiche di Venezia ma dell'isole ancora circonvicine*
    (Venice: Nicolini, 1664)
Cornaro, Flaminio, *Notizie storiche delle chiese e monasteri di Venezia e di Torcello*
    (Padua: Manfrè, 1758)
Gennari, Giuseppe, *Notizie spettanti al beato Nicolò Giustinian Monaco di S. Nicolò
    del Lido* (Venice: Naratovich, 1845)
Gozzi, Gasparo, *Opere scelte di Gaspare Gozzi* (Venice: Tipografia dell'editore
    G. Antonelli, 1833)
Martinioni, Giustiniano, *Venetia città nobilissima et singolare* (Venice: Curti, 1663)

Moschini, Giannantonio, *Guida per la città di Venezia all'amico delle belle arti opera di Giannantonio Moschini*, 2 vols (Venice: nella tipografia di Alvisopoli, 1815)

Ridolfi, Carlo, *Le maraviglie dell'arte overo le vite de gl'illustri pittori veneti, e dello Stato*, [1648], 2 vols (Rome: Società multigrafica editrice Somu, 1965)

Sansovino, Francesco, *Venetia città nobilissima et singolare* (Venice: Iacomo Sansovino, 1581)

Sanudo il Giovane, Marin, *I diarii*, [1496–1533], ed. by Rinaldo Fulin, 58 vols (Venice: Tipografia del commercio di Marco Visentini, 1879–1903)

Zanetti, Antonio Maria, *Rinnovazione delle Ricche minere di Marco Boschini* (Venice: P. Bassaglia a S. Bartolomeo, 1733)

Secondary Works

Andrews, Frances, *The Other Friars: The Carmelite, Augustinian, Sack and Pied Friars in the Middle Ages* (Woodbridge: Boydell, 2006)

Bisceglia, Michelina Anna, *Pietro Vecchia nell'ambiente veneto del '600*, ed. by Danilo Sergio Pirro (Scotts Valley: Create Space, 2017)

Bouwsma, William J., *Venice and the Defense of Republican Liberty: Renaissance Values in the Age of the Counter Reformation* (Berkeley: University of California, 1984)

Caburlotto, Luca, ed., *Sebastiano Mazzoni: storie di Santa Caterina* (Milan: Electa, 2004)

Caputo, Gianmatteo, ed., *Tintoretto: il ciclo di Santa Caterina e la quadreria del Palazzo Patriarcale* (Milan: Skira, 2005)

Chauvard, Jean-François, *La circulation des biens à Venise. Stratégies patrimoniales et marché immobilier, 1600–1750* (Rome: École française de Rome, 2005)

Concina, Ennio, *Venezia nell'età moderna. Struttura e funzioni* (Venice: Marsilio, 1989)

——, *Dell'arabico. A Venezia tra Rinascimento e Oriente* (Venice: Marsilio, 1994)

Cozzi, Gaetano, *Il doge Nicolò Contarini. Ricerche sul patriziato veneziano agli inizi del seicento* (Venice-Rome: Istituto per la collaborazione culturale, 1958)

Crouzet-Pavan, Élisabeth, 'La conquista e l'organizzazione dello spazio urbano', in *Storia di Venezia dalle origini alla caduta della Serenissima*, vol. II: *L'età del comune*, ed. by Alberto Tenenti and Ugo Tucci (Rome: Istituto della Enciclopedia italiana Treccani, 1995), pp. 549–75

——, 'La maturazione dello spazio urbano', in *Storia di Venezia dalle origini alla caduta della Serenissima*, vol. V: *Il Rinascimento. Società ed economia*, ed. by Alberto Tenenti and Ugo Tucci (Rome: Istituto della Enciclopedia italiana Treccani, 1996), pp. 3–100

——, *Venice Triumphant: The Horizons of a Myth* (Baltimore: Johns Hopkins University Press, 2002)

De Maria, Blake, *Becoming Venetian: Immigrants and the Arts in Early Modern Venice* (New Haven: Yale University Press, 2010)

Favero, Giovanni, and others, 'Le anime dei demografi. Fonti per la rilevazione dello stato della popolazione di Venezia nei secoli XVI e XVII', *Bollettino di demografia storica*, 15 (1991), 23–110

Ferrari, Sarah, 'Tiziano Vecellio. Tobiolo e l'Arcangelo Raffaele', in *Pietro Bembo e l'invenzione del Rinascimento*, ed. by Guido Beltramini, Davide Gasparotto, and Adolfo Tura (Venice: Marsilio, 2013), pp. 206–08

Fortini Brown, Patricia, 'Becoming a Man of Empire: The Construction of Patrician Identity in a Republic of Equals', in *Architecture, Art, and Identity in Venice and Its Territories, 1450–1750*, ed. by Nebahat Avcioğlu, and Emma Jones (Farnham: Ashgate, 2013) pp. 231–49

Galeazzo, Ludovica, 'Dinamiche di crescita di un margine urbano. L'insula dei Gesuiti a Venezia dalle soglie dell'età moderna alla fine della Repubblica' (unpublished doctoral thesis, Doctoral School Ca' Foscari-Iuav of Venice, 2014)

—— , *Venezia e i margini urbani. L'insula dei Gesuiti in età moderna*, Memorie, Classe di scienze morali, lettere ed arti, 144 (Venice: Istituto Veneto di Scienze, Lettere ed Arti, 2018)

Gardner, Julian, 'Nuns and Altarpieces: Agendas for Research', *Römisches Jahrbuch der Bibliotheca Hertziana*, 30 (1995), 27–57

Giuliani, Innocenzo, 'Genesi e primo secolo di vita del magistrato sopra monasteri, Venezia 1519–1620', *Le venezie francescane*, XXVIII, 1/2 (1961), 42–68 and 160–69

Grubb, James, 'Elite Citizens', in *Venice Reconsidered: The History and Civilization of an Italian City-state, 1297–1797*, ed. by John Martin, and Dennis Romano (Baltimore: Johns Hopkins University Press, 2000), pp. 339–64

Hochmann, Michel, 'Le collezioni veneziane del Rinascimento: storia e storiografia', in *Il collezionismo d'arte a Venezia: dalle origini al cinquecento*, ed. by Michel Hochmann, Rossella Lauber, and Stefania Mason (Venice: Fondazione di Venezia-Marsilio, 2008), pp. 3–39

Humfrey, Peter, *Titian: The Complete Paintings* (Ghent: Ludion, 2007)

Joannides, Paul, *Titian to 1518: The Assumption of a Genius* (New Haven: Yale University Press, 2001)

Laven, Mary, *Virgins of Venice: Enclosed Lives and Broken Vows in the Renaissance Convents* (London: Penguin, 2003)

Lowe, Kate J. P., *Nuns' Chronicles and Convent Culture in Renaissance and Counter-Reformation Italy* (Cambridge: Cambridge University Press, 2003)

—— , 'Power and Institutional Identity in Renaissance Venice: The Female Convents of S.M. delle Vergini and S. Zaccaria', in *The Trouble with Ribs: Women, Men and Gender in Early Modern Europe*, ed. by Anu Korhonen and Kate Lowe (Helsinki: Helsinki Collegium for Advanced Studies, 2007), pp. 128–52

Lucco, Mauro, ed., *Tiziano e la nascita del paesaggio moderno*, exhibition catalogue (Florence: GAMM Giunti, 2012)

Lunardon, Silvia, 'L'ospedale dei Crociferi', in *Hospitale S. Mariae Cruciferorum. L'ospizio dei Crociferi a Venezia*, ed. by Silvia Lunardon (Venice: IRE, 1984), pp. 18–85

Mantioni, Susanna, *Monacazioni forzate e spazi di auto-affermazione femminile. Norma e prassi nel serenissimo dominio di età moderna* (Rome: Gangemi, 2017)

Moschini Marconi, Sandra, 'Note per la chiesa di Santa Caterina', *Quaderni della soprintendenza ai beni artistici e storici di Venezia*, 7 (1978), 31–39

Murat, Zuleika, 'Medieval English Alabaster Sculptures: Trade and Diffusion in the Italian Peninsula', *Hortus Artium Medievalium*, 22 (2016), 399–413

Pavanini, Paola, 'Venezia verso la pianificazione? Bonifiche urbane nel XVI secolo a Venezia', in *D'une ville à l'autre. Structure matérielles et organisation de l'espace dans les villes européennes, XIIIe-XVIe siécles*, ed. by Jean-Claude Maire Vigueur (Rome: École Française de Rome, 1989), pp. 485–507

Pedani, Maria Pia, 'Monasteri di agostiniane a Venezia', *Archivio Veneto*, s. 5, 124–25 (1985), 35–78

Penco, Gregorio, and Trolese, Francesco Giovanni, *Monastica et humanistica: scritti in onore di Gregorio Penco* (Cesena: Badia di Santa Maria del Monte, 2003)

Piasentini, Stefano, 'Aspetti della Venezia d'acqua dalla fine del XIV secolo alla fine del XV secolo', in *Venezia la città dei rii*, ed. by Giovanni Caniato (Sommacampagna: Cierre, 1999), pp. 41–67

Salomon, Xavier F., *Veronese: Magnificence in Renaissance Venice* (London: National Gallery Company, 2014)

Sperling, Jutta Gisela, *Convents and the Body Politic in Late Renaissance Venice* (Chicago: University of Chicago Press, 1999)

Stella, Aldo, 'La proprietà ecclesiastica nella repubblica di Venezia dal secolo XV al XVII', *Nuova Rivista Storica*, 42 (1958), 50–77

Svalduz, Elena, 'Al servizio del magistrato. I proti alle acque nel corso del primo secolo d'attività', in *"Architetto sia l'ingegniero che discorre". Ingegneri, architetti e proti nell'età della Repubblica*, ed. by Giuliana Mazzi, and Stefano Zaggia (Venice: Marsilio, 2004), pp. 233–68

——, 'Procedure materiali, decisioni tecniche e operative nella realizzazione delle Fondamente Nuove', in *L'edilizia prima della rivoluzione industriale secc. XIII– XVIII*, ed. by Simonetta Cavaciocchi (Prato: Istituto Internazionale di Storia Economica Datini-Le Monnier, 2004), pp. 555–85

Tafuri, Manfredo, 'Documenti sulle Fondamenta Nuove', *Architettura, storia e documenti*, 1 (1985), 79–95

Toffolo, Francesca, 'Art and the Conventual Life in Renaissance Venice: The Monastery Church of Santa Caterina de' Sacchi' (unpublished doctoral dissertation, Princeton University, 2005)

Trebbi, Giuseppe, 'La società veneziana', *Storia di Venezia dalle origini alla caduta della Serenissima*, vol. VI: *Dal Rinascimento al Barocco*, ed. by Gaetano Cozzi and Paolo Prodi (Rome: Istituto della Enciclopedia italiana Treccani, 1994), pp. 129–213

Vio, Gastone, *Le Scuole Piccole nella Venezia dei dogi. Note d'archivio per la storia delle confraternite veneziane* (Costabissara: Colla, 2004)

KIMBERLYN MONTFORD

Musical Networks and the Early Modern Italian Convent

Introduction

The paternalism of the early modern Roman Catholic Church fostered female monastic communities as systems that derived their power from their interaction with other institutions, both secular and sacred. The constant transformative drive inherent in a Church administration that substantially changed with each new pope or the rise of new, powerful cardinals created tension with the unchanging, traditional elements of religious liturgy and hierarchy. A common thread through each Church administration, however, was an overarching obsession with the control of women, especially their chastity. Religious influence overlaid that of a patchwork of wealthy principalities, all jealous of their rule over their lands and people. Yet from these tensions arose a physical and cognitive landscape rife with possibilities for self-promotion, determination and celebration in the music-making activities of female religious communities.

This essay examines the myriad musical connections that nuns fostered not only to maintain a presence in early modern society, but also to craft, protect, and preserve their own autonomy. It considers the notions of gender and religiosity that form the philosophical underpinning of the Church's view of nuns' music-making. Grounded in recent studies on nuns' activity and convent music in various Italian cities, it presents a comparative overview that focuses on strategies that utilized musical connections to strengthen and exploit convent networks in the wake of the Tridentine reforms and subsequent efforts to regulate convent music in the late sixteenth and seventeenth centuries. Despite occasional conflicts between the Church, nobility, and convent leadership, each of these constituencies understood and employed convent music as a mechanism for imparting prestige, establishing important alliances, and creating potential spiritual benefit. This essay locates these shifting relationships, their underlying motivations, and their consequences within the particular social and religious character of different Italian cities.

Kimberlyn Montford, Ph.D., (kmontfor@trinity.edu) is Associate Professor of Music History and co-director of African American Studies at Trinity University.

Convent Networks In Early Modern Italy, ed. by Marilyn Dunn and Saundra Weddle, ES 25 (Turnhout: Brepols, 2020) pp. 231–259   BREPOLS✠PUBLISHERS   DOI 10.1484/M.ES-EB.5.119518

Cloister and Tridentine Reform

Early Christian patristic writings established the notion that woman was less capable of achieving perfection of the soul because of her physical variance from the image of God and her role as originator of sin. Her physical state required the monitoring and control of loving, paternalistic supervision. Nowhere was this notion more visible than in the fervour for the administration of nuns.

The simplest form of controlling nuns' physical state, separating them from temptation, had the secondary effect of striking at nuns' identity and their means to maintain a presence in their society. One of the earliest efforts of official Church supervision of nuns, Boniface VIII's papal decretal *Periculoso* ('Dangerous'), issued in 1298, sought to change and normalize female monastic practices by requiring strict, systematic enclosure of all nuns in the western Church. *Periculoso* marked a shift in enclosure's purpose, enforcing *clausura* to protect nuns from the dangerous temptations of the outside world, but also, and more importantly, from their own sinful natures, thereby allowing them 'to serve God more freely, wholly separated from the public and worldly gaze, and, occasions for lasciviousness having been removed, may most diligently safeguard their hearts and bodies in complete chastity'.[1] While inconsistently applied across Europe, the institution of new protocols limiting contact between the outer world and nuns exemplified a new conceptualization of enclosure. It was no longer one means among many of defending the religious environment; it became 'an end in itself to which other values of religious life were increasingly subordinated'.[2] As such, *Periculoso* provided the authoritative foundation for Church authorities' efforts to reform and control the convents. During the Council of Trent (1545–1563), three centuries later, the delegates' focus on the enclosure of nuns was prevalent enough that they declared that it was 'the primary obligation for nuns', citing *Periculoso* in their deliberations.[3]

The implementation of the conciliar decrees varied from locale to locale. Important factors in the wielding of Church control included the nature, quality, and strength of the other affiliations within which nuns operated. In one such affiliation, the power and standing of the families associated with a convent bolstered its prestige in its community, city and the Church, as well as the individual standing of the nun within the convent's hierarchy. In tacit reciprocity for providing homes and communities for unmarriageable daughters, families contributed funds through dowries and donations, and patronage by building chapels, commissioning art, and sponsoring memorials and music. In short, noble families throughout Italy were highly invested in the convents where their daughters were installed, and it was exactly that type of investment that the Church sought to disrupt.

---

1 Makowski, *Canon Law and Cloistered Women*, p. 135.
2 Brundage and Makowski, 'Enclosure of Nuns', p. 153.
3 Evangelisti, *Nuns: A History of Convent Life*, p. 45.

The Council tasked bishops with overseeing the rich diversity of customs and practices in convents. The proposed changes threatened many of the conventions upon which nuns had based their acceptance of monastic life, as well as the privileges that families had enjoyed in their relations with the convents. This included the necessity for bishops to address the role of music, not only as a liturgical requirement but also as a cultural signifier for the sisters, their families, and the community. The personality of the individual bishops and their philosophy regarding nuns' musical activities, the strength and flexibility of community and familial ties to the convents, and the ability of religious women to control their circumstances were all factors in how successfully the decrees were enacted.[4]

Implementing Reform: Trent and beyond

The Tridentine decrees on cloister formalized a paternalistic relationship between the Church and nuns that had been implied in *Periculoso*. The reforms, particularly those related to music, reflected not only the bishops' interpretation of the final decree, they also signalled the bishops' interpretation of the Church's position on female religiosity and the role that musical activities played in the convent. As examples from Bologna, Milan, Siena, and Rome demonstrate, convent practices and authorities' efforts to control them differed from place to place, and evolved over time.

Gabriele Paleotti, whose exacting proposals during conciliar deliberations would have eliminated any music in the convents but the singing of plainchant, found that while his proposed regulations did not garner the approval of the other conciliar delegates, the final decrees themselves left the door open to a more rigorous application of their intentions, as can be seen in his own diocese in Bologna. Upon his promotion to bishop there in 1566, just a few years after the Council closed, his severe restraints on convent music laid the groundwork for decades of struggles between local episcopal, regular, monastic, civic, and noble authorities.

Despite being a musician himself — or perhaps because, as a musician, he was especially aware of the power of music — Paleotti was adamant about regulating the performance of music in Bologna's convents. In 1580, he issued his *Ordine da servarsi dalle suore nel loro cantare e musica* (Orders to be used by nuns for their singing and music), which was based on his conciliar proposals. The *Ordine* was specific in its directives, indicating clearly what repertoire and performance styles were approved and prohibiting anything else. It required the nuns to sing their services mainly in plainchant, allowing for some performance of *falsobordone*, and severely limited polyphony to psalms performed on patronal feasts, and motets only in important masses

---

4   See Medioli, 'An Unequal Law', pp. 136–52.

and vespers services.[5] It also restricted performance to group singing, with a few exceptions wherein a solo voice might sing, always in Latin. Instruments were forbidden with the exception of rare occasions — when the organ accompanied a solo voice or a viol supplied the bassline when polyphony was performed. Finally, under no circumstances were men to either teach, rehearse, or perform with the nuns.[6]

Paleotti's *Ordine* began his campaign to eradicate what he considered to be the abuses caused by convent music. While the foremost issue was that such activities distracted the nuns from their duties, singing and playing inappropriate music, sometimes with male musicians, cultivated an unseemly atmosphere and encouraged lack of discipline and worldliness. In addition, the focus on music led to vanity and rivalries among singers, further thwarting the goal of communal devotion:

> Experience demonstrates that the excessive study that the nuns devote these days to their songs not only fails to serve the end to which music was permitted them, [which is] to praise God and be aroused themselves to the contemplation of celestial harmony; but [rather] it impedes them from greater goods and encumbers their souls in perpetual distraction. It causes them vainly to expend precious time that they could use more fruitfully. And, while they stand with their bodies within the sacred cloisters, it causes them to wander outside in their hearts nourishing within themselves an ambitious desire to please the world with their songs.[7]

A few years later, Paleotti issued further restrictive measures when he prohibited nuns from hiring secular musicians to perform in the outer church, and even more drastically, required the removal of organs to the inner church of all convents, thereby eliminating the presence of even a soloist's voice in the 'outside world'. While designed to further separate nuns from outside influences and maintain the sanctity of the cloister, these directives also struck at music's ability to forge even aural links outside the convent walls.

Reactions to these edicts differed. In many cases, nuns responded with an outpouring of letters to the Congregation of Bishops and Regulars in Rome, lobbying for exemptions to the regulations, and calling upon the most appropriate members of their network — many of whom served in the local Church hierarchy — to do the same.[8] However, a number of convents

---

5   Plainchant is the traditional single-line melody of the Catholic liturgy. *Falsobordone* is a Renaissance recitation style in which a plainchant melody is harmonized by root position triads. Polyphony is compositional style in which a number of independent musical lines are crafted to be performed simultaneously and harmonize with each other.

6   Monson, *Disembodied Voices*, pp. 37–38.

7   Cited and translated in Monson, *Disembodied Voices*, p. 37; see p. 260, n. 6 for transcription of document found in Bologna, Archivio Generale Arcivescovile, Misc. vecchie 808, fasc. 6, 'Ordine da servarsi dalle suore nel loro cantare et musica'.

8   Convents appealed to local nobility, confessors, superiors within their orders, and members

countered by simultaneously following and circumventing the restrictions, moving the organ to the inner nuns' church but then enlarging it so that it could be heard quite clearly in the public church.[9] While the women were enclosed within convents walls and gradually became more and more invisible to the world outside the convent walls, they devoted their efforts to keeping their music, and thereby their presence, a part of the layperson's religious and social experience within the church.

As archbishop of Milan, Carlo Borromeo was mindful of both the prominence of nuns' music in urban culture and the power of the noble families. At least initially, his primary concern was maintaining the respectability of nuns' music-making; for example, in 1565, he approved the hire of male teachers of 'mature age and blameless life' to teach in the convents.[10] Shortly thereafter, however, he changed his position. Pope Pius V's decree *Circa pastoralis* of 1566 reinforced the Tridentine decree establishing cloister as the normative practice for all female convents, and Borromeo's strict interpretation of the papal decree had serious implications for Milanese convent music.

Borromeo first had the Tridentine decrees (along with the more drastic proposals of Gabriele Paleotti) translated into Italian, to be distributed to each convent. He then instituted a diocesan *vicario delle monache* (vicar of nuns) for Milan, and implemented a visitation procedure that left few areas of monastic life unexamined. Borromeo's tenure (1564–1584) initiated changes both in the physical configuration of the convents and in the procedures of convent administration. The reforms issued by him and the *vicario delle monache* involved increasing the size of the walls surrounding the buildings and sealing off gates, parlours, and the connections between the public and private sections of double churches. It was in the overhaul of convent administration and liturgical expression, though, that Borromeo's most drastic intrusion into monastic affairs could be seen. He sought to curtail the power of the noble families within the convents by regulating the election of abbesses and the assignment of confessors, setting controls on individual ownership of property among the nuns, and severely limiting the visits of clergy (including confessors) and laity to convents. In contrast to his temperance when he first arrived in Milan, he reacted rigorously to the interference with enclosure regulations caused by musical activities, eventually trying to restrict the ability of convents to draw upon professional musicians to perform in their external churches on feast days.[11]

While the programmes of Paleotti and Borromeo were notable for their severity and breadth, other reformers were more careful in incorporating the

---

of the local Church hierarchy for support and advocacy before the Congregation. See Monson, *Disembodied Voices*, pp. 39–48.

9   Monson, *Disembodied Voices*, pp. 40–41.
10 Cited in Kendrick, *Celestial Sirens*, p. 60.
11 Kendrick, *Celestial Sirens*, pp. 62–70.

conciliar decrees in their management of their diocese. In Siena during the years immediately after Trent, the bishop did not reside in the city, and the coadjutors who administered in his stead were themselves members of the Sienese elite. Siena's annexation by the Grand Duchy of Tuscany in the 1550s informed this approach to oversight. Urban musical programmes, including those of female convents, contributed to the city's proud and distinctive cultural identity, which centred on its republican government. The convents were significant symbols of elite status, and the coadjutors were initially unwilling to implement any of the decrees that might change long-standing practices, in particular, access to monastic liturgies by the lay public.[12] However, the election of Archbishop Francesco Maria Tarugi in 1597 led to the implementation of the long-delayed changes. The focus of his tenure, as well as those of his successors, was mainly enforcement of cloister which had the potential of dramatically changing the musical soundscape of Siena. But, as Reardon notes, convent music continued to be a valued enterprise in Siena into the eighteenth century. This acceptance of Sienese nuns' music-making seems due in part to their avoidance of the internal disputes over music that erupted in convents in some other cities, and to the fact that the city's archbishops, most of whom were members of the Sienese patriciate themselves, esteemed the nuns' musical performances.[13]

As in Siena, the years immediately following the Council showed little change of business from usual in Rome. In the conciliar sessions addressing abuses of Church practices, the papacy had been alert to any questioning of its authority. The papal delegates' obstructionism in those areas that threatened established procedures meant that few substantial changes were made in curial systems. Thus, the earliest post-Tridentine visitations, dating from the beginning of the seventeenth century, reflected none of the reformers' eagerness for change; they simply listed buildings and their state of repair, holdings, and the condition of the monastic accounts.[14]

Nuns' Networks within the Church

Whether enactment of conciliar reforms was prompt and rigorous or relatively gradual, nuns, seeing their traditional way of life threatened, marshalled their forces to protect it. They found that they could draw upon their connections with members of the Church hierarchy, exploiting the complicated administration that had developed rather organically over the centuries and itself resisted change. In the Tridentine sessions on reform of the clergy, the papacy had resisted any challenges to its authority. It insisted that the Council's zeal to reform the Church focus on the members and leave the head — the papal

---

12 Reardon, *Holy Concord within Sacred Walls*, pp. 20–21.
13 Reardon, *Holy Concord within Sacred Walls*, pp. 22–29.
14 For a discussion of reform in Roman convents, see Montford, 'Holy Restraint'.

Curia — to take care of itself.[15] Thus, papal legates and vice-legates, ecclesiastical visitors, members of the secular or regular clergy, or anyone in the Curia with whom nuns or their families had any affiliation, as well as convent chaplains, curates, or confessors were all sources of influence to whom nuns appealed when they saw the restrictions limiting their activities.

For example, the pope's *cardinale vicario* (cardinal vicar) administered the convents of the diocese of Rome, but another layer of complexity was added with the position of the cardinal protector. As the liaison between the convent and the Curia, the cardinal protector was often extremely involved in a monastic institution's policies, finances, and social and curial status. Sometimes these institutions benefitted from the relationship through patronage of architectural improvements, artwork, musical programmes, and financial assistance. More importantly, the cardinal protectors sometimes called in favours with the *cardinale vicario*, or even used their curial connections to appeal to the pope himself to grant concessions to their charges.[16] Often the convents were a part of wide-ranging campaigns to further the political fortunes of the cardinal protector, his family, his social circle, and by association, the convents themselves. This symbiotic relationship tied the fortunes of the cardinal protector and the convent together, and either could gain or lose prestige accordingly.[17]

Another significant node of connection with the Church was that between the members of a monastic community and their confessor. In the minds of Catholic reformers, the spiritual guidance of nuns had to be an integral element of the reformed communities, with the confessor providing guidance for the individual nuns and the convent as a whole.[18] Officially given the power to influence and guide the nuns, the confessor often developed familial, sometimes indulgent feelings for his charges, as in the words of Girolamo da Vigevano, confessor for the convent of S. Agnese in Bologna, 'I shall love them always, as mothers, sisters, and daughters, most dear, with no partiality'.[19] Such an important relationship was another source of support

---

15 See *Canons and Decrees of the Council of Trent*, ed. and trans. by Schroeder, pp. 154–57, 198–99, 204–05, 253 and Bungener, *History of the Council of Trent*, pp. 111–12, 146–48, 171–79. The latter, though aggressively antagonistic regarding the Council, and Catholicism in general, is nevertheless useful in providing the diplomatic and social context of the conciliar debates.

16 For example, Gian Garzia Mellini, *cardinale vicario* of Rome, was also the cardinal protector of S. Cecilia in Trastevere. Only two years after Pope Urban VIII's ban on licences to enter convents, Mellini obtained the pope's permission to issue a licence for the Duchess of Sora and two companions to enter the convent to visit her sick daughter, an *educanda*, and her infirm sister-in-law, who was a nun in the convent. See Rome, ASR, CRF, Benedettine Cassinesi in S. Cecilia in Trastevere, 4032, no. 6.

17 Montford, 'Holy Restraint', p. 1014.

18 Ranft, 'A Key to Counter Reformation Women's Activism', pp. 16–18.

19 Cited in Monson, *Disembodied Voices*, pp. 45–46. This is most likely a reference to — and in this case, a denial of — the close relationships that sometimes developed between holy

and promotion for nuns in their efforts to maintain autonomy in the face of increasing curial regulation.

Confessors could be utilized in petitioning the authorities, and many lent their backing to requests for licences. However, as the only officially sanctioned men who were allowed regular contact with female convents, they served a more valuable role as the public voice for the cloistered community.[20] They were also less formal intermediaries between the convents and civic and legal authorities. Their function providing religious and emotional comfort to the nuns under their care, their inclination to identify with the problems of their charges, and the tendency of the nuns to call upon, and sometimes subvert, their aid made the Church hierarchy extremely cautious about assigning confessors. Many of the reformers demanded that confessors be of a certain age and level of experience, and that they be rotated every three to five years, though following up on the latter regulation proved to be difficult.[21] The caution was deserved. The potentially claustrophobic atmosphere of any enclosed community could exacerbate familial, social, and political tensions within the convent, and being a part of the convent community encouraged confessors to take sides, promote their own agendas, and get drawn into the nuns' drama.[22]

In some cases, nuns' networks included the very bishops elected to administer monastic institutions. Many of the Sienese archbishops in the sixteenth and seventeenth centuries were members of the local nobility. As noted above, as members of the Sienese elite, they valued the inclusion of convents in the city's ceremonial environment. Publicly acknowledging the involvement of convents in the well-being of the greater community obliged the local Sienese to make the concessions necessary to allow conventual musical activities, avoiding much of the conflict between reformers and convents seen in other Italian cities. The greater cause of representing Sienese identity seemed to take precedence over any decrees initiated by outsiders.

In Milan, Borromeo's uncompromising efforts implementing his stringent interpretation of the Tridentine decrees gave way to the more accommodating programme of his successor, Gaspare Visconti (archbishop 1584–1595). However, it was under the administration of Borromeo's nephew, Federico Borromeo (archbishop 1595–1631), that Milanese nuns' music bloomed. He was an ardent

---

women and their confessors. Here, Girolamo da Vigevano may have simply meant to imply a paternalistic affection towards all of the women under his care.

20   The hagiographical efforts of confessors in crafting the biographies of holy women are probably the best-known example of this role. See Coakley, *Women, Men, and Spiritual Power*; Dolan, 'Reading, Work, and Catholic Women's Biographies'; Mayne Kienzle, 'Margherita of Cortona'; and Copeland, *Maria Maddalena de' Pazzi*; while the Sienese nun Maria Francesca Picccolomini was convinced to write her spiritual autobiography by Padre Sebastiano Conti, he wrote a biography that prefaced it; see Reardon, *Holy Concord within Sacred Walls*, pp. 108–22.

21   Laven, 'Sex and Celibacy in Early Modern Venice', p. 872.

22   For a psycho-social exploration of the development of the close relationships between confessors and nuns, see Laven, 'Sex and Celibacy in Early Modern Venice', pp. 865–88.

champion for nuns' music-making and believed that when appropriately guided, music could strengthen nuns' spiritual growth. His directives were rarely prohibitive; instead they encouraged music that reinforced humility and penitence, the elements that he felt formed the foundation of monastic spirituality. As such, Federico was intensely occupied with musical activity that cultivated contemplation and religious comfort.[23]

Nuns' Networks: Political Implications

As noted above, the retroactive imposition of strict *clausura* in the latter part of the sixteenth century represented a dramatic departure from the tacit contract upon which many women had entered the convent. Strict claustration forced renegotiation of the links between convents and their lay communities, but also required changes in the performance of liturgical services of convent churches. The rigorous interpretation of the Tridentine decrees by reformers meant that nuns could no longer sing in the outer churches of the convent, nor could they sing from the inner choirs with male musicians present in the outer churches, and the regulations prohibited the entrance of male music teachers into the cloister.[24] Rigorously observed, these regulations drastically diminished the presence of nuns in society.

The ability of nuns to maintain their presence in the musical landscape was a testimony to the adaptive quality of their networks and their facility working from their place in those networks. In many cases, religious institutions followed the letter of the regulations, while engaging in subversive interpretations of the spirit of those same regulations. In other cases, the nuns and their advocates flooded the Congregation of Bishops and Regulars with letters requesting licences and exceptions. In some convents, the regulations were simply ignored for as long as possible. A common thread, though, was the utilization of every connection that nuns had to maintain a role in their society. In a way, the attempts of the reformers to wrest control of convents from extra-ecclesiastical influences had the opposite effect of the intended purpose: their transformative drive to implement conciliar reforms was mirrored in the rejuvenation of those very same networks to meet the challenges sparked by the changes taking place throughout the Catholic Church.

Even though they were ecclesiastical entities, female convents could not wield official power in the exclusively male hierarchy of the Church. By definition a system in which people or groups are ranked one above the other according to degree of authority, position and status within that system

---

23 For a discussion of the use of music in Federico's programme for Milanese nuns, see Macy, 'Geronimo Cavaglieri, the Song of Songs and Female Spirituality in Federigo Borromeo's Milan', pp. 349–57, and Kendrick, *Celestial Sirens*.

24 Montford, 'Holy Restraint', p. 1013; Monson, *Disembodied Voices*, pp. 58–59.

is expressed by means of the impact of one's voice in the decision-making of the hierarchy. Although they sometimes had influence, women had no voice in the structure of Roman Catholicism, and thus could not participate in making, implementing, or carrying out decisions. Decision-making takes place in the centre, internal parts of such a system, like a heart beating, pulsing blood out to the body.

The Church as an institution shared the notion of women's chastity as an integral element of their familial and social worth, a notion heightened by monastic vows founded upon chastity (among other virtues). Consequently, paternalistic treatment of women's bodies, views, and role in the Church to protect that chastity was constant. In general, women were strictly discouraged from deciding or acting; they were to be decided for or acted upon. In such a system, women were viewed as objects or symbols rather than actors or agents. Nevertheless, the domain created by the social constructs developed to guard and defend women's chastity — inhabited only by those so protected, and defined by its very isolation from the sphere of male activity — also allowed women to forge a degree of autonomy.

The potential of the bonds developed within this domain could be formidable, as can be seen in the battle of the nuns of S. Cristina della Fondazza in Bologna to reinstate the Sacra. A consecration ritual by the bishop that could only be performed once a nun reached the age of twenty-five, the Sacra was a unique rite of passage that allowed her to serve in the highest monastic offices. Many of these ceremonies featured lavish gifts, decoration, food, and musical performance. Reformers saw these activities as ephemera that ate away at the nun's dowry and distracted the sisters from their devotional activities, while the nuns saw such expenditures as investments in the community that furthered the relationships upon which their social networks were based.[25]

Because of the imposition of *clausura* and sumptuary controls, the ritual had fallen out of practice in many institutions, and was held infrequently even in Bologna. When the nuns asked Archbishop Giacomo Boncompagni to consecrate twelve nuns in 1696, he required that the ceremony be held in a small chamber in the inner church; the nuns found this unacceptable. In a campaign that was breathtaking not only in its breadth, but also in its subtlety and adroitness, the nuns of S. Cristina set out to reinstate the Sacra in all of its glory.[26]

Madre Donna Luigia Orsina Orsi, the house's bursar, initiated the endeavour. Her first step was to enlist the aid of her brother, Ludovico Maria Orsi, the prior of a Camaldolese hermitage. S. Cristina belonged to the female branch of the Camaldolese order and the prior general of that order had administered the convent until the late 1620s. Ludovico Maria suggested hiring Giovanni Battista Sabbatini, a former protégé, as procurator for the convent before the

---

25   For the traditions of the Sacra, see Monson, *Disembodied Voices*, pp. 182–98.

26   For a detailed discussion of the campaign, see Monson, *Disembodied Voices*, pp. 199–224.

Curia in Rome.[27] Sabbatini then presented the case to the Congregation of Sacred Rites and requested that Cardinal Leonardo Colloredo oversee the case in the Congregation.

Colloredo was an inspired choice as his family was linked to Donna Luigia Orsina's family by marriage. He was the first of many connections utilized in this venture, and he, in turn, led to numerous other advantageous associations. For example, Sabbatini advised the abbess to develop a relationship with individuals who were well placed to advocate for their cause, including Cardinal Ferdinando Borromeo d'Adda, papal legate in Bologna and cardinal protector of the Camaldolese order, who could work on the nuns' behalf with the cardinals in the Congregation, and Don Agostino, Camaldolese procurator general.

The nuns had already begun to tap their own networks to find attendees of the consecrations of 1658 and 1675, and asked them for testimonials describing the respectability of those events. A distant Camaldolese connection produced a testimonial from the nuns at S. Maglorio in Faenza, who attested that in 1686, they had celebrated a consecration in their external church presided over by Bishop Antonio Pignatelli, who was elected in 1691 to the papacy as Pope Innocent XII. This set a precedent that the nuns of S. Cristina could exploit in their case.

Many of the nuns scrutinized their connections and enlisted members of the nobility who were outside of their immediate and obvious relationships. Among these was Count Paolo Bolognetti, whose efforts among the cardinals would be persuasive and unflagging. Working within the sphere available to them while Sabbatini pressed their case in the Congregation, the nuns also requested assistance from Princess Flaminia Pamphili Pallavicina, Countess Lisabetta Bargellini-Bolognetti, as well as Maria Moretti Ottoboni in Venice. The sisters asked the latter to intercede on their behalf with her son, Cardinal Pietro Ottoboni, who was not only a music lover and vice-protector of the Camaldolese order, but had also advocated to have music restored at the convent church of the nuns of S. Radegonda in Milan earlier in the decade. What was significant about the advocates the sisters enlisted was that many were not in their immediate circle nor had ever been in the convent church. They were acquaintances of acquaintances, but nevertheless those relationships were strong enough to forge more links as needed.

After more discussion and manoeuvering, Sabbatini's meticulously drawn documentation of precedent going back as far the writings of Carlo Borromeo on the topic, combined with testimonials and gentle pressure from members of the highest level of elite society, proved enough for S. Cristina to triumph.

---

27 The Sabbatini were a noble family of Bologna, most noted for the antiquarian, Marcantonio Sabbatini. He served as papal curator to Pope Clement XI and mentor to the pope's nephew, Alessandro Albani, who was a prominent collector of antiquities and art patron in Rome during the eighteenth century.

Attended by an impressive array of members of the Bolognese nobility, the consecration took place in 1699 in the church, which glowed with candlelight and was adorned with silver vessels and silk streamers; and every ritual act was accompanied by song.

The significance of the consecration reflected the nuns' appreciation for their individuality and the uniqueness of their traditions. Just as they expended every effort to maintain those ceremonial traditions, they recognized and laboured to maintain their music-making activities, retaining their sonic presence even as their physical presence was increasingly constrained.

Nuns' Musical Programmes

The traditional musical programme of most convents in the early modern period consisted of chanting the prayers, psalms, antiphons, canticles, and hymns of the Office. An early seicento *visitatore* (visitor) in Rome, Monsignor Antonio Seneca reveals this relatively simple practice as representing the 'ideal' of many of the Church reformers, who felt that plainchant was the purest form of musical realization of the liturgy:

> Tra tutte le funtioni Ecclesiastichi, et regulari quelle senza dubio sono le maggiori, che toccano il culto divino, delle quali vengono in caminate et ben regulate tutte l' altre attione monastiche, per tanto le Religiose alle quali sopratutte spetta occuparsi nelle laudi divine, poìche a quest' effetto abandonato il mondo, si sono sposate a Giesu Christo, et fra le mura del Monastero, devono la notte et il giorno esser presenti nel Choro alli (ill.)-ni officij et (ill) secondo (ill) della sua Religione recitarli con devotione, attentatione, et con la devita distintione di punti con voce equae, chiara, et spiccata, et con le parole bene, et intelligibilmente espresse.[28]

> (Among all of the ecclesiastical and regular functions, without doubt those are the greatest which regard the divine worship, by which all of the other monastic actions were set up and well-regulated. For many women religious, to whom especially it is their duty to be occupied

---

28 Città del Vaticano, ASV, A. A., Arm. I–XVIII, MS 6492, Antonio Seneca, Prattica del governo spirituale e temporale de monasterii delle monache secondo le regole et constitutioni de Santi Padri loro fondatori et del Sacro Concilio di Trento e di Sommi Pontefici, fol. 77ᵛ–78. In another hand, a note indicates the intended readers: 'Autore Antonio Seneca Decano di Milano, Riformatore apostolico l'anno 1604 per uso delle monache di Roma. Congionto il Trattato spirituale fatto nel visitar monasteri'. Seneca was unusual for a member of the Roman Curia in the intensity with which he approached his duties. His commitment to reorganization and reform advanced his efforts as *visitatore*, as aide to Carlo and Federico Borromeo in Milan, and as bishop of the diocese of Anagni. His 'Praxis', a treatise on the proper means of conducting an apostolic visitation, was the result of his strong commitment to the use of the visitation as an episcopal tool. See Fiorani, 'Le visite apostoliche', pp. 77–78.

in divine songs; to this effect they have abandoned the world, are wed to Jesus Christ, and closed between the walls of the monastery. They must be present day and night in the choir for the Divine Offices and according to the rite of their order, recite these with devotion, attention and with the proper distinction of points in an even, clear, and distinct voice, with good words, expressed intelligibly).

Plainchant formed a vital link to the early Church, and was the basis for the musical programmes of most monastic houses. The perception of chant — traditional and beautiful in its simplicity — was that it supported the spiritual desire of the singers and listeners, prepared the heart for prayer, and provided succour and comfort: *Qui bene cantat bis orat* (He who sings well prays twice). The selection, preparation, and rehearsal of the chants for service were the duties of the chant mistress, and the responsibility for the performance was shared between a small group of soloists and the plainchant choir. Even those preparations — reading through the texts of the chants assigned for the day, handling the manuscript to prepare for rehearsal, and the rehearsal itself — were considered elements of the performance of devotion. Singing the ancient melodies reinforced the spiritual development, discipline, and fortitude of pious women dedicated to prayer, in humble obedience to their vows.[29]

The gradual addition of polyphony during the sixteenth century created a new aural experience in the monastic setting. Ornate polyphonic settings were the aural equivalent to the highly ornamental architectural detail and opulent visual arts of the Baroque monastic church. Both embellished and intensified the liturgy and, combined with candles and the internal choreography of the service, presented an awe-inspiring sensory spiritual experience. A report on the 1649 procession of a relic to the Sienese monastic church of Ognissanti describes the decoration of the church with decorative tapestries and paintings, the candles, and the press of people attending as the context for the musical experience:

> At the very moment the [sacred head] entered [the church], the nuns sang the Confessor's hymn from the organ loft in two distinct choirs with most beautiful music combined with various instruments and after that, a lovely motet in praise of the saint, such that it seemed as if paradise had opened up.[30]

Church authorities were ambivalent about women singing polyphony.[31] The most commonly cited reason was disruption to the smooth operation of

29 See for example, the commentary of Alexander VII on the historical precedents of women singing in the ancient church, Città del Vaticano, ASV, Congr. Visita Ap., vol. 7, fols 223–27.

30 Cited and translated in Reardon, *Holy Concord within Sacred Walls*, p. 46; see p. 196, Doc. 12A, for transcription from *Relatione della general processione fatta in Siena nella Domenica in Albis*.

31 For a discussion of the efforts of Church authorities addressing the issue of polyphony in

the convent. The amount of rehearsal to perform polyphonic or the newer, monodic works might take the nuns away from their other duties.[32] There was the danger of the sisters being caught up in vanity, self-promotion, and competitiveness.[33] In addition, the threat to cloister was ever-present, between the possibility of interaction with crowds flocking to hear the choirs of monastic churches with strong musical programmes, the fear that the nuns might manage to perform with male musicians in the outer church, and the concern as well about male musicians entering the houses to teach the nuns. While many religious foundations included polyphonic performance in their services without problems, enough disputes and scandals occurred that reformers' concerns seemed well founded.

One such dispute that dominated the relations of the Benedictine sisters of S. Radegonda in Milan from 1659 to 1690 was ostensibly about cloister, but quickly revealed the connection between cloister, music, and power, and provides an excellent example of the intertwined networks of convents. The accusation of a breach in cloister provoked by rivalries among the singers in the convent exacerbated long-simmering tensions about convent control and music that exploded into a city-wide scandal, wrested control of the convent from the Cassinese, and eventually resulted in a ban on polyphony at S. Radegonda, which had been renowned for its music.

During Lent of 1659, Donna Maria Faustina Palomera was accused by other nuns of leaving the cloister overnight in the company of two men.[34] The abbess reported the accusation to her superior in the order, as S. Radegonda was subject to the local Cassinese abbot rather than the archbishop, Alfonso Litta. As an anonymous Cassinese monk wrote to Rome during the investigation:

> Palomera was charged with having broken *clausura*; the abbess told her superior, the Cassinese abbot Melzi. He decided that such a crime, if it were true, should not remain unpunished and considered informing Monsignor Archbishop of what had happened. But in the light of his [the Archbishop's] character, and the irreconcilable hatred he had shown the Cassinese (especially the abbot himself) on all occasions, he [Melzi] (agitated by many thoughts) decided to consult the President of the Senate, his relative, who … advised that the nuns be examined … which

---

Roman houses, see Montford, 'Holy Restraint', pp. 1007–26.

32 Monody is a style of accompanied solo song consisting of a vocal line, which is frequently embellished, and simple, often expressive, harmonies; it developed among humanistic circles in Italy.

33 A particularly pithy example of this complaint was that of Alfonso Paleotti, who succeeded his cousin Gabriele Paleotti as archbishop in Bologna, 'Throughout the time that I have been coadjutor and archbishop, I have felt from my experience that the thing that removes the spirit, devotion, and peace within the nunneries is music, which they compete to present in the choirs of their convents', cited in Monson, *Disembodied Voices*, p. 38.

34 For a detailed discussion of this period of discord at S. Radegonda see Kendrick, *Celestial Sirens*, pp. 96–106.

he did, discovering only the words of the two Vimercati sisters, ill disposed towards the accused.[35]

The abbess drew upon her connection with the local official of her order for advice and sanction. Abbot Vincenzo Melzi, recognizing the sensitivity of the issue and hoping to forestall involvement by the archbishop, called upon his relative, a secular official. Unfortunately, they were unable to contain the news, which spread quickly throughout the city and reached the ears of the archbishop.

Archbishop Litta was a member of the Milan nobility. After earning his doctorate in canon and civil law, he served in the tribunals of the Apostolic Signature, and as governor in the Papal States, and he was consecrated as a bishop immediately before his return to Milan. His relationship with the local nobility was initially cordial, but that changed upon the death of his older brother when he inherited the family holdings. As a cleric, Litta was expected to remain outside of mundane politics, and should have relinquished the patrimony to an adult male relative. Because of his high ecclesiastical position, his ensuing efforts to promote himself and his family would have been considered highly irregular, creating hostility and mistrust among the other noble families.

Ever protective of his personal status, Litta took the Cassinese abbot to task both for not reporting the incident to the archbishop and for discussing the incident with the President of the Senate. He saw it as another insult to his position and used it as proof that the Cassinesi were not competent supervisors of the sisters — a common argument of many reformers.

In the ensuing investigation, it was discovered that there had been past conflicts over music between the accused and accusers, who belonged to rival choirs. S. Radegonda was so blessed with singers that it had two polyphony choirs, which often contended for performance rights on significant feast days. The dispute was eventually settled with Palomera punished, with restrictions placed on her participation in convent governance and the right to sing in the choir. However, when she later sang in public despite having been expressly forbidden, Litta found that her singing gave rise to another issue. In direct opposition to the spirit of cloister, some of the nuns were socializing with the men who came to the monastic church to hear the music and stayed after the services. Litta called on the Congregation to support a temporary ban on polyphony.[36]

---

35 Cited and translated in Kendrick, *Celestial Sirens*, p. 98; see p. 456, Appendix A, Doc. 46 for transcription of document found in Città del Vaticano, Archivio Segreto Vaticano (ASV), Sacra Congregazione dei Vescovi e Regolari sez. Monache, 1660, February–March, packet dated 5 March 1660.

36 Cited and translated in Kendrick, *Celestial Sirens*, p. 102, found in Città del Vaticano, ASV, Sacra Congregazione dei Vescovi e Regolari, sez. monache, 1664, June–August.

In this ban, however, Litta attacked an important element of monastic identity, the foundation's religious and musical presence in the city. In spite (or perhaps because) of *clausura*, music was an aural symbol of the sisters' religious devotion that soared out of the religious houses and connected them to their communities. The convent churches with strong musical programmes provided a city's most attended services, offering opportunities for devotion, musical entertainment, displays of prestige on the part of the churches and their audiences, and usually, a significant influx of funds through alms. For many convents, their ability to supply music was a significant component of their status, as can be seen in a letter from a nun at S. Radegonda to her Cassinese superiors:

> Since our choir has been notably depleted by the departure of the five above-named and of others who stopped singing unexpectedly, it cannot fulfill its duty; thus it will be necessary either to fall under this burden or to abandon singing [resulting] in the lessened fame and esteem of both this monastery and the city.[37]

The implication is that as one of the foremost musical foundations in the city, S. Radegonda had to work to maintain its urban prestige. This was certainly one of the major reasons for the inability of reformers to eliminate polyphony in monastic liturgy, despite the accompanying problems. The religious foundations were solidly embedded in the urban landscape — liturgically, socially, and culturally — and music provided one means to forge and maintain connections with the lay community. Indeed, during a temporary suspension of polyphony in 1665, the nuns presented a polyphonic Mass and Vespers service for the Protestant Duke Ernst August and Duchess Sophie of Brunswick-Lüneburg, infuriating Litta. Traditionally, local nobility would escort important foreign visitors to Milan to the services at the renowned convent churches, S. Radegonda among them, and the nuns refused to abandon their part in the diplomatic and political custom, even under sanctions.[38]

The connections among musicians inside and outside the convent also demonstrated the significance of nuns' music in Italian cities. Collections of published music by male composers often contained individual pieces dedicated to nuns. Kendrick opines that some dedications referenced the status of the dedicatee's family or her own reputation for piety, while others reflect the dedicatee's status as someone in the position to either programme or perform the work.[39] While rare, some dedications reference occasions

---

37 Cited and translated in Kendrick, *Celestial Sirens*, p. 105; see p. 105, n. 50 and Appendix A, Doc. 69 for transcription of document found in Milan, Archivio Storico Diocesano Milanese, Carteggio Ufficiale, vol. 92, 1675, petition of 14 Nov 1675.

38 Kendrick, *Celestial Sirens*, p. 103.

39 Such composers included Costanzo Antegnati, Orfeo Vecchi, Giovanni Paolo and Andrea Cima, See Kendrick, *Celestial Sirens*, pp. 187–89; 209–10; 244; 251.

wherein the dedicatee had already performed several of the composer's works, as in Paolo Quagliati's dedication of spiritual madrigals to a singer at S. Lucia in Selci in Rome.[40]

Deploying high-quality convent music programmes to convey status was a common practice that contributed to civic distinction in many cities. For example, Sienese nuns were also expected to present music for visitors. The convent churches Ognissanti, Il Refugio, S. Abbondio, and S. Maria degli Angeli hosted such noted guests as archbishops, cardinals, a Polish countess, and relatives of Alexander VII. However, in Siena, monastic music was seen not only as an expression and source of urban prestige but as a means of celebrating their unique Sienese heritage. Indeed, visiting the churches, participating in the religious calendar that celebrated local holy men and women, and hearing the voices of the city's daughters forged a communal experience built of ancient, yet continually renewed, musical and religious ties.[41]

As in Milan and Siena, visitors to Rome would try to see as many of the pilgrimage basilicas as possible, but for many, attending services at the convent churches renowned for their musical programmes was imperative. S. Caterina da Siena in Monte Magnanapoli, S. Chiara, SS. Domenico e Sisto, S. Lucia in Selci, S. Maria della Concezione in Campo Marzo, S. Silvestro in Capite, and Spirito Santo were also among Rome's oldest and wealthiest convents. Contemporary accounts note the type of music that was performed — plainchant, polyphony, or the new monodic style — and often remark on the singular skill of the performers or the beauty of the music. Pietro della Valle enthusiastically recounted his experience at one of these:

> Alcuni anni addietro, poco dopo il mio ritorno in Italia, un lunedì della Pentecoste io sentii un vespero nella Chiesa dello Spirito Santo, cantata appunto dalle sole monache, tutto da capo, a piedi di musica ornata, che io giuro certo a V. S. che mai a' miei dì non ho inteso più bella cosa in tal genere.[42]

> (One Monday during Pentecost I heard a vespers service in the church of the Spirito Santo, sung just by the nuns only, all from head to foot in ornate music, that I certainly swear to your Lordship that in all my days I have never perceived a more beautiful work in this style).

---

40 He wrote of his compositions as 'first cherished and favored by you when sometimes it pleased you to sing and embellish them with your artful refinements and most delicate voice' ('gli stessi componimenta accarezzati prima, & favoriti da lei, quando tal volta s' è compiaciuta cantarli, & abbellirli con le sue artificiose maniere, & soavissima voce'). Quagliati, *Affetti amorosi spirituali*, p. 2. It should be noted that Quagliati appeared to have had a close association with the nuns of S. Lucia in Selci. In his will, he left his harpsichord to them. For a discussion of the use of devotional music as a support for monastic life, see Montford, '*Gli Affetti amorosi spirituali*'.

41 Reardon, *Holy Concord within Sacred Walls*, pp. 28–29, 42–49.

42 Della Valle, 'Della musica dell'età nostra', p. 173, cited in Montford, 'Holy Restraint', p. 1015.

Another traveller alludes to the custom of attending monastic services, describing the music of S. Maria in Campo Marzo as

> the best in the world without dispute … where I heard divers times a Nunn sing with such perfection both of skill and voyce, that (and I speak it truly) a journey to Rome were well spent to heare that woman sing thrice.[43]

Depending on the day, time, and type of service, attendees could either hear a liturgy performed by the nuns themselves or with music provided by male musicians in the outer church. During this period, nuns never performed side by side with male musicians in Rome. As can be seen in the monastic financial documents, male musicians were often behind the scenes, as teachers, or writing and rehearsing music for special occasions, yet in the seat of the Roman Catholic Church, every effort was given to maintaining the appearance of the inaccessibility of nuns.

The experience was a complex layering of aural versus visual effects. In many convent churches, while the outer church would be filled with candlelight, ceremonial pieces of silver and gold, and the ornate vestments of the clergy if at Mass, the music of the sisters, partially muted by thick walls, drifted through grates from the inner church choir, creating a distance between what was seen and heard. Many female convents exploited the sensory disconnect; in the absence of visible bodies producing the sound, the nuns took on the mystique of unearthly voices singing from paradise. That perception is compounded when parts of the service are sung in polyphony. In a seventeenth-century performance, the individual melodies produced their own lacy intertwining, while the resonance generated by the harmonies had to have infused the liturgy with a rich sense-memory that also created momentary sonic connections between the listeners and the distant singers. It was a complicated combination of the real and the symbolic.[44]

Religious foundations were symbols of spiritual prestige for the Church as well as for their families and cities. While their presence alone was an emblem and source of divine grace, their prayers were also deemed more compelling than those of worldly women, and were sought for extraordinary situations. During the plague years of 1629–1631, Pope Urban VIII published a decree directing nuns to recite the litanies of the saints each evening. Such prayers were amplified by their status, noted above, as liminal beings living in grace for the betterment of their families and communities. Combined with their singing, which served to mark their status as earthly angels, whose music sonically and symbolically represented the celestial choirs', nuns became mediators to heaven prized even above the prayers of the successor of St Peter.[45]

---

43 Lassels, *An Italian Voyage*, p. 150, cited in Montford, 'Holy Restraint', pp. 1015–1016.
44 For a more detailed analysis of self-presentation and image in nuns' music, see Montford, 'Musical Marketing', pp. 153–75.
45 Kendrick posits the high tessitura of nuns' music, combined with the select occasions during

Roman Convents during the Holy Year of 1675

The Church drew upon the spiritual prestige of nuns in other ways. In Rome, at least, the music and liturgy of religious houses was one facet of a unique celebration designed to demonstrate to the world the glory of the Church. Established in 1300, the *anno santo* — Holy or Jubilee Year — is observed every twenty-five or fifty years as a special year of remission of sins and universal pardon. The main conditions are confession, Communion, prayer for the pope, complete renunciation of all attachment to sin, and visits to the four patriarchal basilicas.[46] However, in order to serve the large number of pilgrims in the city, every institution and organization of the Church contributed to the pageantry of the commemoration, and convents were no exception.

The *anni santi* from 1575 to 1700 were significant as demonstrations of the magnificence and strength of post-Tridentine Catholicism for two major reasons. The first reason was that after the defection of innumerable souls to Protestant confessions and the unpleasant but crucial period of introspection, infighting, and restructuring of reform, it was important that the Church project an image of serenity and strength. The second reason was that the spectacle and religiosity of the event distracted attention from two realities of seventeenth-century religion: the Roman Catholic Church had lost the complete control that it had held over religious and political life in the western Christian world, and even within the Holy Roman Empire, papal influence was dwindling.

In spite of those obstacles, or perhaps because of them, the Church projected an image of stability and influence through the displayed wealth, art, and architecture in the basilicas and churches, through the performance of sumptuous liturgies and music, and through the *avvisi* (notices), collections of music, devotional treatises, guidebooks, and published descriptions of *apparati* (furnishings) disseminated throughout the Catholic world.[47] The demonstrations of religiosity and grandeur throughout the year involved many nodes of social, religious, and political interaction. Participants in the pomp and ceremony included the curial hierarchy, priests, confraternities, monastics, pilgrims, citizens, and convent churches.

---

which only women's voices were heard, contrasted sharply with the music performed by male musicians heard elsewhere in the urban setting, contributing to the association of nuns' singing with angelic choirs. See *Celestial Sirens*, p. 166.

46 These basilicas were S. Giovanni Laterano, S. Pietro, S. Paolo fuori le Mura, and S. Maria Maggiore.

47 By the mid-seventeenth century, the *apparato* included not only candlesticks, reliquaries, and vases of precious metals decorating the altar and sanctuary, but also incorporated painted hangings of allegorical scenes back lit by hundreds of candles and oil lamps. For an examination of the significance of *apparati*, see Weil, 'The Devotion of the Forty Hours', pp. 218–48.

The Holy Year of 1675 was musically notable for a number of reasons. The convent churches offered lavish liturgical services throughout the year, the composers associated with the convent services were some of the most prestigious in the city, and most importantly, the year-long celebration was thoroughly documented. The convent churches programmed their most impressive music, ignoring along the way prohibitions against polyphonic performance, playing instruments other than the organ, and calling upon male music teachers to assist in their preparations. It can only be assumed that this was with the tacit acceptance of cardinals of the Congregation responsible for overseeing the convents, many of whom were reported in the audience of these performances.[48] Clearly, the religious foundations played an important part in the spectacle and self-celebration of the *anno santo*.[49]

The diversity of offerings by convent churches included nuns performing the liturgy in plainchant or polyphony for their patronal feasts and major feasts of the Church. On occasion, convents renowned for their singers and their performances were accompanied by instruments, as at S. Lucia in Selci.[50] This is one of the few references to the fact that nuns had instruments other than organ, harpsichord, or lute and that they were willing to perform on the instruments in public.

Three other convents known for nuns' singing — S. Caterina da Siena a Monte Magnanapoli, S. Maria della Concezione in Campo Marzo and S. Silvestro — engaged some of the most skilled musicians in the city to organize and conduct some of their music for the Holy Year. Being able to assure the music and presence of musicians at the top levels of the Roman musical world indicated both the wealth and importance of a church, as well as its ability to manoeuvre within Roman musical networks. In addition, professional male musicians allowed more variety in a convent's offerings over the course of a year. The convent churches were in competition with the large parish churches, basilicas, and each other to get the musicians they needed for patronal feasts or other important days of the Church calendar. However, the convents known for their musical programmes were also respected by the city's male musicians, so those institutions could usually get the musicians they wanted with only a little negotiation. The quality of convent services displayed their status while the nuns shared their music and liturgy with the local nobility, pilgrims, and Church officials.

---

48 These included Cardinals Borromeo, Franciotti, Omodeo, Ottoboni, Pallavicini, and Rospigliosi, and Monsignors, De Vecchi, Fagnani, De Rossi, De Angeli, Ugolini, Ferrini, and Mellini.

49 For more detailed discussion of the debates regarding nuns' music, the edicts and enforcement, see Montford, 'L'Anno santo and Female Monastic Churches'.

50 'Venerdì a li 13. La festa di Santa Lucia Vergine, e Martire fu celebrata in diverse Chiese … da le Reverende Monache, dette in Selci a li Monti: ove le medesime cantarono li Vesperi, & accompagnarono con le loro Voci, e Sinfonie il Canto de la Messa'. Caetano, *Le memorie de l'anno santo*, p. 440.

The process of contracting outside musicians varied, partly because at various times throughout the years, it was outlawed. During the periods in which it was acceptable, the abbess, through an agent (usually a relative or a city musician with connections to the convent), would normally engage the *maestro di cappella* (director of music); with his input the abbess would then decide on the number of musicians he would hire and would also choose the music. In many cases, the pieces the *maestro* had composed for that year would be among the choices, and the convents were not above repeating some of their larger, polychoral works for festive occasions. For the year's major feasts, the agents would sometimes confer with each other to ensure that each convent had the programming it wanted. Among the most important *maestri di cappella* during the 1675 Holy Year were Alessandro Melani, Giovanni Battista Giansetti, Antonio Masini, and Francesco and Antonio Foggia.

Alessandro Melani — the *maestro di cappella* of S. Luigi dei Francesi, the national church of the French community in Rome — led the music at a number of convent churches, among them S. Caterina da Siena in Monte Magnanapoli for its patronal feast.[51] Melani's political networks, as well as those of his older brothers Jacopo and Atto, were complex, and included Louis XIV, Giulio Rospigliosi, the Medici family, and Francesco II d'Este.[52] Alessandro's reputation as a composer and *maestro di cappella* was only enhanced by his relationships with powerful political and religious figures, so acquiring his talents and his music represented a triumph for any church during the *anno santo*.

Giovanni Battista Giansetti played an important role in the *anno santo* of 1675, in part due to his status as *maestro di cappella* at S. Giovanni in Laterano, one of the four basilicas visited in procession to earn the Holy Year indulgence. In addition to his duties there, he provided special music for many of the other important institutions in Rome. During the *anno santo* of 1675, he directed the music at the convent of S. Silvestro in Capite for two of their services, preparing and directing music for multiple choirs.[53]

S. Silvestro's collaboration with Giansetti connected the community to Rome's broader musical context, but the convent was also an attraction in its own right. It housed a cherished relic, the head of St John the Baptist (hence, 'in Capite'). On that saint's feast, 24 June, the head was traditionally uncovered for veneration by the congregation. On this occasion the nuns themselves sang, using only the plainchant assigned for that martyr, rather than more contemporary music. Compared to the elaborate music heard during the rest of the year, the stark, simple sound of the chant must have been striking, and

51 Caetano, *Le memorie de l'anno santo*, p. 191. Cited in Montford, '*L'Anno santo* and Female Monastic Churches', 5.5.

52 For a discussion of Atto Melani's activities as diplomat and spy, as well as an investigation of his extant compositions, see Freitas, *Portrait of a Castrato*.

53 Caetano, *Le memorie de l'anno santo*, pp. 59, 318. Cited in Montford, '*L'Anno santo* and Female Monastic Churches', 5.2–5.3.

particularly dramatic for the audience while it gazed upon the relic. Displaying the relic and singing the ancient chant also highlighted the convent's link to the early Christian Church and its first martyrs, an indisputable signifier of religious and civic status in the Eternal City.

The feast of St Cecilia, the patron saint of musicians (22 November), was an also important musical event in Rome. Antonio Masini, *maestro di cappella* at St Peter's basilica and chamber musician in the court of Queen Christina of Sweden, supplied the music for the patronal feast of the convent of S. Cecilia. Masini had distinguished himself earlier in the year during Lent, which was marked by the presentation of an extraordinary cycle of oratorios performed at the Oratorio della Pietà, contributing eight of the fourteen oratorios. That musical coup and his service to Queen Christina meant his star was rising, and that reflected glory shone on the entertainments in which he participated.[54]

Francesco Foggia, the most prestigious *maestro di cappella* in mid-seventeenth-century Rome, having served at the basilicas of S. Maria in Trastevere, S. Giovanni in Laterano, and S. Maria Maggiore, was also among the most published *maestri* of the seventeenth century. It should be noted that his son Antonio was also a gifted musician, and the training he received from his father fitted him to serve as assistant *maestro di cappella* at S. Maria Maggiore, later succeeding his father.[55] They directed the music at a number of churches during the year, among them the convent churches of S. Maria della Concezione in Campo Marzo and SS. Domenico e Sisto.[56]

The efforts of such noted musicians in convent musical programmes locates nuns' churches very securely within the rich interwoven circles of Roman musical society. Musicians had their regular place of employment, but it was expected that they would freelance at other institutions on important feasts. Singers at prominent churches would supplement the choirs of other institutions to provide large-scale, polychoral works that impressed attendees with sonic grandeur and visual spectacle. Of course, the *maestri di capella* supplied their music, their musicians, and their own status as directors at the major basilicas and churches. While nuns were unable to be physically visible to their congregations, their own music and that provided in their exterior churches by other talented performers sounded a significant note in the musical tapestry of Rome.

---

54 Caetano, *Le memorie de l'anno santo*, p. 414. Cited in Montford, 'L'Anno santo and Female Monastic Churches', 5.4.

55 This was not unusual: like the Nanini, Aneri, and Allegri families, there seemed to be a cottage industry producing gifted musicians for the Roman musical scene. What was interesting was that the same families supplied the convents as well, with musical daughters, sisters, cousins, and aunts populating a number of Roman convents.

56 Caetano, *Le memorie de l'anno santo*, pp. 106, 298. Cited in Montford, 'L'Anno santo and Female Monastic Churches', 4.6.

The *anni santi* of the post-Tridentine Church presented the opportunity to demonstrate to the world, embodied in the innumerable pilgrims to the Holy City, the magnificence, glory, and above all, the permanence of the Holy Roman Church. Participation in the *anni santi* gave religious houses a means of contributing to the propaganda through their architecture, art, music, and liturgy. By presenting music and musicians of the highest quality and reputation, their services added to the rich, vibrant soundscape of the Jubilee in Rome. In return, during the Holy Year and for a few years afterwards, they enjoyed a level of freedom and visibility that was rare for women in general — and nuns in particular — in early modern Rome.

Entering the Convent

The use of music to establish and reinforce social and patronage connections between nuns and outside constituencies was not limited to public performances. While the *anni santi* represented the means for religious foundations to present their offerings to the world at large, on a smaller, more informal scale, nuns used music in private audiences to consolidate their links among female networks. The facility with which laywomen could enter the cloister was one of the areas that reflected Church authorities' fluctuating attitudes. Cloister was supposed to restrict outsiders entering the convent and sisters leaving it. However, reformers' primary concern was limiting sisters' contact with men. Recognizing this underlying fear, women exploited inconsistencies in the use of licences, and often just blatantly ignored edicts banning the entrance of non-monastic personnel to the cloister.

Not all convents sought out these interactions, as the efforts of those who fought to maintain their enclosure and limit the admittance of laywomen reveal. For example, Chiara Colonna, founder of the ultra-observant Roman house of Regina Coeli, complained so much that she stopped writing to the Congregation of the Apostolic Visit, and sent her letters directly to Pope Clement IX and Pope Clement X. She took issue with the number of exceptions granted to noble women, allowing them to ignore the prohibitions. In one such letter to Pope Clement X, she pleads for a rigorous ban on the practice, since

> by virtue of their apostolic permits various leading ladies of the city enter frequently, and with them many people of any station and quality, sometimes fifty or sixty people at a time, proving not only of great disorder to the enclosure that was recommended by the Sacred Council of Trent, but also disturbing to spiritual discipline.[57]

57 'Perchè entrando frequentemente in essi, in virtù de' loro brevi apostolici diverse dame primarie della città e con esse introducendo moltissime persone, talvolta ancosa d' ogni conditione e qualità sin al numero di 50 o 60 per volta, riesce non solo di gran disordine alla

The facts associated with Colonna's complaints may have been exaggerated, but the practice was indeed common amongst the nobility. In 1592 Pope Clement VIII gave Christine of Lorraine permission to enter any Florentine house of her choice with her daughters.[58] Despite Pope Urban VIII's 1624 prohibition of the granting of licences to enter Roman convents, Eleanora Zapata Boncompagni, Duchess of Sora prevailed upon the *cardinale vicario* to enter the convent of S. Cecilia in Trastevere to visit her daughter and sister-in-law.[59] And in a set of circumstances that can only be attributed to an aristocrat quite used to getting her way, Olimpia Chigi Gori had no compunction about entering a Sienese convent to treat her *educande* daughters with a visit to the opera:

> The opera began at 6:30 in the evening and ended at 12:30 a.m., and truly it was most beautiful, sung and conducted very well ... I assure you I was entranced, and I do not think that one can hear more refined or elegant music than this ... for that reason, I am thinking of going to all the performances, and yesterday I took all my girls out of the convent and escorted them to the opera.[60]

Nuns capitalized on the opportunity to entertain their relatives and woman dignitaries inside the enclosure, forming bonds of intimacy that recreated — or reestablished — those of women sharing household or familial ties, linking home, palace, and convent. In these cases, music was not only used as a marker of prestige and a gesture of homage. Opening their private sphere, with the implication that their guests belonged there, served to convey a particular kind of kinship between the women creating music and the women listening to it.

Berenice Della Ciaia received permission from her brother-in-law, Pope Alexander VII to visit all of Siena's religious foundations. A native of Siena, she and her husband, Mario Chigi, had been called to Rome when he was named commander of the papal armies. Allowing her entrance to Sienese houses celebrated both her papal and local connections and the reflected prestige shone upon the houses that honoured her. Della Ciaia spent a day in S. Maria degli Angeli accompanied by her daughter, sister-in-law, two of the pope's nieces, and one of his grand nieces. The ladies

> were admitted into the cloister and received with great joy by our superiors and by all of us nuns. Six most elegant chairs of crimson velvet, fringed in gold, were prepared and placed near the cloister door. Once the women were seated, the musical nuns sang the following five-voice madrigal in

---

clausura de' medesimi tanto raccomandata da s. Conc. di Trento, ma di molta distrattione dalle cose spirituali'. Città del Vaticano, ASV, Misc. Arm., VII, 37, fol. 341.

58   Cited in Harness, *Echoes of Women's Voices*, pp. 248–49.

59   Rome, ASR, CRF, Benedettine Cassinesi in S. Cecilia in Trastevere, 4032, no. 6.

60   Cited and translated in Reardon, *Holy Concord within Sacred Walls*, p. 127; see p. 262, n. 22 for transcription of document found in Città del Vaticano, BAV, Archivio Chigi 3871, fols 92[r-v].

honor of Her Excellency [Berenice Della Ciaia], composed by me, the writer of these chronicles. The work featured concerted instruments and lovely sinfonias.[61]

The visitor's status determined the significance of the laywoman's visit. The presence in Rome of Queen Christina of Sweden was considered a religious and political triumph for the Church. Christina's abdication and conversion, making her home in the seat of the Catholicism, and embracing Catholic institutions were considered symbolic of the resurgence of the Catholic Church and the universality of Catholicism. Her entrance to Rome was conducted like a triumph of the post-Tridentine Church and she was honoured and feted by both the Church hierarchy and the local nobility. The most noted female Catholic convert of the era, she was denied nothing, and her fascination with the notion of the female convent prompted her to visit many houses in Rome, sometimes staying overnight, and in one instance, for four days.[62] At S. Caterina, Christina was welcomed 'by a concert of diverse musical instruments, hearing also with much satisfaction an exquisite motet sung by a beautiful voice'.[63]

While she did not share familial or community ties with the sisters, over the course of her thirty years in Rome, Christina was to visit musical foundations numerous times, receiving gifts and developing correspondences with several learned nuns who sought to strengthen ties to this celebrity. The reciprocity of her visits went far beyond the obvious: her renown enhanced the reputation of the convent while its sanctity reflected upon her. By entering one of the secret holy spaces of the Church, she was offered entrance into a sorority that connected her with the network of monastic women.[64]

Conclusion

The music-making activities in convents in early modern Italy were constrained by varying levels of enforcement of cloister. The ideas of reformers, the Roman Curia, and the local Church hierarchy often conflicted with the needs and desires of the local nobility, musicians, and the religious women themselves. As noted, women were not a part of the Church's hierarchy, and thus the most

61 The anonymous chronicler is cited and translated in Reardon, *Holy Concord within Sacred Walls*, p. 43; see p. 195, Appendix 1, Doc. 10 for transcription of document found in Siena, Archivio Arcivescovile, Con. sopp. 2542.

62 Reports of Christina's visits to convents can be found in BAV, Vat. Lat. 8028, fols 10, 15, 25.

63 Priorato, *Historia della sacra real maestà di Christina Alessandra regina di Svetia*, p. 272.

64 By virtue of their networks, she could have also been freely admitted to the society of noble Roman women. However, Christina developed acrimonious relations with several women of Rome, often shocking them with her free language, and masculine posture and mannerisms. For her relationships, particularly her patronage of artists, musicians, writers, and intellectuals in Rome, see Akerman, *Queen Christina of Sweden and Her Circle*.

significant role that female monastics could play was as intermediaries between this world and heaven, living separate, holy lives so that their prayers had an unparalleled power. The unworldly isolation of cloister allowed the Church to invoke elaborate images of piety in the form of brides of Christ, or as angels on earth. At the same time, the music of the sisters, which in some cases was their only presence in the outside world, sonically reinforced those images.

Nuns constructed and used their relationships to implement their self-determined goals, and music was a vehicle for these activities. Women religious recognized that in trying to control and discipline convent communities, the Church found itself able to exploit the power of monastic music only infrequently, on extraordinary occasions. Convents seized the promise of these opportunities, however, and intentionally utilized music to spark interest, develop intimacy, and cement bonds. Their networks included and extended beyond family, encompassing civic, political, or religious associations, united and sustained by the sounds of religious song.

Works Cited

Manuscripts and Archival Sources

Città del Vaticano, Archivio Segreto Vaticano (ASV)
    Archivum Arcis (A.A.)
    ——, Arm. I–XVIII, MS 6492
    Congregazione della Visita Apostolica (Congr. Visita Ap.)
    Miscellanea (Misc. Arm.)
    ——, VII
Città del Vaticano, Biblioteca Apostolica Vaticana (BAV)
    MS Vat. Lat. 8028
Rome, Archivio di Stato di Roma (ASR)
    Congregazioni Religiose Femminili (CRF)
    ——, Benedettine Cassinesi in S. Cecilia in Trastevere

Primary Sources

Caetano, Ruggiero, *Le memorie de l'anno santo MDCLXXV celebrato da Papa Clemente X e consecrate alla santità di N. S. Papa Innocenzo XII, descritte in forma di giornale da l' Abb. Ruggiero Caetano romano* (Rome: Marc' Antonio e Orazio Campana, 1691)

Della Valle, Pietro, 'Della musica dell'età nostra (1640)' in *Le origini del melodramma*, ed. by Angelo Solerti (Turin: Fratelli Bocca, 1903), pp. 148–79

Lassels, Richard, *An Italian Voyage; or A Compleat Journey through Italy*, 2nd edn (London: Richard Wellington & B. Bernard Lintott, 1697)

Priorato, Galeazzo Gualdo, *Historia della sacra real maestà di Christina Alessandra regina di Svetia* (Modena: Soliani, 1656)

Quagliati, Paolo, *Affetti amorosi spirituali* (Rome: Robletti, 1617)

Secondary Works

Akerman, Susanna, *Queen Christina of Sweden and Her Circle: The Transformation of a Seventeenth-Century Philosophical Libertine* (Leiden: Brill, 1991)

Baernstein, Prudence Renée, 'The Counter-Reformation Convent: The Angelics of San Paolo in Milan, 1535–1635' (unpublished doctoral dissertation, Harvard University, 1993)

Blainey, Geoffrey, *A Short History of Christianity* (Lanham: Rowman and Littlefield, 2011)

Brundage, James A., and Elizabeth M. Makowski, 'Enclosure of Nuns: The Decretal *Periculoso* and Its Commentators', *Journal of Medieval History*, 20.1 (June 1994), 143–55

Bungener, L. F., *History of the Council of Trent*, ed. by John McClintock, D.D. (New York: Harper and Brothers, 1855)

Canons and Decrees of the Council of Trent, ed. and trans. by H. J. Schroeder (St Louis: Herder, 1941)

Coakley, John W., *Women, Men, and Spiritual Power: Female Saints and Their Male Collaborators* (New York: Columbia University Press, 2006)

Copeland, Clare, *Maria Maddalena de' Pazzi: The Making of a Counter-Reformation Saint* (Oxford: Oxford University Press, 2016)

Dolan, Frances E., 'Reading, Work, and Catholic Women's Biographies', *English Literary Renaissance*, 33 (2003), 328–57

Evangelisti, Silvia, '"We Do Not Have It, and We Do Not Want It": Women, Power, and Convent Reform in Florence', *Sixteenth Century Journal*, 34 (2003), 677–700

——, *Nuns: A History of Convent Life, 1450–1700* (Oxford: Oxford University Press, 2007)

Fiorani, Luigi, 'Le visite apostoliche del cinque-seicento e la società religiosa romana', *Ricerche per la Storia Religiosa di Roma*, 4 (1980), 53–148

Freitas, Roger, *Portrait of a Castrato: Politics, Patronage, and Music in the Life of Atto Melani* (Cambridge: Cambridge University Press, 2009)

Gilmore, David D., *Misogyny: The Male Malady* (Philadelphia: University of Pennsylvania Press, 2001)

Glixon, Jonathan E., *Mirrors of Heaven or Worldly Theaters? Venetian Nunneries and Their Music* (New York: Oxford University Press, 2017)

Harness, Kelley, *Echoes of Women's Voices: Music, Art, and Female Patronage in Early Modern Florence* (Chicago: University of Chicago Press, 2006)

Kendrick, Robert L., *Celestial Sirens: Nuns and their Music in Early Modern Milan* (Oxford: Oxford University Press, 1996)

Laven, Mary, 'Sex and Celibacy in Early Modern Venice', *The Historical Journal*, 44 (2001), 865–88

Macy, Laura, 'Geronimo Cavaglieri, the Song of Songs and Female Spirituality in Federigo Borromeo's Milan', *Early Music*, 39.3 (2011), 349–57

Makowski, Elizabeth M., *Canon Law and Cloistered Women: Periculoso and its Commentators 1298–1545* (Washington, DC: The Catholic University of America Press, 1997)

Mayne Kienzle, Beverly, 'Margherita of Cortona: Women, Preaching, and the Writing of Hagiography', *Medieval Sermon Studies*, 54 (2010), 38–50

Medioli, Francesca, 'An Unequal Law: The Enforcement of Clausura Before and After the Council of Trent', in *Women in Renaissance and Early Modern Europe*, ed. by Christine Meek (Dublin: Four Courts, 2000), pp. 136–52

Monson, Craig, *Disembodied Voices: Music and Culture in an Early Modern Italian Convent* (Berkeley: University of California Press, 1995)

Montford, Kimberlyn, '*L'Anno santo* and Female Monastic Churches: The Politics, Business and Music of the Holy Year in Rome (1675)', *Journal of Seventeenth-Century Music*, 6 (2000) http://www.sscm-jscm.org/v6/no1/montford.html (Online journal)

——, 'Gli *Affetti amorosi spirituali* (Roma, 1617): Devozione nei Monasteri femminili della Roma post-tridentina' in *Il Tempio Armonico: Giovanni Giovenale Ancina e le musiche devozionali nel contesto internazionale del suo tempo*, ed. by Carla Bianco (Lucca: Libreria Musicale Italiana, 2006), pp. 265–82

——, 'Holy Restraint: Religious Reform and Nuns' Music in Early Modern Rome', *The Sixteenth Century Journal*, 37 (2006), 1007–26

——, 'Musical Marketing in the Female Monasteries of Early Modern Rome' in *Patronage, Gender and the Arts in Early Modern Italy: Essays in Honor of Carolyn Valone*, ed. by Katherine A. McIver and Cynthia Stollhans (New York: Italica, 2015), pp. 153–75

——, 'Within and Without: Women's Networks and the Early Modern Roman Convent' in *Mapping Gendered Routes and Spaces in the Early Modern World*, ed. by Merry E. Wiesner-Hanks (Farnham: Ashgate, 2015), pp. 213–27

Ranft, Patricia, 'A Key to Counter Reformation Women's Activism: The Confessor-Spiritual Director', *Journal of Feminist Studies in Religion*, 10 (1994), 7–26

Reardon, Colleen, *Holy Concord within Sacred Walls: Nuns and Music in Siena, 1575–1700* (Oxford: Oxford University Press, 2002)

Tuana, Nancy, *Less Noble Sex: Scientific, Religious, and Philosophical Conceptions of Woman's Nature* (Bloomington: Indiana University Press, 1993)

Weil, Mark S., 'The Devotion of the Forty Hours and Roman Baroque Illusions', *Journal of the Warburg and Courtauld Institutes*, 37 (1974), 218–48

MARILYN DUNN*

Family Dynasties and Networks of Alliance in Post-Tridentine Convents in Rome and its Environs

As the papal city, Rome was not dominated by a dynastic ruling family like the Gonzaga in Mantua, or the Medici in Florence where convents could become parallel courts for family noblewomen, but its convents in the seventeenth century were predominately populated with the daughters of the city's many noble families.[1] Some of these convents were restricted to only titled and noble women and enjoyed exalted reputations for the nobility of their nuns.[2] In the fluid but highly competitive social structure of Rome the noble classes were comprised of the titled feudal nobility, papal nobility, and civic nobility, and members of all of these noble families frequently had ties to the Curia and the cardinalate. Family members collaborated in a team effort to advance the success and prestige of their families in the social and political hierarchy of Baroque Rome, and their strategies and networks extended into Rome's convents.[3]

* This research was partially supported by a Loyola University Chicago Summer Stipend Award (2015). I wish to thank Suor Raffaella, prioress of SS. Rosario in Marino, for granting me permission to consult the convent's archive and for her most gracious hospitality. A particular debt of gratitude is owed to Dr Ugo Onorati for his generosity in assisting me to gain admittance to the archive, helping me to consult its holdings, and generously sharing his photographed documents. His professional assistance and friendship along with that of his wife Dr Assunta Colazza contributed greatly to my research. I am also grateful to Dr Elia Mariano and Fra D. Romano di Cosmo for their kind assistance at the Archivio Colonna in Subiaco.

1 Some convents in Rome, however, accommodated less elite or wealthy postulants. See Lirosi, *I monasteri femminili*, pp. 87–90. For convents in Mantua see Hickson, *Women, Art and Architectural Patronage in Renaissance Mantua*; Gladen, 'Suor Lucrina Fetti, Pittrice in una corte monastica', pp. 123–41; and Bourne, 'From Court to Cloister and Back Again', pp. 153–79. For the Medici at La Crocetta in Florence see Harness, *Echoes of Women's Voices*.

2 See Rome, ASR, Camerale III, Roma Chiese e monasteri, Busta 1893, SS. Domenico e Sisto and Zucchi, *Roma domenicana*, p. 287.

3 See Nussdorfer, *Civic Politics in the Rome of Urban VIII*; Ago, *Carriere e clientele nella Roma barocca*; Ago, 'Giochi di squadra', pp. 256–64; and Borello, *Trame sovrapposte*. Honours,

Marilyn Dunn (mdunn@luc.edu) is Associate Professor of Art History and associate faculty member of the Women Studies and Gender Studies Program at Loyola University Chicago.

Convent Networks In Early Modern Italy, ed. by Marilyn Dunn and Saundra Weddle, ES 25 (Turnhout: Brepols, 2020) pp. 261–301   BREPOLS ☙ PUBLISHERS   DOI 10.1484/M.ES-EB.5.119519

Family influence and interference in convent life that had traditionally marked female monastic culture was an abuse targeted by the reforms of the Council of Trent (1563).[4] By re-establishing strict enclosure and regulating convent governance, Church reformers hoped to break the perceived pernicious effects of the close relationships that families formed with particular convents,[5] a practice that had contributed to powerful family cliques which undermined communal life, distracted from spiritual duties, and reproduced the social hierarchies and politics of the secular world in the supposedly sacred space of the convent.[6] While Tridentine reforms were well established by the seventeenth century in Rome and the worst abuses of family interference curtailed,[7] prescriptive literature in the seventeenth century continued to manifest concerns about the influence of family groups within convents. Antonio Seneca in his treatise on the government of Roman convents (1604) declared that in convents with fewer than forty nuns, no more than two sisters from the same family or four relatives of the second degree should be admitted, and Carlo Andrea Basso (1627) warned of the distracting influence of an aunt's affection for her niece in the convent.[8] In fact even after the Tridentine reforms, many convents remained favoured sites for particular families to place their daughters, creating clusters of related nuns who sometimes continued multi-generational family lineages or dynasties within their convents. Novices still often joined sisters or aunts already in a religious community, and a nun's natal family remained an essential part of her identity. Even though a new nun symbolically shed her connection with the external world and marked her entry into a religious community by changing her secular name to a new religious name, she still remained identified with her paternal family's last name as well.

Focusing on the elite Dominican convent of SS. Domenico e Sisto in Rome and on two reformed Dominican convents it spawned outside of Rome, this essay examines family dynastic patterns within the convent and the networks

---

prestigious appointments, important offices in civic or papal government, and art patronage all contributed to advancing family reputation and success.

4   *Canons and Decrees of the Council of Trent*, ed. and trans. by Schroeder, pp. 218–29.

5   Families had manipulated the management of convents especially through kinswomen elected to the abbacy for lifetime terms. See Sperling, *Convents and the Body Politic*, p. 116.

6   See Monson, *Disembodied Voices*, pp. 110–17, 131–51.

7   Religious communities were placed under the supervision of the Ordinary or, in the case of Rome, the cardinal vicar or other prominent cardinal protectors; a congregation of male deputies was mandated to oversee financial expenditures; and terms of abbesses and other elected officials were limited to three years. See Lirosi, *I monasteri femminili*, pp. 107–13; De Luca, *Il religioso pratico*, pp. 226–45; Città del Vaticano, ASV, A.A., Arm. I–XVIII, 6492, fols 140ʳ–41ʳ; Città del Vaticano, ASV, A.A., Arm. I–XVIII, 6493, fols 36ᵛ–37ʳ. Despite a few scandalous incidents, most abuses of cloistered life in seventeenth-century Rome were of a more minor nature with over-frequentation of the parlour, where nuns could converse with family and friends, ranking as most common. See Fiorani, 'Monache e monasteri romani', pp. 76–77.

8   Città del Vaticano, ASV, A.A., Arm. I–XVIII, 6492, fol. 6ʳ; De Luca, *Il religioso pratico*, p. 235; Basso, *La monaca perfetta*, p. 319. Cardinal De Luca advised that a third sister could be admitted to a convent with special permission and a double dowry but without a voice in convent affairs.

of alliance that existed between nuns and their families both inside and outside the convent, as well as networks established between nuns of different families and between convents. It seeks to illuminate both the impact and complexity of family relations in the post-Tridentine convent and the extensive networks of alliances forged by cloistered nuns that reached beyond natal families. The first part of this study is devoted to a consideration of family dynasties and networks at SS. Domenico e Sisto in Rome, while the second part shifts perspective from the aristocratic dynastic character of the Roman convent to examine the role of family ties and multiple networks of alliance in the context of two little-studied reformed Dominican convents founded outside of Rome by Colonna family nuns from SS. Domenico e Sisto whose austere character and circumstances differed notably from their Roman source. By examining these diverse but interrelated Dominican convents in Rome and its environs this essay seeks to reveal a more nuanced understanding of the nature and function of family and other networks of alliance in the lived experience of seicento nuns and their convents.

SS. Domenico e Sisto

Clusters of family members and multi-generational family lineages were prevalent at the large Dominican convent of SS. Domenico e Sisto, considered second to none for the nobility of its nuns and its conspicuous patrimony.[9] The significance of lineage is documented in the careful recording of family relationships in the biographies of nuns contained in the chronicle of the convent and in the family *stemmi* (coats of arms) placed by many nuns on the decorations they sponsored in their public church.[10] Related nuns frequently occupied key administrative positions, collaborated as patrons, or succeeded family members in these roles. Within the confines of the cloistered environment these religious noblewomen assumed an active agency in parallel to their relatives in the secular world or the Curia. In seventeenth-century Rome projects of construction, renovation, and decoration of convents and their public churches were frequently financed by convents as a corporate body or by individual nuns within the community who enjoyed *livelli* (allowances) provided by their families.[11] The image-consciousness that motivated much

---

9   Zucchi, *Roma domenicana*, p. 287. In 1626, there were 130 nuns; 92 of these were choir nuns (Città del Vaticano, ASV, Congr. Visita Ap., 3), while by 1662 there were 116 nuns of whom 84 were choir nuns (Lirosi, *I monasteri femminili*, p. 330). The origins of the community of nuns at SS. Domenico e Sisto dated back to the foundation of the first Dominican convent in Rome by St Dominic at S. Sisto all'Appia (1221). Due to unhealthy conditions around S. Sisto, outside the well-populated areas of Rome, the nuns moved to a new complex on the Monte Magnanapoli in 1575.

10 Rome, AMR, Salamonia, 'Memorie'.

11 De Luca (*Il religioso pratico*, p. 168) noted that it was common for nuns to have at their

of the patronage of Rome's noble classes extended to its religious institutions whose patronage constructed religious identities, and in the case of enclosed female convents their physical complex and public church represented the public face of the cloistered nuns. In marking public decorations with family *stemmi*, noble nuns functioned as representatives of their families, commemorating lineage, as well as sponsoring works that benefitted their convents.[12]

Among the family dynasties at SS. Domenico e Sisto was that of the Mattei family from which between the late sixteenth and early eighteenth centuries at least ten women, representing several groups of sisters, were members of the community. Four Mattei nuns were elected as prioress between 1656 and 1672.[13] During the rule of the last of these seicento Mattei prioresses, Madre Suor Maria Angela Mattei, the decoration of the vaults of the tribune and church with the illusionistic frescoes of Domenico Maria Canuti and Enrico Haffner (1674–1675) was begun. Canuti had arrived in Rome in 1672 to execute paintings for the Mattei family, and Maria Angela's family connections may have influenced or facilitated his commission at SS. Domenico e Sisto.[14]

The convent's inhabitants also included many nuns of one of the most preeminent noble families of Rome, the Colonna. Women of the Colonna family had been represented in this community from its thirteenth-century origins at S. Sisto all'Appia, and this tradition continued after the nuns' move in 1575 to a new site at Monte Magnanapoli on the Quirinal Hill, not far from the Colonna family palace at SS. Apostoli. Nuns deriving from two branches of the family were active in the convent in the Seicento. Three daughters of Don Marzio Colonna, duke of Zagarola and member of the vice-regal advisory council of Naples,[15] joined the convent of SS. Domenico e Sisto between 1597 and 1605, distinguishing themselves in various ways within the convent.[16] Suor Clarice

disposition 'qualche rendita vitalizia, che volgarmente si dice livello' (an annuity commonly called an allowance). While *livelli* were technically under the control of their superiors, in practice they were available for nuns' use. Amounts of *livelli* varied according to the circumstances of individual nuns and were different from the set amount of the dowry paid for a nun's maintenance in the community. See Città del Vaticano, ASV, A.A., Arm. I–XVIII, 6493, fol. 36^r; Dunn, 'Nuns as Art Patrons'; and Radke, 'Nuns and Their Art'.

12   See Dunn, 'Nuns, Family, and Inter-Familial Dynamics of Art Patronage'.

13   Mattei women had been present in the community since the Trecento. Madre Suor Aurora Mattei was prioress (mother superior) during the 1656 plague, and her sister Cherubina Mattei was prioress in 1662. They were daughters of Mario Mattei, duke of Paganica. Another pair of sisters, Maria Luigia Mattei and Maria Angela Mattei, served as prioress in 1670–1672 and 1672–1674 respectively. Maria Luigia and Maria Angela were daughters of Marchese Asdrubale Mattei (d. 1638), noted collector and patron of Palazzo Mattei di Giove in Piazza Mattei. See Rome, AMR, Pannilini, 'Biografie delle Religiose', nos 956, 963, 975, 982.

14   Malvasia, *Vite di pittori bolognesi*, p. 33.

15   Petrucci, 'Colonna, Marzio'.

16   Rome, AMR, Pannilini, 'Biografie delle Religiose', no. 926 and Spiazzi, *Cronache e fioretti del monastero di San Sisto all'Appia*, pp. 487–88. The first daughter to profess, Suor Beatrice

IESA DI S-DOMENICO COL MONASTERO DELLE MONACHE DELL'ORDINE DELL'ISTESSO SANTO A MONTE MAGNANAPOLI.
sul quirinale la facciata e Architettura di Vincenzo della Greca
1 *Monastero delle Monache.*   *Gio-Batta Falda di se fece*   *Per Gio Iacomo Rossi in Roma alla Pace e Priv del s Pont.*   2 *Giardino Aldobrandino.*   15

Figure 8.1. SS. Domenico e Sisto Façade, Rome. 1628–1663. From Giovanni Battista Falda, *Il nuovo teatro delle fabriche, et edificii, in prospettiva di Roma moderna,* 1665–1669. Wikimedia Commons, image in the public domain.

Colonna,[17] perhaps taking after her father who was an active patron of sacred and secular buildings in Zagarolo, devoted herself to extensive patronage for her convent, donating two silver angels for the church, constructing a new sepulchre for the nuns under the altar of St Catherine (1632–1634), erecting an altar to St Onuphrius (Onofrio) in the dormitory, and decorating a chapel dedicated to the Virgin in the convent garden with paintings of Sts Mary Magdalene, Mary of Egypt, and other hermit saints that evoked the reclusion and contemplation of the cloister.[18] Clarice's sister Raimonda, elected prioress in 1654 and again in 1660, oversaw the completion of the church's façade and the construction of its scenographic staircase (Figure 8.1) and at her own

---

(Porzia in secular life), noted for her virtues and devotion to Christ's Passion, served the community in various offices.

17　Named Vittoria in her secular life, she entered the convent in 1600 after her arranged marriage to Francesco Maria della Rovere, duke of Urbino fell through (Spiazzi, *Cronache e fioretti del monastero di San Sisto all'Appia,* p. 502).

18　Spiazzi, *San Domenico,* pp. 394, 404, 426; Hills, 'The Housing of Institutional Architecture', pp. 139–40. While the convent chronicle does not record any offices held by Suor Clarice, it notes her observant spirit, generosity to the poor, and patronage, as well as her particular devotion to virgin martyr St Catherine and hermit saints Onuphrius and Romuald (Spiazzi, *Cronache e fioretti del monastero di San Sisto all'Appia,* p. 503).

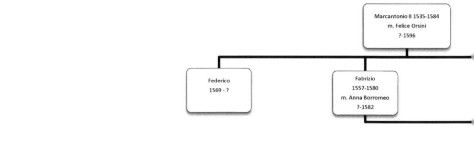

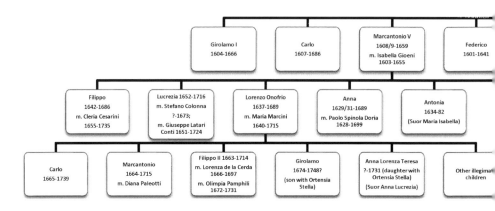

expense had made the ciborium for the public church (1646) and constructed a new sacristy (1655).[19]

These Colonna nuns were described in the convent chronicle as aunts[20] of four daughters of Isabella Gioeni and Contestabile Marcantonio V Colonna, head of the Paliano branch of the family (Figure 8.2), who represented the next generation of Colonna women at SS. Domenico e Sisto — Maria Isabella, Maria Girolama, Maria Colomba, and Maria Alessandra Colonna (entered 1649, 1654, 1656, and1659 respectively).[21] Since SS. Domenico e Sisto was a large convent the rule regarding the limit of two sisters in smaller communities did not apply.[22] Their brother Lorenzo Onofrio (1637–1689), who succeeded his father as Contestabile of the kingdom of Naples in 1659, was also closely associated with SS. Domenico e Sisto, serving as one of its advisory deputies

19 Rome, AMR, Pannilini, 'Biografie delle Religiose', no. 951; Spiazzi, *Cronache e fioretti del monastero di San Sisto all'Appia*, pp. 532, 534–35 and Spiazzi, *San Domenico*, pp. 425–26. The stairs were begun in 1655 using money from funds for the *educande* (female boarding students), a donation of fifty scudi from Suor Maria Calora, and Suor Raimonda's own contribution.

20 Rome, AMR, Pannilini, 'Biografie delle Religiose', no. 1037.

21 Rome, AMR, Pannilini, 'Biografie delle Religiose', nos 1034, 1037, 1042, 1043; Marino, ASRM, Arm. 2, no. 1, 'Fatti notabili' pp. 5–6.

22 See notes 8 and 9.

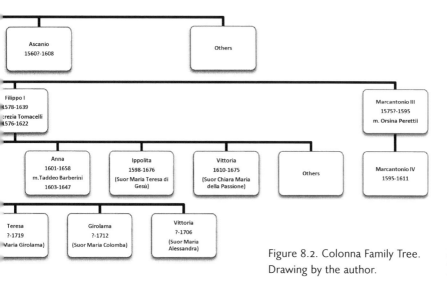

Figure 8.2. Colonna Family Tree. Drawing by the author.

during the period when the convent undertook the embellishment of the vaults of the church's tribune and nave with the frescoes of Canuti and Haffner. He may have played some role as agent in this commission for the church so closely associated with his family since, as in the case of the Mattei, Canuti had also previously worked for him.[23] These spectacular illusionistic frescoes not only enhanced the prestige of SS. Domenico e Sisto but also reflected lustre onto the reputations of families closely tied to the convent through dynasties of nuns. Influential, well-connected relatives of nuns were valuable intermediaries for convents with the public world, assisting these cloistered institutions to undertake corporate projects. While nuns typically initiated and financed their projects of construction and decoration, male agents were necessary to mediate with the secular world.[24]

Lorenzo Onofrio Colonna's cloistered sisters were active patrons within their convent. Maria Isabella donated silver candlesticks and reliquary busts of Sts Agnes and Barbara to the church, while Maria Girolama and Maria

---

23   His name appears along with Prioress Maria Angela Mattei's on payment orders for scaffolding for the ceiling paintings. See Ontini, *La chiesa di S. Domenico in Roma*, p. 96 and Malvasia, *Vite di pittori bolognesi*, p. 34.
24   Dunn, 'Nuns, Agents, and Agency'.

Colomba each gave a pair of silver candlesticks.[25] Like many of the nuns at SS. Domenico e Sisto, these Colonna sisters contributed to creating sacred spaces within the cloister as patrons of religious images or chapels. In gratitude for a miraculous cure she attributed to her patron, St Nicholas of Bari, Maria Isabella richly decorated a convent chapel with marbles and stuccoes to which an image of St Nicholas,[26] originally located on an altar in a room off a convent staircase, was moved in 1665. Maria Girolama Colonna replaced the transferred image with one of the Three Magi on the staircase altar.[27] Ultimately these two Colonna nuns turned their efforts to more ambitious spiritual projects by founding new Dominican convents in the Colonna territories of Marino and Avezzano (to be discussed below).

Related nuns frequently allied as patrons as in the case of four daughters of Marchese Prospero Costaguti, Maria Agnese, Prospera Vincenza, Paola Maria and Maria Candida, who collaborated in decorating the Chapel of St Dominic marked with their family *stemma* (coat of arms) in the public church with marbles, gilded stuccoes, and an altarpiece by Pier Francesco Mola in 1648.[28] Around this time Mola also painted frescoes in the Palazzo Costaguti for their brother, Cardinal Vincenzo Costaguti, who may have facilitated their commission of the artist. Nearly simultaneous decorations in the family palace by the cardinal and in the church of SS. Domenico e Sisto by the Costaguti nuns exemplify collaborative efforts by brother-sister siblings from both sides of the cloister walls that functioned to celebrate family reputation.[29] Suor Maria Agnese also donated 400 scudi to decorate the church's façade with statues of the Dominican saints Dominic and Sixtus in 1653.[30] She and her sister Prospera Vincenza would later collaborate with the Colonna nuns in establishing their new convents.[31] In the Colonna and Costaguti examples

---

25 Rome, AMR, Pannilini, 'Biografie delle Religiose', nos 1034, 1037; Spiazzi, *San Domenico*, pp. 426, 428.

26 According to the convent chronicle of SS. Rosario, Marino, Suor Maria Isabella Colonna throughout her life was especially devoted to the Virgin Mary and to St Nicholas of Bari (Marino, ASRM, Armadio 2, no. 1, 'Fatti notabili', p. 9). The Dominican order also held St Nicholas of Bari in special devotion because when St Dominic went to Bologna in 1218 he was given the church of St Nicholas of the Vineyards (Hinnebusch, *The History of the Dominican Order*, vol. 1, pp. 64–65, 106–07 and Dominican Nuns, 'St Nicholas', unpaginated).

27 Spiazzi, *San Domenico*, pp. 407, 409; Rome, AMR, Pannilini, 'Biografie delle Religiose', no. 1034; Marino, ASRM, Armadio 2, no. 1, 'Fatti notabili', p. 9.

28 In female monastic communities, nuns worshiped in a nuns' choir separated by walls and grilles from the convent's attached public church, outside of the cloistered precinct, where the lay public worshiped.

29 Bernardini, Draghi, and Verdesi, *SS. Domenico e Sisto*, pp. 84–86; Rome, AMR, Salamonia, 'Memorie', vol. 5, fol. 72ᵛ; Rome, AMR, Pannilini, 'Biografie delle Religiose', nos 1018, 1022, 1026, 1030; and Spezzaferro, 'Pier Francesco Mola e il mercato artistico romano', p. 42.

30 Her donation was combined with other convent funds by Prioress Lorenza Molara. See Spiazzi, *San Domenico*, p. 425 and Bernardini, Draghi, and Verdesi, *SS. Domenico e Sisto*, p. 33.

31 Suor Paola Maria Costaguti was also connected with a Colonna project, adding painting and decoration to and caring for the altar of St Onuphrius erected by Suor Clarice Colonna. Spiazzi, *San Domenico*, p. 404.

we can see fluid patterns of alliances shifting between family members within the convent, collaborations with family outside the convent, and alliances between nuns of different families in support of common goals.

Different last names of nuns sometimes obscure the extent of familial relationships that existed between nuns in religious communities related along matrilineal and mixed lines.[32] These relationships are more difficult to trace, but in the case of SS. Domenico e Sisto, the convent chronicle's attention to family relationships reveals networks of interrelations. For instance, in the sixteenth and seventeenth centuries three nuns from the noble Jacovacci family, whose male members included two cardinals and many conservators and officials of the civic government in Rome, resided in the community.[33] Among the Jacovacci nuns were two women descended from different fathers. Suor Angela Jacovacci, daughter of Marc'Antonio Jacovacci, was elected prioress several times (1604, 1614, and 1620), presiding over the embellishment of the nuns' choir with wooden choir stalls, financed by the community with monies donated to the convent in excess of their dowries by Suor Raimonda Colonna and Suor Eufemia Carpegna, and large frescoes paid for by other individual nuns during her first tenure. During her second term as prioress she enlarged the organ with a wooden balustrade.[34] Madre Suor Serafina Jacovacci, daughter of Domenico Jacovacci, professed in 1577 and distinguished herself in many offices in the convent, culminating in her term as prioress, during which the nave of the church of SS. Domenico e Sisto was commenced in 1628. Through her mother, Suor Serafina was related to a cluster of nuns from the Margani family.[35] She had made her profession when her aunt Cristina Margani was prioress.[36] Two other nieces of Cristina, sisters Raffaella and Maddalena Margani had joined the convent in 1554. By 1599 Raffaella was serving as prioress while her sister Maddalena fulfilled the role of under prioress, suggesting a concentration of family power. After Maddalena's death, Raffaella went on to be elected prioress two more times (1606, 1613).[37] In 1577 Gabriella Farsegni, whose mother was a Jacovacci, entered the convent. Madre Suor Gabriella proved a devoted patron of her church, donating a pair of precious silver candlesticks while she was sacristan

---

32 See Medioli, 'Reti famigliari'. Centuries of marriages between noble families in Rome created a vast network of interrelations that resulted in some degree of relationship between nuns from many of the families represented at SS. Domenico e Sisto.

33 Amayden, *Storia delle famiglie romane*, vol. 1, pp. 457–58 and Nussdorfer, *Civic Politics in the Rome of Urban VIII*, pp. 44–47. Suor Maria Mauri Jacovacci joined the convent in 1559 and died in 1603 during her term as under prioress (Spiazzi, *Cronache e fioretti del monastero di San Sisto all'Appia*, p. 395).

34 Spiazzi, *Cronache e fioretti del monastero di San Sisto all'Appia*, pp. 395, 527.

35 The Margani, an ancient and powerful Roman noble family, were intermarried with many other Roman noble families. Amayden, *Storia delle famiglie romane*, vol. 2, pp. 54–56.

36 Spiazzi, *Cronache e fioretti del monastero di San Sisto all'Appia*, pp. 424–25, 530–31. Cristina (d. 1581) had professed in 1545.

37 Spiazzi, *Cronache e fioretti del monastero di San Sisto all'Appia*, pp. 386, 388.

and commissioning the decoration of the tribune with gilded stuccoes and paintings after her election as prioress in 1634. She conceived the idea of constructing a grated corridor inside the convent that encircled the church's nave at its upper level so that her nuns could listen to the Mass, a project paid for by another nun, Suor Maria Lucrezia Lanti.[38] Having some money from an inheritance at her disposal, Suor Gabriella planned to construct a chapel in the new church, but before she could bring her plan to fruition she became ill and died in 1638. Before her death, she entrusted the completion of the chapel project to her niece, Madre Suor Gregoria Boccarini, who introduced yet another family name into this extended familial network of nuns. Suor Gregoria, who added some funds of her own, completed the chapel dedicated to St Peter Martyr in 1648, though apparently only after some prodding from her deceased aunt, who supposedly appeared to her in a dream and chastised her for her procrastination.[39]

The multiple generations of nuns from noble families like those discussed and others such as the Giustiniani, Fonseca, Capizucchi, Alli, Altemps, and Frangipane as well as the presence of numerous clusters of multiple sisters (two to four) from the Colonna, Giustini, Leni, Conti, Celsi, Altemps, and other families within the community at SS. Domenico e Sisto attests to the favoured relationship between particular families and this prestigious Dominican convent. While familial dynasties are evident in the convent population and in the leadership and patronage roles assumed by the female religious of particular families, the nuns also very strongly identified with the institutional family of their convent community, creating their own conventual family dynasty.[40] This is evident in the practice of 'remaking' an earlier deceased nun in the community by a novice taking her name for her own religious name, a custom to which Sharon Strocchia has called attention in fifteenth-century Florentine convents.[41] The practice both honoured the deceased and cast the new nun in her convent lineage. After her father died when she was still a child, the aforementioned Suor Angela Jacovacci was placed under the tutelage of Alessandro Colonna, who provided her convent dowry. Thus, she chose Angela as her religious name in memory of Suor Angela Colonna who had preceded her in the convent.[42] Sometimes the name 'remade' an earlier blood relative in the community. When Madre Suor Marta Tenaglini chose her religious name Marta she did so to renew

---

38   Spiazzi, *Cronache e fioretti del monastero di San Sisto all'Appia*, pp. 436–37; Rome, AMR, Pannilini, 'Biografie delle Religiose', no. 1007.

39   Spiazzi, *Cronache e fioretti del monastero di San Sisto all'Appia*, p. 437; Rome, AMR, Pannilini, 'Biografie delle Religiose', no. 973.

40   See Hills, 'The Housing of Institutional Architecture', pp. 136–40.

41   Strocchia, 'Naming a Nun', pp. 236–40.

42   Suor Angela Colonna was *camerlenga* (financial administrator) of the community during the turbulent events of the Sack of Rome (1527) and was noted as a guide and example for her fellow nuns. Spiazzi, *Cronache e fioretti del monastero di San Sisto all'Appia*, pp. 312–14.

the pious memory of her deceased maternal aunt. Additionally, her choice of religious name reflected her special devotion to St Martha, a saint whom she emulated in her own active character, exercising a multitude of administrative functions in the convent.[43]

Although a certain sense of competitiveness may have stimulated nuns' patronage, as Kate Lowe has noted in the case of rival family groups at the convent of S. Cosimato,[44] nuns were not simply motivated by personal aggrandizement or family honour, but also by their investment in their corporate culture and identity. Noble nuns empowered by family wealth and prestige and possessing independent *livelli* were avid patrons of art, architecture, and liturgical objects in their convents and churches. As well as competitiveness, we should also think of collaboration as a model of convent patronage. Individual nuns and family groups of nuns contributed toward the realization of larger projects. As related in the chronicle of SS. Domenico e Sisto, they contributed funds to build their public church (1628),[45] and once it was completed various nuns assumed responsibility for decorating the presbytery (1636–1646) by acting as patrons of specific parts of it. Sisters Lucrezia and Antonia Leni paid for the high altar (Figure 8.3), marked with their *stemma*, designed by Gianlorenzo Bernini, on which the ciborium (later altered) donated by Raimonda Colonna was placed; sisters Maria Grazia and Flavia Domitilla Capizucchi assumed responsibility for the marble pavement of the tribune; while Suor Maria Maddalena Fonseca paid for the marble balustrade; and Suor Benedetta Vipereschi gave money for the stairs to the high chapel.[46] These donations for specific parts of the

---

43 Suor Marta Tenaglini, who entered the convent in 1577, sought to honour her aunts, Suor Marta and Suor Innocenzia Tomarozzi (Tomarossi), who had entered the community in 1544, joining their aunt Suor Felice Tomarozzi (Spiazzi, *Cronache e fioretti del monastero di San Sisto all'Appia*, pp. 335, 425–26).

44 Lowe, *Nuns' Chronicles and Convent Culture*, pp. 63, 67–71, 390. See BAV, Vat. Lat. 7847, fol. 288ʳ. At SS. Domenico e Sisto, the chronicle in relating how Madre Suor Maria Girolama Colonna founded the new convent in Avezzano, states that she did not want to be less than her older sister (Madre Suor Isabella who had founded the convent in Marino) in bringing honour to her convent and to the entire Dominican order (Rome, AMR, Pannilini, 'Biografie delle Religiose', no. 1037).

45 Suor Paola Giustini, who donated 1000 scudi, secured a 500 scudi donation from their cardinal protector Scipione Borghese and encouraged donations from many fellow nuns. See Rome, AMR, Salamonia, 'Memorie', vol. 4, fols 53ʳ–53ᵛ; vol. 5, 71ʳ–71ᵛ and Spiazzi, *San Domenico*, pp. 421–23.

46 Spiazzi, *Cronache e fioretti del monastero di San Sisto all'Appia*, pp. 454–55, 463–64, 484–85 and Rome, AMR, Pannilini, 'Biografie delle Religiose', nos 993, 999//1000. The Leni nuns were sisters of Cardinal Giambattista Leni (1573–1627), patron of the Barnabite church of S. Carlo ai Catinari, and cousins of Paul V's papal nephew Cardinal Scipione Caffarelli-Borghese on their mother's side (Spiazzi, *San Domenico*, pp. 335–36 and Amayden, *Storia delle famiglie romane*, vol. 2, pp. 6–8). The Capizucchi nuns were daughters of Paolo Capizucchi, the head of one of the oldest noble families in Rome, and sisters of Dominican cleric and future cardinal Raimondo Capizucchi (1681), patron of the family's chapel (1685)

presbytery were combined with corporate funding. Even the *converse* (lay nuns), who derived from more modest social classes and performed manual tasks in the convent, contributed to the church's construction and as a group to the expense of the church's windows.[47]

The church's six lateral chapels were all decorated between 1632 and 1652 under the patronage of the convent's nuns, either acting individually or in collaboration with convent family members, as previously discussed in the case of the Costaguti and Farsegni-Boccarini chapels (1648). Following in the footsteps of her elder sister Paola, patron and catalyst of the church's construction, Innocentia Giustini in 1632 undertook the decoration of the Chapel of St Catherine of Siena to whom she was especially devoted, utilizing an inheritance from her father and brother.[48] Anna Margherita Altemps, member of one of the most prestigious families of Rome, embellished the Chapel of the Crucifix (1646) with marbles, stuccoes, and an altarpiece by Giovanni Lanfranco, while Suor Maria Eleonora Alaleone decorated the altar of the Chapel of St Mary Magdalene (1649–1652) with a sculpture of the *Noli me tangere* by Antonio Raggi.[49] Sisters Ortensia and Maria Caterina Celsi, whose family belonged to the civic nobility, collaborated in decorating the Chapel of the Rosary (1652) with marbles, stuccoes, and an altarpiece of the *Madonna of the Rosary with Saints Dominic and Catherine* by Giovanni Francesco Romanelli.[50] The circle of artists employed for the chapel decorations also worked for many of the families of nuns in SS. Domenico e Sisto suggesting possible family networks of intermediaries.[51]

---

in S. Maria in Campitelli (Rome, AMR, Pannilini, 'Biografie delle Religiose', nos 999//1000; Amayden, *Storia delle famiglie romane*, vol. 1, pp. 243–52; and 'Raimondo Capizucchi', unpaginated). Maria Maddalena Fonseca, whose sister Celeste was also at SS. Domenico e Sisto, was a daughter of Emanuele Fonseca. Of Portuguese origin, their family, established in Rome since the 1400s, were members of the titled and civic nobility and were related to Nuñez family nuns in the convent (Amayden, *Storia delle famiglie romane*, vol. 1, p. 414 and Spiazzi, *San Domenico*, p. 371). The Vipereschi were members of the civic nobility who served as conservators of Rome (Amayden, *Storia delle famiglie romane*, vol. 2, p. 231 and Spiazzi, *Cronache e fioretti del monastero di San Sisto all'Appia*, pp. 484–85).

47 *Converse* at SS. Domenico e Sisto were daughters of members of the working and artisan classes, such as cooks, pastry chefs, saddle-makers, or gardeners. Initially lay nuns had been admitted to the community without a dowry, but in 1628, as part of the effort to raise funds to build the public church, a dowry of 200 scudi began to be required for *converse*. See Spiazzi, *Cronache e fioretti del monastero di San Sisto all'Appia*, pp. 402, 499, 500, 501.

48 She supplemented money from her inheritance with additional funds earned from some unspecified work, spending 900 scudi on marbles, gilded stuccoes, and silver lamps, and she endowed the chapel with a fund of 400 scudi (Spiazzi, *Cronache e fioretti del monastero di San Sisto all'Appia*, p. 410).

49 She reportedly spent 3000 scudi on the chapel (Spiazzi, *Cronache e fioretti del monastero di San Sisto all'Appia*, p. 533).

50 Spiazzi, *Cronache e fioretti del monastero di San Sisto all'Appia*, pp. 530–34 and Bernardini, Draghi, and Verdesi, *SS. Domenico e Sisto*, pp. 58–67, 84–91.

51 See Dunn, 'Nuns, Family, and Inter-Familial Dynamics', pp. 343–44.

Family *stemmi* marked many of these public decorations undertaken by nuns acting as autonomous patrons who simultaneously represented their natal families and benefitted their convent family. But SS. Domenico e Sisto nuns also eagerly made improvements to the less visible interior of their convent to enhance their devotional lives by filling its cloistered spaces with small chapels and altars that represented personal piety and served communal devotion. In the convent chronicle a picture emerges of the rich and extremely active devotional lives that the nuns created within their institution in which chapels, altars, images, and relics functioned in the rituals, ceremonies, and devotions of the convent community.[52] Acts of patronage expressed a nun's devotion, ensured her memory within the lineage of the convent family, served as an exemplar of piety, and contributed to a spiritual patrimony for future nuns within the community. The public church and convent of SS. Domenico e Sisto were aesthetically and spiritually enriched by the generosity of its noble nuns who acted as independent, internal art patrons and contributed as 'team players' to the prestige of both their families and community as well as actively shaping the spiritual environment of their convent complex. The nuns' own patronage expanded the convent's potential to make improvements and embellishments, making it less reliant on external patronage, and gave the community more control over its spaces.[53] Though frequently allied with family members within the convent in patronage projects, nuns also engaged in collaborative efforts outside their family circle, forming networks that crossed beyond natal family lines to embrace a collective communal family identity.

Colonna Convents in Marino and Avezzano

In some cases, family networks and alliances facilitated the extension of nuns' patronage even beyond their cloistered convent and its public church by enabling these enclosed women to found new convents that promoted spiritual goals of Catholic reform and to impact the broader religious landscape. In this way noble nuns participated in religious patronage like their secular female counterparts who were active patrons of reformed religious institutions in

---

52 Rome, AMR, Salamonia, 'Memorie', vol. 5, 'Erario di sacre gioie', 1656. Hills, 'The Housing of Institutional Architecture', pp. 136–40.

53 Lay nuns joined professed nuns as patrons of spiritual embellishments in their cloistered spaces. For instance, among the four nuns who were patrons of Christologically-themed paintings in the nuns' choir in 1605 was a *conversa*, Suor Felicita, who worked in the kitchen (Spiazzi, *Cronache e fioretti del monastero di San Sisto all'Appia*, pp. 494, 527). While the nuns were ultimately under the control of male religious authorities, the negative assessment of their capacity to make decisions suggested by some scholars is belied by documentary evidence of autonomy and their own embrace of post-Tridentine spirituality that directed their choices. Lowe, *Nuns' Chronicles and Convent Culture*, p. 394 and Rome, AMR, Salamonia 'Memorie'.

Figure 8.3. High Altar and Tribune in SS. Domenico e Sisto, Rome, 1636–1646. Photo courtesy of William McGuire.

Counter-Reformation Rome.[54] Two Colonna nuns, Maria Isabella (1634–1682) (Figure 8.4) and Maria Girolama (d. 1719), whose patronage at SS. Domenico e Sisto has already been noted, focused their greatest efforts on founding Dominican convents devoted to a strict observance of a common life with no dispensations in contrast to the more privileged atmosphere of the aristocratic SS. Domenico e Sisto. With the assistance of their brother, Contestabile Lorenzo Onofrio Colonna, their new foundations were established in feudal territories of the Colonna family.

Educated along with her sisters at the Clarissan convent of S. Silvestro in Capite in Rome and destined for marriage to the prince of Caserta, Maria Isabella (Antonia in secular life) had been temporarily placed in SS. Domenico e Sisto by her mother, Isabella Gioeni Colonna, who bore great affection for this convent, so that the vivacious teenager could help cheer the community saddened by the death of two of its members when a wall had collapsed.[55] At SS. Domenico e Sisto, Antonia was inspired to embrace the religious life, taking the habit there in 1649 and assuming the name Maria Isabella in honour of her mother. Upon her profession the following year she renounced an inheritance of 30,000 scudi from her maternal grandmother in favour of her brother Lorenzo Onofrio.[56] Like many other aristocratic nuns, she was provided with an annual *livello* of 400 scudi by her family and a *conversa* for her service; and in the initial years of her vocation she did not manifest a particularly observant spirit.[57] But a serious illness and the influence of her male spiritual directors eventually led her to desire a more austere, contemplative religious life dedicated to poverty, and she resolved to found a new, more strictly observant Dominican convent.[58] She won the support and approval of Dominican Father Master General, Tommaso Roccaberti, for

54 See Valone, 'Women on the Quirinal Hill'; Dunn, 'Spiritual Philanthropists'; Andretta, 'Il governo dell'osservanza'; and Lirosi, *I monasteri femminili*, pp. 48–65.

55 See Spiazzi, *Cronache e fioretti del monastero di San Sisto all'Appia*, p. 465.

56 Marino, ASRM, Armadio 2, no. 1, 'Fatti notabili', pp. 8–9.

57 Marino, ASRM, Armadio 2, no. 1, 'Fatti notabili', pp. 8–9. Suor Violante took the habit as a *conversa* in the service of Maria Isabella. Although *converse* were supposed to serve the whole religious community, in practice they often served particular nuns or members of the same family. From the time of Gregory XIII (1572), *converse* were obligated to observe the rules of enclosure and followed the sequence of vestition, novitiate, and profession (Lirosi, *I monasteri femminili*, pp. 96–97).

58 Suor Maria Domenica del SS. Rosario, author of the convent chronicle of SS. Rosario in Marino, notes the esteem in which Maria Isabella held her spiritual advisors, particularly Padre Fra Michele Arcangelo Nanni, who recommended to her Jesuit father Fabio Ambrogio Spinola's *Delle meditationi sopra la vita di Giesu Signor Nostro: per ciascun giorno* (1652–1653). Although, at first, she brushed off his suggestion, claiming already to have lots of books, she came to value the meditations of Father Spinola, which were eventually read twice a day during communal mental prayer at her convent of SS. Rosario. After her illness, she dedicated herself to the spiritual direction of her confessor, Padre Maestro Mauritio del Bosco. See Marino, ASRM, Armadio 2, no. 1, 'Fatti notabili', pp. 10, 13–14.

the new foundation, confirmed in a papal brief of 8 May 1675.[59] To realize her ambitious undertaking, the cloistered Maria Isabella enlisted the assistance of her brother Lorenzo Onofrio who determined that the new observant convent, dedicated to SS. Rosario, should be located in Marino, the Colonna fief closest to Rome to which the Colonna held the title of duke.[60] He travelled to Marino accompanied by Roccaberti and Maria Isabella's confessor, Father Mauritio del Bosco, to scout out an appropriate site for the convent, and on 27 May 1675 a group of houses with stables, hay-lofts, cantinas, and gardens in Borgo delle Grazie (now Piazza Garibaldi) just outside the city walls was acquired from Ferdinando Leoncelli di Cave to be adapted into the convent complex. With the sale of the property valued at 2165 scudi, Leoncelli extinguished some *censi* (loans secured by property) which he owed the Colonna and that Lorenzo Onofrio had transferred to his sister for the foundation of the convent, which then became creditor of Leoncelli's remaining *censi*.[61]

The dedication of the Marino convent to SS. Rosario was doubly significant, tying the foundation to both the Dominicans and the Colonna family. Traditionally believed to have been given to St Dominic by the Virgin Mary, the Rosary, a cycle of meditations devoted to the Virgin and aided by a chaplet of beads, had been espoused by the Dominicans as a form of prayer since the fifteenth century. Emphasizing the significance of this prayer, Maria Isabella's community at SS. Domenico e Sisto had expanded the custom of the personal daily recitation of the Rosary to a communal recitation that included both choir nuns and *converse*.[62] Furthermore, the Rosary was associated with the Colonna family through its greatest military hero Marcantonio II, a native of Marino and commander of the papal fleet at Lepanto where Christian forces won a decisive victory over the Otttoman Turks in 1571. Pius V had placed the naval expedition to Lepanto under the protection of the Madonna of the Rosary, and the Virgin's intercession in the battle became closely linked with the Rosary thereafter.[63]

Assisting his sister in the foundation of the Marino convent allowed Lorenzo Onofrio to attest to his piety and zeal for the greater service of God and the Virgin Mary, to provide for the spiritual consolation of his subjects,

---

59 A copy of the papal brief exists in Marino, ASRM, Armadio 3, *palchetto* B, no. 2.

60 The Colonna acquired Marino during the reign of Pope Martin V Colonna (1417–1431). Pope Paul V elevated Marino to the status of *ducato* (duchy) in 1606, and Pope Urban VIII in 1633 confirmed the title in favour of Filippo Colonna and his descendants. See Tomassetti, *La campagna romana*, vol. 4, pp. 204–07, 230.

61 See Marino, ASRM, Armadio 2, no. 1, 'Fatti notabili', pp. 15–16; Subiaco, AC, AA 80, n. 41; Tomassetti, *La campagna romana*, vol. 4, p. 253; and Onorati, *La chiesa del SS. Rosario*, p. 15. Suor Maria Isabella's *procuratore* (attorney) Raffaele Marchesi stipulated the purchase contract on her behalf. Marino, ASRM, Armadio 1, no. 2, 'Magistrale 1699', fol. 2ʳ.

62 Dunn, '*Invisibilia per visibilia*', p. 196 and Spiazzi, *Cronache e fioretti del monastero di San Sisto all'Appia*, pp. 409–10.

63 Onorati, *La chiesa del SS. Rosario*, pp. 4–7 and Tomassetti, *La campagna romana*, vol. 4, pp. 214–21.

Figure 8.4. Anonymous, *Portrait of Suor Maria Isabella Colonna*, Marino, Italy, Convent of SS. Rosario. Photo courtesy of Ugo Onorati, reproduced with permission of the Mother Superior of SS. Rosario, Marino, Italy.

and to enable honest virgins to live in the security of enclosure devoted to their divine spouse.[64] Through the pious act of co-founding a strictly reformed convent in the Holy Year 1675, Lorenzo Onofrio, ever conscious of his social status, also burnished his reputation. His social and political prestige had suffered setbacks since his wife Maria Mancini had abandoned him and fled Rome in 1672, and his promotion of the convent in his Marino fief may be seen within the context of other patronage that aimed at enhancing family reputation. In this same period, he assisted his sisters' Roman convent of SS. Domenico e Sisto, closely linked to the family through the dynasty of Colonna nuns, by serving in an intermediary capacity for frescoes in its church, and he

---

64 Subiaco, AC, AA 199, n. 22, copy of *memoriale* for the erection of the convent of Marino.

Figure 8.5. Giovanni Coli and Filippo Gherardi, *Battle of Lepanto*, Rome, Palazzo Colonna Galleria. 1675–1678. Photo Sailko, Wikimedia Commons, reproduced under the Creative Commons Attribution-Share Alike 3.0 Unported (https://creativecommons.org/licenses/by-sa/3.0/deed.en) license.

was engaged in the redesign and decoration of the gallery of the family palace in Rome with frescoes by Giovanni Coli and Filippo Gherardi (1675–1678), glorifying the Colonna through the heroic accomplishments of Marcantonio II at Lepanto (Figure 8.5).[65]

The site Lorenzo Onofrio chose for the convent of SS. Rosario on the north side of Borgo delle Grazie served to anchor the Colonna presence at the western outskirts of Marino. Opposite, across the ample piazza of the Borgo was a small palace owned by the Colonna and used as an *osteria* (inn) for travellers from Rome,[66] and nearly adjacent in the southwestern corner of this urban space was the Augustinian church and monastery of S. Maria delle Grazie to which earlier members of the Colonna family had been donors.[67] Ascending from the piazza on the east, a street constructed by Marcantonio II and his son Cardinal Ascanio Colonna (late sixteenth to early seventeenth century) led past the Colonna gardens through the Porta Romana (1596) to the Colonna Palace rebuilt by Marcantonio II Colonna and his successors.[68] In a piazza outside the northern entrance of the palace, the Colonna in 1632 erected the *Fontana dei Quattro Mori* (Figure 8.6) in which sirens, a Colonna heraldic emblem, support four sculpted figures of Turks chained to the base of a column, another heraldic symbol of the Colonna. Alluding to Marcantonio's victory at Lepanto, the fountain celebrated the Colonna family, but through its water supply it also functioned to benefit the populace.[69] On the piazza adjacent to the palace, the basilica collegiata of S. Barnaba,[70] patron saint of Marino, had been constructed (1640–1662) on the designs of Vincenzo della Greca and Antonio Del Grande under the patronage of Lorenzo Onofrio's uncle, Cardinal Girolamo Colonna (1604–1666), whose heraldry prominently embellishes its façade (Figure 8.7).[71] Maria Isabella's convent can be viewed within this context of Colonna family patronage in Marino as another site for

---

65   Strunck, "'The Marvel Not Only of Rome, but of All Italy'", pp. 80–91.

66   The palace was designed in 1615 by Girolamo Rinaldi. See Piperno and Moore, 'Rome in the Footsteps of an XVIII Century Traveller, Marino', unpaginated and Tomassetti, *La campagna romana*, vol. 4, p. 252 n. 1.

67   Tomassetti, *La campagna romana*, vol. 4, p. 252. Filippo I Colonna (1578–1639) had systematized the Borgo as a site for fairs and markets, enclosing its western side with a row of houses opposite the city walls on the east (Calabrese, *Marino e I Colonna*, p. 24).

68   Benedetti, 'La chiesa del SS. Rosario in Marino', pp. 9–11; Calabrese, *Marino e I Colonna*, pp. 12–20.

69   Sculpted by Pompeo Castiglia and erected under the direction of Filippo Colonna, the fountain was paid for by the priors of Marino. The fountain, from which wine flows during the celebration of the Sacra dell'Uva festival, was relocated to Piazza Matteotti in 1969. See Onorati, *La chiesa del SS Rosario*, pp. 7–8; Tomassetti, *La campagna romana*, vol. 4, pp. 245–47; and Strunck, 'Old Nobility versus New', pp. 139–41.

70   The basilica collegiata of S. Barnaba was served by a college of canons directed by a bishop abbot (*abate mitrato*). Onorati, *La basilica collegiata*, p. 5.

71   Onorati, *La chiesa del SS. Rosario*, pp. 6, 8–9; Onorati, *La basilica collegiata*, pp. 5–12; and Tomassetti, *La campagna romana*, vol. 4, pp. 247–50.

Lorenzo Onofrio to signify the authority and glory of the Colonna as well as demonstrate his beneficence toward his feudal subjects.

Beyond Suor Maria Isabella's reliance on networks of male family members or religious superiors, she drew upon the expansive networks that united religious and secular women and convents of various religious orders. Monastic women were consulted for advice and through their counsel played a role in religious reform. To accomplish her goal of establishing a strictly observant convent, Maria Isabella sought the advice of Suor Maria Giulia Lancellotti, a nun at the Dominican convent of S. Maria Maddalena al Quirinale in Rome, located nearby SS. Domenico e Sisto. Founded in 1581 by Suor Maria Maddalena Orsini, S. Maria Maddalena was renowned for its austerity, and Suor Maria Giulia Lancellotti possessed the experience in governing an observant convent that Maria Isabella lacked.[72] Daughter of Marchese Scipione Lancellotti (1609–1663) and Claudia De Torres, whose marriage united two prestigious noble Roman families, Giulia Lancellotti followed a path to a religious life that illustrates the connective fabric of family and female networks operative in Rome. As a young woman, uncertain about what state of life to embrace, she was taken by her paternal aunt Portia Gabrielli to visit Suor Francesca di Gesù Maria Farnese, founder of several reformed Clarissan convents, including SS. Concezione in Rome (1641),[73] who inspired Giulia to profess as a nun at S. Maria Maddalena. Suor Francesca Farnese also had served as a source of inspiration for her sister-in-law Camilla Virginia Savelli Farnese's foundation of Augustinian Oblates at S. Maria dei Sette Dolori (1641) in Rome after she had accompanied her on visits to Francesca's foundations outside of Rome.[74] Another Colonna family nun, Maria Isabella's aunt, Suor Maria Teresa di Gesù (Ippolita Colonna) in the Discalced Carmelite community at S. Egidio in Trastevere, had also exercised an advisory role, contributing to the foundation of the first community of the austere and strictly cloistered *Turchine* nuns in Rome. Through her correspondence with Prioress Maria Maddalena Centurioni, co-founder of the order of SS. Annunziata (called the *Turchine*) in Genoa (1604), she had gained a favourable impression of this institution and often spoke of it when her friend Camilla Orsini Borghese visited her to discuss spiritual matters, ultimately inspiring her to found a convent for the *Turchine* in Rome (1670).[75] Beyond advice, the accomplishments of other women within family and social networks in support of Catholic reform provided models to emulate. Two other aunts of Suor Maria Isabella Colonna, Ippolita's sisters Anna Colonna Barberini and Suor Chiara Maria

72 Valone, 'Women on the Quirinal Hill', pp. 132–33 and Borselli, *Breve narratione della vita*.

73 Farnese (1618), Albano (1631), and Palestrina (reformed 1638). Later an *educanda* at one of these convents, SS. Concezione in Albano, would become the first novice to take the habit at SS. Rosario in Marino (1676) (Marino, ASRM, Armadio 2, no. 1, 'Fatti notabili', pp. 3–4, 11–12, 26–27).

74 Dunn, 'Spiritual Philanthropists', p. 164.

75 Dunn, 'Piety and Patronage in Seicento Rome', pp. 654–56.

Figure 8.6. Pompeo Castiglia,
Fontana dei Quattro Mori,
Marino, Italy. 1632. Photo
courtesy of William McGuire.

della Passione (Vittoria Colonna), who cofounded the Discalced Carmelite
convent of S. Maria Regina Coeli in Trastevere (1654), undoubtedly served as
exemplars for her own later activity as convent founder.[76] As these examples
attest, networks among convents and women were not bound by affiliation

---

76 Dunn, 'Piety and Patronage in Seicento Rome', pp. 644–53. When Biagio della Purificazione's
*Vita della venerabile madre suor Chiara Maria della Passione carmelitana scalza fondatrice del
monastero di Regina Coeli* was published (1681), shortly before Maria Isabella's death, she
desired to read it aloud to her nuns in the refectory for four consecutive weeks, but her
deteriorating health prevented it. Marino, ASRM, Armadio 2, no. 1, 'Fatti notabili', p. 40.

with a particular religious order but through shared religious goals to support a more authentically spiritual convent life.

Maria Isabella Colonna obtained permission to transfer to S. Maria Maddalena in May 1676 in order to gain a better understanding of strictly observant convent life and to induce Suor Maria Giulia Lancellotti to join her in her new foundation, of which Lancellotti would become the first prioress. Once the complex in Marino was sufficiently systematized to accommodate the nuns, Suor Maria Isabella, joined by Suor Maria Giulia Lancellotti and Suor Agata Maria Serafini, left S. Maria Maddalena on 18 September 1676 for a three-day visit to SS. Domenico e Sisto, where Maria Isabella had lived as a nun for twenty-seven years. Although her new foundation was conceived as a more austerely reformed Dominican convent it was viewed by Maria Isabella and the community of SS. Domenico e Sisto as a small branch growing from the magnificent tree of her former convent.[77] Before leaving Rome she also paid visits to other churches in her Dominican network — S. Sisto, the oldest convent of the order in Rome (1221), and S. Sabina on the Aventine where her spiritual director, Father Giacinto da Sestola, was prior, receiving from him an image of St Dominic for her new convent.[78] On 21 September, twelve postulants escorted by Countess Ortensia Ianni Stella and Abbot Giuseppe Moscardini set out for Marino. These escorts were trusted associates of the Colonna family. Various members of the Moscardini family served as agents for the Colonna in this period,[79] but the role of Ortensia Stella as escort for the postulants might seem a bit ironic. Having come to Rome as a lady-in-waiting of Maria Mancini following the latter's marriage to Lorenzo Onofrio in 1661, she remained as part of the *famiglia* (household staff) of the Colonna even after Mancini fled her marriage and Rome in 1672. The marriage was finally dissolved by Pope Innocent XI in February 1681 after Lorenzo Onofrio was frustrated in his attempts to return his wife to Rome. But in the meantime, he had entered into a relationship with Ortensia which produced two children whom he openly acknowledged, and until shortly before his death (1689) he resisted papal pressure to send her away from Rome. Thus, Ortensia Stella appears to have fulfilled a role of trusted female companion for Lorenzo Onofrio, deprived of his wife's presence, in the period of SS. Rosario's foundation.[80]

---

77   Marino, ASRM, Armadio 2, no. 1, 'Fatti notabili', pp. 19–20.

78   Marino, ASRM, Armadio 2, no. 1, 'Fatti notabili', p. 21.

79   See Subiaco, AC, I B 28, Libro Mastro (1668–1678), fols 51[bis], 74, 367–67[bis], 455 for payments made by Oratio Moscardini for Colonna. Also, Subiaco, AC, Carteggio di Lorenzo Onofrio Colonna, Suor Isabella Colonna 1679, *camicia* 197, 14 October 1679; Maria Isabella sent this letter with Lorenzo Moscardini who included a note in which he offered to serve Lorenzo Onofrio as loyal vassal.

80   For Lorenzo Onofrio's marital troubles with Maria Mancini, and for Ortensia Stella and her children by Colonna see Gozzano, *La quadreria di Lorenzo Onofrio Colonna*, pp. 70–73, 79–87. Lorenzo Onofrio sold the palace formerly used as an *osteria* opposite the convent on Borgo delle Grazie to Ortensia Stella on 24 September 1683 for 2500 scudi. Assuming the name Palazzina Stella (today Collegio Bandinelli), it was inherited by her son by Colonna,

Figure 8.7. Basilica Collegiata di S. Barnaba, Marino, Italy. 1640–1662.
Photo courtesy of William McGuire.

Delayed in Rome on the day of the postulants' departure by the election of Pope Innocent XI, the founding nuns journeyed to Marino the following day accompanied by members of the Colonna family and their court — Lorenzo Onofrio, Maria Isabella's sister Lucrezia, duchess of Bassanello, and her sister-in-law Cleria Cesarini Colonna, as well as Dominican Master General Tommaso Roccaberti and other religious dignitaries. This entourage manifested both family and ecclesiastical support for the new convent. The group's arrival was greeted by a jubilant local population and the ringing of bells, as the cortege made its way to the Duomo and then to the Colonna Palace where the nuns were hosted for lunch with the postulants before visiting their church and entering into the cloister of their new convent, which was characterized by its simple, austere architecture (Figures 8.8 and 8.9) in contrast to other more celebratory Colonna monuments.[81]

Suor Maria Domenica del SS. Rosario (Girolama Buffardi), first nun to receive the habit at SS. Rosario and author of the convent's chronicle, significantly follows these descriptions of family display and ceremony by relating an anecdote about the humble first meal of the new community that contrasts the poverty embraced by Maria Isabella and her convent to the opulence of the secular world of her illustrious family. Lorenzo Onofrio had ordered that the abundant leftovers from the sumptuous meal provided earlier in the day at his palace be sent to his sister and her convent, but through a miscommunication only some fruit and fresh beans were delivered. When the beans were cooked, not even a spoon could be found to serve them, so Suor Maria Isabella, noted for her great humility and willingness to perform the humblest tasks, knelt on the ground and extracted them from the pot with a wooden stick. Suor Maria Domenica interpreted the circumstances of this meal as directed by divine providence so that the community could begin to devote itself to a life of poverty from their first meal.[82]

When the convent of SS. Rosario had been instituted, Lorenzo Onofrio had agreed to provide annually 300 scudi from Suor Maria Isabella's yearly *livello* of 400 scudi to her new convent during her lifetime and after her death until the interest derived from dowries equalled that amount annually.[83] Dowries were to be set at 500 scudi for professed choir nuns from Marino or 600 scudi for nuns from other towns, while dowries of *converse* were 100 scudi. These amounts were considerably less than most aristocratic convents in Rome where dowries for choir nuns were commonly 1000 scudi.[84] The

---

Girolamo. Thus, the convent of Lorenzo Onofrio's sister and the palace of his mistress faced each other across the Borgo, apparently in harmonious coexistence.

81 Marino, ASRM, Armadio 2, no. 1, 'Fatti notabili', pp. 21–22 and Armadio 1, no. 2, Magistrale 1699, fol. 2ᵛ; Rome, AMR, Pannilini, 'Biografie delle Religiose', no. 1034.

82 Marino, ASRM, Armadio 2, no. 1, 'Fatti notabili', pp. 23–25.

83 Subiaco, AC, III AA 199, no. 22.

84 The Magistrale 1699, however, records payments of 700 scudi for the first group of choir nuns who professed on 9 January 1678, except for Eufemia Zenobia Desclavi of Genazzano

Figure 8.8. Convent of SS. Rosario, Façade, Marino, Italy. 1676–1677.
Photo Gino il Pio, Wikimedia Commons, image in the public domain.

reconstruction of the buildings purchased in 1675 to be converted into a
space appropriate to accommodate the needs of a convent was seriously
underfunded, however, relying on the initial capital of Suor Maria Isabella's
livello of 400 scudi. In order to help finance the building project she successfully
appealed to Dominican Father General Roccaberti for a loan of 1500 scudi,[85]
and secured some other donations from pious supporters, notably 100 *doppie*
from the duchess of Modena, who while in Rome for the Holy Year (1675) had
visited Maria Isabella at SS. Domenico e Sisto.[86] Even after the establishment
of strict enclosure noblewomen still gained permission to visit convents
and sometimes enter into the cloister for spiritual counsel or retreats. The
aristocratic character of SS. Domenico e Sisto attracted visits by prestigious
laywomen like the duchess and was a locus of elite networks.[87]

---

who, as a favour to Constestabile Colonna, was allowed to profess having only paid 500 scudi
of the owed 700 since her mother had been the nursemaid of the Colonna princes. In this
case, the family network extended to include servants. Marino, ASRM, Armadio 1, no. 2,
Magistrale 1699, fols 2ᵛ–3ʳ. At SS. Domenico e Sisto, dowries for choir nuns had been set at
1000 scudi in 1595, while dowries of 200 scudi were established for *converse* in 1628. Spiazzi,
Cronache e fioretti del monastero di San Sisto all'Appia, pp. 402, 462.

85 Marino, ASRM, Armadio 2, no. 1, 'Fatti notabili', p. 18.
86 Marino, ASRM, Armadio 1, no. 2, Magistrale 1699, 2ʳ; Rome, AMR, Pannilini, 'Biografie delle
    Religiose', no. 1034. Sandro Benedetti also cites a loan of 1000 scudi from the Comune di
    Marino ('La chiesa del SS. Rosario in Marino', p. 11).
87 See Borello, *Trame sovrapposte*, pp. 35–37. Roman noblewomen received papal authorization
    to visit the Chapel of St Dominic, containing a copy of the miraculous image of St Dominic

Figure 8.9. Convent of SS. Rosario, Interior, Marino, Italy. 1676–1677. Photo courtesy of William McGuire reproduced with permission of the Mother Superior of SS. Rosario, Marino, Italy.

The patronage of the duchess of Modena, a woman inscribed into Maria Isabella's network of friends and family, contributed to the convent's completion in 1677. Described as being very close to Maria Isabella,[88] Duchess Laura Martinozzi (d. 1687) was a niece of Cardinal Jules Mazarin[89] and the widow of Duke Alfonso IV d'Este of Modena. She held the title of duchess of Modena from 1658 until her death in 1687, ruling as regent (1662–1674) until her son Francesco II claimed power, after which she returned to Rome where she was residing in the late 1670s when Maria Isabella was establishing her convent.[90] Laura Martinozzi had kinship ties to the Colonna family since she was the

---

in Soriano, located in the dormitory of SS. Domenico e Sisto. Spiazzi, *San Domenico*, pp. 401–02.

88   Marino, ASRM, Armadio 2, no. 1, 'Fatti notabili', p. 26.

89   She was one of the 'Marzarinettes', seven Italian nieces of Cardinal Mazarin whom he brought to France.

90   Tamalio, 'Laura Martinozzi'. Also see Iotti, 'Da fille de France a dux Mutinae', pp. 11–69.

cousin of Maria Isabella's sister-in-law, Maria Mancini, the estranged wife of Lorenzo Onofrio.[91] The devout duchess, skilled in promoting her status while exercising her noted piety, had engaged in an active patronage of secular and religious projects in Modena and elsewhere, including the foundation and decoration of a Visitandine church and convent adjacent to the Ducal Palace and connected to her apartments (1668–1673), and the decoration of a sumptuous altar in honour of her protector, St Francis de Sales, in the church of the Visitandine convent of Notre Dame de la Visitation in Aix-en-Provence (1665–1675).[92] On the occasion of the first vestitions at SS. Rosario in Marino (13 December 1676) the duchess, accompanied by her court, visited the convent where they lunched and then escorted the postulants in two coaches to visit the Duomo and the church of SS. Trinità before returning,[93] heralded by trumpets and escorted by a throng of populace, to SS. Rosario where Maria Isabella's uncle, Monsignor Egidio Colonna, Patriarch of Jerusalem, delivered a sermon for the vestition ceremony.[94] Among the first novices was a young Modenese noblewoman, Lanora Renati, from the court of the duchess, who sponsored her entrance into the convent.[95] The ceremonial pomp surrounding the vestitions, more common to aristocratic convents than reformed ones, again functioned to reinforce Colonna family connections and prestige.[96]

The duchess maintained her relationship with SS. Rosario through service and patronage. She was entrusted with escorting one of the founding nuns, Suor Agata Maria Serafini, back to Rome when she decided to return to S. Maria Maddalena after instructing the first group of novices, and in 1677 the duchess donated 100 *doppie* to construct a *parlatorio* (parlour) which the convent still lacked. This *parlatorio* was modelled on the one St Dominic had built for the first Dominican nuns in Rome at S. Sisto Vecchio and on the nuns' parlour that existed at SS. Domenico e Sisto, thus architecturally linking

91 Her help was solicited in 1660 during Colonna's negotiations to arrange his marriage with Maria Mancini, celebrated 11 April 1661. See Gozzano, *La quadreria di Lorenzo Onofrio Colonna*, p. 67.

92 See Cavicchioli, 'Una principessa dall'animo grande', pp. 89–117. On her way from Rome to Paris (*c.* 1653), Laura Martinozzi spent time in spiritual retreat at the Visitandine convent in Aix-en-Provence from which she later brought nuns for the foundation of the order she established in Modena. Also see Iotti, 'Da fille de France a dux Mutinae', p. 20. On the Visitandines in France see Diefendorf, *From Penitence to Charity*, pp. 174–83. Martinozzi also promoted the establishment of the Ursulines in Rome (1684) (Lirosi, *I monasteri femminili*, p. 256).

93 The postulants' visit of other churches in a coach accompanied by noblewomen prior to the vestition ceremony emulated the vestition ritual at SS. Domenico e Sisto. See Spiazzi, *San Domenico*, p. 199.

94 Marino, ASRM, Armadio 2, no. 1, 'Fatti notabili', pp. 26–27.

95 Marino, ASRM, Armadio 2, no. 1, 'Fatti notabili', pp. 28–29.

96 Church officials sought to forbid elaborate display and instrumental music accompanying vestitions in seventeenth-century Rome, but the practice still appeared in some wealthy patrician convents. See Città del Vaticano, ASV, A.A., Arm. I–XVIII, 6493, fols 35^r–35^v and Lirosi, *I monasteri femminili*, pp. 200–04.

SS. Rosario to its Dominican heritage.[97] The duchess of Modena, who gave a further 100 *doppie* for liturgical furnishings and a gift of a statue of the Christ Child, was esteemed as a special benefactor of the convent.[98]

Maria Isabella's example inspired her younger sister, Suor Maria Girolama (Teresa), to found a second strictly observant Dominican convent, dedicated to S. Caterina Martire in Avezzano,[99] another Colonna territory, again with the practical and financial assistance of her brother, Lorenzo Onofrio.[100] Like SS. Rosario, the Avezzano convent was to be under the protection of a cardinal from the Colonna family.[101] With four other professed choir nuns from SS. Domenico e Sisto, Prospera Vincenza Costaguti, Angela Eletta Nuñez, Maria Antonia Nuñez, and Maria Bonaventura Cavallarini, five choir nun postulants, and four lay nun postulants from Rome, Maria Girolama established the Avezzano convent on 15 May 1677, after visiting her sister's Marino convent on her trip from Rome.[102] Relying on somewhat broader sources of initial funding than the Marino foundation, S. Caterina Martire was founded through the application of annual income (*rendite*) from an earlier pious bequest by Avezzano native Alessandro Felli (87 *ducati*), property donated by Lorenzo Onofrio (57 *ducati*), and donations of other pious residents of Avezzano (51 *ducati*) plus 30 *ducati* from S. Antonio delle Fratte along with 1200 *ducati* of S. Antonio's income to apply to investments in favour of the new convent. To these resources would be joined the dowries of the original twelve choir nuns and four *converse* (300 *ducati* for choir nuns from Avezzano, 400 for those from other cities, and 100 for *converse*).[103]

---

97 Marino, ASRM, Armadio 2, no. 1, 'Fatti notabili', p. 29.
98 Marino, ASRM, Armadio 2, no. 1, 'Fatti notabili', p. 29.
99 Fourth-century martyr St Catherine of Alexandria was especially venerated by the Dominican order.
100 Rome, AMR, Pannilini, 'Biografie delle Religiose' no. 1037. A copy of the foundation bull of Clement X dated 19 October 1675 is found in Marino, ASRM, Armadio 1, Avezzano volume. By 1910 due to their dwindling population, the nuns of S. Caterina Martire had joined the sisters at SS. Rosario. The volume in Marino is the only extant document from the Avezzano convent destroyed in a devastating earthquake of 1915. Thus, less information is available for this convent.
101 For SS. Rosario see Subiaco, AC, III AA 199, no. 22, *Memoriale* for the erection of the convent; for S. Caterina Martire see Marino, ASRM, Armadio 1, Avezzano volume, copy of papal bull of 19 October 1675.
102 Marino, ASRM, Armadio 1, Avezzano volume and Armadio 2, no. 1 'Fatti notabili', p. 28. Prospera Vincenza Costaguti, co-patron of the Chapel of St Dominic in SS. Domenico e Sisto, returned to her former convent after five months; Angela Eletta Nuñez remained in Avezzano until June 1680; Maria Bonaventura Cavallarini returned to Rome in 1682; Maria Antonia Nuñez remained through 1684; and Maria Girolama Colonna returned to Rome in 1686 when the foundation was well-established. See Rome, AMR, Pannilini, 'Biografie delle Religiose', nos 1030, 1037.
103 Marino, ASRM, Armadio 1, Avezzano volume. Lorenzo Onofrio Colonna had the right to name a nun with no dowry. The surviving volume records investments made with the dowries of nuns who joined the convent.

While Lorenzo Onofrio's influence and monetary contribution were crucial in facilitating the establishment of his sisters' religious foundations in his territories, his level of financial patronage scarcely met the degree of munificence that his aunt, Anna Colonna Barberini, bestowed upon the Discalced Carmelite convent of S. Maria Regina Coeli which she had founded in 1654, providing for its construction, decoration, furnishings, and endowment.[104] By contrast, the early years of their new foundations presented challenges for both Maria Isabella and Maria Girolama, who frequently appealed to their brother to exercise his social and political clout on behalf of their institutions. For example, letters from Maria Girolama sought his help in negotiating the acquisition of 200 sheep (useful to the community that abstained from meat and relied on dairy products) or reminded him of his earlier promise to pay for the delivery of water.[105] Writing on 2 February 1679, Maria Girolama asked Lorenzo Onofrio to write to Marchese di Banigiano in support of her and her convent because local vassals were spreading malicious rumours that he (Lorenzo Onofrio) held her and her foundation in low esteem.[106] The vassals of Avezzano were apparently still causing Maria Girolama problems in July 1679 when she reported to her brother that some construction work on the convent had begun, but she fumed about difficulties with rude and impertinent vassals who caused her to lose her patience.[107] Lorenzo Onofrio's absence from his feudal territories of Marino and Avezzano during his tenure as viceroy of Aragon (1678–1681) limited his direct influence during the initial years of his sisters' foundations, and Maria Girolama's letters express the impact of this absence, conveying her hopes for an improved situation upon his return and lamenting that without his presence 'sembrano Corpi senza Anima' (they are like bodies without a soul).[108]

At SS. Rosario, Maria Isabella's spiritual goal of establishing a convent dedicated to the ideal of strict poverty soon met the harsh reality of inadequate finances and other difficulties.[109] On 2 October 1678 Maria Isabella informed her brother of the convent's great need and appealed for his assistance in obtaining promised money from the *Grano del Murte* (a granary), expressing

---

104   Dunn, 'Piety and Patronage in Seicento Rome', pp. 644–53.

105   Subiaco, AC, Carteggio di Lorenzo Onofrio Colonna, Suor Maria Girolama Colonna 1679 *camicia* 87, letters of 2 February 1679, 15 August 1679, and 15 November 1679.

106   Subiaco, AC, Carteggio di Lorenzo Onofrio Colonna, Suor Maria Girolama Colonna 1679 *camicia* 87.

107   Subiaco, AC, Carteggio di Lorenzo Onofrio Colonna, Suor Maria Girolama Colonna 1679 *camicia* 87, 4 July 1679.

108   Subiaco, AC, Carteggio di Lorenzo Onofrio Colonna, Suor Maria Girolama Colonna 1679 *camicia* 87, 15 August and 28 October 1679. Also, Gozzano, *La quadreria di Lorenzo Onofrio Colonna*, pp. 72–73.

109   This was probably exacerbated by the fact that only seven of the original twelve postulants persevered to vestition. By 9 January 1678 five choir nuns and one lay nun had professed (Marino, ASRM, Armadio 2, no. 1, 'Fatti notabili', pp. 23, 31).

her belief that she would not face such resistance if Lorenzo Onofrio were in residence.[110]

The convent also struggled in its early years with staffing key positions. After Suor Agata Maria Serafini returned to Rome in July 1677, the novices remained without a designated *maestra* (novice mistress) for two years.[111] Unwilling to dispense with the practice in observant convents of a five-year novitiate,[112] Suor Maria Isabella requested permission to bring two nuns from Dominican convents in Rome who were adept at teaching the choir devotions, in particular *canto fermo* (plainchant), a skill the other nuns lacked. But her request was denied.[113] On 14 October 1679 she wrote to her brother that there were nuns willing to come, but the convent lacked someone who could influence the pope to favour their request, lamenting that without Lorenzo Onofrio's return, 'è impossibile che il Monastero possa andar avanti' (the convent could not survive).[114] In a letter of 18 January 1680, Maria Isabella related the continuing struggle to secure either additional nuns from S. Caterina a Magnanapoli in Rome or her sister Suor Maria Colomba and two others from SS. Domenico e Sisto, with Cardinal Vicar Gaspare Carpegna refusing to grant permission. She perceived his lack of cooperation as stemming from an animosity toward her convent and family ('nostra casa'), having learned that the cardinal had intended to suppress her convent if she had succumbed to a recent illness from which she recovered, a sign, in her eyes, that God and the Blessed Virgin did not want her convent to perish.[115] Ultimately in October 1680 Maria Isabella succeeded in gaining permission for two nuns from S. Agnese in Rieti, Suor Corona Vittoria Corona [*sic*] and Suor Colomba Caterina Agostini who desired to join the community, to enter the convent in Marino where the former assumed the office of novice mistress. Though both were noted for their religious virtue, neither brought the desired expertise in instruction for the choir.[116]

---

110   Subiaco, AC, Carteggio di Lorenzo Onofrio Colonna, Suor Maria Isabella Colonna 1678 *camicia* 84, 2 October 1678. Lorenzo Onofrio had entrusted the governance of his fiefs to his sister Lucrezia in his absence, but despite this latter's good intentions Maria Isabella felt that she lacked the clout of her brother. Also, Gozzano, *La quadreria di Lorenzo Onofrio Colonna*, p. 90.

111   After her initial service to the new convent, Suor Agata Maria desired to return to a quieter life at S. Maria Maddalena. Marino, ASRM, Armadio 2, no. 1, 'Fatti notabili', pp. 29, 33.

112   The observant Dominican convents of S. Maria Maddalena al Quirinale and S. Maria dell' Umiltà in Rome also required a five-year novitiate. Lirosi, *I monasteri femminili*, p. 188.

113   Marino, ASRM, Armadio 2, n. 1, 'Fatti notabili', 33–34.

114   Subiaco, AC, Carteggio di Lorenzo Onofrio Colonna, Suor Maria Isabella Colonna 1679, *camicia* 197, 14 October 1679.

115   Subiaco, AC, Carteggio di Lorenzo Onofrio Colonna, Suor Maria Isabella Colonna 1680, *camicia* 54, 18 January 1680. The reasons for this perceived animosity and the difficulty in gaining permission for nuns to transfer to SS. Rosario is not clear.

116   Marino, ASRM, Armadio 2, no. 1, 'Fatti notabili', p. 34.

Family bonds and supportive networks are evident in the coordinated appeal in separate letters to their brother Lorenzo Onofrio from Maria Colomba at SS. Domenico e Sisto and Maria Isabella concerning the continuing difficulties facing SS. Rosario. Writing on 15 January 1681, Maria Colomba informed Lorenzo Onofrio that after much reflection and prayer she desired to transfer to SS. Rosario for the good of the convent, the reputation of the *casa* (family), and the consolation of her sister who, after so much effort, should not see her pious work destroyed. She asked for his help gaining permission from Cardinal Carpegna to obtain a papal licence for her, a companion, and two *converse* to go to Marino. She suggested that he ask his son, Filippo II, to request that his future father-in-law[117] to write to the Spanish ambassador to ask that he use his influence to persuade Carpegna.[118] On the following day Maria Isabella wrote reminding Lorenzo Onofrio that without the help of God and himself the Marino convent would not endure. She explained that Maria Colomba's *entrate* (income) could increase the capital of the convent and conserve it, noting that available funds only paid for food and that the dowries of nuns did not yet render sufficient interest. Citing various attempts to procure the papal licence for Maria Colomba's transfer through Cardinal Carpegna, who she believed preferred to destroy her convent rather than advance it, she, like her sister, proposed that Lorenzo Onofrio ask the Duke de la Cerda to secure the influence of the Spanish ambassador. The seemingly unworldly nun who had renounced aristocratic wealth and privilege in founding a reformed convent devoted to poverty showed herself to be remarkably politically astute, stating that what was needed to convince Carpegna was someone he esteemed and feared, and this had to be someone from the Spanish faction. Observing that her convent served both God and the reputation of the Colonna family (*casa*) she noted how this would be harmed if the convent at the gates of Rome, in the best territory of Lorenzo Onofrio, failed so soon after its founding.[119] This was surely the right card for the nuns to play with their intensely prestige-conscious brother, but their concern for

---

117   His bride-to-be was Lorenza de la Cerda and her father was the Duke of Medina Coeli Juan Francisco de la Cerda Aragona. The marriage of Filippo II Colonna, first-born son of Lorenzo Onofrio and Maria Mancini, and Lorenza de la Cerda took place on 7 April 1681 in Madrid, after which time Lorenzo Onofrio returned to Rome having completed his term as viceroy of Aragon. Gozzano, *La quadreria di Lorenzo Onofrio Colonna*, p. 73.

118   Subiaco, AC, Carteggio di Lorenzo Onofrio Colonna, Suor Maria Colomba Colonna 1679 [*sic*], *camicia* 86, 15 January 1681. Also, Marino, ASRM, Armadio 2, no. 1, 'Fatti notabili', p. 38. This example illustrates the complexity of networks, which involved multiple relationships.

119   Subiaco, AC, Carteggio di Lorenzo Onofrio Colonna, Suor Maria Isabella Colonna 1681, *camicia* 52, 16 January 1681. Maria Isabella and Maria Colomba must have conferred regarding their appeal to their brother and their suggestion of utilizing the occasion of the upcoming marriage of Filippo II and Lorenza de la Cerda to solicit her father's help. Maria Isabella's letter offers more detail on the politics behind the strategy of involving the Spanish ambassador.

family reputation also reflects their own continued family ties that coexisted with their commitment to the strict observance espoused at SS. Rosario.

Greatly desiring her sister's admittance to SS. Rosario, Maria Isabella also appealed to powers much higher than her brother, engaging in strenuous prayer and penitence. Remaining in the choir after Matins for prayer, she would leave the floor bloody from her rigorous discipline, and each day she made her way around the dormitory on her knees while reciting the Rosary. But despite these ardent devotions, her prayers were to remain unanswered in her lifetime. Often suffering from fragile health, she finally succumbed to her afflictions on 5 February 1682 at the age of forty-eight.[120] During her final illness Lorenzo Onofrio sent his personal physician to assist in his sister's care, and when she died he sent a painter from Rome to record her portrait.[121] Her death left the community feeling orphaned without their founder and greatly worsened its fiscal crisis, having lost her annual income of 400 scudi.[122]

In the face of their loss, the struggling convent pressed on with its efforts to bring nuns from Rome, petitioning the Sacred Congregation of Bishops and Regulars to grant permission for Suor Maria Colomba Colonna and Suor Maria Agnese Costaguti, accompanied by their *converse*, to come from SS. Domenico e Sisto in Rome to SS. Rosario for a few years to help complete the foundation of the young convent by contributing their expertise. Prioress Maria Giulia Lancellotti pointed out that the community had evolved from its initial group of novices, requiring only one *maestra*, to eight newly professed nuns, four *converse*, and six to eight *educande* and noted that to conform to the decrees of the Sacred Congregation three *maestre* were now necessary in order to bring the new foundation to required perfection. At least two other mature, experienced nuns besides herself and the two nuns from Rieti were needed to exercise the offices of the convent and to teach plainchant and direct the choir. The nuns requested from SS. Domenico e Sisto had expressed their willingness to come, and they possessed the needed choral expertise. Additionally, their annual *livelli* of 400 scudi (Colonna) and 120

---

120 Marino, ASRM, Armadio 2, no. 1, 'Fatti notabili', pp. 39, 41, 44.

121 Marino, ASRM, Armadio 2, no. 1, 'Fatti notabili', pp. 44. A payment of 6 scudi to painter Pietro Paolo Vegli (active 1672–1692) for a portrait of Suor Maria Isabella was issued on the day of her death (Gozzano, *La quadreria di Lorenzo Onofrio Colonna*, pp. 245–46). The portrait's present location is unknown, but portraits of Suor Maria Isabella, possibly based on Vegli's original, exist at the convent. Vegli also contributed to a series of portraits of nuns from the Chigi family, some of whom were members of the community at SS. Domenico e Sisto. He also copied many works of Flemish painter Jacob Ferdinand Voet (1639–1689) who painted portraits of members of the Colonna family, including Lorenzo Onofrio. See Nigrelli, 'Le velate di Casa Chigi'.

122 After Suor Maria Isabella Colonna's death, convent chronicler Suor Maria Domenica del SS. Rosario, engaging in apt word play, claimed she could barely express the profound sense of grief felt by the community at the loss of 'quella colonna in qui stava appoggiato l'ancora fresco edificio' (that column which supported the still fresh edifice). See Marino, ASRM, Armadio 2, no. 1, 'Fatti notabili', pp. 39–45.

scudi (Costaguti) would benefit the financially challenged convent, which practised the common life.[123]

Finally, Pope Innocent XI issued a brief granting the long-sought permission, and on 24 May 1683 Suor Maria Colomba Colonna, Suor Maria Agnese Costaguti, and two *converse*, Suor Apollonia and Suor Amata, from SS. Domenico e Sisto arrived in Marino accompanied by the Contestabile Lorenzo Onofrio Colonna and the duchess of Paliano (Lorenza de la Cerda). Lorenzo Onofrio's presence demonstrated his support for the convent, but it is unclear what role, if any, he or his influential contacts had played in ultimately bringing about this desired outcome. The Roman nuns brought essential aid that stabilized the struggling convent, and Maria Colomba functioned as a surrogate for her deceased sister. But their projected three-year residence was cut short slightly more than a year after their arrival when poor health necessitated the four nuns' return to Rome in June 1684. On this occasion, Maria Giulia Lancellotti, who had served as prioress of SS. Rosario since its foundation and had borne the vicissitudes of firmly establishing and perfecting the community, decided to relinquish this responsibility and return to SS. Domenico e Sisto with them.[124] Though they left SS. Rosario, these nuns did not forget their spiritual sisters in Marino. Maria Colomba continued her support of SS. Rosario, for example donating 100 scudi for a new vineyard (*vigna*) contiguous to the cloister in 1693, and the community regarded her as its protector, claiming it was through her that God had maintained the convent. After her death in 1712 her role as '*protetrice*' (protectress) was assumed by two other nuns from SS. Domenico e Sisto, Maria Girolama Colonna, her sister who had founded S. Caterina Martire in Avezzano, and Anna Costanza Gaetani.[125] At her death in 1695 former prioress Maria Giulia Lancellotti left a *memoria perpetua* to remember her and her noble family, instructing her brother Marchese Ottavio Maria Lancellotti to consign 1000 scudi in *luoghi di monti* (shares of papal bonds) to SS. Rosario.[126] The networks forged between nuns at SS. Domenico e Sisto and SS. Rosario through family relations, shared

---

123 Subiaco, AC, Marino Miscellanea III KB 3, no. 52, 'Marino. Memoriali delle Monache e Notizie di Marino e di S. Domenico e Sisto a Roma'.

124 Marino, ASRM, Armadio 2, no. 1, 'Fatti notabili', pp. 46–48 and Armadio 1, no. 2, Magistrale 1699, fol. 4'. Although she had professed at S. Maria Maddalena al Quirinale, she obtained permission to spend her final years at SS. Domenico e Sisto so she could remain with her companion nuns who had laboured with her at SS. Rosario (Rome, AMR, Pannilini, 'Biografie delle Religiose', no. 1072).

125 Marino, ASRM, Armadio 2, no. 1, 'Fatti notabili', pp. 56–58, 83–84. Maria Colomba had desired to return to the Marino community in 1694, but was denied a licence. In an effort to force permission for her return the nuns at SS. Rosario elected her prioress, but this tactic failed. Maria Girolama had returned to SS. Domenico e Sisto in 1686 after her foundation in Avezzano was well-established (Rome, AMR, Pannilini, 'Biografie delle Religiose', no. 1037).

126 Marino, ASRM, Armadio 2, no. 1, 'Fatti notabili', pp. 58–59.

religious goals and activities, and respect earned through exemplary spiritual behaviour helped to sustain the Marino convent in its formative years.[127]

Documents suggest that the official request for the foundation of the Marino and Avezzano convents of Maria Isabella and Maria Girolama Colonna was made by their brother, Lorenzo Onofrio Colonna, whose prestige and influence lent crucial support for his sisters' spiritual initiatives of establishing these reformed Dominican convents.[128] By locating the convents in two of his feudal territories he was able to offer ready sites and enhance the spiritual and moral well-being of these towns along with Colonna *casa* prestige. Though the primary motivations of Lorenzo Onofrio and his sisters for these foundations varied in degree, they no doubt overlapped, and the projects were a mutually beneficial collaboration between siblings. After his initial support, it is difficult to ascertain the tangible results of Lorenzo Onofrio's influence, but his sisters certainly regarded him as a valuable and potent source of aid and frequently appealed to him. Their letters, however, were not just occasioned by requests for help. In some, his sisters functioned as intermediaries for others seeking favours, while many letters revolve around inquiries about his health or reports of their own health. But even these mundane epistolary tropes attest to the sustained bonds of family affection and sense of family identity maintained by the Colonna nuns even within their strictly reformed convents that renounced aristocratic privileges in favour of austerity. These family bonds were especially evident between the Colonna sisters who helped sustain each other, but their ties of alliance extended beyond natal family to convent families and to a network of female mentors and patrons.

Conclusion

Convent chronicles and other primary documents attest to nuns' sense of institutional identity and religious devotion at the Dominican convent of SS. Domenico e Sisto and its daughter convents of SS. Rosario and S. Caterina Martire, but the character of the Roman community and those in Marino and Avezzano differed significantly. In both, however, family and various other networks of alliance played key roles. Tracing its origins from near the beginning

---

127 By the early eighteenth century the nuns at SS. Rosario were able to expand their complex with the construction of a second dormitory, storage rooms, and a guest house in 1706, assisted by their Padre Vicar Tomasso Sala, who was noted for his charitable zeal. Between 1712 and 1713 a new public church on the design of architect Giuseppe Sardi was constructed by the convent to replace its original temporary chapel. The *contestabilessa* Colonna had donated 100 scudi for the new church in 1710. Its gracious interior decoration of stucco reliefs, statues, and three altarpieces was owed to the generosity of Dominican Father General Fra Antonio Cloche (Marino, ASRM, Armadio 2, no. 1, 'Fatti notabili', pp. 60, 72, 80–81, 85–91).

128 Marino, ASRM, Armadio 1, no. 2, Magistrale 1699, fol. 2ʳ; Armadio 1, Avezzano volume, loose folio; Armadio 2, no. 1, 'Fatti notabili', pp. 14–15.

of the Dominican order in the thirteenth century, the elite SS. Domenico e Sisto became a traditional site of prominent noble family dynasties of nuns and clusters of interrelated nuns, and even after the reforms of Trent and efforts to curb family ties with convents, it retained its close relation to Rome's aristocratic families. The distinguished lineages of its nuns that enhanced its reputation were carefully recorded in its convent chronicle, and this legacy of family nuns became intertwined with the history and identity of the convent. In contrast, the nuns at SS. Rosario in Marino in 1703 voted to drop their secular surnames and choose a saint's name as a spiritual last name, making official a practice already adopted by some of the nuns.[129]

Empowered by *livelli* or inheritances, social prestige, and networks of alliance, SS. Domenico e Sisto's cloistered nuns continued to represent and contribute to the prestige of their families through their roles as patrons, administrators, or exemplars of devotional life. By identifying with both their natal and institutional families, the nuns formed networks of alliance within and beyond family groups and created alliances between family and convent not unlike a secular bride's role in linking two families. Their family ties brought benefits to the convent by connecting it to intermediary networks and enabling individual nuns to act independently as internal patrons, significantly expanding the convent's potential to undertake projects of construction and decoration, thus making the convent more autonomous and less dependent on external patronage. In renouncing the privileged status of SS. Domenico e Sisto to found convents devoted to poverty in the spirit of Catholic reform, Maria Isabella and Maria Girolama Colonna chose a more difficult path for the Marino and Avezzano communities. Away from the centre of wealth and power of Rome, these convents drew nuns from less elite social backgrounds that did not have allowances at their disposal to help augment the patrimonies of their convents.[130] While their nuns' more modest dowries were invested, it is clear, especially at the better-documented SS. Rosario, that this was not sufficient to establish a stable financial base for at least the first few decades, and the nuns truly did experience the life of poverty to which they had devoted themselves.[131] This rendered the Marino and Avezzano foundations more dependent on Colonna family ties and other networks of alliance outside the convents. Although they founded strictly reformed convents, Maria Isabella and Maria Girolama certainly did not adhere to the advice of seventeenth-century treatises that urged nuns to forget their families except in their prayers,[132] since Colonna family influence or material assistance was

---

129   Marino, ASRM, Armadio 2, no. 1, 'Fatti notabili', p. 66.
130   Transplants from SS. Domencio e Sisto who could contribute their *livelli* to the convent's patrimony were an exception, and this was one reason why their transfers to SS. Rosario were so desired.
131   See Marino, ASRM, Armadio 2, no. 1, 'Fatti notabili' for accounts of the convent's early financial struggles.
132   Basso, *La monaca perfetta*, pp. 344–53.

crucial to help their foundations negotiate the challenges of their formative years and survive.[133] Even while embracing an austere monastic life they nonetheless remained conscious of family reputation and maintained affectionate familial bonds. Patterns of family relationships and other networks of alliances inside and beyond the cloister walls manifested themselves in multiple and diverse ways within the distinct characters of the Roman convent of SS. Dominico e Sisto and the communities at Marino and Avezzano but reveal the integral nature of such networks within the functioning of post-Tridentine convents.

---

133   While S. Caterina Martire survived in Avezzano until the early twentieth century, a small community of Dominican nuns still exists at SS. Rosario in Marino.

Works Cited

Manuscripts and Archival Sources

Città del Vaticano, Archivio Segreto Vaticano (ASV)
    Archivum Arcis (A.A.),
      ——, Arm. I–XVIII, 6492, Antonio Seneca, 'Prattica del governo delle monache', 1604
      ——, Arm. I–XVIII, 6493, 'Decreti Generali, 1625'
    Congregazione della Visita Apostolica (Congr. Visita Ap.)
Città del Vaticano, Biblioteca Apostolica Vaticana (BAV)
    MS Vat. Lat. 7847, 'Istoria del monastero di San Cosimato'
Marino, Archivio SS. Rosario (ASRM)
    Armadio 1, no. 2, Magistrale 1699
    Armadio 1, Avezzano volume, unnumbered volume labelled 'Questo libro appartiene all'ex Monastero S. Caterina V. M. di Avezzano (Aquila) fondato nel 1675 dalla madre Girolama Colonna sorella della nostra M. Fondatrice M. Isabella Colonna'
    Armadio 2, no. 1, 'Fatti notabili, e prodigiosi, occorsi intorno all'erettione, e progresso del Venerabile Monastero del SS. Rosario fondato non senza speciale concorso di S. D. Maestà in Marino l'anno 1676 adi 22 settembre'
    Armadio 3, palchetto B, no. 2
Rome, Archivio del Monastero del SS. Rosario (AMR)
    Suor Domenica Salamonia, 'Memorie del Monastero di SS. Domenico e Sisto'
    Tommasa Angelica Pannilini, 'Biografie delle Religiose del Ven. Monastero dei SS. Domenico e Sisto dal 1218 al 1820'
Rome, Archivio di Stato di Roma (ASR)
    Camerale III, Roma Chiese e monasteri
Subiaco, Archivio Colonna (AC)
    AA 80, no.41
    AA 199, no. 22
    Carteggio di Lorenzo Onofrio Colonna
    I B 28, Libro Mastro (1668–1678)
    Marino Miscellanea III KB 3, no. 52, 'Marino. Memoriali delle Monache e Notizie di Marino e di S. Domenico e Sisto a Roma'

Primary Sources

Basso, Carlo Andrea, *La monaca perfetta* (Venice: Pezzana, 1674)
Borselli, Bonaventura, O. P., *Breve narratione della vita e virtù della Ven. Suor Maria Maddalena Orsini* (Rome: Nicol'Angelo Tinassi, 1668)
De Luca, Giovanni Battista, *Il religioso pratico dell'uno e dell'altro sesso* (Rome: Stamperia della Reverenda Camera Apostolica, 1679)
Malvasia, Carlo Cesare, *Vite di pittori bolognesi (appunti inediti)*, ed. by Adriana Arfelli (Bologna: Commissione per I Testi di Lingua, 1961)

Secondary Works

Ago, Renata, *Carriere e clientele nella Roma barocca* (Bari: Laterza, 1990)

——, 'Giochi di squadra: Uomini e donne nobili del XVII secolo', in *Signori, patrizi, cavalieri in Italia centro-meridionale nell'età moderna*, ed. by Renata Ago and Maria Antonietta Visceglia (Rome: Laterza, 1992), pp. 256–64

Amayden, Teodoro, *Storia delle famiglie romane* (Rome: Edizioni Romane Colosseum, 1987)

Andretta, Stefano, 'Il governo dell'osservanza: poteri e monache dal Sacco alla fine del seicento', in *Roma, città del papa, Storia d'Italia*, Annali 16, ed. by Luigi Fiorani and Adriano Prosperi (Turin: Giulio Einaudi, 2000), pp. 397–427 ·

Benedetti, Sandro, 'La chiesa del SS. Rosario in Marino', *Quaderni dell'istituto di storia dell'architettura*, serie 12, fasc. 67–70 (1965), 7–32

Bernardini, Virginia, Andreina Draghi, and Guia Verdesi, *SS. Domenico e Sisto* (Rome: Istituto Nazionale di Studi Romani and Fratelli Palombi, 1991)

Borello, Benedetta, *Trame sovrapposte: La socialità aristocratica e le reti di relazioni femminili a Roma (XVII–XVIII secolo)* (Naples: Edizioni Scientifiche Italiane, 2003)

Bourne, Molly, 'From Court to Cloister and Back Again: Margherita Gonzaga, Caterina de' Medici and Lucrina Fetti at the Convent of Sant'Orsola in Mantua', in *Domestic Institutional Interiors in Early Modern Europe*, ed. by Sandra Cavallo and Silvia Evangelisti (Farnham: Ashgate, 2009), pp. 153–79

Calabrese, Ferdinando, *Marino e I Colonna (1500–1800)* (Rome: De Luca, 1981)

Canons and Decrees of the Council of Trent, ed. and trans. by H. J. Schroeder (St Louis: Herder 1941)

Cavicchioli, Sonia, 'Una principessa dall'animo grande: Laura Martinozzi mecenate negli anni della reggenza (1662–1674)', in *Laura Martinozzi d'Este fille de France, dux Mutinae. Studi intorno a Laura Martinozzi reggente del Ducato di Modena (1662–1674)*, ed. by Sonia Cavicchioli (Modena: Il Bulino edizioni d'arte, 2009), pp. 89–117

Diefendorf, Barbara B., *From Penitence to Charity: Pious Women and the Catholic Reformation in Paris* (Oxford: Oxford University Press, 2004)

Dominican Nuns of Dominican Monastery of St Jude, Marbury, AL, 'St Nicholas', 2011 http://www.stjudemonastery.org/2011/st-nicholas/ [accessed 12 October 2015]

Dunn, Marilyn, 'Nuns as Art Patrons: The Decoration of S. Marta al Collegio Romano', *The Art Bulletin*, 70 (1988), 451–77

——, 'Piety and Patronage in Seicento Rome: Two Noblewomen and Their Convents', *The Art Bulletin*, 76 (1994), 644–63

——, 'Spiritual Philanthropists: Women as Convent Patrons in Seicento Rome', in *Women and Art in Early Modern Europe: Patrons, Collectors, and Connoisseurs*, ed. by Cynthia Lawrence (University Park: Pennsylvania State University Press, 1997), pp. 154–88

——, '*Invisibilia per visibilia*: Roman Nuns, Art Patronage, and the Construction of Identity', in *Wives, Widows, Mistresses, and Nuns in Early Modern Italy: Making the Invisible Visible through Art and Patronage*, ed. by Katherine A. McIver (Farnham: Ashgate, 2012), pp. 181–205

——, 'Nuns, Agents, and Agency: Art Patronage in the Post-Tridentine Convent', in *Patronage, Gender and the Arts in Early Modern Italy: Essays in Honor of Carolyn Valone*, ed. by Katherine A. McIver and Cynthia Stollhans (New York: Italica, 2015), pp. 127–51

——, 'Nuns, Family, and Inter-Familial Dynamics of Art Patronage in Post-Tridentine Roman Convents', *Sixteenth Century Journal*, 48 (2017), 323–56

Fiorani, Luigi, 'Monache e monasteri romani nell'età del Quietismo', *Ricerche per la storia religiosa di Roma*, 1 (1977), 63–111

Gladen, Cynthia A., 'Suor Lucrina Fetti, Pittrice in una corte monastica sei-centesca', in *I monasteri femminili come centri di cultura fra Rinascimento e Barocco*, ed. by Gianna Pomata and Gabriella Zarri (Rome: Edizioni di Storia e Letteratura, 2005), pp. 123–41

Gozzano, Natalia, *La quadreria di Lorenzo Onofrio Colonna: Prestigio nobiliare e collezionismo nella Roma barocca* (Rome: Bulzoni, 2004)

Harness, Kelley, *Echoes of Women's Voices: Music, Art, and Female Patronage in Early Modern Florence* (Chicago: University of Chicago Press, 2006)

Hickson, Sally Anne, *Women, Art and Architectural Patronage in Renaissance Mantua: Matrons, Mystics and Monasteries* (Farnham: Ashgate, 2012)

Hills, Helen, 'The Housing of Institutional Architecture: Searching for a Domestic Holy in Post-Tridentine Italian Convents', in *Domestic Institutional Interiors in Early Modern Europe*, ed. by Sandra Cavallo and Silvia Evangelisti (Farnham: Ashgate, 2009), pp. 119–50

Hinnebusch, William, *The History of the Dominican Order: Origins and Growth to 1500* (Staten Island: Alba House, 1965)

Iotti, Roberta, 'Da fille de France a dux Mutinae: La parabola biografica e politica di Laura Martinozzi d'Este', in *Laura Martinozzi d'Este fille de France, dux Mutinae. Studi intorno a Laura Martinozzi reggente del Ducato di Modena (1662–1674)*, ed. by Sonia Cavicchioli (Modena: Il Bulino edizioni d'arte, 2009), pp. 11–69

Lirosi, Alessia, *I monasteri femminili a Roma tra XVI e XVII secolo* (Rome: Viella, 2012)

Lowe, K. J. P., *Nuns' Chronicles and Convent Culture in Renaissance and Counter-Reformation Italy* (Cambridge: Cambridge University Press, 2003)

Medioli, Francesca, 'Reti famigliari. La matrilinearità nei monasteri femminili fiorentini del seicento: il caso di Santa Verdiana', in *Nubili e celibi tra scelta e costrizione (secoli XVI–XX)*, ed. by Margareth Lazinger and Raffaella Sarti (Udine: Forum, 2006), pp. 11–36

Monson, Craig A., *Disembodied Voices: Music and Culture in an Early Modern Italian Convent* (Berkeley: University of California Press, 1995)

Nigrelli, Gianni, 'Le velate di Casa Chigi: Una singolare galleria di monache nella Roma del tardo seicento', in *Velo e velatio: Significato e rappresentazione nella cultura figurative dei secoli XV–XVII*, ed. by Gabriella Zarri (Rome: Edizioni di Storia e Letteratura, 2014), pp. 110–30

Nussdorfer, Laurie, *Civic Politics in the Rome of Urban VIII* (Princeton: Princeton University Press, 1992)

Onorati, Ugo, *La basilica collegiata di San Barnaba Apostolo* (Marino: Associazione *Senza frontiere* O.n.l.u.s., 2010)

——, *La chiesa del SS. Rosario di Marino* (Marino: Barocco in Sagra, 2014)

Ontini, Bianca Rosa, *La chiesa di S. Domenico in Roma* (Rome: Edizione Cateriniane, 1952)

Petrucci, Franca, 'Colonna, Marzio', *Dizionario biografico degli Italiani*, vol. 27 (1982) http://www.treccani.it/enciclopedia/marzio-colonna_res-090c0884-87eb-11dc-8e9d-0016357eee51_(Dizionario-Biografico) [accessed 16 August 2018]

Piperno, Roberto, and Rosamie Moore, 'Rome in the Footsteps of an XVIII Century Traveller: Marino' http://www.romeartlover.it/Marino.html [accessed 30 May 2018]

Radke, Gary M., 'Nuns and their Art: The Case of San Zaccaria in Renaissance Venice', *Renaissance Quarterly*, 54 (2001), 430–59

'Raimondo Capizucchi' https://en.wikipedia.org/wiki/Raimondo_Capizucchi [accessed 30 May 2018]

Sperling, Jutta Gisela, *Convents and the Body Politic in Late Renaissance Venice* (Chicago: University of Chicago Press, 1999)

Spezzaferro, Luigi, 'Pier Francesco Mola e il mercato artistico romano: atteggimenti e valutazione', in *Pier Francesco Mola, 1612–1666*, ed. by Manuela Kahn-Rossi (Milan: Electa, 1989), pp. 40–59

Spiazzi, Raimondo, *Cronache e fioretti del monastero di San Sisto all'Appia* (Bologna: Edizioni Studio Domenicano, 1993)

——, *San Domenico e il monastero di San Sisto all'Appia. Raccolta di studi storici tradizioni e testi d'archivio* (Bologna: Edizioni Studio Domenicano, 1993)

Strocchia, Sharon, 'Naming a Nun: Spiritual Exemplars and Corporate Identity in Florentine Convents, 1450–1530', in *Society and Individual in Renaissance Florence*, ed. by William J. Connell (Berkeley: University of California Press, 2002), pp. 215–40

Strunck, Christina, '"The Marvel Not Only of Rome, but of All Italy": The Galleria Colonna, Its Design History and Pictorial Programme 1661–1700', in *Art, Site, and Spectacle. Studies in Early Modern Visual Culture*, ed. by D. R. Marshall (Melbourne: The Fine Arts Network, 2007), pp. 78–102

——, 'Old Nobility versus New: Colonna Art Patronage during the Barberini and Pamphilj Pontificates (1623–1655)', in *Art and Identity in Early Modern Rome*, ed. by Jill Burke and Michael Bury (Aldershot: Ashgate, 2008), pp. 135–54

Tamalio, Raffaele, 'Laura Martinozzi, duchessa di Modena e Reggio', *Dizionario biografico degli Italiani*, vol. 64 (2005) http://www.treccani.it/enciclopedia/laura-martinozzi-duchessa-di-modena-e-reggio_(Dizionario-Biografico) [accessed 16 August 2018]

Tomassetti, Giuseppe, and Francesco Tomassetti, *La campagna romana. Antica, mediovale, e moderna*, vol. 4 (Rome: Maglione and Strini, 1926)

Valone, Carolyn, 'Women on the Quirinal Hill: Patronage in Rome, 1560–1630', *The Art Bulletin*, 76 (1994), 129–46

Zucchi, Alberto, *Roma domenicana. Note storiche* (Florence: Memorie Domenicane, 1943)

SHEILA BARKER and JULIE JAMES

Art as a Conduit for Nuns' Networks

*The Case of Suor Teresa Berenice Vitelli
at S. Apollonia in Florence*[*]

Introduction: A Nun Among Artists

Near the Raphaels, Titians, and Caravaggios of the Medici grand dukes' art collection at Palazzo Pitti are the works of a Florentine nun, Suor Teresa Berenice Vitelli (1687–1738).[1] Three of her artworks are kept in the Sala delle Vetrine, a small room reserved for diminutive works called miniatures, most of which, including hers, are painted on vellum. From a technical point of view, Suor Teresa Berenice's artworks are every bit as virtuosic as those made by professional miniaturists. What sets her miniatures apart is not their manuality so much as their ingenious compositional arrangements that bring the natural history subjects to life and infuse them with gentle wit. In one of her miniatures, for instance, field lizards (*Podarcis sicula*) play hide-and-seek around a perforated *búcaro* (a Mesoamerican clay vessel), while an African parrot (*Agapornis pullaria*) politely offers a Eurasian blue tit (*Cyanistes caeruleus*) a drink of water from a black *búcaro*, serving it from a dainty Chinese porcelain cup (Figure 9.1).

---

[*] All dates have been converted from the Florentine year to the modern year, unless noted. Whenever folio numbers have been omitted, this indicates that the folio was unnumbered.

[1] Essential bibliography on the artist includes Borroni Salvadori, 'Le esposizioni d'arte a Firenze', p. 133; Meloni Trkulja, 'Teresa Berenice (Suor Veronica) Vitelli', pp. 141–43; Mosco, entry in *La natura morta in Italia*, p. 600; Casale, *Gli incanti dell'iride*, p. 120; Casciu, 'Violante Beatrice di Baviera', pp. 330–31; Casciu and Navarro, *La Galleria Palatina*, p. 486; Tongiorgi Tomasi, 'La femminil pazienza', pp. 176–77; Fortune, *Invisible Women*, pp. 55, 218; and Matilde Simari and Acanfora, eds, *Flowers on Vellum*, pp. 13–16, 98–114.

Sheila Barker (barker@medici.org) (PhD Art History, Columbia University, 2002) directs the Jane Fortune Research Program on Women Artists, which she founded in 2010 at the Medici Archive Project in Florence. She has recently curated an exhibition on Giovanna Garzoni for Palazzo Pitti in Florence, and is currently preparing a monograph on Artemisia Gentileschi.

Julie James (jmjames03@gmail.com) is a doctoral candidate at Washington University in St Louis.

Convent Networks In Early Modern Italy, ed. by Marilyn Dunn and Saundra Weddle, ES 25 (Turnhout: Brepols, 2020) pp. 303–330   BREPOLS ✠ PUBLISHERS   DOI 10.1484/M.ES-EB.5.119520

Figure 9.1. Suor Teresa Berenice Vitelli, *Parrot, Blue Tit, and Two Lizards*, Florence, Galleria Palatina. 1706. Photograph reproduced with the permission of the Ministero per i Beni e le Attività Culturali.

In light of Suor Teresa Berenice's monastic status, it is indeed surprising that her miniatures feature an array of exotic animals and foreign objects. Her preferred subject matter is much more readily associated with the natural curiosity collections of Europe's nascent museum culture than with the Benedictine convent of S. Apollonia that the artist entered at age fifteen in 1703.[2]

---

2 There is a large body of research on early modern curiosity collections. See for instance Findlen, *Possessing Nature*; MacGregor, *Curiosity and Enlightenment*; Ruggieri Tricoli, *Il richiamo dell'Eden*; Evans and Marr, eds, *Curiosity and Wonder*; and Felfe and Lozar, eds, *Frühneuzeitliche Sammlungspraxis und Literatur*. By contrast, there is comparatively little bibliography on the nuns of S. Apollonia, and what does exist tends to focus on the artistic and architectural commissions for this convent. See for instance Davis, 'Cosimo Bartoli', pp. 261–76; Bertucci, 'A Leaf from the Scholz Scrapbook', pp. 93–100; Bacarelli, 'Sant'Apollonia'; Bacarelli, 'Per l'architettura fiorentina del quattrocento'; Hayum, 'A Renaissance Audience Considered'; Proto Pisani, *Il cenacolo di Santa Apollonia*; Lenzi Iacomelli, *Vincenzo Meucci*, pp. 187–88. Regarding Suor Teresa Berenice's entrance to the convent as a choir nun and her later vows, see Matilde Simari and Acanfora, eds, *Flowers*

Also part of the Medici collections at Palazzo Pitti, although not currently on display, are nine small-scale works that Suor Teresa Berenice rendered in pastel. In 1729 these pastels, as well as two of her oil paintings, were put on public view in Florence alongside the artworks of the most prominent artists of that time in an exhibition organized by the Accademia delle Arti del Disegno and held in the cloister of the church of the SS. Annunziata.[3] Like a number of the paintings displayed in this exhibition, Suor Teresa Berenice's works were copies of originals made by other artists. The works that had served as models for her pastels were a group of religious history paintings executed by Livio Mehus (1630–1691), whereas her two oil paintings were made after portraits done by Rembrandt and Francesco Trevisani. Remarkably, all of the original works that Suor Teresa Berenice studied belonged at that time to the family of Grand Duke Cosimo III de' Medici, a fact indicating that our cloistered nun had somehow gained privileged access to this princely art collection.

Suor Teresa Berenice's artistic oeuvre vividly testifies to the fact that, despite monastic enclosure, she studied from life not only exotic flora and fauna, and luxury objects such as Chinese porcelain and Mesoamerican *búcaros*, but also a number of paintings in the Medici collections. It will be demonstrated here that Suor Teresa Berenice's ability to make reference to this wide range of subject matter stemmed from her advantageous family connections, and that her incorporation of these objects into her artistic imagery served to reinforce these family ties. Despite the Tridentine decrees legislating strict enclosure and the Church's effort to sever nuns' family attachments, art allowed Suor Teresa Berenice to cultivate a family identity within her convent (where she found herself among three other Vitelli relatives) and to remain vitally connected to her kin in the secular world.[4] Moreover, when Suor Teresa Berenice's paintings and pastels entered other collections such as that of the Medici grand dukes or the Accademia delle Arti del Disegno, they extended her social

---

on Vellum, pp. 15, 22 n. 32. Payments for her first stay at the convent *in serbatoio* during her father's travels in 1699 are in Florence, ASF, CRSGF 82, vol. 66, fol. 1 right. Suor Teresa Berenice's sister, Suor Clemente Felice, who had entered the convent in 1702 (ASF, RV 69 insert 38), was the convent's *speziale* from 1723 (Florence, ASF, CRSGF 82, vol. 94, fol. 73 left) until her designation as *camarlinga* in 1729 (Florence, ASF, CRSGF 82, vol. 45, fol. 61ᵛ). Suor Teresa Berenice herself served the convent and its nuns in a variety of roles during her time at S. Apollonia. Convent records from 1724 name her as the *bucataia*, a position in which she controlled the whitening and bleaching of fabrics (Florence, ASF, CRSGF 82, vol. 69, fol. 158 left). This role indicates she held an understanding of chemical processes. Two years later, she is described as the *sagrestana*. (Florence, ASF, CRSGF 82, vol. 69, fol. 186 right), and, upon her sister's death in 1732, Suor Teresa Berenice assumed the role of *camarlinga* (Florence, ASF, CRSGF 82, vol. 94, fol. 232 left).

3 *Nota de' quadri*, pp. 25, 39–43; Borroni Salvadori, 'Le esposizioni d'arte a Firenze', pp. 27–28, 133.

4 The other three Vitelli nuns at S. Apollonia during Suor Teresa Berenice's time were Suor Placida Maria (born Berenice Vitelli), Suor Maria Clemente Felice (born Isabella Vitelli) and Suor Maria Ancilla (born Luisa Vitelli). Suor Anna Teresa (born Berenice Vitelli) was an *educanda* there since 1733 but only took the veil in 1739.

connections well beyond her kinship network. Through the circulation of her inherently mobile small-scale artworks with secular subject matter, Suor Teresa Berenice's network came to transcend conventual enclosure, enabling her to take her virtual place in the Medici grand ducal court and to establish symbolic links with other artists. Suor Teresa Berenice Vitelli exemplifies the capacity of nuns to interact with the secular world largely on the basis of shared interests and discourses, driven in part by familial network strategies but also by an uncontainable curiosity about natural and manmade wonders in every corner of the globe.

Paintings Rooted in Family Identity

Baptized in Florence on 21 January 1687 with the name Aluisa Maria Caterina Vitelli, the artist later known as Suor Teresa Berenice Vitelli could claim two important kinship networks by birthright.[5] Suor Teresa Berenice's mother, Berenice, bore the surname of Zondadari, an illustrious and noble Sienese family. One of Berenice Zondadari's brothers, Antonfelice Zondadari, was elevated to the purple in 1712; another, Alessandro Zondadari, was named Archbishop of Siena in 1715; and a third, Marcantonio Zondadari, served as Grand Master of the Order of Malta beginning in 1720. All of them had benefitted from the long reign (1655–1667) of their mother Agnese Chigi's Sienese uncle, Pope Alexander VII Chigi, just as had Berenice Zondardari's two Chigi relatives, Flavio Chigi *senior* and Sigismondo Chigi, both of whom reached the cardinalate.[6]

Suor Teresa Berenice Vitelli's mother married into a family no less illustrious than her own Sienese clan. Her husband, Marquise Clemente Vitelli of Bucine, descended from the ruling family of the Vitelli of Città di Castello, several branches of which had honourably served the Medici in their military endeavours for over a century.[7] During the recent peaceful

---

5 Florence, OSMF, Registri Battesimali, Reg. 288, fol. 58 (under the Florentine style year 1686), first published in Matilde Simari and Acanfora, eds, *Flowers on Vellum*, p. 21 n. 24.
6 There had also been a cardinal in the Vitelli family in the previous century: Vitellozzo Vitello (1531–1568).
7 At the time of the marriage of Suor Teresa Berenice's parents, Cardinal Buonvisi characterized the Vitelli family as 'una Casa delle più conosciute d'Italia per la nobiltà e per gl'uomini grandi che hanno avuto nell'Armi' (one of the most renowned families of Italy due to its nobility and due to the great men it sent to battle). See the copy of a letter of Cardinal Buonvisi to Cardinal Sigismondo Chigi, dated 30 November 1683, Florence, ASF, RV 41, insert 6. On the various branches of the Vitelli family and their exploits, see Litta, *Le famiglie celebri d'Italia*; and Florence, ASF, Ceramelli Papiani 4895. On their role in overseeing the German guard, see Florence, ASF, GM 896, insert 1, no. 296, first noted in Matilde Simari and Acanfora, eds, *Flowers on Vellum*, p. 21 n. 26. Another branch of the large Vitelli family, the counts of Montone, had important ties with the Florentine convent of Le Murate; see Weddle, 'Enclosing Le Murate', pp. 155, 158, 299, 304–10.

times, the fierce loyalty of the marquises of Bucine to the Medici had evolved into sentimental expressions and gestures of deep friendship. Suor Teresa Berenice's grandfather Pier Francesco Vitelli had enjoyed close relationships with several members of Tuscany's ruling family. Cardinal Giovan Carlo de' Medici consoled Pier Francesco over the death of the famous elephant Hansken;[8] Cardinal Pietro Leopoldo de' Medici addressed Pier Francesco as *'compare'* (godparent) to confirm his closeness to the family;[9] and, as a youth, Cosimo III enthusiastically corresponded with Pier Francesco about his hunting exploits.[10] These historic bonds between the Vitelli and the Medici were still strong during Suor Teresa Berenice Vitelli's lifetime. The grand duke's brother Francesco Maria de' Medici served as her godfather in 1687, having already attended the marriage of her parents in 1683.[11] In 1699, Grand Duke Cosimo III honoured Clemente Vitelli by designating him as ambassador extraordinary to the court of Pope Innocent XII.[12] When Clemente Vitelli died in 1700 leaving behind eleven orphaned children, Cosimo III responded with avuncular affection, receiving Suor Teresa Berenice's brothers with a special audience and reassuring them that 'egli le sarebbe stato in luogo di Padre' (he would take the place of their father).[13]

Prior to entering the convent, Suor Teresa Berenice lived with her six brothers and four sisters in the family's stately riverfront mansion now known as Palazzo Serristori, located in the Florentine neighbourhood of San Niccolò just a short walk from the Medici grand ducal seat in Palazzo Pitti. Her summers were divided between the family's villas in Fiesole and Scandicci, and on the occasion of her mother's funeral in 1697, she was able to visit her father's princely home in their ancestral base of Città di Castello. Drawn up upon her father's death, inventories of the furnishings in these four homes show that Suor Teresa Berenice was raised amidst nearly the same the

---

8 Letter of Giovan Carlo de' Medici in Rome to Pier Francesco Vitelli in Florence dated 22 November 1655, Florence, ASF, RV 41, insert 6, fol. 64ʳ.

9 The identity of the child in question has not yet been determined.

10 See letters of Prince Cosimo III in Artimino and Pisa to Pier Francesco Vitelli in Florence dated 23 September 1665 and 25 January 1666, Florence, ASF, RV 41, insert 6, unnumbered fols, between fols 93 and 94.

11 On Suor Teresa Berenice's baptism, see Matilde Simari and Acanfora, eds, *Flowers on Vellum*, p. 15; Letter of Francesco Maria de' Medici to Pier Francesco Vitelli, dated 19 October 1683, Florence, ASF, RV 41, insert 6. In the letter, the grand prince referred to Suor Teresa Berenice's mother as a 'Dama molto riguardevole' (very eminent lady).

12 On Clemente's ambassadorial service, see Florence, ASF, RV 42, insert 1; Florence, BNCF, Magl. Cl. XXV, cod. 42, fols 302–03.

13 Clemente died 15 December 1700. Two days later, Cosimo III received her brothers 'con segni di grand'affetto'; Florence, ASF, RV 7, insert 17, fol. 15ᵛ. The children's mother had died three years earlier in 1697 following a difficult birth. Although in the fifteenth century, nuns from several pro-Medici elite families had populated S. Apollonia, according to Strocchia, *Nuns and Nunneries in Renaissance Florence*, p. 108, in Suor Teresa Berenice's century, the Medici do not seem to have taken an interest in the convent.

cultural refinements as the Medici themselves.[14] The Vitelli family shared the Medicis' passion for music as demonstrated by their exceptionally important collection — even by Florentine standards — of costly musical instruments, which included three guitars, a thiorbo, two Cremona violins, a wall organ, and two harpischords, one of which had a double register.[15] Like the grand dukes, the Vitelli family also took a deep interest in botany and horticulture, appointing their villas as well as their Florentine *palazzo* with ornamental gardens abounding in exotic flowers and prized cultivars.[16] In step with the Medicis' advancement of scientific knowledge through their sponsorship of the Accademia del Cimento, the Vitelli family had acquired a number of rare and expensive scientific instruments like those used at the Accademia, including an odometer of English manufacture, a small telescope, two large 'Galilean' telescopes, and, with particular relevance for Suor Teresa Berenice's minutely observed natural history paintings, three compound microscopes.[17]

The Vitelli emulated the splendour and taste of the Medici also when collecting art and natural wonders.[18] In the first half of the seventeenth century,

---

14 Florence, ASF, RV 75, insert 4 contains the following inventories detailing the extensive collections of Suor Teresa Berenice's family: 'Inventario delle piante e vasi che si ritrovano nel giardino dell'Illustrissimo Signore Marchese Niccolò Vitelli alla sua Villa di Fiesole'; 'Inventario de' mobili, biancheria, argenti, rami, stagni, et ottoni biancheria, et altro che si ritrova nella Casa Piano Nobile posta nel Fondaccio di san Niccolò dell'Illustrissimo Signore Marchese Niccolò Vitelli' (hereafter referred to as 'Inventario de' Mobili'); 'Inventario di masserizie e mobili del Illustrissimo Signore Marchese Giovanni Niccolò Vitelli lasciati di lui in Palazzo su Renai per servitio di Illustrissimo Reverendissimo Arcivescovo Nunzio Apostolico'. Insert 5 of the same volume contains the following inventories: '1700, Inventario di tutte l'argenterie, gioie, ori e mobili qualsivoglia ritrovati in essere negli appie luoghi alla morte del Signore Illustrissimo Clemente Vitelli Capitano della Guardia a Cavallo di SAR 16 Dec 1700'; 'Inventario generale di tutte le masserizie tanto della casa di Firenze, che di Fiesole, Scandicci, Città di Castello, e Fonte Segale' (hereafter abbreviated as 'Inventario generale'); 'Inventario e stima i tutti quadri fatti nel mese di febraio 1700 a Firenze dal Signore Marini e Signore Gabbiani Pittore'; 'Inventario di tutte le masserizie e mobili che si ritrovano nel Palazzo dell'Illustrissimo Signore Marchese Vitelli' (hereafter abbreviated as 'Inventario di tutte le masserizie e mobili').

15 Florence, ASF, RV 75, insert 5, Inventario generale, fol. 49ᵛ.

16 All of the plants mentioned in the Vitelli inventories were prized for their beauty, rarity, or fragrance. Potted citrus and jasmine plants kept in a 'stanzone di vasi' are named in Florence, ASF, RV 75, insert 5, 'Inventario generale', fols 54ʳ–56ᵛ. Potted citrus plants, lily of the valley, double jonquils, double hyacinths, ranuculus, anemonies, Mexican tuberose, and Catalonian jasmine appear in the 1732 and 1738 inventories of the garden of Fiesole, located in Florence, ASF, RV 75, insert 4. Historical maps confirm that during Suor Teresa Berenice's life the Florentine palazzo had large, walled, parterred gardens on both the east and west sides of the building.

17 The Accademia del Cimento was an early scientific academy sponsored by Cardinal Leopoldo de' Medici and Grand Duke Ferdinando II de' Medici, and served as a place for Galileo's students and followers to perform experiments and share their discoveries. For the instruments in the Vitelli collections, see Florence, ASF, RV 75, insert 5, 'Inventario generale', fols 33ᵛ, 34ʳ, 38ʳ, 43ᵛ, 50ᵛ; Florence, ASF RV 75, insert 5, 'Inventario di tutte le masserizie e mobili', fol. 46ʳ.

18 An overview of Medici tastes at this time is offered in Tosi, 'Tra scienza, arte e diletto'.

Suor Teresa Berenice's great-grandfather Giulio Vitelli had given the Vitelli art collection new lustre with his purchases of works by such Florentine painters as Francesco Curradi, Cesare Dandini, and especially Francesco Furini, whose thirty-four canvases dominated the collection.[19] Her grandfather Pier Francesco Vitelli subsequently acquired works by a wide swathe of seventeenth-century artists including Giacinto Brandi, Guercino, Luca Giordano, Massimiliano Soldani Benzi, and various Flemish landscape specialists.[20] Although he too collected paintings, Suor Teresa Berenice's father much preferred exotic luxury items from the East and West Indies. His treasures included such rarities as three ostrich eggs, a set of cups made of Mesoamerican cacao seeds, a Turkish tea kettle, an inkwell and several fans from China, both a needle case and a crucifix carved from coconut, ivory tobacco cases, two elk hoofs encased in gold and pearls, tea services made of Oriental lacquerware, and Chinese porcelain.[21] Among the exotic and precious objects Clemente Vitelli valued most were his clay *búcaros* imported from Chile, Mexico, Portugal and Spain, as these *búcaros*, along with his silver, porcelain, and paintings, were explicitly mentioned in Clemente Vitelli's final testament as part of the inheritance assigned to his first-born son.[22]

Whereas the vast majority of early modern painters had to borrow the luxury items that appeared as props in their paintings, Suor Teresa Berenice had access in her childhood home to a vast gamut of extraordinary artworks, curios, and natural specimens, an advantage she fully exploited. In her above-mentioned painting of two birds sharing a drink, for example, a porcelain cup and two *búcaros* of the sort collected by her father figure prominently in the composition. In this painting, and indeed whenever Suor Teresa Berenice drew upon her family's refined collecting interests for the imagery of her miniature paintings, she was effectively laying claim to the cultural legacy of the Vitelli and underlining her identity as one of them. The implications of this strategy of linking herself to the Vitelli patrimony depended in part upon where her artworks were displayed. The following paragraphs will thus address the three principle venues to which our nun consciously directed her art: the Vitelli family's residence in Florence, the Medici court, and the public exhibition organized by the Accademia delle

---

19 Florence, ASF, RV 75, insert 5, 'Inventario e stima di tutti quadri fatti nel mese di febraio 1700 a Firenze dal Signore Marini e Signore Gabbiani Pittore doppo la morte del Signore Marchese Clemente Vitelli'.

20 The corresponding inventories as well as letters between Leopoldo and Pierfrancesco can be found in Florence, ASF, RV 75, insert 5, 'Inventario generale', fol. 12^v.

21 Florence, ASF, RV 75, insert 5, 'Inventario generale', fols 8^v–9^r, 24^v, 32^r–42^r.

22 Florence, ASF, NM 19446, notaio Pandorzi Panezio, fol. 126^r: 'Item per ragione di presegnato, et in ogni altro miglior modo, lassò e legò al Signore Niccolò suo figliuolo primogenito le sue argenterie del tavolino di camera, i suoi buccheri e porcellane e scatolini et alcuni quadri, tutte robe acquistate da esso Signore Testatore col danaro de' proprii avanzi, da dichiararsi circa all'identità e quantità dall'Illustrissimo Signore Marchese Camillo'.

Arti del Disegno in 1729. In doing so, it will consider how art could be used to maintain or establish channels with a range of Florence's most important nodes of secular culture, and to effectively evoke both her individual and her corporate identities beyond the convent walls.

Gifts for a Nun's Secular Kin

Throughout the years, Suor Teresa Berenice made gifts of her miniature paintings of both still-lifes and religious histories to her oldest brother, who, by the time of his death in 1739, had hung a dozen of them amidst the large number of devotional subjects, religious histories, portraits, and still-life paintings in the more public rooms of the family's Florentine palazzo.[23] By giving artworks to her brother Niccolò for display in the family residence, our nun ensured that she would not be forgotten despite living under monastic enclosure in the convent of S. Apollonia. She was not alone in this concern: the problem of staying in touch had long preoccupied Suor Teresa Berenice's family due to their dispersion across Florence, Siena, Città di Castello, and Rome. In order to stay closely connected and reinforce familial bonds, both the secular and religious members of Suor Teresa Berenice's family embraced gift giving in addition to the exchange of letters and visits.[24] During Suor Teresa Berenice's reclusion at S. Apollonia, her uncle Camillo Vitelli and her brother Niccolò gave the four Vitelli nuns at this convent both money as well as items such as lard, cheese, roasted pork, citrus fruit, writing paper, a Nativity scene, damask silk curtains, and other fabrics.[25] In return, the Vitelli nuns at S. Apollonia

---

23   Florence, ASF, RV 75, insert 4, 'Inventario de' mobili', fol. 3ʳ: 'Item 56. Sei quadrini con orna-mento alla Salvadora dorati con suo cristallo dipinti a pastello fatti di mano dell'Illustrissima Teresa Berenice Vitelli Monaca in Santa Apollonia'; 4ᵛ: 'Item 107. Sei quadretti alla Salvadora dorati entrovi copie in pastelli con suo cristallo fatti di mano dell'Illustrissima Teresa Berenice Vitelli'. The latter group presumably consisted of pastel copies that Suor Teresa Berenice had executed of religious history paintings by such artists as Livio Mehus.

24   A representatively large selection of the epistolary exchange among the Vitelli and their cognatic kin is preserved in the Rondinelli-Vitelli family archive housed at the Florentine State Archives (Florence, ASF, RV). On the practice of gift giving by nuns to maintain or reinforce their connections outside the convent, see Weddle, ''Tis Better to Give than to Receive'; and Turrill, '*Compagnie* and *Discepole*'. A study of the epistolary exchange used for the same purpose is found in Sobel, *Letters to Father*.

25   See letters of Niccolò Vitelli to Jacopo Grechi dated 16 September 1624, 28 March 1725, and 26 February 1726, in Florence, ASF, RV 52, insert 2; in particular, the letter of Suor Placida Vitelli to Camillo Vitelli dated 20 November 1730, in Florence, ASF, RV 57, insert 1, part 1. See Florence, ASF, RV 75, insert 5, Inventario generale, fol. 25ᵛ for the transfer of the damask curtains ('un cortinaggio piccolo di dommasco rosso cremisi con suoi finimenti da letto da campagna & un simile turchino'). Additionally, writing paper was promised to the Vitelli nuns of S. Apollonia by Camillo Vitelli: see the letter of Suor Placida to Camillo Vitelli dated 29 April 1730, Florence, ASF, RV 57, insert 1, part 1. The Nativity scene was given to Suor Teresa Berenice's niece while she was an *educanda* at the convent: see the letter of Berenice Vitelli to

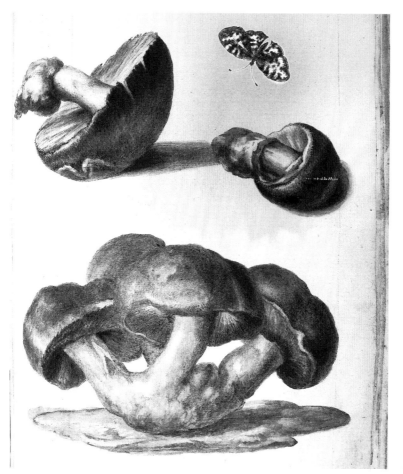

Figure 9.2. Suor Teresa Berenice Vitelli, *Mushrooms*, Florence, Biblioteca Nazionale Centrale di Firenze. Completed by 1738. Photograph by Sheila Barker, and reproduced with the permission of the Ministero per i Beni e le Attività Culturali.

regaled their relatives with candied citrus fruits, orange flowers, medicines, lace collars, and various handcrafted textile items.[26] Compared to these other gifts circulated among the Vitelli, Suor Teresa Berenice's paintings of birds

Camillo Vitelli dated 9 January 1733, Florence, ASF, RV 57, insert 1, part 1. For the identities of the three Vitelli nuns at S. Apollonia during Suor Teresa Berenice's time there, see n. 4.

26 Accompanying a letter of 20 November 1730, in Florence, ASF, RV 57, insert 1, part 1, Suor Placida sent Camillo Vitelli gifts ('una scatola con alcune poche cose'); other letters in the same location describe further gifts (10 January 1731, 'una scatola entrovi alcune poche arance confette perdoni e poca cosa'; 8 July 1731, 'una scatola alle cedrati'). Medicines were sent by Suor Teresa Berenice's niece Suor Anna Teresa to Niccolò Vitelli; see Florence, ASF, RV 56, insert 8, part 1, undated letter of 2 April 1747. Orange flowers are noted in the

and flowers carried a special resonance because they evoked her family's distinctive scientific and artistic interests. By creating further opportunities for dialogue about shared intellectual pastimes, these paintings strengthened the affective bond between giver and recipient.

While Suor Teresa Berenice's gifts of paintings to her first-born brother (who was the chief heir to the family fortune) no doubt were meant to reinforce the bond between the two siblings, the introduction of her artworks into the family painting collection proved her to be a contributor to the Vitellis' cultural legacy. Furthermore, since she had made use of her family's own gardens and collections for the subject matter of her painted miniatures, recording the appearance of flora and fauna in a large sketchbook that she later brought with her into the convent (Figure 9.2), these paintings insured that future Vitelli would see her as an appreciative beneficiary of their ancestors' cultural legacy.

As first a beneficiary of, and later a contributor to, the Vitelli collections, our nun had effectively interpolated herself into the otherwise patrilineal transmission of her family's cultural legacy.

Gifts for the Medici Grand Princess

In addition to placing several of her artworks in the Vitelli collection, Suor Teresa Berenice donated an equal or greater number of them to the Medici court, most or all of which were designated for Violante Beatrice of Bavaria (1673–1731), the consort of Grand Prince Ferdinando de' Medici (1663–1713), the son of the reigning grand duke of Tuscany.[27] Given the notable difference in status and power between the two women, these donations ought to be understood as bids for patronage and protection from the Medici court, presumably for the benefit of her convent.[28]

Although our nun had tenuous connections with other members of the Medici dynasty, including her godfather Francesco Maria de' Medici, Violante Beatrice of Bavaria was the most logical target for her overtures for a number of reasons. First, the grand princess had shown favouritism towards Sienese noblewomen, beginning with her appointment of Bichi Piccolomini as her first-ranked lady-in-waiting and culminating in Violante's nomination as governess of Siena in 1717.[29] This put Suor Teresa Berenice at a decisive advantage for gaining her favour, especially since the grand princess maintained open

---

unnumbered letter of Suor Placida to Camillo Vitelli dated 29 April 1730, Florence, ASF, RV 57, insert 1, part 1.

27 Violante was identified as Vitelli's principal patron at the Medici court in Casciu, 'Violante Beatrice di Baviera', pp. 329–37. Other possible patrons include Suor Teresa Berenice's godfather Cardinal Francesco Maria de' Medici and Grand Prince Ferdinando.

28 For the discussion of the political valance of the convent, see n. 13.

29 On Violante's favouring of Sienese nobility, see Calvi, 'Connected Courts', pp. 302–21, particularly p. 311.

diplomatic channels with Suor Teresa Berenice's Sienese Chigi and Zondadari relatives and particularly with her uncle Cardinal Antonfelice Zondadari.[30] Second, Violante's courts in Florence and Siena offered many positions for pages and ladies, and even though Suor Teresa Berenice was not a candidate for such positions, some of her family members were.[31] As a case in point, her sister Agnesa's daughter, Maria Maddalena Bagnesi, joined Violante's household in 1727 as her maid of honour.[32] Third, Violante offered her patronage to nuns throughout Italy, as revealed by her frequent correspondence with abbesses and her championing of their predilect cults, such as those of Margherita da Cortona and Maria Maddalena de' Pazzi.[33] Finally, as recently demonstrated by Silvia Benassai's archival discoveries, Violante was a fervent art collector who not only appreciated female artists such as Giovanna Fratellini, but who also collected artworks made by amateur artists among the Florentine

30 See the letters of Violante Beatrice of Bavaria to Archbishop Zondadari dated 18 July 1724 (Florence, ASF, MdP 6294); and 17 February 1725 and 7 March 1725 (Florence, ASF, MdP 6295). Also, see the letter of Agostino Chigi to Violante Beatrice of Bavaria dated 30 October 1725 (Florence, ASF, MdP 6295). As for her relationship with Cardinal Antonfelice Zondadari specifically, see the Violante's letters dated 28 June 1724, 19 September 1724, and 4 November 1724 (Florence, ASF, MdP 6294); and dated 7 March 1725, 22 September 1725, and 25 November 1725 (Florence, ASF, MdP 6295); see also the letters of Cardinal Zondadari to Violante Beatrice of Bavaria, dated 12 September 1724 and 30 October 1724 (Florence, ASF, MdP 6294), and dated 1 September 1725 and 14 March 1726 (Florence, ASF, MdP 6295). In 1719, the Cardinal visited Violante Beatrice of Bavaria in Florence; eight years later, he wrote to console Violante on the death of her brother. Their relationship was so well established that in 1728 Violante was asked to intercede with the Cardinal on behalf of the Collegiata di S. Venanzio. She did favours for him as well, writing in favor of his nephew, Suor Teresa Berenice's brother Paolo Vitelli, in 1725 (see the letter of Violante Beatrice of Bavaria dated 7 April 1725, Florence, ASF, RV 52, insert 3). For the close relationship between Cardinal Zondadari and Suor Teresa Berenice's brother Paolo, see the correspondence in Florence, ASF, RV 56, insert 8.
31 Calvi, 'Connected Courts', p. 311.
32 See the letters from Violante Beatrice of Bavaria to Ippolito Antonio Bagnesi dated 9 March 1727, in Florence, ASF, MdP 6297, fol. 526.
33 Violante's interest in Margherita da Cortona is demonstrated by two letters she sent to Pope Benedict XIII regarding her beatification; see Florence, ASF, MdP 6297, fols 342, 1315. As for Maria Maddalena de' Pazzi, Violante sent a portrait of the saint to Suor Maria Clemente Albani of the Convent of the SS. Incarnazione in Rome (see the letter from Suor Maria Grazia to Violante Beatrice of Bavaria, dated 7 December 1726, Florence, ASF, MdP 6296; the minutes of Violante's letter to Madre Suor Maria Clemente Albani dated November 1726 (the specific day is not given), Florence, ASF, MdP 6296; and a document regarding the painting's receipt in Abbatelli, Lirosi, and Palombo, ed., Un monastero di famiglia, pp. 331–32; many thanks to Marilyn Dunn for this last reference. Violante obtained papal rights for the convent of Amor Divina in Rome to observe double rites for Maria Maddalena de' Pazzi (see the letter from Suor Maria Laura, 1 March 1728, Florence, ASF, MdP 6296). Violante also appealed to the pope for other holy women such as Suor Domenica da Paradiso, the founder of the convent of the S. Croce (La Crocetta) in Florence (see the letter of Violante Beatrice of Bavaria to Pope Benedict XIII of 3 May 1726, Florence, ASF, MdP 6296 and Madre Suor Serafina from the convent of SS Salvatore in Naples, Florence, ASF, MdP 6297, fols 1464–66).

Figure 9.3. Suor Teresa Berenice Vitelli, *Two Sparrows and a Mouse*, Florence, Galleria Palatina. 1720. Photograph reproduced with the permission of the Ministero per i Beni e le Attività Culturali.

nobility, and by painters who specialized in representations of animals and flowers.[34] Suor Teresa Berenice ticked all of these boxes.

Several of Suor Teresa Berenice's miniature paintings for the Medici have survived, including six images of birds combined with fruits, insects, and flowers; a floral bouquet; and her two dated paintings, namely the previously discussed *Parrot, Blue Tit, and Lizards* (Figure 9.1), dated 1706, and the *Two Sparrows and a Mouse* (Inv. 1890, no. 4774), dated 1720 (Figure 9.3).[35]

As outlined above, since all of these paintings contain imagery that is emblematic of the Vitelli family's collecting penchants (e.g. porcelain, *búcaros*, birds, and flowers), they declaim her origins in the Vitelli household. Yet, as we have also argued here, the grand ducal Medici family nourished the very

34 Benassai, 'Tra le carte di Violante', pp. 80–112.

35 The *Two Sparrows* is noted in the inventory of the Villa of Lappeggi from 1732, drawn up after Violante's death, Florence, ASF, GM 1393, fol. 8ᵛ.

same interests. In this light, it would appear that Suor Teresa Berenice carefully selected her subject matter and imagery in order to emphasize the families' cultural commonalities, almost as if to recast the ancient feudal bonds between the Vitelli and Medici in terms of mutual friendship and similar tastes.

As experienced art collectors, the Medici family would have been able to recognize in Suor Teresa Berenice's miniatures not merely representations of the things they collected, but also a stylistic approach that was perfectly aligned with the still-life paintings displayed in their villas.[36] In particular, those familiar with the Medici collections would have detected in her art the influence of Giovanna Garzoni (1605–1670) and Jacopo Ligozzi (1547–1627), each of whom had worked at the Medici court for extended periods in the first half of the seventeenth century.[37] The resemblance to these two artists is not coincidental: Suor Teresa Berenice's painting sketchbook at the Biblioteca Nazionale di Firenze, probably begun well before she entered S. Apollonia as a choir nun in 1703, proves that she emulated both of them.[38] Among the leaves of this sketchbook are two of her juvenile attempts to paint fruit arranged in porcelain bowls in the manner of Garzoni, Ligozzi's original miniature of a narcissus flower, and a half-deteriorated drawing of a South American *Passiflora caerulea* plant by Ligozzi that she completed with her own substantial additions (Figure 9.4).[39]

Since neither Garzoni's nor Ligozzi's works were present in the Vitelli family's art collection, it is reasonable to conclude that Suor Teresa Berenice fell under the spell of Garzoni's and Ligozzi's artworks while visiting the Medici collections as a child, perhaps in the company of her father. (Since both Ligozzi and Garzoni were Medici court artists, their works were not readily found in the collections of other Florentine families). Suor Teresa Berenice may have even been encouraged in her youth to adopt Garzoni as an artistic role model, in light of Garzoni's highly praised display of female virtuosity during her first visit to the Medici court at the age of fifteen, and her successful return to Florence as an established artist in the 1640s.[40]

---

36 On the Medici still-life collection, see Ciardi and Tongiorgi Tomasi, eds, *Immagini anatomiche*; Mosco, ed., *Natura viva in Casa Medici*; Chiarini, ed., *La natura morta*; Chiarini, ed., *Botanica come arte*; Tongiorgi Tomasi and Hirschauer, eds, *The Flowering of Florence*; and Chiarini and Casciu, eds, *Il giardino del granduca*.

37 On Giovanna Garzoni, see Casale, *Gli incanti dell'iride*; on Ligozzi, see Cecchi, Conigliello, and Faietti, eds, *Jacopo Ligozzi*.

38 Suor Teresa Berenice used the sketchbook as a repository of nature studies that she would draw upon when assembling her imaginative compositions. Daniel Seghers had employed his sketchbook in a similar way: in Italy and Antwerp he recorded exotic flowers and plants in his notebooks that served as his models throughout his artistic career. Fleming, 'Daniel Seghers', p. 731.

39 Florence, BNCF, Conventi Soppressi A. I. 830 'Ornithologiae vivis expressae coloribus', vol. 4, fols 111, 114ʳ–1115ʳ, 140ʳ.

40 On Garzoni's visit to the Medici court around 1618, see Barker, '"Marvellously Gifted"'; on Garzoni's stay in Florence in the 1640s, see Meloni Trkulja and Fumagalli, eds, *Giovanna*

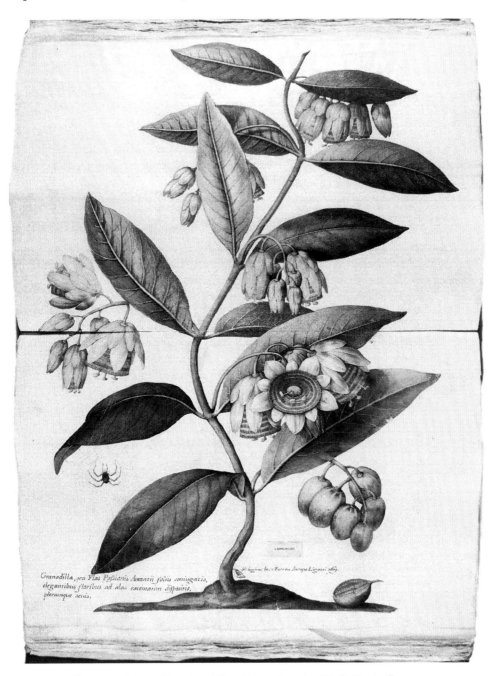

Figure 9.4. Jacopo Ligozzi and Suor Teresa Berenice Vitelli, *Passionflower*, Florence, Biblioteca Nazionale Centrale di Firenze. Begun 1609 and completed by 1738. Photograph by Sheila Barker, and reproduced with the permission of the Ministero per i Beni e le Attività Culturali.

Suor Teresa Berenice's artworks connoted the identity of the Vitelli family even when they were hung amongst the Medici collections. This is especially true of Suor Teresa Berenice's *Two Sparrows and a Mouse* when it was displayed at Violante's Villa Lappeggi outside of Siena.[41] Following a strategy instigated in the early seventeenth century by the Grand Duchess Christine of Lorraine with her so-called 'Bellezze di Artimino' series,[42] the grand princess displayed a large number of portraits at Lappeggi representing her favourite ladies among an elite and multi-national nobility, thereby reifying a sphere of influence that extended far beyond the limited number of ladies in Violante's retinue, and that existed independently of her kinship network. Nearly all of these portraits had been purposefully commissioned by the grand princess, including the portrait of Suor Teresa Berenice's sister-in-law, Anna Frescobaldi, executed by Giovanna Fratellini (1666–1731).[43] In a clever innovation upon the use of portraits to flaunt a network of *clientes*, Violante also put on exhibit at Lappeggi a series of artworks made by dilettante noblemen and noblewomen, each accompanied by a cartouche with the author's illustrious name to make immediately evident to viewers the identity of the maker.[44] Among the noblewomen who made these special artworks were Leopoldina Berzighelli, Sestilia Bardi di Vernio, Ortenzia Caccini Vernacci, Elena Bagnesi (Suor Teresa Berenice's sister-in-law), Caterina San Miniati Dati, and Suor Teresa Berenice Vitelli herself.[45] Encountered in this context, our nun's painting could be appreciated not only as an artistic object, but also as an emblem of the grand princess's privileged relationship with a member of a powerful family. The inclusion of Suor Teresa Berenice's painting among the works of noblemen and noblewomen at Villa Lappeggi strongly suggests that, although she was a nun, her aristocratic lineage continued to be a widely-recognized aspect of her identity.

This does not mean that the grand princess discounted Suor Teresa Berenice's status as a nun at S. Apollonia, where Suor Teresa Berenice's professed relatives included two aunts and a sister, and where her secular relatives, including two additional sisters and her niece, stayed *in serbatoio*.[46] In fact, Violante took a

---

Garzoni, p. 6, and Casale, *Giovanna Garzoni*, p. 10. The Medici grand dukes were highly appreciative of female artists. Besides Garzoni, others who enjoyed their patronage include Artemisia Gentileschi (1593–1656?), Arcangela Paladini (1599–1622), Camilla Guerrieri (1628–after 1690), Agnese Dolci (1635–1686), and Giovanna Fratellini (1666–1731).

41   On the display of this and the earlier image of *A Parrot, a Blue Tit, and Lizards* (Inv. 1890, no. 4775), see Meloni Trkulja, 'Teresa Berenice (Suor Veronica) Vitelli', pp. 142–43.

42   On the purpose of this series, see Chappell, 'Le "Bellezze di Artimino"', pp. 59–64.

43   Giovanna Fratellini executed a number of these; see Benassai, 'Tra le carte di Violante', pp. 97–98. For Fratellini's portrait of Anna Frescobaldi, see Florence, ASF, GM 1393, fol. 63ᵛ.

44   Florence, ASF, GM 1393, 2ᵛ–10ᵛ.

45   Other than Suor Teresa Berenice, none of these artists has received any scholarly attention thus far.

46   For Suor Teresa Berenice's family members at her convent, see n. 4 above. On her sisters' time at S. Apollonia, see Florence, ASF, CRSGF 82, vol. 67, fol. 9ᵛ, payment entry on

deep interest in nuns as a means of tapping into family networks connected through maternal lines. To help her instrumentalize her relationships with the women of Siena, the territory over which she governed, Violante commissioned a large and detailed document that profiled the social connections of every well-born woman in that community.[47] Each of the secular women in this report was portrayed in terms of her kinship ties through father, husband, and sons. By contrast, the religious women in this report were portrayed in terms of their matrilineal ties, going back to their maternal grandmothers. Two conclusions can be drawn from these social profiles. First, as Giulia Calvi has argued, Violante viewed convents as 'centers from which a tight network of relations between professed nuns and women of civil society and the court branch off', which suggests that the grand princess saw Suor Teresa Berenice as a point of mediation between multiple spheres.[48] Second, it can be extrapolated from these reports that Violante would have been particularly mindful of Suor Teresa Berenice's maternal connection to the Chigi and Zondadari families two generations back. Both of these lines were Sienese, and they linked our nun in Florence to a Sienese cardinal of the Catholic Church and to the archbishop of Siena — both of whom were highly useful to the grand princess in her efforts to obtain favours from the ecclesiastical hierarchy for her allies and clients.

Gifts to the Accademia delle Arti del Disegno and the Exhibition of 1729

Extending her network beyond her family and the grand ducal court, Suor Teresa Berenice's participation in the Florentine Accademia delle Arti del Disegno exhibition of 1729 marks a third context in which the nun artist produced art that called attention to herself, her convent, her family, and her relationship with the Medici.[49] Of the eleven small-scale compositions which Suor Teresa Berenice contributed to the Accademia delle Arti del Disegno's exhibition in 1729, nine pastels closely followed paintings by Livio Mehus in the Medici collection, illustrating scenes from the lives of the Virgin Mary and Christ (Figure 9.5).[50] She also presented two oil paintings to the

---

7 October 1707: 'Da alimenti di nostre fanciulle quaranta pagaseco contanti il Signore Marchese Camillo Vitelli gli alimenti anticipati della Signora Agnesa e Virginia Vitelli sue nipoti, recò il Procuratore, 40'; for that of her niece, Florence, ASF, CRSGF 82, vol. 69, fol. 61ᵛ, payment entry on 26 September 1730: 'Da alimenti di nostre fanciulle ducati dieci, pagatici il Signore Marchese Niccolò Vitelli per gl'alimenti d'un anno, da decorrere il dì 15 gennaio primo avvenire, della Signora Berenice sua figliuola'.

47   Calvi, 'Connected Courts', p. 314.
48   Calvi, 'Connected Courts', p. 314.
49   The entire exhibition catalogue survives as the *Nota de' quadri e opere*.
50   These include *Presentation at the Temple*, the *Annunciation to the Virgin Mary*, the *Nativity*, the *Annunciation to the Shepherds*, the *Rest on the Flight into Egypt*, the *Massacre of the Innocents*, the *Last Supper*, the *Agony in the Garden*, and the *Crucifixion*.

Figure 9.5. Suor Teresa Berenice Vitelli, *The Last Supper* (after Livio Mehus), Florence, Gallerie degli Uffizi. *c.* 1729. Photograph reproduced with the permission of the Ministero per i Beni e le Attività Culturali.

exhibition: a copy of a self-portrait by Rembrandt, as well as a copy of a head by Francesco Trevisani.

Over the decades, the Accademia delle Arti del Disegno held many exhibitions in the Chapel of the Painters in the church of the SS. Annunziata. The earliest extant documents refer to a show held in 1673, which was likely their first exhibition.[51] The notice for the 1673 show, which was described as 'quaranta quadri di pittori grandi e de' più rinomati maestri antichi e moderni'

51 Borroni Salvadori, 'L'esposizione di opere d'arte del 1674', p. 366.

(forty paintings by great painters and the most renowned ancient and modern masters), suggests that the curators designed a highly selective exhibition to showcase the talent of only the most prominent artists.[52] Surviving reports of the Accademia delle Arti del Disegno exhibitions record that fourteen successive exhibitions were mounted between 1674 and 1737.[53] While it is unclear how works were chosen for inclusion in the shows, Florentine citizens selected as donors must have felt great pride in having art from their private collections featured in a public setting and recognized in the exhibition pamphlet.[54] At the same time, dilettantes and professional artists alike were honoured by having their works hung alongside those of the great Florentine masters of past ages.

While Suor Teresa Berenice herself never became a member of the Accademia delle Arti del Disegno, several proximate male family members joined the organization as 'gentlemen', thus linking her to Florence's professional artistic community.[55] In addition, though he never contributed dues as a member of the Accademia, her older brother Niccolò sent seven paintings to the exhibition of 1729, including a *Saint Anthony of Padua* by Mehus, the same artist whose compositions inspired our nun. This 1729 exhibition was also the only instance in which Niccolò supplied works from the vast Vitelli collection, a point that may have influenced the decision to include Suor Teresa Berenice in this important public event. However, this family connection alone does not entirely account for Suor Teresa Berenice's participation, which was extraordinary in several other ways as well, including the direct reference in her submissions to paintings owned by the Medici, her status as a cloistered nun, and the exceedingly high number of her artworks in the exhibition, even in comparison to the quantities supplied by male artists.

Livio Mehus, the artist whose paintings provided the compositions for Suor Teresa Berenice's nine pastel entries, was represented posthumously in the very same exhibition by eighteen of his original paintings. Mehus, born in Flanders, had migrated to Milan at a young age and had received his artistic training in Italy.[56] He later attracted the attention of Prince Mattias de' Medici

---

52 Quoted in Borroni Salvadori, 'L'esposizione di opere d'arte del 1674', p. 366.
53 Borroni Salvadori, 'Le esposizioni d'arte a Firenze', p. 5.
54 Several hypotheses are proposed in Borroni Salvadori, 'Le esposizioni d'arte a Firenze', pp. 4–5.
55 Her uncle Camillo Vitelli began paying taxes as a gentleman member of the Accademia del Disegno in 1708. He maintained his membership until at least 1733 (Florence, ASF, AdD 131, fol. 162^r; AdD 132, fol. 74^r; AdD 110, fol. 35^v). After his first tax payment in 1715, Ippolito Bagnesi, father-in-law to Suor Teresa Berenice's sister Agnesa, continued his association with the Accademia until at least 1738 (Florence, ASF, AdD 132, fol. 17^r; AdD 111, fol. 90^r). Cavaliere Pietro Frescobaldi, related to Suor Teresa Berenice's sister-in-law Anna Frescobaldi, joined the Accademia as a gentleman in 1717 and remained a member until 1728 (Florence, ASF, AdD 132, fol. 99^r; AdD 111, fol. 17^v).
56 For more information on Mehus, see Gregori, 'Livio Mehus', pp. 177–226; Chiarini, ed., *Livio Mehus*; Barbolani di Montauto, 'Livio Mehus e Anton Domenico Gabbiani per il Granprincipe', pp. 74–70; Chiarini, 'Il "mezzanine delle meraviglie"', pp. 82–91; Paliaga, '"Mi trovo totalmente preso da un vivo amore alla nobil arte della pittura"', pp. 92–103.

and served as a court painter to him as well as to Grand Prince Ferdinando de' Medici, Violante's consort. Ferdinando was an avid collector of Mehus's work, eventually amassing forty-five paintings by the Flemish artist.[57] The grand prince's continued collecting of Mehus's artistic production long after the artist's death, as well as the large number of Mehus's paintings in the Accademia delle Arti del Disegno exhibition in 1729, both indicate that the Flemish artist maintained an uneclipsed reputation in Florence well into the early eighteenth century.

Aside from the esteem in which Mehus was held by the late husband of her patron the grand princess, another impetus for Suor Teresa Berenice's choice of artistic inspiration may have been her family's personal connection to the Flemish artist. In 1674, Mehus arrived at the Vitelli family's *palazzo* in Città di Castello with a letter of introduction from Cardinal Leopoldo de' Medici, who wished for the artist to appraise paintings in the Vitelli collection that had been offered to the Cardinal for purchase.[58] Though Leopoldo never pursued the purchase, Mehus's visit to the Vitelli family's seat in Città di Castello as a mediating agent signalled the alignment of the Medici and the Vitelli in matters of artistic networks and patronage. Thus, when Suor Teresa Berenice chose to replicate Mehus's paintings, she implicitly emphasized her status as a Vitelli woman and drew attention to the ties between her family and the Medici court in matters of artistic taste.

The significance of Suor Teresa Berenice's involvement in the 1729 exhibition can only be fully appreciated when it is seen in comparison with other women's participation in this event. A close examination of the pamphlets from the exhibitions held between 1706 and 1729 elucidates the role of women in the Accademia during a time in which both amateur and professional women artists were beginning to enjoy unprecedented prominence in the public sphere.[59] Prior to 1706, no women had taken part in the Accademia delle Arti del Disegno exhibitions, either as contributing artists or as lenders. In 1706, however, the first painting by a woman artist, Cassandra Riccardi, was included in the exhibition. From that point on, female participation increased in these public showings of art. In 1715, Violante donated two paintings to the exhibition, while other patrons provided a floral painting by the Venetian painter Margherita Caffi and three pastel portraits by the Florentine artist Giovanna Fratellini. In the exhibition of 1724, four women acted as lenders, supplying a total of fourteen paintings; at the same event, two of Fratellini's portraits were displayed.[60]

---

57 Moro, *Viaggio nel Seicento toscano*, p. 220.

58 See Florence, ASF, RV 41, insert 6, for the letters from Cardinal Leopoldo de' Medici to Pierfrancesco Vitelli in Città di Castello dating to 18 May 1674 and 26 May 1674 discussing Mehus's visit to the Vitelli villa.

59 The following analysis of female participation in Accademia del Disegno shows is based on information gathered from Borroni Salvadori, 'Le esposizioni d'arte a Firenze'.

60 Fratellini's portrait of Signora Principessa Eleonora Gonzaga was supplied by Ortensia

By the exhibition of 1729, the one in which Suor Teresa Berenice made her debut, women had established a pattern of participation in these public events. That year, five female donors and the Sienese convent of SS. Abundio e Abundanzio lent a total of sixteen paintings to the show. The same exhibition showcased works of art by four women artists: Rosalba Carriera, Maria Maddalena Gozzi Baldacci, Giovanna Fratellini (with four pastel portraits), and Suor Teresa Berenice (with nine pastels and two oils), for a total of eighteen works by female artists. Except for Suor Teresa Berenice, these female artists were all secular women who were established amateur or professional painters. The inclusion in the show of our artist, a cloistered nun with no known professional training, is remarkable, especially in consideration of the quantity of works she presented. Not only did her works greatly outnumber those of her fellow female artists, but her eleven compositions rivalled the size of the contributions to the show made by many of the best-represented male artists. Suor Teresa Berenice's admittance into the exhibition with such a large selection of her works suggests that her art was well received by Florence's artistic community of Florence. In this light, it should be noted that Suor Teresa Berenice was identified as a nun of S. Apollonia in the exhibition catalogue. Very likely, then, Suor Teresa Berenice's status as a cloistered religious artist had heightened the interest in her artistic production.

The emergence of women participants in Accademia delle Arti del Disegno exhibitions does not seem to be the result of a deliberate cultivation of female ties by this artistic institution. Instead, it can be more closely linked to Violante's strategic propagation of female artistic networks. As mentioned previously, Violante's decision to display both portraits representing women and works of art created by women recalls the series of female portraits established at Villa Artimino by Grand Duchess Christine of Lorraine in the early years of the seventeenth century; however, the grand princess's decision also demonstrates her advocacy of amateur and professional female artists. Moreover, Violante's role as one of the first female donors to Accademia exhibitions testifies to her involvement in the flourishing community of women artists and patrons, and further confirms her as a leading link between aspiring female artists and the professional artistic community in Florence. It is surely no exaggeration to state that women artists would not have been admitted to the exhibitions of the Accademia delle Arti del Disegno without the aid of the grand princess.

Beginning in the eighteenth century, Italian women artists achieved a series of noteworthy milestones. As noted above, in 1706, Cassandra Riccardi became the first woman artist to participate in the Accademia delle Arti del Disegno's exhibitions. In that same year, Agnese Dolci and Giovanna Fratellini each matriculated into the Accademia delle Arti del Disegno. Both Dolci and Fratellini were elected as professors of the Accademia in January of 1710,

---

Caccini Vernacci, a noblewoman whose own artwork hung on the walls of Violante's villa at Lappeggi (Florence, ASF, GM 1393, fol. 4^r).

making them two of the earliest women to hold this honour in Florence.[61] No less meaningful was Suor Teresa Berenice's contribution to the exhibition of 1729. To a certain degree, our nun's participation in this event was a tangible outcome of Violante Beatrice of Bavaria's efforts to promote the public visibility of women artists. However, unlike the display of Suor Teresa Berenice's artwork at Violante's villa, where the cartouches only provided our artist's name (with its clarion aristocratic associations), the pamphlet from the 1729 Accademia delle Arti del Disegno exhibition identified our nun along with the name of her convent. Suor Teresa Berenice's participation in the Accademia's exhibition therefore confirmed that the rising tide of female artists' public visibility had reached the pinnacle of Florentine society's artistic organizations and was now penetrating Florence's most prestigious convents.[62]

Conclusion: An Artist Among Nuns

At first glance Suor Teresa Berenice's painting practice would seem to have been an individualistic pursuit, and thus quite unlike the workshop production of art by nuns under the guidance of Suor Plautilla Nelli (1524–1588) at S. Caterina da Siena.[63] The manufacture of her pictures involved only one pair of hands, as opposed to the lacemaking and sewing work that were the most frequent artisanal occupations of Florentine nuns. Further underlining Suor Teresa Berenice's independence in undertaking her paintings is the fact that her artist's materials were apparently never purchased through the convent's coffers, and thus were probably supplied to her directly by her kin. Only in marginal ways was her skill in painting relevant to the ordinary exigencies of her religious community: once in 1715 she made repairs to the convent's nativity scene ('Capannuccia'), presumably repainting many of the paper-maché figurines, and a few of S. Apollonia's accounting books bear her painted decorations on their parchment covers.[64]

---

61 The archival notices of Dolci's and Fratellini's status as members and then academicians at the Accademia delle Arte del Disegno are noted in Luigi Zangheri, ed., *Gli accademici del disegno*, pp. 115, 139. For further information on Dolci, see Benassai, 'Carlo Dolci', p. 152; on Fratellini, see Bozzi, 'Giovanna Marmocchini Cortesi'. The following year of 1711, the Sienese noblewoman Aretafila Savini De' Rossi was elected as an academician; a painter and poet, she later went on to write a tractate in defense of the education of women. For comparison to the Roman Accademia di San Luca, see Harris and Nochlin, *Women Artists*, p. 135 n. 6; Cesareo, '"I cui nomi sono cogniti per ogni dove"', pp. 93–145, and Primarosa, 'Nuova luce su Plautilla Bricci', pp. 145–60. For comparison to the Bolognese Accademia Clementina, see Giacometti, 'Rosalba Carriera', pp. 354–59.

62 On the growing visibility of women artists in Florence, see Barker, 'The Female Artist in the Public Eye'.

63 On nuns' art workshops, particularly in Florence, see Turrill, '*Compagnie* and *Discepole*'; Barker, 'Painting and Humanism'.

64 On the nativity scene, see 22 November 1715, Florence, ASF, CRSGF 82, vol. 67, fol. 277 left;

It has been shown here that the circulation of Suor Teresa Berenice's art fostered multiple connections: between our nun and her secular family, between the Vitelli family and the Medici court, between Suor Teresa Berenice's Sienese matrilineal line and Violante Beatrice of Bavaria, and between our nun and the artistic community of Florence. In part at least, the efficacy of her art in bringing so many individuals in rapport with each other hinged on the fact that Suor Teresa Berenice's subject matter and stylistic approach reflected the common cultural interests linking her family with the Medici, as well as her access to the art collections of both families. The other major factor in its efficacy stemmed, as we have argued throughout this essay, from the multiple facets of Suor Teresa Berenice's identity: noblewoman, nun, and artist at the Medici court.

Upon Suor Teresa Berenice's entrance into the convent, her ability to dedicate time to making artworks whose subject matter was not explicitly religious probably hinged upon her family connections to a fair degree. Many of these critical family connections were within the convent itself: in 1713, Suor Teresa Berenice's aunt, Suor Maria Ancilla, was elected as abbess of S. Apollonia, a position which she held until her death the following year; by 1725, another aunt, Suor Placida Maria, was elected abbess, serving in this capacity through 1740.[65] Her family's wealth and influence could not be disguised in these circumstances, given that two generations of Vitelli women had brought vital economic support to S. Apollonia, particularly in the form of *sopradoti* that were paid for the privilege of placing multiple family members in the same convent. Not to be overlooked were Suor Teresa Berenice's own generous donations for the benefit of the other nuns.[66] There is no direct evidence that the other nuns of S. Apollonia believed Suor Teresa Berenice's practice of gifting her miniatures and pastels to the Medici would benefit the whole convent, however the inscription of the convent's name alongside her own name in the Accademia delle Arti del Disegno's exhibition catalogue surely reveals that S. Apollonia reaped benefits from Suor Teresa Berenice's art, even if only in terms of public renown.

Suor Teresa Berenice, who lived her entire adult life in reclusion, is not known to have left behind any letters or personal documents in her own hand, and yet her art found its way into multiple collections beyond her convent's walls. It is worth mentioning, however, that while her name and identity could certainly add valences of significance to her artworks, her naturalistic imagery held great appeal even when her identity was not known. Shortly

---

for the convincing attribution of the accounting book decorations to Suor Teresa Berenice, Simari and Acanfora, eds, *Flowers on Vellum*, pp. 16–17.

65   See Florence, ASF, CRSGF 82, vol. 67, fol. 253 right, and Florence, ASF, CRSGF 82, vol. 94, fol. 88 right.

66   She donated extra food to the convent on 11 September 1703 (Florence, ASF, CRSGF 82, vol. 66, fol. 168 right). Additionally, on 10 July 1716 she paid for a sacristan's funeral (Florence, ASF, CRSGF 82, vol. 67, fol. 253 right).

after her death, Suor Teresa Berenice's sketchbook of nature studies was carried off to the Benedictine monastery of Vallombrosa by a botanist of that religious house named Bruno Tozzi. Following Tozzi's death, Giovanni Targioni Tozzetti, a Florentine naturalist and prefect of the Magliabechiana library who knew very well the contents of the library of Vallombrosa, brought her sketchbook to the attention of John Strange (1732–1799), a member of the Royal Society in London. By that time, her authorship of the notebook had been forgotten and it was instead presumed to have been made by one of the male artists at the late Medici court who were renowned for the expert depiction of *naturalia*.[67]

Remarkably, some of Suor Teresa Berenice's religious artworks, despite being unsigned, continued to be associated with her identity as a nun, nearly a century after her death. In 1815, in the wake of the redistribution and dispersion of artworks during the Napoleonic occupation, the Servite friars of the church of the SS. Annunziata realized that the convent of S. Apollonia had come into the possession of several paintings by a Servite painter named Padre Mascagni. The Servite father Federigo Vannini sought to recuperate the paintings from the convent of S. Apollonia by offering in exchange several pastel paintings that had been made by Suor Teresa Berenice and which were kept in the SS. Annunziata's sacristy of the Chapel of the Painters, a consecrated space under the supervision of the Accademia del Disegno since 1565. Described by Vannini as 'alcune quadri piccoli a pastello oper[e] di una Religiosa del suo convento' (some small pictures in pastel made by a nun from her convent [of S. Apollonia]), there is strong reason to believe these artworks were the very same pastels Suor Teresa Berenice had sent to the SS. Annunziata exhibition of 1729, based on their location.[68] The conservation of Suor Teresa Berenice's drawings in the sacristy of the Chapel of the Painters, the symbolic sanctuary

---

67   Targioni Tozzetti described Suor Teresa Berenice's sketchbook as 'Un volume grosso in foglio che contiene molte bellissime figure miniate coi propri colori, di fiori di giardino, di frutte, di uccelli, di bestie, e di pietre, raccolte dal Padre Tozzi. Alcune di queste figure mi paiono dipinte dallo Scaviati, altre dal Bimbi, ed altre dal Chellini, ma queste sono le inferiori' (A large, folio-sized volume that contains many beautiful figures depicted in their true colours, representing garden flowers, fruits, birds, beasts, and stones, all collected by Father Tozzi. Some of these figures seem to me to have been painted by Scaviati, others by Bimbi, and others still by Chellini, with these last being inferior to the others). Letter of Giovanni Targioni Tozzetti to John Strange, dated 18 May 1771, BL, Add. 23729, fols 235ᵛ–236ʳ.

68   Florence, AABFi, Soppressioni, Carteggio e Atti Processi Verbali … del 1810, fasc. 5, insert A 'Indice dei Fogli Continenti nel Presente Inserto A', numero 8, fol. 525ʳ. This letter was first cited in Meloni Trkulja, 'Teresa Berenice (Suor Veronica) Vitelli', p. 141, but with an invalid shelf number; moreover, Meloni Trkulja's summary of the letter contains several errors of interpretation. In her discussion of the letter, Meloni Trkulja was the first to propose Suor Teresa Berenice as the nun artist. Even though Vannini did not mention the nun artist by name, it must have been Suor Teresa Berenice, for no other nun at her convent is known to have practiced painting, let alone the novel medium of pastel. According to Vannini, the abbess from S. Apollonia hoped to have the pastels returned so that she might sell them, which might explain how the pastels came to be a part of the Medici collection.

for the Florence artistic community, would seem to testify to the esteem in which our nun's pastels were held by her professional artist peers, many decades after their public debut in 1729.

Because of Suor Teresa Berenice's amateur status and her reclusion, her name faded from historical memory rather quickly, and yet her delicate and small artworks survive in some of Italy's premier cultural institutions. This remarkable situation is as much a consequence of the evident skill and ingenuity of her art as it is a consequence of her position at the vertex of multiple overlapping networks that connected this cloistered nun to her relatives with aristocratic and ecclesiastical titles, to her Medici patrons, to the Benedictine community, to the amateur and professional artists of her times, and ultimately to the world at large.

Works Cited

Manuscripts and Archival Sources

Florence, Archivio di Accademia delle Belle Arti di Firenze (AABFi)
    Soppressioni, Carteggio e Atti Processi Verbali ... del 1810
Florence, Archivio di Stato (ASF)
    Accademia del Disegno (AdD)
    Ceramelli Papiani
    Corporazioni religiose soppresse dal governo francese (CRSGF)
    ——, 82 (S. Apollonia)
    Guardaroba Medicea (GM)
    Mediceo del Principato (MdP)
    Notario Moderno (NM)
    Rondinelli Vitelli (RV)
Florence, Biblioteca Nazionale Centrale di Firenze (BNCF)
    Conventi Soppressi
    MS Magliabecchiana (Magl.), Cl. XXV, 4
Florence, Opera di Santa Maria del Fiore (OSMF)
    Archivio storico delle fedi di battesimo
    ——, Registri Battesimali
London, British Library (BL)
    Additional (Add.) 23729

Primary Sources

Nota de' quadri e opere di scultura esposti per la festa di S. Luca dagli Accademici del Disegno: Nella loro Cappella, e nel Chiostro secondo del Convento de' PP. della SS. Nonziata di Firenze l'Anno 1729 (Florence: Nella Stamperia di S. A. Reale, Appresso Gio. Gaetano Tartini e Santi Franchi, 1729)

Secondary Works

Abbatelli, Valentina, Alessia Lirosi, and Irene Palombo, eds, *Un monastero di famiglia: Il Diario delle barberine della SS. Incarnazione (secc. XVII–XVIII)* (Rome: Viella, 2016)

Bacarelli, Giuseppina, 'Sant'Apollonia: Novità iconografiche e una leggenda inedita', *Paragone*, 33 (1982), 101–06, 383–85

——, 'Per l'architettura fiorentina del quattrocento: Il chiostro di Sant'Apollonia', *Rivista d'Arte*, 37 (1984), 133–63

Barbolani di Montauto, Novella, 'Livio Mehus e Anton Domenico Gabbiani per il Granprincipe: Note sui mezzanini di Palazzo Pitti', in *Arte collezionismo conservazione: scritti in onore di Marco Chiarini*, ed. by Miles Chappell, Mario di Giampaolo, and Serena Padovani (Florence: Giunti, 2004), pp. 64–70

Barker, Sheila, 'The Female Artist in the Public Eye: Women Copyists at the Uffizi, 1770–1859', in *Women, Femininity and Public Space in European Visual Culture, 1789–1914*, ed. by Temma Balducci and Heather Belnap Jensen (Farnham: Ashgate, 2014), pp. 65–79

——, 'Painting and Humanism in Early Modern Florentine Convents', in *Artiste nel chiostro: Produzione artistica nei monasteri femminili in età moderna*, ed. by Sheila Barker and Luciano Cinelli, Memorie Domenicane, 46 (Florence: Nerbini, 2016), pp. 103–37

——, '"Marvellously gifted": Giovanna Garzoni's Visit to the Medici Court', *The Burlington Magazine*, 160 (August, 2018), 654–59

Benassai, Silvia, 'Tra le carte di Violante: Note sul mecenatismo della Gran Principessa di Toscana', *Valori Tattili*, 3–4 (2014), 80–112

——, 'Carlo Dolci: i discepoli, l'eredità, il ricordo', in *Carlo Dolci (1616–1687)*, ed. by Sandro Bellesi, Anna Bisceglia, and Cristina Accidini Luchinat (Livorno: Sillabe, 2015), pp. 144–55

Bertucci, Carlo, 'A Leaf from the Scholz Scrapbook', *Metropolitan Museum Journal*, 12 (1977), 93–100

Borroni Salvadori, Fabia, 'Le esposizioni d'arte a Firenze dal 1674 al 1767', *Mitteilungen des Kunsthistorichen Institutes in Florenz*, 18 (1974), 1–166

——, 'L'esposizione di opere d'arte del 1674 alla SS. Annunziata di Firenze', *Mitteilungen des Kunsthistorischen Institutes in Florenz*, 22 (1978), 366–68

Bozzi, Sonia, 'Giovanna Marmocchini Cortesi', *Dizionario Biografico degli Italiani*, 70 (2008), http://www.treccani.it/enciclopedia/giovanna-marmocchini-cortesi_(Dizionario-Biografico) [accessed 10 August 2018]

Calvi, Giulia, 'Connected Courts: Violante Beatrice of Bavaria in Florence and Siena', in *Medici Women: The Making of a Dynasty in Grand Ducal Tuscany*, ed. by Giovanna Benadusi and Judith C. Brown (Toronto: Centre for Reformation and Renovation Studies, 2015), pp. 302–21

Casale, Gerardo, *Giovanna Garzoni: 'Insigne miniatrice', 1600–1670* (Milan: Jandi Sapi, 1991)

——, *Gli incanti dell'iride: Giovanna Garzoni pittrice nel Seicento* (Cinisello Balsamo: Silvana Editoriale, 1996)

Casciu, Stefano, and Fausta Navarro, eds, *La Galleria Palatina e gli appartamenti reali di Palazzo Pitti: catalogo dei dipinti* (Florence: Centro Di, 2003)

Casciu, Stefano, 'Violante Beatrice di Baviera, gran principessa (1676–1731)', in *Il giardino del granduca: natura morta nelle collezioni medicee*, ed. by Marco Chiarini and Stefano Casciu (Turin: Edizioni Seat, 1997), pp. 329–37

Cecchi, Alessandro, Lucilla Conigliello, and Marzia Faietti, eds, *Jacopo Ligozzi: Pittore universalissimo* (Livorno: Sillabe, 2014)

Cesareo, Antonello, '"I cui nomi sono cogniti per ogni dove…": Caterina Cherubini Preciado e la presenza femminile nell'Accademia di San Luca tra secondo Settecento ed inizi Ottocento', in *Francisco Preciado de la Vega: Un pintor español del siglo XVIII en Roma*, ed. by Alfonso Rodríguez G. de Ceballos (Madrid: Real Academia de Bellas Artes de San Fernando, 2009), pp. 93–145

Chappell, Miles, 'Le "Bellezze di Artimino": Una nota sull'attribuzione', *Prospettiva*, 25 (1981), 59–64

Chiarini, Marco, ed., *Botanica come arte: Dipinti dalle collezioni medicee: Villa medicea di Poggio a Caiano* (Florence: Centro Di, 1990)

——, ed., *La natura morta a palazzo e in villa: Le collezioni dei Medici e dei Lorena* (Livorno: Sillabe, 1998)

——, ed., *Livio Mehus: Un pittore barocco alla corte dei Medici, 1627–1691* (Livorno: Sillabe, 2000)

——, 'Il "mezzanino delle meraviglie" e la collezione di bozzetti del Gran Principe Ferdinando a Palazzo Pitti', in *Il Gran Principe Ferdinando de' Medici (1663–1713): collezionista e mecenate*, ed. by Riccardo Spinelli, Ilaria Ferraris, and Franco Angiolini (Florence: Giunti, 2013), pp. 82–91

Chiarini, Marco, and Stefano Casciu, eds, *Il giardino del granduca: Natura morta nelle collezioni medicee* (Turin: Edizioni Seat, 1997)

Ciardi, Roberto Paolo, and Lucia Tongiorgi Tomasi, eds, *Immagini anatomiche e naturalistiche nei disegni degli Uffizi: Secc. XVI e XVII* (Florence: Olschki, 1984)

Davis, Charles, 'Cosimo Bartoli and the Portal of Sant'Apollonia by Michelangelo', *Mitteilungen des Kunsthistorichen Institutes Florenz*, 19.2 (1975), 261–76

Evans, R. J. W., and Alexander Marr, eds, *Curiosity and Wonder from the Renaissance to the Enlightenment* (Aldershot: Ashgate, 2006)

Felfe, Robert, and Angelika Lozar, eds, *Frühneuzeitliche Sammlungspraxis und Literatur* (Berlin: Lukas, 2006)

Findlen, Paula, *Possessing Nature: Museums, Collecting, and Scientific Culture in Early Modern Italy* (Berkeley: University of California Press, 1993)

Fleming, Alison, 'Daniel Seghers (1590–1661)', in *Cambridge Encyclopedia of the Jesuits*, ed. by Thomas Worcester, SJ (New York: Cambridge University Press, 2017), pp. 730–32

Fortune, Jane, *Invisible Women: Forgotten Artists of Florence* (Florence: The Florentine Press, 2009)

Giacometti, Margherita, 'Rosalba Carriera', in *Dictionary of Women Artists*, vol. 1, ed. by Delia Gaze (London: Fitzroy Dearborn, 1997), pp. 354–59

Gregori, Mina, 'Livio Mehus o la sconfitta del dissenso', *Paradigma*, 2 (1978), 177–226

Harris, Ann Sutherland, and Linda Nochlin, eds, *Women Artists: 1550–1950* (New York: Knopf, 1976)

Hayum, Andrée, 'A Renaissance Audience Considered: The Nuns at S. Apollonia and Castagno's Last Supper', *The Art Bulletin*, 88 (2006), 243–66

Lenzi Iacomelli, Carlotta, *Vincenzo Meucci (1694–1766)* (Florence: Edifir, 2014)

Litta, Pompeo, *Le famiglie celebri d'Italia*, vol. 24 (Milan: Giulio Ferrario, 1832)

MacGregor, Arthur, *Curiosity and Enlightenment: Collectors and Collections from the Sixteenth to the Nineteenth Century* (New Haven: Yale University Press, 2007)

Meloni Trkulja, Silvia, 'Teresa Berenice (Suor Veronica) Vitelli', in *Natura viva in Casa Medici: dipinti di animali dai depositi di Palazzo Pitti con esemplari del Museo Zoologico 'La Specola'*, ed. by Marilena Mosco (Florence: Centro Di, 1985), pp. 141–43

Meloni Trkulja, Silvia, and Elena Fumagalli, eds, *Giovanna Garzoni: Nature morte* (Paris: Bibliothèque de l'Image, 2000)

Moro, Franco, *Viaggio nel Seicento toscano: Dipinti e disegni inediti* (Mantua: Paolini, 2006)

Mosco, Marilena, ed., *Natura viva in Casa Medici: Dipinti di animali dai depositi di Palazzo Pitti con esemplari del Museo Zoologico 'La Specola'* (Florence: Centro Di, 1985)

——, entry in *La natura morta in Italia*, ed. by Federico Zeri and Francesco Porzio, vol. 2, (Milan: Electa, 1989), pp. 600–01

Paliaga, Franco, '"Mi trovo totalmente preso da un vivo amore alla nobil arte della pittura": I dipinti di Ferdinando de' Medici del "gabinetto d'opere in piccolo" della villa di Poggio a Caiano', in *Il Gran Principe Ferdinando de' Medici (1663–1713): Collezionista e mecenate*, ed. by Riccardo Spinelli, Ilaria Ferraris, and Franco Angiolini (Florence: Giunti, 2013), pp. 92–103

Primarosa, Yuri, 'Nuova luce su Plautilla Bricci pittrice e "architettrice"', *Studi di storia dell'arte*, 25 (2014), 145–60

Proto Pisani, Rosanna Caterina, *Il cenacolo di Santa Apollonia: Il primo cenacolo rinascimentale a Firenze* (Livorno: Sillabe, 2002)

Ruggieri Tricoli, Maria Clara, *Il richiamo dell'Eden: Dal collezionismo naturalistico all'esposizione museale* (Florence: Vallecchi, 2004)

Simari, Maria Matilde, and Elisa Acanfora, eds, *Flowers on Vellum: Floral Paintings from the Medici Collections* (Florence: Sillabe, 2014)

Sobel, Dana, *Letters to Father: Suor Maria Celeste to Galileo, 1623–1633* (New York: Walker and Company, 2001)

Strocchia, Sharon T., *Nuns and Nunneries in Renaissance Florence* (Baltimore: Johns Hopkins University Press, 2009)

Tongiorgi Tomasi, Lucia, '"La femminil pazienza": Women Painters and Natural History in the Seventeenth and Early Eighteenth Centuries', in *The Art of Natural History*, ed. by Therese O'Malley and Amy R. W. Meyers (New Haven: Yale University Press, 2008), pp. 158–85

Tongiorgi Tomasi, Lucia, and Gretchen A. Hirschauer, eds, *The Flowering of Florence: Botanical Art for the Medici* (Washington, DC: National Gallery of Art, 2002)

Tosi, Alessandro, 'Tra scienza, arte e diletto: collezioni naturalistiche in Toscana nell'età di Cosimo III', in *La Toscana nell'età di Cosimo III*, ed. by Franco Angiolini, Vieri Becagli, and Marcello Verga (Florence: Edifir, 1993), pp. 377–87

Turrill, Catherine, '*Compagnie* and *Discepole*: The Presence of Other Women Artists at Santa Caterina da Siena', in *Suor Plautilla Nelli (1532–1588): The First Woman Painter of Florence*, ed. by Jonathan Nelson (Florence: Cadmo, 2000), pp. 83–102

Weddle, Saundra, 'Enclosing Le Murate: The Ideology of Enclosure and the Architecture of a Florentine Convent, 1380–1597' (unpublished doctoral dissertation, Cornell University, 1997)

——, ''Tis Better to Give than to Receive: Client-Patronage Exchange and its Architectural Implications at Florentine Convents', in *Studies on Florence and the Italian Renaissance in Honour of F. W. Kent*, ed. by Cecilia Hewlett and Peter Howard, Europe Sacra, 20 (Turnhout: Brepols, 2016), pp. 295–315

Zangheri, Luigi, ed., *Gli accademici del disegno* (Florence: Leo S. Olschki, 2000)

Index

Note that nuns changed their name when they entered religious life. Names of abbesses, nuns, and prioresses reflect those used within the convent rather than a woman's given name. Italian provinces are abbreviated and placed between parentheses.

Europa Sacra

All volumes in this series are evaluated by an Editorial Board, strictly on academic grounds, based on reports prepared by referees who have been commissioned by virtue of their specialism in the appropriate field. The Board ensures that the screening is done independently and without conflicts of interest. The definitive texts supplied by authors are also subject to review by the Board before being approved for publication. Further, the volumes are copyedited to conform to the publisher's stylebook and to the best international academic standards in the field.

Titles in Series

Darius von Güttner-Sporzyński, *Poland, Holy War, and the Piast Monarchy, 1100–1230* (2014)

Tomas Zahora, *Nature, Virtue, and the Boundaries of Encyclopaedic Knowledge: The Tropological Universe of Alexander Neckam (1157–1217)* (2014)

Line Cecilie Engh, *Gendered Identities in Bernard of Clairvaux's Sermons on the Song of Songs* (2014)

Mulieres religiosae: Shaping Female Spiritual Authority in the Medieval and Early Modern Periods, ed. by Veerle Fraeters and Imke de Gier (2014)

Bruno the Carthusian and his Mortuary Roll: Studies, Text, and Translation, ed. by Hartmut Beyer, Gabriela Signori, and Sita Steckel (2014)

David Rosenthal, *Kings of the Street: Power, Community, and Ritual in Renaissance Florence* (2015)

Fabrizio Conti, *Witchcraft, Superstition, and Observant Franciscan Preachers: Pastoral Approach and Intellectual Debate in Renaissance Milan* (2015)

Mendicant Cultures in the Medieval and Early Modern World: Word, Deed, and Image, ed. by Sally J. Cornelison, Nirit Ben-Aryeh Debby, and Peter Howard (2016)

Adriano Prosperi, *Infanticide, Secular Justice, and Religious Debate in Early Modern Europe* (2016)

Studies on Florence and the Italian Renaissance in Honour of F.W. Kent, ed. by Peter Howard and Cecilia Hewlett (2016)

Relics, Identity, and Memory in Medieval Europe, ed. by Marika Räsänen, Gritje Hartmann, and Earl Jeffrey Richards (2016)

Boundaries in the Medieval and Wider World: Essays in Honour of Paul Freedman, ed. by Thomas W. Barton, Susan McDonough, Sara McDougall, and Matthew Wranovix (2017)

Marie-Madeleine de Cevins, *Confraternity, Mendicant Orders, and Salvation in the Middle Ages: The Contribution of the Hungarian Sources (c. 1270–c. 1530)* (2018)

Authority and Power in the Medieval Church, c. 1000–c. 1500, ed. by Thomas W. Smith (2020)

In Preparation

Renaissance Religions: Modes and Meanings in History, ed. by Peter Howard, Nicholas Terpstra, and Riccardo Saccenti